Excerpt

Matthew Lau on systemic racism

If the typical anti-racism activist today is looking for widespread institutional or systemic racism of the kind that existed before the mid-twentieth century, which was directed at minorities or women, they simply will not find it. Ironically, the most socially accepted and likely most common form of institutional racism today is the discrimination practiced in the name of social justice or anti-racism.

Greg Piasetzki on Sir John A. Macdonald

A proper and balanced consideration of Macdonald's life as it was actually lived reveals that, through his own actions and policies, Canada's first prime minister was directly and deliberately responsible for saving the lives of untold numbers of indigenous people.

Bruce Pardy on Critical Theory and Canada's compromised institutions

Modern Western civilization grew out of the Enlightenment of the 17th and 18th centuries. The ascendancy of reason in human affairs produced the scientific method and later the Industrial Revolution. Add in the rule of law, individual liberty, private property, and capitalism, and you have the basic recipe that has raised much of humanity out of poverty and oppression over two centuries. Four academic doctrines—Critical Theory, Postmodernism, Social Justice, and Critical Race Theory—are moving the world, or at least the West, from this triumph to decline. These doctrines reject Enlightenment values such as open inquiry, individual autonomy, free speech, scientific skepticism, and even reason itself.

Jamil Jivani on idea diversity among black Canadians

Black Canadians who want to genuinely help our communities often risk having our authenticity attacked by people who believe black men and women should only think and speak in one way. It is far easier to remove oneself from the public square than to be verbally assaulted by those who believe a black person's ideology should mirror the *Toronto Star* editorial page or the CBC newsroom. But the continued pursuit of justice, which black Canadians have contributed immensely to, requires perseverance.

Rima Azar on identity politics

To grasp the danger of modern identity politics, one must realize that in this movement we are both defined by our identity, and trapped by others into it, according to those who see all of us not as individuals but as an extension only of our colour, gender, ethnicity, religion and so forth. It thus helps to remember that dividing people in such ways is not new. However, history teaches us it is also dangerous.

Gourav Jaswal on the error of Canadian self-loathing

Among my correspondents, the group that most fiercely disputed the view that minorities in Canada are subject to indignities were minorities themselves. The most vocal and heartfelt defence of Canada came from almost every first-generation immigrant who wrote in—whether they arrived in Canada 50 years ago or just five years previous.

Chris Champion on the British Empire

Contemporary people too easily fall into what they assume is good progressive thinking but whose origin is actually Leninist dogma: namely that colonialism was a "moribund" phase of capitalist exploitation, the last-ditch attempt of the rich to cheat the poor and of the white to oppress the non-white. In reality, some empires—French, Spanish, Portuguese and others in the Middle East, Africa, and Asia in previous centuries—took a spoils approach, while others, like the British, progressively developed their colonies economically and politically.

Joseph Quesnel on over-governed First Nations

Reflecting on the evolution of federal policy, it should be obvious in the third decade of the 21st century that one significant mistake made by the federal government in history was to federalize every issue involving indigenous peoples.

THE 1867 PROJECT

WHY CANADA SHOULD BE CHERISHED—NOT CANCELLED

Twenty Distinct Voices Make the Case for Canada

MARK MILKE, EDITOR

Contributing authors to *The 1867 Project*

Rima Azar, PhD, is an Associate Professor of Health Psychology at Mount Allison University in Sackville, New Brunswick, where she joined the Psychology Department in 2008, earned tenure in 2011, and is the founder/director of the Psychobiology of Stress and Health Lab (PSHL). Taking a biopsychosocial approach to health, Dr. Azar's work focuses on the biobehavioural mechanisms linking stress and health from a developmental perspective. Over her career, she has worked with newborns, children, adolescents, and their families both as a stress researcher and as a developmental clinician.

Peter Best is a retired Sudbury lawyer and the author of the 2020 book *There Is No Difference An Argument for the Abolition of the Indian Reserve System* endorsed by retired Supreme Court of Canada Justice Jack Major.

Chris Champion, PhD, FRCGS, is the author of *Relentless Struggle: Saving the Army Reserve* (Durnovaria, 2019) and *The Strange Demise of British Canada* (McGill-Queen's University Press, 2010) and editor of *The Dorchester Review*. He was born in Calgary, grew up in West Vancouver, and attended the University of British Columbia , Magdalene College, Cambridge, and McGill University. He worked as a researcher in Parliament and later as policy advisor to a federal cabinet minister. He has served seven years in the Army Reserve (Infantry) and was appointed a Visiting Research Fellow at Queen's University's Centre for International and Defence Policy in 2020-21.

Gordon Clark was employed as a daily newspaper reporter, editor, and columnist for 36 years, including stints at the *Vancouver Sun*, the *Prince George Citizen*, the *Edmonton Journal*, and the *Province*. He holds a degree in history from the University of British Columbia, where he got his start in journalism on the *Ubyssey* student newspaper.

Leo J. Deveau is an author, acquisitions editor, public historian and researcher, and former public librarian. He is the author of *400 Years in 365 Days: A Day by Day Calendar of Nova Scotia History* (2017) and *Fideliter: The Regimental History of the Princess Louise Fusiliers* (2020). He is a member of the Writer's Federation of Nova Scotia, the Creative Nonfiction Collective, the Royal Nova Scotian Historical Society, the Genealogical Association of Nova Scotia, the Royal United Services Institute – Nova Scotia Branch, and is past chair of the Halifax Military Heritage Preservation Society.

Janice Fiamengo, PhD, retired in 2019 from her position as Professor of English at the University of Ottawa where she taught for 16 years. Before that, she taught full time at the University of Saskatchewan for four years. She earned a PhD from the University of British Columbia in 1996 and held a two-year Post-Doctoral Fellowship at Simon Fraser University. She is the author of *The Woman's Page: Journalism and Rhetoric in Early Canada* (2008) as well as many peer-reviewed articles and book chapters on early Canadian writers. In retirement, she is at work on a history of feminist thought in English (from a non-feminist, non-adulatory perspective), and is the author of the *Fiamengo File 2.0*, a YouTube series showcasing the dark side of feminism. She lives in British Columbia with her husband, poet, and singer-songwriter David Solway.

Marjorie Gann is a retired elementary school teacher and a children's author. Her 1994 book, *Discover Canada: New Brunswick* (Grolier), surveyed the geography, history, economy, and culture of the province for young readers. Her history of world slavery, *Five Thousand Years of Slavery* (Tundra), co-authored with Janet Willen, was recognized as a 2012 Notable Book for a Global Society by the International Reading Association. Her book *Speak a Word for Freedom: Women Against Slavery* (Penguin Random House), also co-authored with Willen, was published in 2015. She sits on the executive of the Association of Jewish Libraries – Canada, and is a frequent reviewer of children's books for *AJL News and Reviews* and for the Committee for Accuracy in Middle East Reporting and Analysis (CAMERA).

Bruce Gilley, PhD, is Professor of Political Science and Public Policy at Portland State University, and President of the Oregon Association of Scholars. His research centers on comparative and international politics and public policy. His work covers issues as diverse as democracy, climate change, political legitimacy, and international conflict. He is a specialist on the politics of China and Asia.

David Millard Haskell, PhD, is a professor at Wilfrid Laurier University where he researches and teaches media and cultural trends. As a member of the Society for Academic Freedom and Scholarship and leader of the Waterloo Region Chapter of FAIR (Foundation Against Intolerance and Racism) he advocates publicly for freedom of expression, freedom of conscience, facts over feelings, and equality instead of equity. Mike Ramsay contributed files to Dr. Haskell's chapter.

Gourav Jaswal is an entrepreneur based in Goa, India, who has founded a venture studio that has catalysed multiple profitable companies. He can be reached at GJ@Prototyze.com.

Jamil Jivani is a lawyer, author, and policy advisor. Currently, Jamil serves as president of the Canada Strong and Free Network. Jivani has also served as special advisor to the Premier of Ontario, policy advisor to the Government of Alberta and visiting professor at Osgoode Hall Law School. Jamil grew up in the Toronto area. At 16 years old, he was labelled illiterate by the public school system. But Jamil turned his life around with the support of role models and mentors. He went on to graduate from Yale Law School, Humber College and York University and has dedicated his career to supporting youth facing challenges like he did growing up. Jamil's leadership has been recognized by the International Development and Relief Foundation, Cardus, Observer Research Foundation and the Canadian Association of Black Lawyers. His first book, *Why Young Men: The Dangerous Allure of Violent Movements and What We Can Do About It*, was published in 2018.

Matthew Lau, a financial analyst by trade, is an adjunct scholar with the Fraser Institute and writer for the *Financial Post* editorial page in the *National Post*. His writing covers a wide range of subjects including fiscal policy, economic theory, government regulation, and Canadian politics. He holds a Bachelor of Commerce degree with a specialization in finance and economics from the University of Toronto, and is a CFA charterholder.

Lynn McDonald, CM, PhD, LLD (hon), is a professor emerita of sociology at the University of Guelph, a Fellow of the Royal Historical Society, a former president of the National Action Committee on the Status of Women, and was the New Democratic Party Member of Parliament for Broadview-Greenwood from 1982 until 1988. She is the author or editor of 28 academic books including the 16-volume *Collected Works of Florence Nightingale*. She is a co-founder of the Friends of Egerton Ryerson.

Mark Milke, PhD, editor of *The 1867 Project*, is executive director of the Aristotle Foundation for Public Policy, president of the Sir Winston Churchill Society of Calgary, past president of Civitas, and co-founder of the think tank SecondStreet.org. Mark is a public policy analyst, author, and columnist who has written six books and dozens of studies in the last three decades. His policy work has been published by various think tanks including the Fraser Institute, Frontier Centre, the Montreal Economic Institute, Canadian Energy Centre, Canadian Taxpayers Federation, Cardus, American Enterprise Institute, Heritage Foundation, and the Centre for European Studies. Mark also spent two years with a major donor to help create an internal guideline for philanthropic giving in North America.

Bruce Pardy is Executive Director, Rights Probe, and Professor of Law, Queen's University. Professor Pardy is a classically liberal legal academic for whom equal application of the law, negative rights, private property, limited government, and separation of powers are foundational to the Canadian and Western legal tradition. A critic of legal progressivism, social justice, and the discretionary administrative state, he has written on a range of pressing legal subjects at the front lines of the culture war inside the law, including environmental governance, climate change, energy policy, human rights and freedoms, professional and university governance, property and tort theory, free markets, and the rule of law. He has taught at law schools in Canada, the United States, and New Zealand, practiced civil litigation at Borden

Ladner Gervais LLP in Toronto, served as adjudicator and mediator on the Ontario Environmental Review Tribunal, and has published and commented widely in traditional and online media. He serves as senior fellow at the Fraser Institute, and helped to birth the Runnymede Society, a branch of the Canadian Constitution Foundation. He spearheaded resistance to and ultimate repeal of the Law Society of Ontario's statement of principles (SOP) policy that required Ontario lawyers to attest to their ideological purity to maintain their licence to practice. He is one of the co-creators of the Free North Declaration, a public petition and movement to protect civil liberties in Canada from COVID-19 irrationality and overreach.

Greg Piasetzki is an intellectual property lawyer with an interest in Canadian history. He was born on CFB Shiloh in Manitoba, grew up in Ottawa, and now lives in Toronto. After obtaining a BSc (Honours) in Chemistry from Trent University he spent a year in graduate school before entering Law School at Queen's University. Greg has spent more than 30 years researching his family history, which includes French, Acadian, and Métis ancestors on his mother's side and military service for Canada in two wars on his father's. This led to a more general interest in Canadian history and to his writing several articles on historical topics of current interest.

Joseph Quesnel is a writer and researcher based in Nova Scotia. He has been a policy analyst for the Frontier Centre for Public Policy where he focused on Indigenous policy, especially First Nation economic development and governance. He has also been program manager for the Aboriginal Canada and the Natural Resource Economy project at the Macdonald Laurier Institute. He holds an undergraduate degree in political science and history from McGill University and a master of journalism degree from Carleton University.

John Robson, PhD, is the Executive Director of the Climate Discussion Nexus, a documentary filmmaker, a *National Post*, *Epoch Times,* and *Loonie Politics* columnist, a contributing editor to *The Dorchester Review*, and an adjunct professor at Augustine College in Ottawa. He holds a BA and

MA in history from the University of Toronto and a PhD in American history from the University of Texas at Austin and is the author of the documentary and companion book *Magna Carta: Our Shared Legacy of Liberty.*

Peter Shawn Taylor was the only member of the Queen's University's Economics class of 1987 to find work as a wrangler in Wyoming after graduation. He later earned a Master's in Economics from the University of Alberta and served as senior analyst for the Alberta Liberal Caucus in the early 1990s. Since then, he has written for numerous and diverse publications including *Alberta Report, Maclean's, National Post, Globe and Mail, Toronto Star, Canadian Business, Canadian Geographic, Reader's Digest, National Review, Waterloo Region Record,* and *Walrus.* He is currently senior features editor at *C2C Journal.*

Ven Venkatachalam, PhD, is a research scholar who currently writes on public policy issues. Previously, he was a Research Associate at the School of Public Policy, University of Calgary. In addition to publishing through the School of Public Policy, he has also played a role in several projects consulting for governments, NGOs, and private sector organizations across Asia, Europe, and America. His academic and policy work has touched everything from the financial sector, taxes, international relations, trade, energy, governance, immigration, tourism, and NGOs.

Published by The Aristotle Foundation for Public Policy.

ISBN: 978-1-7775432-1-1
eISBN: 978-1-7775432-2-8

Photo on page 54 used under license from Getty Images.
Book design and cover design by Milan Szabo.

Printed in Canada by Friesens.

CONTENTS

FOREWORD

Canada: The centuries-long project

Mark Milke

It is with infinite caution that any man ought to venture upon pulling down an edifice which has answered in any tolerable degree for ages the common purposes of society.
—EDMUND BURKE, *Reflections on the Revolution in France,* 1790

Utopians have long been a problem.

In the late 18th century, Jacobin revolutionaries destroyed the existing, imperfect order of French society and imposed a dictatorship of terror in their quest to end injustices overnight. The result was repression, mayhem, bloodshed, and the eventual rise of a general on horseback who rose to power to restore order out of the utopian/revolutionary-inspired chaos.

In the 20th century, the main utopians were Marxists. They sought to pull down institutions such as the family, free enterprise, and civil society to construct a social order that was perfectly equal. Profit and poverty were to be eliminated so everyone could be equal and free to "hunt in the morning, fish in the afternoon, rear cattle in the evening, [and] criticize after dinner" to quote Karl Marx. The actual result was entrenched poverty, privilege for the politically-connected, widespread repression, and state-directed murder, be it individual East Berliners shot while fleeing across the no-man's land between East and West Berlin, to communist mass genocides in Ukraine, China, and Cambodia.

History has given us other examples of utopians at work. In the early Renaissance, in Florence, frustrations with corruption in the Catholic

Church led to the rise of an Italian friar, Girolamo Savonarola, who devoted himself to the cause of reforming the Catholicism of Renaissance Italy, and what he saw as Florence's insufficient devotion to a purer faith.[1] Savonarola's rhetorical skills were remarkable and the preacher took dead aim at the moral hypocrisy of Florence's rulers and the corrupt Pope, Alexander VI.

Savonarola was not wrong to condemn the excesses of Rome and its religiously connected rulers in Florence. But his utopian purism became evident when he used his words and his clerical and political power to condemn and in some cases ban horse races, ribald carnival songs, gambling, dancing, playing cards, wearing masks, attendance at music schools, and for women, make-up, jewelry, and "fancy" hair and dress. The friar and his political allies instituted religious police to discourage such behaviour and pressed servants to report on such activities among their "masters."[2] While Florentines initially welcomed some of the reforms against the more corrupt behaviours, Renaissance-era Italians eventually rebelled against the overly severe measures which expected purity and conformity to a vision they did not share and which brooked no tolerance for human weaknesses or even normal desires. In 1498, Florentines executed Savonarola and his allies in the town square.[3]

Whether possessed by a purist vision of equality or morality, utopians in past centuries at least had this excuse: they were looking to the future when they sought to construct their perfect societies. But today we are beset by new utopians: ones who look back at the past and expect people in history to have been perfect, or at least to have acted with 21st century sensibilities whether they lived in the 19th century AD or the 9th century BC.

The beliefs of the new utopians bring us to *The 1867 Project.* This book originated with the observation that the Burkean, "organic" project that is Canada has been relentlessly attacked in recent years. (I use the word "organic" because the working assumption is that communities and civilizations are built on the backs and on the success, failures, imperfections, and ideals of previous generations.) Such attacks include removing a statue of Sir John A. Macdonald in Victoria and tearing down another of him in Montreal, renaming universities (Ryerson), and pretending that a pro-indigenous 19th century British Columbia chief justice (Sir Matthew Begbie) was the opposite. Many other examples could be added to the list.

Canada is an ongoing project, not a utopian destination

A common impulse among current history-vandals is the just-noted utopianism directed at the past. Oddly, extreme revisionists expect Canada's founders and others to have fully worked out the implications of their laudable liberty-seeking 19th century presumptions as if they lived in our century. But even reformist-minded men and women of previous eras had major battles to win before later generations could build on their successes. Those battles included "persuading" the few white slave-owners that still existed in early 19th century Canada (or, in the case of some indigenous communities in British Columbia, later in the 19th century) that such practices were a moral abomination and should be abolished; that males without property, and then women, and then indigenous and minority Canadians were equal and deserved the vote and all rights more generally; that minorities as defined by religion, or colour, or ancestry deserved the chance to immigrate to Canada and the chance to succeed.

Meanwhile, while visionaries from previous generations gradually instituted reforms to achieve those goals, most citizens lived and died poor, facing nearly insurmountable barriers just to earn enough income and grow or buy enough food to support their families. Past generations, whether indigenous who first settled in the Americas via the Bering Plains, or much later arrivals who began to arrive a half millennium ago, also all faced famines, plagues, and wars, but persevered and carved out Canada nonetheless. Some, such as French fur traders in parallel with indigenous peoples, helped construct a nascent economy and both contributed to the growth of the early, pre-nation-state we now call home.

Some among the earlier generations of pre-Confederation Canadians and their British colonial predecessors tried to act fairly in critical instances. The British deserve credit for signing treaties across much of Canada and setting up the North-West Mounted Police to enforce the rule of law and thereby ensure that Canada's first settlers would be protected from later settlers.

Later generations had their own challenges: Some survived two world wars and two destructive ideologies, Nazism and communism, along with the tyrants that promoted both, after having endured the Great Depression just prior to the Second World War. On war, consider how many people alive in Canada today have ancestors who fought in previous wars. They include the 4,000 indigenous servicemen and women in World War One among the 650,000 other Canadians who fought.[4] Similar numbers of indigenous servicemen and women served in World War Two,[5] as did over one million fellow Canadians.[6] In the latter war, Canadian servicemen and women helped saved Europe from Adolf Hitler and Nazism, Asia from imperial Japan's predations, and themselves and us today from a world that would have seen even more tyranny had they not fought and sacrificed to preserve a freer world then and now.

Consider that it is only after people climb out of absolute poverty that work on needed reforms in the societies they live in is even feasible. Consider that and the question looking back then becomes not an accusatory one—why did more Canadians not advance reforms earlier?—but a sympathetic one: Is it not remarkable that anyone managed to advocate for the abolition of slavery, for suffrage, for the legal equality of all regardless of one's background or skin colour, and for other policies that would create greater opportunity for all instead of a fixed economic "pie" to be fought over by a few?

Consider all that and then again ponder the problems wrought by utopians today. They look back and accuse farmers, soldiers, nurses, and nuns, long-dead immigrants and their progeny today of privilege when poverty for most was the norm. The critics assume that the previous Canada compares easily with today's more tolerant, opportunity-rich country. Instead, the relevant comparison is: How did other people in other nations fare in 1867, or 1960, and in any other year? On that comparison, Canada and its peoples were mostly ahead of much of the rest of the world on matters related to slavery, women's rights, and rights for minorities, often in eras and in nations where slavery, the oppression of women, and top-down racism from those in power was assumed "normal."

The 19th century is not calling and no one wants it back

None of this means the authors of *The 1867 Project* have romantic ideas about the 19th century and think it a golden age. Some Canadians, at least pre-1950s, did restrict the freedoms of many and in some instances egregiously so in a way that caused permanent harm to those alive at the time.

Previous generations of Canadians were imperfect by our standards, and in some instances even by theirs. Those imperfections are why those of indigenous or Asian ancestry, or of Catholic, Jewish, or Sikh religious affiliation, or without property, or female, or black, indeed suffered: because the idea of the equality of the individual had not yet bloomed robustly enough to change the hearts and minds of a large enough proportion of the population. The imperfections explain why earlier generations wrongly applied a "head tax" to Chinese immigrants, forced Japanese Canadians into internment camps in World War Two, did not treat black Canadians as equal under the law until the 1950s, and withheld the vote from indigenous Canadians (unless they gave up treaty status) until 1960.

Those and other examples were denials of our ideals as Canadians, but the ideas of freedom and order that we did inherit were always desirable. They served as a North Star to guide previous generations of Canadians to greater freedom, internal peace, and prosperity. Such "North Star" ideas include the rule of law inherent in the Royal Proclamation of 1763 which properly assumed that indigenous peoples were able negotiators capable of concluding treaties; the British North America Act of 1867 and its guarantee of elections and parliamentary supremacy vis-à-vis the Crown; the desirability of freedom as enunciated by, to use just one example, Wilfrid Laurier in 1896 (see chapter 20); and the idea of human rights in the 1960 Bill of Rights and in the 1982 Constitution. All Canada's foundational principles and ideas, no matter how imperfectly delivered in history, were always superior to the faulty or weaker ideas enunciated in selected other countries, civilizations, and eras. In much of human history and in every civilization if one goes back far enough – and even in some societies today – error-prone and illiberal assumptions were and are rife: the divine right to rule; the belief that a philosopher-king should govern; anti-scientific and racist beliefs inherent in National Socialism; top-down organizational assumptions of the economy and populations inherent in Marxism; or the belief that religion and state should be one as was generally assumed to be normal in ancient Greece and Rome, in medieval Europe, and is still the case today among Iran's ruling theocrats.

In contrast, the preferred North Star ideas of ordered liberty articulated by past generations of Canadians and for which some of them shed blood would, over time and with justified challenges to status quo, allow for a freer, more flourishing Canada.

Welcome to a book with natural diversity

Now to the topics and authors of this book. Readers will discover a compendium of chapters written by diverse thinkers who would likely disagree with each other on multiple issues. In asking for submissions for *The 1867 Project*, I never inquired about anyone's colour, heritage, faith, philosophy, or political leanings. Instead, I sought out those who sensed and saw that Canada's institutions, peoples, and history have been hit with rhetorical wrecking balls from ideological utopians. If there is any agreement in this book, it is on that. In contrast to those who judge the past from a weaponized present, the authors of this book believe that Canada is worth cherishing, not cancelling, and that in 1867 and since, Canada has been a project: It was not perfect in 1867, 1967, and is not perfect now. And "project" language notwithstanding, Canada will never be "complete" and perfect because it will always be composed of imperfect human beings. And they will necessarily be wrong sometimes, even when guided by their better angels.

The agreement on the idea of Canada as a project led to authors with a natural and not a forced diversity. As a happy accident, *The 1867 Project* reflects every human skin colour and a few different faiths (Christian, Muslim, Jewish, Hindu, or none). Men and women are both "here." The ethnic stock includes those who trace their genetic roots to the first arrivals to the Americas 20,000 years ago to those with roots in Europe, the Anglosphere, Africa, and India. Some authors are a "Heinz 57" mix of multiple national or ethnic ancestries. That is natural given that the human species has been under constant development and mixing since we all departed from our primal ancestral homeland in Africa about eight million years ago.

The authors of *The 1867 Project* tackle present challenges in diverse ways. The first set analyze our compromised institutions and the cancellation of free expression in academic institutions and in the media. As part of such analyses, they examine Critical Theory, Critical Race Theory, and identity politics. They point out the damage that those ideas inflict on schools, higher education, government, and on ordinary Canadians. Bruce Pardy, Gordon Clark, and David Millard Haskell cover much of that territory. Bruce Gilley details the attack on scholarship and empiricism in the firing of Frances Widdowson at Calgary's Mount Royal University. He labels her cancellation as a "witch hunt" prompted by "academic Stalinists on campus" and totalitarian in nature. Gilley is correct on all counts. Rima Azar gives us a first-hand explanation of the dangers of identity politics. Azar, who grew up in civil-war-torn Lebanon, is well-placed to do so. The first section ends with a dive into education and income statistics broken down by race and ethnicity. Matthew Lau asks and answers the question whether Canada in the third decade of the 21st century is institutionally, systemically racist.

The second section in *The 1867 Project* reintroduces three concepts that have been scarce lately: informed history, nuance, and the reality of limited choices in any era. Thus, John Robson explains how modern Canadians owe much to dusty documents such as the 1215 Magna Carta and its limits on tyrants. Greg Piasetzki explores the limited options facing Canada's first prime minister, John A. Macdonald, and concludes, contrary to reflexive critics, that he saved more indigenous lives than any other prime minister. Lynn McDonald, Peter Shawn Taylor, and Leo Deveau explore other Canadian figures instrumental in building Canada from the ground up. McDonald examines Ryerson University's self-created controversy about its founder and finds the justifications for renaming that university unpersuasive. Taylor takes the reader through the judgments and positions of Sir Matthew Begbie, British Columbia's first chief justice. When New Westminster's city council voted in 2019 (four to two) to remove a statue of him from the provincial courthouse, they committed a crime against nuance: Begbie did hang six Tsilhqot'in chiefs for murder and readers can decide for themselves if that was the proper sentence. But in his career, Justice Begbie also commuted the death sentences of other indigenous peoples – something he did not do for white convicts sentenced to hang. He also refused to enforce illiberal laws enacted against indigenous peoples, such as the potlatch ban, and defended British Columbia's Chinese population against white racists. Similarly, Leo Deveau deconstructs a few myths about the founder of Halifax, Edward

Cornwallis. He also details how local politicians disingenuously removed the Cornwallis statue and renamed a local park, in effect sending Cornwallis down a *1984*-like memory hole.

Janice Fiamengo and Chris Champion offer robust chapters on women and the British colonial record, respectively. They provide the historical depth that has been lacking in recent accounts by the popular media, politicians, and academics. Fiamengo asserts that to see women of a century or more ago as only victims, or primarily victims, is simplistic. Canadian women in that earlier era did endure struggles, but some emerged successful. From early lawyers to journalists and in education and in business, Canada has many examples of women who were anything but docile. Champion turns his attention to the colonial British and asks a central question generally ignored in contemporary vilification accounts: The British record as compared with *who* and *what*? With a nod to nuance, informed history, and necessary distinctions, Champion details the many differences between the regressive imperialism of the French, Spanish, Portuguese, and Russians in history, and compares it with the relatively progressive colonialism of the British. Slavery's enforced abolition by the British navy, Champion opines, is one example of the benefits of the British presence. There are others. Of course, no empire was perfect because all of humanity is *imperfect*. Cue again the problem with utopian thinking, including when viewing history and past empires through that lens.

The authors of the third section look to the future by posing and answering the question: What kind of Canada we should consciously create? "Free and flourishing for all" is the easy answer but achieving that vision requires that we all make deliberate choices. Jamil Jivani starts with advice for "woke" progressives: Stop recycling pre-1960s racism under new justifications. Instead, start looking at men and women of colour (and everyone else) as individuals with their own ideas, potential, and character. Along such lines, Peter Best analyses how the Yukon Court of Appeal denied Charter rights to an indigenous woman based on her identity as indigenous. That collective identity trumped her individual identity and there is nothing she can do about that egregious decision unless a higher court reverses such a collectivist-inspired repression of her constitutional rights. Joseph Quesnel explores how an increasing number of First Nations people and leaders are tired of the rhetoric and instead want practical accountability from each other along with freedom and prosperity. Quesnel challenges First Nations and mainstream Canada to think pragmatically and practically about the Canada we all want.

Marjorie Gann's history lesson provides one way to counter the notion that Canadians should feel guilty today about a practice abolished two centuries ago, rather than grasping the fact that what was unique about slavery in Canadian history was its early abolishment. Gann details how slavery was once ubiquitous worldwide. Thus, far from thinking that Canada's relatively rare instances of slavery in our history should make us view Canadian history in only a negative light, we should teach students that while slavery was universal, the movements to abolish it—which happened in the British Empire and the United States—were uniquely Western phenomena, rooted in Protestant Christianity and Enlightenment thought. Gourav Jaswal weighs in on Canada from Goa, India. As an Indian, an entrepreneur, and a father to two young men in Canadian universities, Jaswal is astonished that such a successful nation-state has allowed the negative naysayers to dominate the media, academic, and political landscape—to treat the ongoing Canada project as one worthy of contempt instead of treasuring what has been built since 1867.

The second last chapter in *The 1867 Project* is co-authored by Ven Venkatachalam and me. We explore what immigration flows tell us about Canada's tolerance now and how immigrants are integrating and succeeding in the Canadian mosaic. We conclude that there are multiple reasons for optimism. Finally, I end with a chapter where I argue it is precisely because Canada is so identity-diverse that all Canadians should avoid divisive identity politics and instead unite around laudable ideas.

That is what *The 1867 Project* is about: Renewing and ultimately strengthening the project that is Canada, a centuries-long conscious creation that has provided ever-increasing opportunities to ever-more diverse peoples. It is a project worth continuing and cherishing.

—Mark Milke, editor, and executive director, Aristotle Foundation for Public Policy, Calgary, March 2023

THE 1867 PROJECT

PART I

Addressing the "J'accuse" crowd

CHAPTER 1

The four doctrines of the Apocalypse: Critical Theory and our compromised institutions

Bruce Pardy

Their goal is to destroy the game that we have been playing for the last few centuries and replace it with a game they can never lose.
— JAMES LINDSAY, in New Discourses

I teach at the law school at Queen's University in Kingston, Ontario, which until recently was housed in Sir John A. Macdonald Hall, named after Canada's first prime minister and Kingston's most famous son. In the fall of 2020, the law school's faculty board, consisting of professors, students, administrators, and staff, voted 29 to three to request the University remove Macdonald's name from the building. The University's Board of Trustees thereafter approved a recommendation from the University's Principal to do exactly that. Soon after Macdonald's expulsion from Queen's, Kingston's city council, following similar actions in communities across the country, ordered the removal of his statue from its perch in a city park. Macdonald, without whom Canada might not exist, has been cancelled. He has become a casualty of the cultural revolution currently underway in the country he brought into being.

One of the tasks of any revolution is to tear down the narratives upon which the previous order is built. At universities and other Canadian institutions, that task is all but complete.

Four destructive doctrines

Modern Western civilization grew out of the Enlightenment of the 17th and 18th centuries. The ascendancy of reason in human affairs produced the scientific method and later the Industrial Revolution. Add in the rule of law, individual liberty, private property, and capitalism, and you have the basic recipe that has raised much of humanity out of poverty and oppression over two centuries.

Four academic doctrines—Critical Theory, Postmodernism, Social Justice, and Critical Race Theory—are moving the world, or at least the West, from this triumph to decline. These doctrines reject Enlightenment values such as open inquiry, individual autonomy, free speech, scientific skepticism, and even reason itself. They claim to champion equality, peace, and social cooperation, but instead promote identity politics, elitism, and centralized control. They are the four doctrines of the apocalypse.

Unlike traditional academic inquiry, these "neo-Marxist" doctrines are less theories than programs. They are activist and political. "The philosophers have hitherto only interpreted the world in various ways," Marx famously wrote, "The point, however, is to change it."[1] Critical Theory is not to be confused with critical thinking, for to think critically is to reason, explain, critique, and challenge. Instead, the purpose of these doctrines is to condemn. They largely consist of ideological assertions not based on data or deduction. They lead with their conclusions.

Critical Theory and its related fields do not constitute a singular school of thought but a scholarly umbrella that consists of multiple related approaches and variations that defy easy encapsulation. Its history is messy and convoluted. Its scholarship can be verbose, incoherent, and sometimes impenetrable, while much of its original intellectual project has been overtaken by its modern activist incarnation. Critical Theory is attractive to cultural revolutionaries in part because it is difficult to pin down, like trying to staple jelly to a wall.

Yet these doctrines have become the intellectual foundation for the ascendant ideology of our time, woke progressivism, which is severe, uncompromising, and vengeful. Their commandments have become Canada's secular religion, whose apostles sneer at the foundations of their own society. Cultural contrition has become ubiquitous: Canada is systemically racist. White people are privileged. The nuclear family is misogynist. Capitalism is oppressive. Private property rights cause environmental destruction. Prosperity produces climate change. The most serious threat to the West is not China or Russia but cultural self-hate. No coup is more effective than one committed by a people against itself.

The premises of these four doctrines define the ethos now dominant in major public institutions: government, legacy media, universities, big corporations, public schools, public health authorities, law enforcement, professional regulators and, increasingly, courts. Yet many people are unfamiliar with Critical Theory, would not be able to identify these doctrines by name, and do not realize that they are following their prescriptions. Cultural revolution is complete when the new way of thinking simply becomes the way people think.

Doctrine One: Critical Theory

It all starts with Marx. Between the two world wars, scholars at the Institute for Social Research at the University of Frankfurt began to investigate why Marxism was failing to catch on in the West. They broadened Marx's tight focus on economic oppression of the working class and developed the doctrine known as *Critical Theory*, which is premised on the ideas that power and oppression define relationships throughout society, that knowledge is socially contingent, and that unjust Western institutions should be collapsed and reconstituted.[2]

In his seminal 1937 essay, "Traditional and Critical Theory," Max Horkheimer, sometimes referred to as the father of Critical Theory, distinguished between the scientific or empirical tradition of enquiry and what he called a "critical" approach that integrates numerous disciplines and incorporates historical and social influences in the enterprise of enquiry.[3] Unlike the scientific method, which accepts observation as evidence and reproducibility as confirmation of truth, in Critical Theory, knowledge is contingent upon its origins and the social environment from which it comes. While Critical Theory shares Marx's condemnation of capitalism and the power imbalances that define economic relationships, it rejects Marx's essential empiricism in favour of melding science, philosophy, sociology, and history into a single interdisciplinary enquiry.

Doctrine Two: Postmodernism

Critical Theory is the foundation for numerous other doctrines including Social Justice, Critical Race Theory, and other "critical" theories. Embedded within them is the central tenet of *Postmodernism*, a philosophical movement of the mid- to late 20th century. Postmodernism challenges the premises of Enlightenment reason, particularly the claim that observation and rationality can identify objective truth, whether moral or scientific.[4]

The Postmodernist argument has merit: neither morality nor the scientific premise that what we perceive is real is capable of proof. Postmodernism's Achilles' heel is not its central thesis but its failure to follow it. If there is no objective truth, then no universal conclusions can be reached, and therefore all questions must be left to individuals. To be consistent with their own thesis, Postmodernists should be libertarians. Instead, Postmodernism tends to embrace Critical Theory and vice versa. Modern progressives are apt to insist that truth is relative and subjective when they encounter facts that they do not like, but otherwise eagerly enforce "truths" that they prefer. There is no truth, they say - except the truth that we expect you to embrace.

Doctrine Three: Critical Social Justice

The term "social justice" has been used for centuries to mean various things, but the modern version is *Critical Social Justice*, in which people are not unique individuals but members of identity groups, including those of race, gender, sexuality, disability and so on; and in which power, privilege, and oppression define the relationships between groups, which are either victims or perpetrators.[5] In assessing victimhood and guilt, the social justice concept of "intersectionality" takes account of historically oppressed traits that intersect in any one person and the groups to which the person therefore belongs.[6] Straight white able-bodied males sit at the top of the "privilege pyramid" and disabled, lesbian, transgendered, indigenous women are on the bottom. The objective of critical Social Justice is to flip the pyramid upside down.

Like other features of Critical Theory and its variations, intersectionality makes little sense. Intersectionality's premise, which is obviously correct, is that everyone has a different combination of numerous characteristics: genes and ancestors; parents and childhood circumstances; cultural influences and affiliations; personalities and psychological tendencies; mental and physical attributes and weaknesses; dreams and ambitions; wealth and education; faiths and beliefs; and so on. However, rather than furthering the cause of identity law and politics, this reality should short-circuit the whole enterprise. Imagine a disabled lesbian woman who is part Irish, Mayan and South African; is a Rhodes scholar and specialist in Dutch art; comes from a wealthy family with a reserved father and an alcoholic mother; was home-schooled, is slightly short-sighted, has above average looks and below average height; suffers from eczema, is a chess master, is Roman Catholic, and speaks English and German. This person, who is of course far more complex than even this long list of traits reflects, will share each of these traits with some number of other people but her exact combination with no one. The logical conclusion of intersectionality is that she is the only person who belongs to her group. The smallest minority is the individual. Social justice acolytes profess to protect minorities yet denigrate the autonomy that allows individuals to be unique.

Doctrine Four: Critical Race Theory

According to *Critical Race Theory*, which crystallized in the 1980s in the American legal academy, race is the fundamental organizing feature of Western, especially American, society; power and oppression define race relationships; and racism is "systemic" and "structural," embedded in the culture of capitalism and endemic to white people.[7] Critical Race Theory turns the meaning of racism on its head. Racism used to mean treating people differently because of their race (hence "race-ism") rather than approaching them as individuals. It meant judging them on the colour of their skin rather than on the content of their character, to paraphrase Martin Luther King Jr. In Critical Race Theory, racial identity is fundamental instead of irrelevant. Race indicates whether you are victim or oppressor and therefore deserving of compensation or contempt. In Critical Race Theory, it is racist to deny the intrinsic advantage of white privilege or to claim to be colourblind. The new racism means failing to condemn or favour the right races.

As political tools, Critical Theory and its variations are brilliant. Any challenge to their legitimacy can be interpreted as a demonstration of their thesis: the assertion of reason, logic, and evidence is a manifestation of privilege and power. Thus, any challenger risks the stigma of a bigoted oppressor. James Lindsay, an independent American critic of Critical Theory and Social Justice, calls Critical Theory a "kafkatrap."[8] "Notice race? Because you're racist. Don't? Because you're privileged, thus racist." If you deny that you are a witch, then you are a witch. And if you do not deny it, then you are a witch for sure. Pointing out that Critical Theory makes no sense misses the point: making sense is Western and privileged.[a]

The long march through the institutions

In the decades following its birth at the Frankfurt School, Critical Theory and its variations made an inexorable march through universities, influencing such disparate disciplines as sociology, literary criticism, and linguistics, infiltrating professional schools like teachers' colleges and law schools, and dominating "grievance studies" programs such as women's studies, gender studies, and media studies. Today its reach extends to virtually every field in the arts and social sciences, and its final conquest is now underway inside science, technology, engineering, and medical faculties.

Generations of university graduates, taught to believe in the premises of Critical Theory rather than how to think critically about it, now populate the workplace. Critical Race Theory and Social Justice premises are embedded in elementary school curricula, with white children taught that they are racist and oppressive, and non-white children that they are victimized and without agency. Law societies require lawyers to attest to their belief in the ideology of "equity, diversity, and inclusion," while medical regulators censure doctors for expressing medical opinions about coercive government policies. In the corporate world, ESG, the "Environmental, Social, and Governance" model of business administration, asserts ideological control over corporations and the economy. In the universities themselves, job offers and research grants are now reserved for those who comport with Critical Theory's prescriptions, narrowing the range of acceptable thought and stifling open inquiry. The new order has been established as the ascendant status quo.

---

a) James Lindsay, along with partners Helen Pluckrose and Peter Boghossian, masterminded the "Grievance Studies Hoax," in which they managed to get seven academic papers of Critical Theory and identity studies nonsense accepted for publication in scholarly journals.

The concept of a long march through the institutions can be traced to Italian neo-Marxist Antonio Gramsci, who argued that the cultural hegemony of capitalism features a ruling class that maintains power through cultural institutions rather than with overt force. Therefore, Gramsci warned, direct revolution aimed at simply capturing the means of production was unlikely to succeed without first creating a new hegemony of ideas and beliefs. As he wrote on the state and civil society and why both could not be confronted head-on but had to be undermined akin to physical guerilla warfare:

> The superstructures of civil society are like the trench-systems of modern warfare. In war it would sometimes happen that a fierce artillery attack seems to have destroyed the enemy's entire defensive system, whereas in fact is had only destroyed the outer perimeter; and at the moment of their advance and attack, the assailants would find themselves confronted by a line of defense which was still effective.[9]

The idea, as crystallized by German revolutionary Rudi Dutschke in the 1960s, was that Gramsci's implicit and more effective war could be waged by turning civil society's institutions and processes against itself, especially its altruistic inclinations "vulnerable to exploitation, manipulation, and subversion" by what Lenin called "useful idiots." Many of today's radical "social justice" warriors in the field of feminism, race and gender seem willing or keen to play the latter role."[10] One need only look to the ethos now dominant in public institutions of every description to conclude that Gramsci's vision has been realized.

"Repressive Tolerance" and woke progressivism

Double standards on speech and conduct are baked into our current political order. Burning churches and blocking railways are blows in support of Social Justice, but peacefully protesting vaccine mandates constitutes a public order emergency. Defying pandemic lockdown rules is a threat to public safety when parishioners gather for church services in parking lots, but not when thousands gather for Black Lives Matter marches. The federal government vilifies law abiding gun owners while it eliminates minimum sentences for gun crimes.[11] The hypocrisy of our authorities is no accident. Their choices are deliberate and calculated.

This uneven treatment, according to James Lindsay, is rooted in a single 1965 essay by Critical Theory philosopher Herbert Marcuse called "Repressive Tolerance," whose theme Lindsay encapsulates in one sentence: "movements from the left must be extended tolerance, even when they are violent, while movements from the right must not be tolerated, including suppressing them by violence."[12]

This is the world we now inhabit. If you are not on board with the prevailing program, your speech and behaviour must be crushed. Intolerance should extend to actions as well as to expression. Marcuse wrote:

> ...true pacification requires the withdrawal of tolerance... at the stage of communication in word, print, and picture. Such extreme suspension of the right of free speech and free assembly is indeed justified.... Different opinions and 'philosophies' can no longer compete peacefully for adherence and persuasion on rational grounds.[13]

Once upon a time, when they were cultural mavericks, liberals championed free speech. Establishment conservatives were the censors, urging limits on obscenity, blasphemy, and communist propaganda. In a free society, went the liberal argument, all must be able to express ideas and opinions no matter who has the reins of power. Freedom of expression protected the dissenter, the rebel, and the heretic from the orthodoxy of the prevailing view. Now the shoe is on the other foot. With the help of Critical Theory and its related doctrines, liberalism has morphed into the dominant ideology of woke progressivism and free speech is no longer needed to protect the left, whose sensibilities now prevail. It turns out that progressives were less interested in the principle of free speech than in promoting their own values.

The pattern cannot be missed unless you avert your eyes. The federal government under Prime Minister Justin Trudeau, for instance, has repeatedly promised to pass legislation to monitor social media for "misinformation" and "hate speech."[14] A new orthodoxy is being established: speech consistent with progressive norms is legitimate, while contrary opinions are racist, "alt-right," or violent; whether speech is objectionable depends in part upon the identity of the speaker and the subject; attacking European culture, whiteness, Western values, or Christianity is proper speech but defending them is beyond the pale.

Undermining individualism and equality in the law

Equal treatment under the law means that everyone is subject to the same rules and standards. When justice is blind, the law treats people as individuals rather than as members of groups, without regard to personal characteristics and regardless of disparate outcomes that equal treatment under the law produces. It applies in the same way to rich and poor, black and white, man and woman, straight and gay.

But to Critical Race Theory proponents, social justice advocates, and increasingly lawyers and courts, equality of treatment, also known as "formal equality" or "equality of application," is unjust. Instead, they say, legal equality should mean that identity groups should be equal in outcome, and that different rules and standards should be applied to different groups to achieve this result. Equality of outcome, also known as "substantive equality" or "equity," requires that justice not be blind but instead should inquire into group identity. The law should not treat people the same way but distinguish between them based upon group affiliation and make adjustment to take account of "systemic" advantages and disadvantages.

These two kinds of equality are incompatible. They cannot co-exist. The law cannot apply the same rules to every individual and also apply different rules to different groups. If the law must apply equally to everyone, then equality of outcome is impossible. If all groups are to achieve equal levels of success, then the same rules and standards cannot be applied. Substantive equality assesses whether standards will be more difficult for some to meet than others. A rule might require that all volunteers for military duty be able to run a mile in under ten minutes wearing heavy boots. That rule establishes a common standard for all recruits. It meets the requirements for equality of treatment. However, if the average man runs faster than the average woman, the rule does not comply with the requirements for substantive equality because as a group women will have a greater challenge meeting the standard than men.

In Canada, the right to formal equality appears to be guaranteed in the Charter of Rights and Freedoms. Section 15(1) of the Charter reads: "Every individual is equal... without discrimination..." The section says that it is to apply to individuals, not to groups. The words describe a universal right to equal treatment under the law. The same rules are to apply to everyone "...

without discrimination and, in particular, without discrimination based on race, national or ethnic origin, colour, religion, sex, age or mental or physical disability." The section says that the law should not distinguish between people based on identity and group affiliation.

However, the Supreme Court of Canada has said otherwise. Since the adoption of the Charter 40 years ago, the Court has insisted that section 15(1) protects substantive, not formal, equality. It has said that "identical treatment may frequently produce serious inequality" and that different treatment may be necessary to produce equitable outcomes between groups.[15] According to the Court, equal treatment under the law is not what the Charter requires. Instead, under the Charter, substantive equality means discriminating in favour of "historically disadvantaged" groups. It is available only in select circumstances to a privileged few. The white, straight, Canadian male has the worst of all constitutional worlds. He can neither insist that the same rules be applied to everybody nor claim to belong to the right kind of group to have the rules adjusted in his favour. The words of the Charter say that every individual is equal, but he is not one of them. Substantive equality makes some more equal than others.

Corrupting science: A recent example

In 1840, William Whewell described the scientific revolution of the 16th and 17th centuries as "the transition from an implicit trust in the internal powers of man's mind to a professed dependence upon external observation."[16] Scientific discovery challenged established belief. The sun does not, in fact, go around the Earth, and the world is not, in fact, flat.

Science makes an excellent servant and an imperious master. The scientific method is a method of enquiry, not an approved set of conclusions. As a process for investigating facts and theories, its practical benefits are unmatched. Yet the history of science is a history of error. That is not a flaw but a feature. Scientific inquiry depends on falsification: the use of empirical evidence not to definitively prove the truth of a theory, but to reveal its flaws.[17] When data shows theories to be faulty, those theories can be challenged, improved, or replaced. Thus, the search for truth leads to error that is (often) less erroneous than the previous theory. This process calls for humility, not conceit. Just wait a while and the understanding may change. Skepticism and dissent, not consensus and authority, fuel scientific progress.

But anti-Enlightenment doctrines are not based on skepticism and dissent. For Critical Theory and the woke progressivism that it has begotten, COVID-19 was the perfect storm. An airborne virus that posed little risk to most people empowered a technocratic elite to declare its monopoly on scientific "truth". Like critical theories themselves, the public health-driven COVID imperative led with its conclusions. Doctors and scientists who questioned the accuracy and validity of official medical narratives were censored by their own regulators and institutions. Public health officials stood on The Science to justify government *diktats*, broad bureaucratic discretion, incoherent policies, rituals such as wearing masks that lacked actual benefit, and directives that limited individual agency in the name of collective good. "Obey the science" came to mean "Believe what we tell you and do as you are told." Citing science, officials prevented people from visiting their families at Christmas and closed small businesses and restaurants. Vaccine mandates were the ultimate form of cancel culture, separating the unvaccinated from their jobs, education, travels, and social standing.

Yet these measures were not medical or scientific. Public policies, by definition, involve trade-offs: social, economic, psychological, and political. Trade-offs reflect values, and values are not scientific. Scientific evidence may be relevant but never determinative. While once scientific discovery challenged the supremacy of theological dogma, scientific authorities, not the Church, are now the despots, dictating behaviour from the pulpit of press conferences with the power of compulsory "recommendations."

It is no coincidence that universities, once a crucible for scientific discovery and rationality, were among the most hyper-COVID-vigilant of institutions. Some faculty tended to be irrationally germophobic, supporting the most extreme COVID measures, and expressed a COVID narrative replete with Critical Theory jibber-jabber. One professor wrote in consternation when her university declined to extend mandatory masking and vaccine requirements, "The reference to a 'mask-friendly' campus reveals the university's awareness of the violence embedded in anti-mask ideology and the extent to which white heteronormative nationalism has infiltrated the institution's thinking, as it has the broader social fabric."[18] As the anonymous writer Eugyppius has put it, universities "aren't just eager sponsors of racial hysteria. They have also emerged as some of the most radical centres of Corona containment in the world."[19]

Free people may disagree with scientific theory no matter the claims of consensus, which is no test of truth. For the layman, "confidence in science" was apt to amount to little more than blind faith in the authority of people who claimed to have expertise—and during COVID, blind faith was more popular than skepticism and dissent. Institutions captured by Critical Theory produced the debacle of COVID overreach and undermined the principles of science itself.

Ignoring facts, erasing history

Critical Theory and woke progressives tend to treat history as an Orwellian memory hole where contrary facts are banished in pursuit of a preferred narrative. Queen's University cancelled John A. Macdonald purportedly on the grounds that he was a racist white man. Macdonald is accused, among other things, of forcing indigenous children to go to residential schools and letting Aboriginal people on the prairies starve when the buffalo disappeared. According to Macdonald's defenders, the historical record says otherwise.[20] Residential schools already existed before Macdonald came to power, and they did not become compulsory until the 1920s, 30 years after his death. When the famine struck, Macdonald sent aid to save indigenous lives and was condemned in the House of Commons for providing too much. Looking after people was not something governments commonly did until the welfare state emerged well into the 20th century.

But resorting to the historical record to defend Macdonald misses the point. Macdonald's demise has little to do with the man himself and everything to do with what he has come to represent. That Macdonald was enlightened for his time has made no difference to his denunciation. Macdonald himself is less important than how he is regarded. When any historical figure is cancelled, the real targets are the attitudes of the living. Who controls the past controls the future, Orwell tells us, and who controls the present controls the past.[21]

Despite the facts, Macdonald will be called racist because that is the conclusion Critical Race Theory demands. Facts are socially contingent, the Postmodernists assert, and are the product of privilege and oppressive power relationships, say the Critical Theorists. Facts, in other words, matter only when they support the proper narrative. White men, especially if they are straight, are privileged by definition and therefore racist. Macdonald, as a dead white man who brought into being what is now regarded as an oppressive Western nation, is self-evidently culpable.[b]

Conclusion

Do not expect bedrock principles of Canadian law and society to withstand these subversions. Rome cannot be protected from the Visigoths once the Visigoths run the place. Critical Theory revolutionaries and woke progressives have infiltrated institutions with their own norms and edicts, and a cultural apocalypse is well underway. As James Lindsay has put it, the goal "is to destroy the game that we have been playing for the last few centuries and replace it with a game that they can never lose."[22] Canadians not on board with the new order will find themselves the barbarians on the outside looking in.

It turns out that obscure academic doctrines are among the most serious threats to freedom, prosperity, informed history, and rationality. Henry Kissinger, among others, is credited with the observation that university politics are so vicious precisely because the stakes are so small. That line is funny only if it is true. We now know it is dead wrong.

---

b) I have only touched on Canada's first prime minister given that two other chapters in this book, from John Robson and Greg Piasetzki, deal in detail with Macdonald's record. For my purposes, Macdonald serves as an example of Critical Theory's acidic effect on the legacies of historic figures and on their contribution to Canada.

CHAPTER 2

Cancel culture harms journalists, journalism, and citizenship

Gordon Clark

This is called a purge. It is a mentality that belongs in Stalin's Russia. How bad does this atmosphere we are living in have to get before the people who say cancel culture is overblown admit that it is, in fact, an insanity that is swallowing up the world?
—BILL MAHER

The first sign of trouble arrived as my wife and I were walking our dog one Saturday morning in September 2019. My boss, *Vancouver Sun* editor-in-chief Harold Munro called me and was upset about an opinion piece that ran that day in the *Sun*'s print edition. He said that the column by Mount Royal University lecturer Mark Hecht questioning the "dogma of diversity, tolerance and inclusion"[1] was being criticized on social media, including by members of the *Sun*'s reporting staff, as racist. Munro said he agreed and that the newspaper would publish a public apology for running Hecht's opinion. Also, a staff meeting would be held to discuss the matter given the anger that was being publicly vented by some employees and other voices on social media. Munro had already removed Hecht's article from the *Sun*'s website, a breach of journalistic ethics.[a]

I was shocked by Munro's reaction and plans and—as I would soon learn—those of his superiors at Postmedia's head office in Toronto. I told him that

a) The ethics guidelines of the Canadian Association of Journalists notes: "We generally do not 'unpublish' or remove digital content, despite public requests, or 'source remorse.'" Rare exceptions generally involve matters of public safety, an egregious error, ethical violation, or legal restrictions such as publication bans. See Canadian Association of Journalists (2011), *Ethics Guidelines*, Canadian Association of Journalists <https://bit.ly/3guP6mL>.

we should run another piece countering Hecht's arguments and any letters that arrived disagreeing with what he had written—the time-honoured way one encourages public debate and discussion in newspaper editorial pages. Munro rejected this option to maintain the diversity of opinion in the *Sun*'s pages and online.

Society is not well-served by allowing activists or anyone with an agenda to redefine such a fundamental term as racism, especially when their intent is to weaponize it in order to attack others. The Hecht opinion piece was not racist by the standard definition. Hecht had not argued, as Merriam-Webster defines it, "that racial differences produce an inherent superiority of a particular race."[2] Nor had he engaged in or encouraged "behaviour or attitudes that reflect and foster this belief," another Merriam-Webster entry.[3] Hecht also had not argued that Canada should restrict immigration to certain races or ethnicities. In an article published as the controversy swirled on canadaland.com—a podcast company and news website known for criticizing other media—Hecht also rejected "the characterization of his ideas as racist or white nationalist, because 'I'm talking about culture, not skin colour.'"[4]

That is not to say that Hecht's column was perfect. It contained phrasing that was at times unnecessarily provocative and imprecise, including a line near the end where he wrote that we must "say goodbye to diversity, tolerance and inclusion." I understood him to mean what he described in the essay as the "dogma of diversity"—the officially enforced, uncritical belief in the concept as opposed to diversity itself.

A Black Trinidadian versus blind-faith multiculturalism

Given the uproar, we shortly returned from our walk and I went to visit a long-time friend and neighbour—a Jamaican immigrant who holds progressive views—who subscribed to the *Sun* and likely would have read Hecht's piece. I wanted to hear her thoughts. Not only did she *not* consider Hecht's article racist, her chief concern was "how frightening" it was to learn that the editor of the *Sun* was censoring Hecht's opinion and what that meant both about the newspaper and the climate of political discussion and free speech in Canada. She mentioned Neil Bissoondath, a Trinidadian-Canadian author and Governor General's Award winner whose 1994 book, *Selling Illusions: The Cult of Multiculturalism in Canada*, argues that

Canada's "policy of multiculturalism, with its emphasis on the former or ancestral homeland and its insistence that '*There is more important than Here*,' discourages the full loyalty of Canada's citizens." In the book, Bissoondath argues that multiculturalism in Canada, "encourages exoticism, highlighting the differences that divide Canadians rather than the similarities that unite them." My neighbour's point was that Hecht's general view that unfettered tolerance of diversity can lead to social problems and lack of trust has been stated many times before—in Bissoondath's case by an immigrant person of colour—and that it is not inherently racist to discuss problems with diversity.

That diversity can have negative impacts on social trust has been extensively researched by academics, including social psychologists and business and political science professors. For example, the authors of a 2020 paper, "Ethnic Diversity and Social Trust: A Narrative and Meta-Analytical Review," published in the peer-reviewed journal, *Annual Review of Political Science*, found "a statistically significant negative relationship between ethnic diversity and social trust across all studies" of the 87 they examined.[5] That is not to say that other research has not found positive aspects to diversity, something I generally support. However, aspects of diversity should be up for debate, discussion, and research—people should be free to engage in all of the foregoing without being slammed with accusations of racism.

When I went to work the following Monday morning, it became clear that that approach was not going to survive at the *Vancouver Sun*. The first problem was that Munro had run an apology in that day's paper:

> An opinion article by Mark Hecht published in Saturday's Weekend Review section and online contained views that do not meet the journalistic standards of the *Vancouver Sun* and do not represent the views of our editors and journalists. The *Vancouver Sun* is committed to promoting and celebrating diversity, tolerance and inclusion. Our vibrant community and nation are built on these important pillars.
>
> We apologize for the publication of the article. We are reviewing our local workflow and editorial processes to ensure greater oversight and accountability so that this does not happen again. We value the trust that our community and readers place in the *Vancouver Sun* and we are committed to continuing, every day, to earn that trust...

As I always did on a Monday morning, I began to read the hundreds of emails that flowed in over the weekend into the four email accounts that I managed, including the letters-to-the-editor emails for our two newspapers (the *Province* in addition to the *Vancouver Sun*). What began as a trickle became a torrent of letters condemning Munro's decision to pull the online version of Hecht's column as well as the apology for running it in print. The vast majority of readers who wrote in said they did not view the column as racist, even some who disagreed with it said the same, and many said that it raised important issues that needed to be discussed. Some threatened to cancel their subscriptions over the company's conduct. Many were particularly upset that Munro had written that Hecht's column did "not represent the views of our editors and journalists." Guest columns, they pointed out, are by definition not required to reflect the views of a newspaper's "editors and journalists." Others asked if Munro understood his job, and queried if the apology and new opinion policies meant that in future the *Vancouver Sun* would only run opinions that aligned with the views of the paper's "editors and journalists." Postmedia's attack on free expression upset many readers, with the ratio of letters against the paper's apology versus those that favoured it running at least fifteen to one.

When Munro walked by my desk outside his office that September morning, I told him I needed to speak with him. He said yes but that there was something he needed to do first. He went to his desk, worked on his computer for a few minutes, and then just before calling me in, an email to all editorial staff announcing a staff meeting about the Hecht article popped into my inbox.

In our closed-door meeting, I was frank. I told Munro that I did not think the column was racist, that it should not have been pulled, that the apology was wrong-headed and that I did not believe the paper had broken any journalist standards by running it. The *Vancouver Sun*'s "journalistic standards" referenced in the apology were never provided to me despite multiple requests because no such document exists. It should also be noted that in running the Hecht piece, I was operating under the ethical guidelines opinion editors have used for centuries in Western liberal democracies, the essence of which can be found in the relevant sections of the former B.C. Press Council Code of Practice:

> Newspapers should defend their hard-won right to exercise the widest possible latitude in expressing opinions, no matter how controversial or unpopular the opinions may be, and to give columnists, editorial cartoonists and others the same latitude in expressing personal opinions.[6]

The B.C. Council was merged into the National NewsMedia Council in 2015. The new organization relies on the Ethics Guidelines of the Canadian Association of Journalists (CAJ), which includes in its section on journalistic independence that:

> Columnists and commentators should be free to express their views, even when those views conflict with those of their organizations, as long as the content meets generally accepted journalistic standards for fairness and accuracy.[7]

Ironically, under the section "Diversity," another CAJ guideline states: "News organizations—including newspapers, websites, magazines, radio and television—provide forums for the free interchange of information and opinion. As such, we seek to include views from all segments of the population."[8] All segments of the population include people with conservative views. Given that, I never apologized, as some suggested I should, for running Hecht's words, even if they upset some people. I ran his column because I believed it would generate thoughtful debate and because I believe in free speech. To be blunt, I did my job.

In my meeting with Munro, I also pointed out to him that the reporting staff should not be commenting publicly on pieces in the opinion section. That was necessary in order to maintain the longstanding ethical standard that reporters not make public their political views so they can do their jobs free of accusations of bias. While opposition to actual racism is non-partisan, the claims against Hecht reflected the false accusations of racism currently in fashion among critical race theory proponents and those who push their agenda without necessarily understanding its ideological underpinnings or goals. I also expressed concern about the way some staff were publicly criticizing the paper's decision to run Hecht's column and taking other negative actions against their employer, including talking anonymously to reporters from other media outlets that led to several "newsroom in revolt" stories, not to mention unfair personal attacks on me. I pointed out that such behaviour in other organizations—and in newsrooms previously—would generally end with employees being disciplined, if not fired.

Media management versus journalistic free expression

I told Munro about the many readers who were angry at his decision to pull the column and issue an apology. (Many had also written to him directly.) Munro responded that the decisions to apologize, hold a meeting with staff, and introduce radical changes to how the opinion pages would be managed in future came from head office [in Toronto]. He said he was taking his directions from his boss, Lucinda Chodan, then Postmedia's senior vice president of content. He said, for instance, that she had personally approved the wording of the apology.

Munro explained that his Postmedia superiors were reacting to negative social media comments about the Hecht column, particularly online claims that its publication meant that Postmedia was racist. He said their concern was linked to the fact that Postmedia brass had been stung by an August 2019 article, "You must be this conservative to ride: the inside story of Postmedia's right turn."[9] The article claimed that ahead of the 2019 federal election, CEO Andrew MacLeod had "tapped veteran *National Post* journalist and commentator Kevin Libin, considered by some at the chain to be among its most conservative editorial voices, to oversee federal and provincial political reporting and certain commentary published across Postmedia's newspapers." As the author wrote, "His mandate is straightforward: to make the papers more "reliably" conservative." Thus, some critics on social media falsely linked Postmedia's new "reliably conservative" mandate from head office to what they considered Hecht's alleged white supremacy, sending company executives into a moral panic. Munro told me that his superiors wanted to demonstrate that the company was not racist. To put it another way, it seems I was caught up in a panicky, poorly thought-out corporate marketing exercise in which the company tossed aside longstanding, critically important journalistic principles of free speech and editorial independence in order to address a public perception concern.

My first inkling that my time with Postmedia was coming to an end came with what Munro said next: an order from Munro to me not to run any of the significant majority of letters from readers upset with the company's apology and its decision to remove the Hecht column from the *Sun*'s website. As with a government scared of continuing bad news, or a corporate CEO panicked by critical coverage—i.e., from the media which is to show no fear or favour—Munro asserted that Postmedia wanted to, "take the oxygen" out of the issue by not running anything further.

The *Sun's* decision to censor its readers was particularly unprincipled. The letters sections of newspapers are for the readers; what I have always called the original social media, and have long been a forum for debate of public issues. As editorial pages editor, I always provided a representative range of opinions in the letters section, even when readers criticized the newspaper. By using the letters page to prop up one, in fact, minority view of the Hecht column, and to withhold all criticism of its actions, the *Vancouver Sun* had turned the opinion pages into a corporate propaganda leaflet.

Munro also ignored and refused to run material critical of Postmedia's actions by former journalists such as Trevor Lautens, who worked in newspapers for 65 years, including from 1963 to 2000 in all the roles within the *Vancouver Sun*'s opinion section. He submitted a proposed column a few days after the paper's apology had run which he titled, "A thoughtful, gentle reflection on a *Sun* apology that shafted free expression":

> Which is more reprehensible? *Vancouver Sun* editor-in-chief Harold Munro's craven apology for the exercise of free expression in the paper's printing of Mark Hecht's Sept. 7 opinion piece? Or is it the paper's cowardly throwing raw meat to what I kindly call the New Bullies and New Bigots, cheering a major daily newspaper's humility for expressing opinions the NBNB want permanently banished—and in this case retroactively expunged—from the media, the public forum, the academy, the public school classrooms, the social media's chattering classes whose importance is grotesquely inflated, and finally mainstream political parties, either already onside with or panicked about offending any demographic or special interest?

Lautens also wrote that it was:

> ...incredulous that several top *Sun* editorial staffers . . . endorsed this indefensible suppression. No defence, no debating here of Hecht's academically footnoted essay—noting only that his citing of Danish reaction to Muslim immigration has been widely reported and commented on. The issue is free expression, and the necessity for it to be given vigorous, regular and fearless exercise by all.[10]

Five days after Munro's Saturday morning call and three days after the manic Monday retreat from journalistic principles and standards, I awoke before four a.m. on Thursday, having not slept much over the previous nights. I checked my work email and discovered a shocking reply to Munro's note to staff by Nathan Griffiths, then the most recently-hired person in the newsroom. Not content to discuss his concerns with Munro privately, Griffiths blasted his email to the entire newsroom, where, of course, it was quickly leaked to other media:

> Unfortunately, I was not able to make the meeting on Monday but I have been able to listen to a recording of it and have some thoughts on the meeting & your follow up email. I would like to stress that reading a blatantly racist op-ed of white nationalist talking points disgusted & infuriated me & it has been very difficult trying to work since then. I do not feel that either your published apology or explanations to staff were adequate—nor do they adequately address the the (sic) hateful racism so casually on display in our paper's op-eds.[11]

Griffiths, a "data journalist" who was heralded by Munro on his arrival for his previous experience at the *New York Times*—all seven months of it—had been at the *Sun* less than a year when he wrote his email and complained that the "retracted article was merely the latest in a series of ignorant, bigoted & racist op-eds that have been published on our site that I found in 30 minutes of browsing"[12]—thirty minutes of browsing apparently now passing for thoroughness in modern newsrooms.

"Outrage archaeology"

Griffiths likely "found" what he claimed was a pattern of bigotry in columns I and others had written by punching my name and words such as "Muslim" or "immigration" into an electronic database of previously published articles in Canadian newspapers. There is a term for this, a common technique of the cancel culture cult—outrage archeology—where you dig up what people have written in the past and look for something to express outrage about or to signal one's self-proclaimed personal virtue. It is often about matters that generated no controversy at the time. None of the columns Griffiths hysterically and wrongly labelled as "racist" had ever been identified as such to me by anyone over the years, including my colleagues, bosses, nor my readers.

For instance, Griffiths claimed that a column[13] by Robert Hauknes, a third-generation commercial fisherman from Prince Rupert, was "racist" by raising concerns that commercial fishing lodges, often catering to foreign nationals, were allowed to fish unimpeded while commercial fishermen were barred from fishing. Griffiths also wrote that Hauknes claimed that "'foreigners' are coming to Canada to illegally harvest salmon while on fishing tours in B.C.," something the author did not say. His column was not a racist complaint about "foreigners." Hauknes was raising concerns about the policies of Fisheries and Oceans Canada. As well, the "foreigners" Hauknes wrote about were mostly wealthy, white businesspeople from the United State and Europe, flying in to luxury fishing lodges up the coast of British Columbia, hoping to catch massive salmon they could brag about back home.

Griffiths also claimed the opinion section under my guidance had run an "Islamaphobic op-ed supporting bans on niqabs."[14] The column author, Calvin White, is a veteran high school counsellor from Salmon Arm, a mental-health worker and author who has written opinion pieces for most of the major newspapers in Canada. White was frank that he disliked face-covering niqabs—as do the vast majority of Canadians—because they see it in many instances not as voluntary but as a symbol of oppression for immigrant women. To describe such a column as racist entirely misrepresented the views of White, who, as he wrote to me later, is a "thrice NDP candidate, socialist, counselor who loves all children, with biracial kids and [is married to] an immigrant wife."

One of my columns from 2017 that Griffiths attacked as "evidence" of my alleged racism was about my concerns that Vancouver—already the Canadian city with the highest population density—was getting denser and the negative impacts that was creating.[15] Although the column noted reams of Statistics Canada data and highlighted the numerous problems of too-rapid growth—normally a left-wing concern—on Metro Vancouver, Griffiths distilled my argument to, "we are letting too many people into Canada." That was a grotesque misrepresentation of what I wrote. That column was not motivated by opposition to immigration or immigrants and certainly not by racism. It argued that "we can't keep up with growth, from exorbitant house prices, badly crowded roads, a chronically overburdened transit system, long wait lists for medical specialists and surgery, overcrowded schools and a general over-demand on government services"—the subjects of countless newspaper stories and endless public debate that continues to this day. Since two-thirds of Canada's population growth comes from immigration, which mostly affects its large cities, "Perhaps it is time to ask whether having the fastest growth rate among the top industrialized nations... is best for Canada?" I mused.

I was not alone then or now in wondering if some slowdown—not an end—in immigration numbers, might help moderate soaring housing prices and other costs. Don Wright—who retired in 2020 as British Columbia's deputy minister to the premier, cabinet secretary and head of the public service—made similar points in a 2021 online essay published by the federal government-funded Public Policy Forum. He has called for lower immigration rates to help Canada's struggling middle class:

> There seems to be a reluctance to challenge the arguments for growing immigration levels. Perhaps that is because they have been repeated so often, they are generally believed to be true. At least in part, however, it is because the promoters of large immigration numbers are quick to label as racist, parochial or small-minded any questioning of larger immigration numbers. Canada needs, however, to be a little more nuanced in its thinking than just accepting that more is always better. The question of what the optimal level of immigration should be over time is a legitimate question of public policy debate.[16]

With many *Sun* journalists expressing their disagreement with Hecht's column and anger through Twitter and other social media, journalists with other news outlets produced articles about our allegedly "racist" newsroom. David Beers, the founder of the left-wing media website, The Tyee, and a frequent critic of mainstream media, wrote three pieces about the Hecht controversy, using Griffiths' email as the main source for one. They included unfair, personal attacks on me by a writer who has never met nor interviewed me. Several of his readers agreed.

In the comments section under Beers' first article, a reader who went by the handle "Political Ranger" called the piece "the most abhorrent piece of yellow journalism I have seen in a long, long time, perhaps ever, not least because of its complete capitulation to Orwellianism." Another, "WesNelsonBC," said: "Very disappointed in this article. What started as an analysis suddenly evolved into a hatchet job attacking one specific individual. There was no analysis as to how the decision by Clark to run this opinion piece was out of line with Munro's direction that 'he wants to make more space on the op-ed pages for a wide range of voices.' As the article states, Clark's job description is 'facilitating conversation in the public interest on the pages of two newspapers reaching tens of thousands of local citizens.' How can he do this if [it] is only acceptable to publish opinions is (sic) support of immigration?"

Griffiths concluded his email to Munro by stating he hoped that "moving forward the op-ed pages would reflect the voices of B.C. that are underserved, that are ignored & that face discrimination every day." His suggestion that the editorial pages had ignored marginalized voices was complete nonsense. During my time as editorial pages editor, the *Province* and the *Vancouver Sun* routinely ran columns by members of the LGBTQ community, multicultural and poverty groups, native leaders, environmentalists, leftist think tanks and other progressive groups, as well as works by scientists and researchers on all manner of academic subjects, including rising concerns about climate change. With one exception from a child-poverty group that submitted a too-similar column to one recently published, I do not recall ever turning down the kind of material Griffiths claimed was under-represented in the newspapers.

Moreover, as is typical with cancel culture and outrage archaeology, other aspects of one's work that do not fit the "racist" narrative are ignored, i.e. how I had: written against racism and in defence of multiculturalism; twice defended the right of Chinese merchants in Richmond, B.C to display Chinese-only signs in their windows,[17] a not very popular opinion at the time; expressed horror at a racist attack on a young Muslim woman on a transit train[18]; denounced a white supremacist at Vancouver city hall in 2017, in which I wrote that such people hold "ignorant, despicable and hateful views" and that, "Like many people, I've been heartbroken in recent days about the racist protests and violence south of the border."[19]

Social worker, film producer and author Alex Sangha said he was "surprised" by the information Beers claimed about me, noting in a comment under his story that "I have never met him and I do not know him, however, he published three op-eds in the *Province that I wrote about legalization of the sex trade,*[20] domestic violence in the South Asian community[21] and universal health care. I am a gay South Asian male. I am not sure if Gordon knew that or if he even cared."

I did and I did not. Of course.

The rise of safe-space journalism

Newspaper journalism in North America began, as it frequently remains in Britain, Europe and elsewhere in the world, as an extension of party politics. The journalism presented was a means to promote partisan friends and attack foes. Beginning in the mid-nineteenth century and expanding significantly in the twentieth century, however, a new journalistic ethos of political independence and dedication to reporting the truth in a balanced, apolitical way took over, particularly at quality newspapers in large metropolitan markets. The *New York Times* emerged as a leading example. Its Ethical Journalism: Handbook of Values and Practices for the News and Opinion Departments notes that:

> The goal of the New York Times is to cover the news as impartially as possible—'without fear or favor,' in the words of Adolph Ochs, our patriarch—and to treat readers, news sources, advertisers and others fairly and openly, and to be seen to be doing so. The reputation of the Times rests upon such perceptions, and so do the professional reputations of its staff members.[22]

The handbook goes on: "Our fundamental purpose is to protect the impartiality and neutrality of the *Times* and the integrity of its report."

The acceptance of woke ideology by media companies puts the lie to the impartiality and independence that major North American newspapers and other media claim to value, as summed up in the *New York Times'* ethics handbook. In Canada, the $600 million in tax credits and incentives approved by the federal government in 2018 to prop up the country's ailing newspapers and online publications also add to fears about the independence and impartiality of the media.[23] What happened to me was not the first nor last time a journalist would be attacked by the cancel culture cult in Canada, the United States and elsewhere, often resulting in harms to their health, finances and the end of their careers.

- Veteran CBC journalist and anchor Wendy Mesley was forced out of her job in 2020 for saying the "n-word" in a meeting while quoting the title of a book, clearly in a way meant to inform, not to insult.
- Stan Wischnowski, the senior editor of *The Philadelphia Inquirer*, resigned in June 2020 after an article headlined, "Buildings Matter, Too," about damage to buildings by Black Lives Matter, and which led dozens of his staff to walk off the job in protest.
- James Bennet, who was in the same role as me, editorial pages editor, at the *New York Times* was forced to resign in June 2020 after he ran a column by Senator Tom Cotton, arguing that the military should be deployed to end riots in the wake of George Floyd's murder.
- Tara Henley resigned from the CBC in December 2021 due, she said, to woke culture that forced her and others working there "to embrace cognitive dissonance and to abandon journalistic integrity."[24]
- Esteemed *New York Times* science reporter Donald McNeil resigned under pressure in 2021 after using a racial slur in front of high school students and allegedly being racially insensitive during an educational trip to Peru. McNeil said he used the n-word in a discussion started by the students concerning another student's use of the word.[25]
- Journalist and lawyer Jamil Jivani said he was fired by Bell Media in January 2022 for not being woke enough, including his refusal to do a radio show on how racist Canada was in the days leading up to Canada

Day in 2021. "Bell Media/iHeartRadio was not prepared for a black man who loves his country, rejects victimhood politics, maintains strong ties to his faith community, and shares heterodox views on a wide range of issues."[26]

- Perhaps the most high-profile of all cancel culture incidents in that two-year period was when *New York Times* columnist Bari Weiss quit in July 2020, writing in a public resignation letter that *Times'* management had failed to correct "unlawful discrimination" and a "hostile work environment" by woke colleagues.[27] She opined that her "forays into Wrongthink have made me the subject of constant bullying by colleagues who disagree with my views. Showing up for work as a centrist at an American newspaper should not require bravery."

These are just a few of hundreds of similar stories of cancel culture from within the media, the arts, universities and elsewhere. What was particularly galling was the *New York Times* treatment of Bennet, who said in late 2022 that "when push came to shove at the end," *Times'* publisher A.G. Sulzberger "set me on fire and threw me in the garbage and used my reverence for the institution against me. This is why I was so bewildered for so long after I had what felt like all my colleagues treating me like an incompetent fascist."[28] *Times* staff who complained justified their attacks on Bennet by claiming that Cotton's column made them feel "unsafe." That was a particularly precious and self-absorbed assertion given that 2,119 journalists and other media workers lost their lives while reporting the news around the world between 1992 and 2019, with thousands more before that period.[29]

Free expression: Acerbic comedians value what media head offices disdain

In a 2022 YouTube video clip from his popular HBO show, comedian and talk-show host Bill Maher described the cancelling of people by the woke cult for what they write or say: "This is called a purge," he told his Los Angeles audience. "It is a mentality that belongs in Stalin's Russia. How bad does this atmosphere we are living in have to get before the people who say cancel culture is overblown admit that it is, in fact, an insanity that is swallowing up the world?"[30]

While cancelling anyone for an alleged thoughtcrime is destructive, it has a uniquely critical impact when done to journalists, especially by colleagues, because of the devastating effect it has on free debate within a democracy and the damage it does to the public's view of the media. It harms our democracy, both in not allowing different views to be heard—which is an assault on people's ability to be informed citizens—but also in destroying critical debates that are needed to find the best policy solutions to society's many problems. Journalists have a duty to be knowledgeable, balanced, fair and strictly committed to reporting the truth.

Treating other citizens as enemies and cancelling them because one dislikes their publicly-expressed views is dangerously close to totalitarian. One does not gain a hearing, win respect for a point of view or promote improved conditions of dignity for oppressed groups by attacking or seeking to destroy other people with whom one shares a neighbourhood, country or planet. Besides, attacking people for their views, especially by working to end their ability to earn a living for them and their families, is unlikely to convince them that you are right. Selected journalists may feel a powerful surge of ideological confirmation, and enjoy the moral preening of each other in the progressive bubbles of safety that were once called newsrooms. However, they do themselves no favours by turning off the roughly half of readers who do not think as they do and who desire newspapers and other media with a wide range of views. There is a reason alternative media has arisen.

If you build a society that casually allows the cancelling of people, as authors George Orwell, Arthur Koesler or Hannah Arendt warned, one day the victim might be you. History is filled with examples. American Senator Joseph McCarthy's reckless attacks on the left during the anti-communist frenzy of the 1950s that resulted in blacklisting people out of work is a story with which young, modern progressives should become better acquainted. In some ways the attacks now are worse, with social media and the Internet allowing rushed, unfair and widespread accusations against people to remain permanent stains on their reputations.

Anne Applebaum, the author and staff writer at *The Atlantic*, painted the "grim" future if cancel culture is allowed to continue to thrive in an excellent essay in 2021:

> Foundations will do secret background checks on their potential grantees, to make sure they haven't committed crimes-that-are-not-crimes that could be embarrassing in the future. Anonymous reports and Twitter mobs, not the reasoned judgments of peers, will shape the fate of individuals. Writers and journalists will fear publication. Universities will no longer be dedicated to the creation and dissemination of knowledge but to the promotion of student comfort and the avoidance of social-media attacks.

Worse, if we drive all of the difficult people, the demanding people, and the eccentric people away from the creative professions where they used to thrive, we will become a flatter, duller, less interesting society, a place where manuscripts sit in drawers for fear of arbitrary judgments. The arts, the humanities, and the media will become stiff, predictable, and mediocre. Democratic principles like the rule of law, the right to self-defence, the right to a just trial—even the right to be forgiven—will wither.[31]

Is that really the world we wish to build? I hope not.

CHAPTER 3

How a professor was cancelled by academic Stalinists on campus

Bruce Gilley

Speech is civilization itself. The word, even the most contradictory word, preserves contact—it is the silence that which isolates.
—THOMAS MANN, *The Magic Mountain*

Five days before Christmas 2021, one of Canada's most courageous scholars was fired by her university because she had consistently dissented from its rigid ideology on indigenous issues. There is much to say about the shameful expulsion of Professor Frances Widdowson by administrative bureaucrats at Mount Royal University in Calgary. The pattern of the story will be familiar to the public, long-accustomed to non-left-wing professors being driven from the academy. But the details are important: One wonders if this will be the sort of bare-knuckled Stalinist purge that finally alerts citizens in Western countries to the mortal danger posed to their societies by out-of-control radical movements in contemporary institutions of higher education. For Canada, the Widdowson liquidation could not be more germane to the drift of a once great country into guilt-wracked paralysis.

Widdowson is a political scientist who has spent her career investigating the politics and ideologies of indigenous affairs in Canada. Her 2008 book with Albert Howard, *Disrobing the Aboriginal Industry: The Deception Behind Indigenous Cultural Preservation,* took a critical look at the well-organized industry of indigenous activists and their lawyers whose efforts do such monumental harm to indigenous youth who might otherwise enjoy successful lives as part of Canadian society. Her follow-up 2019 book, *Separate but Unequal: How Parallelist Ideology Conceals Indigenous Dependency*, centered on the intentional segregation and ghettoization of indigenous peoples in the name of "justice" that was anything but just.

Both books were published by university presses—McGill-Queen's and University of Ottawa, respectively—that have been doing penance ever since. Indigenous activists and their academic enablers targeted the presses for rhetorical attack after they published the books. In 2020, for instance, Toronto Metropolitan University professor Ian Mosby declared: "As academics we can make it clear to...whoever is going to publish her next book that they are making a choice: publish this racist nonsense again and we'll stop publishing with or doing peer reviews for you."[1] Mount Royal's first "Coordinator of Indigenization," Liam Haggarty, promoted Mosby's post. Meanwhile, a self-described "coalition of members of the Mount Royal community committed to anti-racist education and mobilization on campus and beyond," tweeting as Mount Royal Anti-Racism Coalition, turned itself into a bilge dump of attacks on Widdowson, all without repercussions. Mosby later called Widdowson "Canada's leading residential school denialist" after noting she had been invited to a conference at Stanford University on academic freedom.[2]

Many more examples of the "witch hunt" against Widdowson by the Canadian academy could be cited. This clarion call by Canadian scholars to go after Widdowson as well as her university publishers for dissenting from the radical orthodoxy on campus was about as bald an example as we have of the totalitarian threat to Canadian society emanating from the universities. In addition to the two books above, Professor Widdowson added two important edited volumes—*Approaches to Aboriginal Education in Canada: Searching for Solutions* (2013) and *Indigenizing the University: Diverse Perspectives* (2021). These documented the sorry depths to which indigenous activism has plunged education and research in Canada. Given the deadening intellectual monoculture that pervades establishment thinking on native issues in Canada (as in the United States), one would think that a university would celebrate having a "critical theorist" who dissents from the dominant paradigm and "unmasks" the structure of knowledge production that empowers the oppression of marginalized groups. Of course, we all know that "critical theory" is only considered valuable when it targets non-left ideologies.

The litany of published attacks on Widdowson even in supposed scholarly journals would astound if it were not so commonplace today. A self-described indigenous scholar and writer Leanne Simpson (who has since renamed herself "Leanne Betasamosake Simpson"), reviewing *Disrobing the Aboriginal Industry*, inveighed: "It is simply stunning that a prominent so-called academic press...(which has lost all credibility as a result), would publish this book...The book is part of a racist colonial machine that still manages to find room to operate in Canada."[3] Simpson's clear declaration that her disagreement with this fellow scholar implied that the latter should not have "room to operate" and that her publisher had "lost all credibility" with the self-professed, self-appointed arbiters of academic gatekeeping in Canada speaks volumes about the very problems that Professor Widdowson sought to diagnose. Imagine if scholars who disagreed on the chemical composition of the sun or on the authorship theories of Shakespeare acted in such a censorious fashion.

As with all totalitarian movements that have haunted Western civilization, the aboriginal or indigenous activist movements in former British colonies are in constant rebellion against liberal society, which they disparage as weakening their ethno-nationalist spirit and providing free rein to ideas that challenge their myths, even as they fuel hatreds using its fruits. Democratic societies deceive themselves if they think that accommodating these ethno-nationalist indigenous movements will satiate their demands. Some indigenous activists in Canada—as distinct from Canadians of indigenous ancestry who fully participate in Canadian life—are explicit in their desires to tear down liberal society. They instead aim to remake Canada into little more than a rent-seeking state where people who have succeeded in the relentless jostling to be categorized as indigenous will be isolated from the mainstream but yet forever dependent on the taxes of other Canadians, including successful indigenous Canadians off-reserve.[a] The self-identification of the movement as composed of permanent and ineluctable victims of the modern Canadian state turns it into a farce of self-absorption and irresponsibility.

Mount Royal was given university status only in 2009. For most of its history (it was founded in 1910[4]), it was a lower-level provincial college with mostly unremarkable faculty. Widdowson was an exception. Her collision course with the university was foreseen in 2016 when it abandoned the Enlightenment for a plan to "indigenize" learning. A new Office of Academic Indigenization would enforce ideological plans to "embrace indigenous knowledge and ways of knowing, to integrate indigenous teachings and practices." In early 2021, the university armed the academic thought police by hiring an Associate Vice-President of Indigenization and Decolonization named Linda ManyGuns. One of her first acts was to literally deck the halls with Cultural Revolution-style posters that accused any student who disagreed with indigenous knowledge claims of having a "colonized mind."[5]

What an actually "indigenized" university would look like is anyone's guess beyond virtue-signalling and constant messaging about indigenous victimization and virtue. The spread of "indigenized" or "decolonized" mandates beyond the already-radicalized confines of the humanities and social sciences into the sciences may be the movement that causes serious damage to be done. In a typical paper on indigenous knowledge in the sciences published 1998, two university of Alaska professors assert that "[n]ative elders have long been able to predict weather based upon

---

a) For more on this, see Mark Milke (2013), *Ever Higher: Government Spending on Canada's Aboriginals since 1947* (Fraser Institute): iii-iv <https://bit.ly/2XQk92h>. Milke notes that inflation-adjusted spending on Canada's Indigenous peoples has been significant, rising from $79 million annually in 1946/47 to almost $7.9 billion in 2011/12, or nearly 99 times higher after adjusting for inflation. Using census data and adjusting for population, Aboriginal/Indian Affairs spending increased from $922 per registered First Nation individual in 1949/50 to $9,056 in 2011/12. That constituted an 882 per cent rise in spending per First Nations person. In contrast, during the same period, total federal program spending per person on all Canadians rose from $1,504 in 1949/50 to $7,316 in 2011/12 or by 387 percent. See also Tom Flanagan (2021), *Fiscal Explosion: Federal Spending on Indigenous Programs*, 2015-2022 (Fraser Institute): 3 <https://bit.ly/3MXBI6J>. Flanagan notes that there are two exceptions to such relentless rise in spending in real terms: "[W]hen it temporarily levelled off—during the fiscal crisis of the mid-1990s when Paul Martin was finance minister in Jean Chrétien's Liberal government; and 2011-15 when Stephen Harper's Conservatives had a majority government."

observations of subtle signs that presage what subsequent conditions are likely to be."[6] In addition to the lack of evidence for the claim, it is probably true of anyone who spends a lot of time outdoors. It is also perfectly consistent with "Western" science (which after all is based on observation) and, more to the point, almost certainly inferior to it because of its lack of appeal to general explanatory and predictive tools.

Mount Royal University was serious in training its many guns on any dissenters. In July 2021, as Canada was succumbing to mass mania over the discovery of alleged "unmarked graves" of children at a former Catholic school for Indian children in Kamloops in the interior of British Columbia (often incorrectly referred to as "mass graves" by residential school activists), Widdowson convened an online panel that countered the hysteria with facts and data. Several experts cast doubt on the claim of "unmarked graves" pointing out that child mortality for all children in Canada at the time was high and that pauper cemeteries were the norm for those without family members to claim them. Then there is the issue of graves that might have been existed and marked at one time but due to time (wooden crosses degrade, for example), have long since moved into the unmarked category. In any event, Widdowson's refusal to be stampeded into early sureties earned her the charges of being a "residential school denier," the highest insult possible for a serious scholar of this topic. For a country whose "woke" federal government lowered all federal flags at half-mast after the Kamloops claims were made in the late spring of 2021, Widdowson's dissent was explosive with powerful academics reflexively incensed. Like censorious Soviet bureaucrats who expressed surprise when people sent to the gulag refused to cease their opposition, these Canadian academics were apoplectic that this enemy of the people remained vocal and undeterred.

By purging her over the Christmas holiday in late 2021, Mount Royal University hoped to keep things quiet, but Widdowson decided instead to be public, conducting interviews and joining podcasts soon after her firing. Not to go without a fight, she also engaged in arbitration through her union. The university sent a private email to all chairs on the day of her firing, as if to reassure them that this inconvenient dissenter from the "indigenization" *diktat* had been sent to the gulag for thought reform. The University of Manitoba native studies professor Niigaanwewidam James Sinclair crowed on social media that her firing "is the holiday present that gives and gives and gives and gives." (Sinclair has since deleted the post.)

Native activists like Sinclair cited the firing as "evidence" that Widdowson was engaged in misconduct (the Party is always right). Sinclair even called on the province of Ontario's state-run broadcaster TVO to apologize for featuring her on one of its programs. Others like the local activist Terrill Tailfeathers and the former Mount Royal University professor Renae Watchman, who left for McMaster University earlier in 2021 citing her unpaid "emotional labour to combat aggressive anti-indigenous sentiments," wanted the university to issue a statement absolving of all blame the faculty radicals who drove her out. "There are already indigenous faculty put in danger by Widdowson's words, actions and misinformation. This is unacceptable," complained Tailfeathers about the university's silence.[7]

Shortly after Widdowson was fired, I tweeted news of the termination and attributed it to the well-documented harassment and bullying that Widdowson has faced from indigenous studies professors and university administrators. In response to my tweet, the chair of humanities, Scott Murray, emailed me demanding I provide evidence for this explanation of Widdowson's firing, "which directly impugns the reputations of several of my very well respected, hard-working department colleagues, as well as that of MRU as a whole." I was too familiar with the totalitarian tactics of contemporary universities to take that bait. What Murray wanted me to do was confess that Widdowson has violated university confidentiality policies on personnel issues by sharing details with me. My thought at the time and now was that Murray would have to find another patsy to help him exercise the dictatorship of the indigenous studies proletariat.

Yet the boilerplate below his email signature (and pronouns) tells you all you need to know. "Mount Royal University is located on or adjacent to the hereditary territories of the Niitsitapi (the Siksika, Kainai, and Piikani), the Îyârhe Nakoda, and the Tsuut'ina nations. This land has become home to non-indigenous peoples and institutions through the negotiation of agreements like Treaty 7, the terms of which have not been honoured amidst the ongoing violence of settler colonialism and white supremacy." (The same land acknowledgement, now *de rigeur* at Canadian universities nationwide, is also on Mount Royal University's website.[8]) This historically inaccurate and anti-intellectual statement speaks volumes about the hostile intellectual environment in which Professor Widdowson operated. Every aspect of her research challenged every word of that catechism.

Universities today will reply that these mandatory ideologies are mere "values" in order to vindicate them from the reality that they practice censorship and thought control—exactly how totalitarian systems infect liberal polities. Canada suffers from an extra burden in having free speech officially denied to speech deemed "hateful" which in the vocabulary of the modern Left is anything that disagrees with left-wing ideology. Calgary's Mount Royal University is a perfect test case of such a claim. It cannot in good faith assert that it protected, much less supported, Widdowson's academic freedom against such an aggressive malignancy—quite the opposite. When the faculty radicals allied to indigenous activists playing victim Olympics put the pressure on the university, it caved.

What the Widdowson affair makes plain is that any university that embraces "indigenization" or "decolonization" or "racial justice" as part of its mission statement is a university that has given up on science, debate, and truth-seeking, much in the way a university that subscribes to a literal reading of the Bible would similarly have proscribed certain lines of inquiry as off-limits. It cannot escape notice that the very things these activists charge the residential schools with—fostering and perpetrating an abusive environment, forced indoctrination and assimilation into intolerant norms, hostile and violent responses to dissenters—are exactly what these universities have done.

I grew up in Calgary and frequently found myself at Mount Royal College, as it was then called. It was for me a place of thrill, seeing all the lecture halls, students, and flyers of events. How sad that today, having attempted to elevate itself as a "university," it has crumbled into a fanatical cult with adherents so unable to think and act clearly in the face of the inevitable disagreements inherent in a liberal society that its only response is fear and anger. Every single person at Mount Royal who has been a party to this disgraceful purge should be hauled up on academic misconduct charges. Perhaps as a symbolic move, it should go back to calling itself Mount Royal College, indicative of a time when it still held fast to the expectations of a democratic and liberal society.

CHAPTER 4

The fight against Critical Race Theory at an Ontario school board

David Millard Haskell

If we decide to again judge people not primarily as individuals, but rather as members of intractable and often squabbling tribes, it will become increasingly difficult to ever find common ground between them.
—WILFRED REILLY

In mid-summer 2022, the Elementary Teachers' Federation of Ontario began distributing new lesson plans that aimed to indoctrinate children—but without their parents finding out. The reason for the secrecy was straightforward: Most parents, if informed, would have objected to having their children instructed in the belief that their skin colour is fundamental to their success and that Western society is fundamentally racist.[a] The pre-made curriculum the federation doled out focused on so-called "white privilege"[1] and was to be used by their members teaching across primary, junior and intermediate grades in the province. The new lesson plans were an extension of the Federation's existing and larger White Privilege Project, which included a workshop for educators.[2]

---

a) In September 2022 the Hamilton Wentworth board sent out a survey to parents of students in their schools asking them to review the board's new "anti-racism" policy. It was explained the ideas of the policy would inform the "anti-racist" instruction in the classroom. Parents were shocked by what they read with two-thirds of survey participants saying they opposed the implementation of the board's anti-racism policy and the ideas it promoted.

Some background: "white privilege" ideology teaches students that, if they are white, their successes are not primarily achieved through personal effort but are bestowed upon them because of the colour of their skin. Conversely, students of colour are taught that despite personal effort, their chances of success are significantly diminished because society, on balance, is systemically racist and thus stacked against them.[3] Tellingly, white privilege instruction always avoids mentioning that Canadians of East Asian and several other non-white ethnic groups have for many years achieved higher average income and educational attainment than Caucasians.[4] One component of white privilege instruction seeks to convince white students that even if they hold no conscious animosity toward non-whites, unconsciously they embody racist tendencies which put them, intractably, in the role of oppressor. As promoters of unconscious bias (sometimes called implicit bias) like to put it, "Even if you know in your heart that you are not racist, remember: It is possible to have implicit (or unconscious) racial biases."[5]

The concept of unconscious racial bias has been debunked as unscientific nonsense.[6] However, that inconvenient truth is ignored by its proponents as they relentlessly push specific rituals meant to expiate this hidden sin. A key ritual of penance is the act of "checking one's privilege." In this, those with white skin are told they can lessen their oppressiveness by recusing themselves from opportunities or silencing themselves in public conversations.[7]

The concept of white privilege is an element of the larger curriculum initiative known as "anti-racism" education. As it is currently applied in educational settings, the term "anti-racism" is misleading.[8] In this pedagogical movement, discrimination based on skin colour is actually encouraged. The top-selling instruction manual on the topic, *How to Be An Antiracist* by American academic Ibram X. Kendi, categorically rejects the idea of treating all people equally. Instead, Kendi insists that to make society "equitable" those with white pigmentation must be denied equal treatment and be made to pay for historical misdeeds and this because someone alive today incidentally shares the skin colour with someone long dead.[9] He claims, "The only remedy to racist discrimination is antiracist discrimination. The only remedy to past discrimination is present discrimination."[10]

Both white privilege and "anti-racist" education are underpinned by a larger philosophical project known as Critical Race Theory (CRT). Critical Race Theory is not really a theory, since a theory must, as a start, be grounded in solid empirical evidence. Instead, this theory is more properly viewed as a worldview that promotes particular truth claims.[11] The truth claims of Critical Race Theory have a Marxist influence because, in fact, it evolved out of Marxist ideology. In particular, the Marxian notion of society being divided into oppressors and the oppressed is appropriated by critical race theory and its proponents.[12] Rather than apply the labels according to economic status (capitalists versus the proletariat), however, this theory applies them according to racial status (whites versus non-white, and so forth).

The growing resistance to Critical Race Theory

Critical Race Theory has received some bad press of late as parents across North America began to realize it heavily influences their local schools and the young minds therein.[13] While parents in Canada are just waking up to this development, since 2020, American parents have been coming before their boards of education to passionately critique the negativity and polarization their children experience on account of CRT instruction in the classroom.[14] In broad terms, conservative-leaning elected officials have been supportive of the parents while those on the radicalized left have tended to demonize anyone challenging the doctrines of Critical Race Theory,[15] casting them as bigots or even "domestic terrorists."[16]

By late 2021, concerns about this new ideology anchored in Marxist assumptions and paired with race had grown sufficient to change the political dynamic in Virginia, a Democratic stronghold where the incumbent governor Terry McAuliffe lost to a relatively unknown Republican, Glenn Youngkin.[17] McAuliffe had led in the polls up to the closing weeks of the campaign, making Youngkin's win an upset. Youngkin's political fortunes changed when he began promising to ban the teaching of CRT in state schools on "day one."[18] His momentum increased following a television debate in which McAuliffe, commenting on some parents' hostility toward Critical Race Theory stated, "I don't think parents should be telling schools what they should teach."[19] In Florida, after making a similar promise to

Youngkin, Governor Ron DeSantis passed legislation making Critical Race Theory instruction illegal in his state.[20] At least 35 states have followed suit.[21]

The increasing negative attention paid to Critical Race Theory in the United States has caused some school board officials to avoid using the term in statements or policy documents.[22] But often, even if the term is gone, the pedagogical concepts from CRT—"anti-racism" training and instruction in white privilege—remain. And parents are noticing this attempted sleight-of-hand. Given the Elementary Teachers' Federation of Ontario's recent actions to push the concept into Ontario elementary schools, it is now a live issue for Canadian parents as well.

A case study in school board obfuscation

The experience in my own community of Waterloo Region in southwestern Ontario, a community of nearly 625,000, is instructive. My day job is that of professor at a local university, but in mid-2022 I founded a local chapter of the Foundation Against Intolerance and Racism (FAIR). FAIR began in the United States when some parents noticed their children's schools were teaching that people should be judged by their immutable traits and not by their actions or character.[23] As leader of the Waterloo Region chapter, hundreds of local parents contacted me with concerns about the Waterloo Region District School Board's embrace of Critical Race Theory; with one of my own children still attending a Waterloo school, I could corroborate and commiserate. Further, many parents have also told me they are equally troubled by the tendency for secrecy and authoritarian-style action among a majority of Waterloo Region school board trustees.

Consider the authoritarian urges first. Many parents recounted the story of the hostile silencing of teacher Carolyn Burjoski. Appearing before trustees in January 2022, Burjoski, a 20-year teaching veteran, attempted to present information on the explicit sexual content of some new library books. When she began questioning the age-appropriateness of such books—found in elementary school libraries and kindergarten to grade six classrooms across the Waterloo region—the Board Chair, Scott Piatkowski, stopped her from speaking and ejected her from the meeting. The books with which Burjoski took issue featured transgendered characters. Piatkowski thus justified his censorship by claiming Burjoski's questions were transphobic and tantamount to "hate speech."[24] Burjoski has since launched legal action against the board.[25]

Parents also highlighted the ouster of trustee Mike Ramsay. In June 2022, a majority of Ramsay's fellow trustees voted to expel him from all meetings of the Waterloo public school board. His exclusion would last until just before the next election of trustees in the fall. The details on why he was sent packing where not forthcoming. Beyond claiming that he had transgressed rules of conduct and that one of his fellow trustees launched a complaint against him, his opponents on the board refused to provide any specifics.[26] Their secrecy appeared even more bizarre given that Ramsay publicly called for the release of all the details. Ultimately, the school board's suppression of information was deemed so extreme that the *Waterloo Region Record* newspaper called for the provincial government to intervene.[27] The re-elected Progressive Conservative government of Doug Ford made no response.

To those following the internal battles within the Waterloo board, the overarching reason for Ramsay's dismissal seemed clear. Ramsay and fellow trustee Cindy Watson stood out on the board because of their calls for greater transparency and open debate on contentious issues. Ramsay's insistence that trustees allow diverse opinions to be voiced repeatedly put him at odds with his less-open-minded colleagues. In a public letter addressing his dismissal, Ramsay confirmed ideological difference were at play, writing that, "The complaint is motivated by disagreement with [my] positions at board meetings and statements made to constituents."[28] In interviews with reporters, Ramsay, who is black and conservative-leaning, went further and condemned the hypocrisy of his ideological opponents (who have strong links to the New Democratic Party)[29] saying, "They pretend to advocate about diversity, inclusion and equity. But the irony of all of this is that when a Black person disagrees with them, they are quick to put me in my place."[30] Getting nowhere with his appeals for transparency, as a measure of last resort—and with the hope of clearing his name—Ramsay launched a lawsuit against the board arguing his constitutional rights to freedom of expression were violated. In early October 2022, after receiving a green light from his legal council, he released a 306-page record of the back-and-forth proceedings between himself and his opponents.[31]

The *Waterloo Region Record* had their political affairs columnist, Luisa D'Amato, review the court document. She determined that Ramsay had done nothing wrong, stating, "What it shows is that Ramsay was punished for disagreeing vehemently with most of his fellow trustees, at the board table and in social media. And nothing more."[32] D'Amato also concluded Ramsay's opponents on the board used its policies and procedures in a vexatious and frivolous manner to censor him. She wrote, "Ramsay's contention that these rules, applied with an authoritarian hand, violated his constitutional right to free speech is highly defensible." Highlighting the frivolous nature of the complaints against Ramsay, D'Amato noted that his opponents claimed he had violated the trustee code of conduct because he had retweeted articles from the local newspaper that were critical of the school board.[33]

The acrimony and authoritarian behaviour documented in Ramsay's court filing was further demonstrated in the board's actions after he was excluded from trustee meetings. Specifically, just prior to his removal, Ramsay and his ally Watson had crafted a motion calling for a detailed account of the board's "anti-racism curriculum." Then, in Ramsay's absence, Watson advanced the motion. It asked staff to answer specific questions related to how Critical Race Theory influenced instruction. In particular, Watson sought clarification as to what was being taught about the concept of white privilege. They were acting out of an obligation to their constituents. Watson and Ramsay had long heard concerns from numerous parents—of multiple backgrounds and not just Caucasian, that such instruction was occurring. The parents worried such instruction could internalize a "sense of shame or guilt" and create "stigma in the school atmosphere" for children of the "wrong" colour.[34]

The Ramsay-Watson motion was easily defeated but, not content in their victory, the opposing trustees piled on Watson, insinuating that her motion was illegitimate. Trustee Jayne Herring depicted the motion as morally corrupt, proclaiming, "We're better than this." Upping emotional extremism, trustee Carol Millar suggested that bringing forth the motion had done harm, saying, "I would suspect that our staff, our students and families have had to deal with the hate and racism as a result of this motion." The motion's very introduction caused the director of education at the Waterloo Region District School Board, Jeewan Chanicka,[b] to weep openly.[35]

---

b) Jeewan Chanicka insists that his name be spelled all lower-case. I hold to the practice of capitalizing names.

Nine minutes to educate school board trustees

The week after the motion's defeat, on June 27, 2022, the last board meeting before summer break, I was allowed to make a presentation to the Waterloo Region trustees on behalf of FAIR. I hoped they might reconsider their earlier vote against Watson's motion and allow parents to know what is being taught regarding Critical Race Theory and "white privilege" instruction. It was certainly within the board's purview to reverse course. Given their track record, I had my doubts. However, I was armed with a trove of empirical evidence that I thought might at least change a few trustees' minds. These were the leaders of our educational system, after all; surely facts grounded in scholarly research could dislodge a few from their ideological intransigence? After reminding the trustees that Section 4 of their governing bylaws require them to "make decisions in a manner which is open, approach all Board issues with an open mind and respect different points of view," I began to review the peer-reviewed data.[36]

- First, I described a 2019 study that was conducted to measure how lessons on white privilege affect students' attitudes. Published in the *Journal of Experimental Psychology: General* the study found such instruction did not make students more sympathetic to people of colour—there were no positive results. It did, however, increase hostility toward poor whites. The researchers concluded that, "Learning about White privilege reduces sympathy, increases blame, and decreases external attributions for White people struggling with poverty."[37]
- Next, I highlighted a study published in May 2022 in the online journal *PLoS One*. The research involved an experiment to see how introducing the concept of white privilege would affect online discussions on issues related to racial equity. The researchers found that doing so actually shuts down open discussion and lowers support for racial harmony. They concluded that, "Mention of white privilege seems to create online discussions that are less constructive, more polarized, and less supportive of racially progressive policies." In fact, receiving white privilege doctrine made *previously supportive* whites less engaged in the conversation and "led to less constructive responses from whites and non-whites."[38]

- I then turned to a lengthy 2021 study published in the *Annual Review of Psychology*. The lead author is world-renowned psychologist Elizabeth Paluck from Princeton University. Paluck and her colleagues performed a meta-analysis of over 400 existing studies. Their goal was to see if mandatory instruction in diversity, equity and inclusion works to decrease prejudice and increase harmony. As white privilege is one of the core modules in most diversity training programs, this meta-analysis was highly applicable. After analyzing hundreds of research papers, Paluck and her team concluded that, despite the bold claims made by people developing and facilitating this kind of instruction, the average impact of diversity, equity, and inclusion training is zero.[39]
- While it offers no measurable positive outcomes, I explained to the trustees that there is evidence that anti-racism-type instruction does actual harm. Specifically, I highlighted the conclusions of Harvard sociologist Frank Dobbin. In *Anthropology Now*, he surveyed hundreds of studies and, like Paluck, found that "anti-bias training doesn't reduce bias, alter behavior, or change the workplace."[40] Conversely, he determined "field and laboratory studies find that asking people to suppress stereotypes tends to reinforce them — making them more cognitively accessible to people."[41] Elaborating on that conclusion, in the *Harvard Business Review* Dobbin cautioned, "a number of studies suggest diversity training can activate bias or spark a backlash."[42] (Indeed, this is exactly what the 2019 research published in the *Journal of Experimental Psychology: General* found.)

It was just after I explained that the research proves this kind of instruction can actually *cause more prejudice* that board chair Piatkowski interrupted my presentation to inform me that I had just one minute remaining. The interruption was not a surprise. I had been informed previously that a one-minute warning signal would flag the end of my 10-minute slot. What was surprising was that Piatkowski shaved a minute off my allotted time. There is a video recording of my delegation and those watching can see I have two minutes left when I am told one minute remains.[43]

Rather than complain and potentially lose more of my time I edited on the fly to get to my finishing statements. The trustees would otherwise have heard about other research that found concepts like white privilege and similar "anti-racism" instruction are likely to do the *most harm* to students of colour. Specifically, I intended to summarize the findings of hundreds of academic studies on the psychological phenomenon called stereotype threat. They show that when racial minorities are taught to perceive themselves as disadvantaged—as happens when instructed about white privilege—such a perception can lead to diminished academic performance.[44] In my rushed conclusion I said, "Racism is real and it is harmful. And for our schools to do much better we must work toward solutions and strategies proven to bring unity. And those solutions need to be based on evidence and open discussion."

Lesson plan for today: Credible research can produce a reaction

My call for an open discussion was met by blank stares and silence. Watson, hoping to spur on other trustees, asked if there was more research to be explored on the effects of diversity-type instruction, to which I answered that there was. No other trustees offered any comment or question. While no trustee, apart from Watson, cared to explore the harm done by propagandizing children into believing they live in a bigoted wasteland where every disparity is due to racism, regular citizens were keen to make comments; immediately following my presentation there was an outpouring of feedback on social media. This was due to the fact the school board meeting, including my presentation, was livestreamed on the internet.

Some viewers expressed gratitude that I had done what the board refused to do by providing information on the effect of teaching so-called "anti-racist" material. Others condemned me for providing the research. In their eyes, only activists speaking from "lived experience" and promoting more white privilege-styled instruction deserved a hearing. One Waterloo high school English teacher posted this to my Twitter account: "@DMillardHaskell you should probably listen to the [pro-white privilege instruction] delegate who spoke after you. Saying white scholars conclude ANYTHING about racism just doesn't cut it anymore."

It is troubling that an employee of a school board with direct influence over high school students would assert in an online public forum that some research should be viewed as worthless if the scholar conducing the study is white. Besides being a textbook example of a racist claim—wherein one's standing or worth is praised or condemned according to one's skin colour—the comment also demonstrated a lack of logical consistency: The woman responding was a "white scholar" (by definition a teacher is a scholar), which meant by her own admission, *anything she says* should also be ignored on the basis of her skin colour.

We cannot ignore what this teacher, and others like her, believe and say. Indeed, such comments deserve careful scrutiny. Consider this: if she has no reservations about making such comments in public, what is she telling the captive audience of students in her class? Perhaps her comments provide a clue as to why the majority of trustees in the Waterloo board voted against Watson and Ramsay's motion to explore how Critical Race Theory influenced the region's schools. But, despite their efforts to obscure transparency, these trustees cannot hide a problem that has become so widespread. Even the board's own equity department has since been exposed as racist, this after one staffer suggested white people are unique in showing aggression toward others and opined on social media that "history is paved with white-led violence."[45] Admittedly, whites have committed their share of atrocities; however, the thousands of non-white tyrants—from Mao Zedong to Idi Amin to Pol Pot—would be right to criticize this equity staffer for her lack of historical inclusivity.

Beyond comments on social media, the harmful ideas now propagated in classrooms seems to be creating a real-world reaction, a "pushback" of sorts. More parents now hear from their children about activist teachers promoting highly biased, factually-questionable, ideological instruction. Some of those parents have joined forces with other mothers and fathers, grandparents, and concerned citizens in grassroots organizations meant to effect change and hold school boards and others accountable. In 2022 alone, the Foundation Against Intolerance and Racism opened chapters in every province; the Waterloo chapter I founded was one of six new chapters launched in Ontario that year.[46] FAIR's growth has been mirrored by other likeminded groups such as Parents as First Educators and Blueprint for Canada. All have made bringing ideological neutrality to classrooms a priority.[47] In more common parlance, they describe their activities as fighting the "woke" agenda in schools—"woke" being a catchall term for the beliefs and practices of the radical political Left.

Fighting woke ideology meant that these organizations became heavily involved in the October 2022 municipal elections of school board trustees in Ontario. In cities, counties, or regions where chapters of different parental groups were established, the disparate bodies sought each other out and did their best to work together recruiting candidates for trustees and providing them with training and volunteer support. In the past, school board elections were often shrugged off as inconsequential but now parents and others—especially those of more conservative worldviews—realize what activists on the Left have known for a long time: the world is run by the people who "show up." Indeed, there is no alternative to having aware, informed people in positions to blunt a harmful 21st century ideology that divides children by colour, race, and ethnicity.

An example of what can happen when such people serve as trustees—people who value education over ideology—arose from the Regional Municipality of Durham, east of Toronto in late spring of 2022. As the last major work before adjourning for the summer, the Durham Catholic District School Board banned concepts and language rooted in Critical Race Theory from its new anti-racism policy.[48] The Durham board is thus able to prevent the kind of problematic instruction that the Waterloo Region board and others support.

In the summer and fall of 2022, across the province, the success of the Durham Catholic board inspired trustee candidates and supporters concerned about the divisiveness of "woke" ideology. However, in the late October elections, fewer succeeded than hoped for. In the Waterloo public board, for instance, there was an anti-woke candidate running to fill each of the 11 trustee seats. (Two were incumbents Ramsay and Watson.) While Ramsay and Watson both kept their seats, only one new candidate campaigning on a platform of ideological neutrality in the classroom and respect for parents wishes was elected. Similar results were seen across the province. We might speculate about the various factors that contributed to this weak showing but at least two forces are indisputable: election outcomes were significantly impacted by teachers' union leaders and also journalists who sought to derail any candidates promising to challenge radical ideologies.

On the former, teachers' union leaders from provincial headquarters and those at the level of the local boards plied their roughly 140,000 members with not-so-subtle direct emails, bolstered by embedded videos, telling them who to vote for (and who not to).[49] Those trustees who received their endorsement were described as "progressive candidates" friendly to "labour and education"—none espoused anti-woke ideas.[50] In their messaging, the union bosses underscored how vulnerable municipal elections are to block voting; when only about one third of eligible voters participate in municipal elections, an army of educators voting exclusively for "approved" candidates can do much to tip the balance.[51]

Journalists were also a problem. In the last few days before the vote reporters at *CBC, Globe and Mail, Toronto Star, CTV News, Global News* and *CityTV* published stories that depicted trustee candidates opposed to woke ideology as far-right, racist, transphobes.[52] In their reports, opposing Critical Race Theory was equated with being racist; opposing radical gender ideology and the sexualization of children was equated with being a transphobe. To substantiate their claims, most relied on the subjective opinion of spokespersons from the Canadian Anti-Hate Network—a self-described activist organization heavily funded by the federal government with a confirmed record of spreading falsehoods and maligning ideological opponents.[53] This quote from *CTV News* is emblematic of the content and slant found in much coverage:

> It's municipal election season, and experts are warning that some far-right groups and individuals are bringing an agenda of anti-diversity and anti-LGBTQ2S+ views to an important, but often-forgotten, ballot battleground: school boards. According to the Canadian Anti-Hate Network (CAHN), far-right lobbying groups are attempting to install school board trustees who will uphold what CAHN calls regressive views... [These] hateful ideologies can have hugely negative impacts on school environments, from creating unsafe policies exposing LGBTQ2S+ students in front of potentially unsupportive families to voting to limit books and speakers that could provide students with more diverse perspectives.[54]

In the United States, well-funded news organizations such as *Fox News, Wall Street Journal, National Review*, and *New York Post* publish reports that question Critical Race Theory and, as such, many Americans are informed about the radical theory and practices that have infiltrated their public schools.

In Canada, fewer media outlets investigate radical theories, which seems especially likely if the theories originate with an ideological perspective that a journalist might share. An additional problem—likely self-censorship—exists, because of federal government funding for both the CBC and private media. The dearth of diverse perspectives from our traditional media has meant most citizens are not just uninformed but misinformed about the state of our public education system.

Given such challenges, removing pedagogy steeped in critical race theory from our public-school systems may seem an improbably task. But we should remember that the ideologues currently promoting what passes for "anti-racism" education in our schools were, for decades, engaged in their own "long march through the institutions." We should not be surprised that a similar long march will be needed to reverse the trend.

However, one thing is clear: Beirut, the capital of the flourishing Lebanon, had been and is a cultural hub where the East meets the West, with a blend of old history and an elegant modernity. It was even known as the Paris of the Middle East, a reference, as one author describes it, to "... its French Mandate architecture, its world-class cuisine, its fashionable and liberated women, its multitude of churches, and its thousand-year-old ties to France...."[5]

Lebanon was a French-designed "hodgepodge" of various peoples and religious traditions, and this seems to have worked for a while, resulting in a mostly peaceful republic.[5] This may perhaps explain why, at first, the Lebanese political system was applauded by some as an ideal model of pluralism and coexistence. Indeed, after its independence from France in 1943, Lebanon even served as a refuge for those fleeing from other regional conflicts. Historically, the country welcomed refugees, including initially, Armenians. Later, Palestinians, Iraqis and Syrians fleeing from their own country's bloody wars would also find refuge in Lebanon. In other words, Lebanon knew a period of harmony and flourished. When peace was prevalent, Beirut, the Lebanese capital, became a vibrant center for commerce, banking, and trade. It also became both an intellectual and a touristic hub. Lebanon's agricultural sector was also prosperous.

However, Lebanon has also been at the geographic and religious crossroads of such disputes, which along with being used as a proxy by other states, exacerbated the identity divisions within Lebanon itself. The result of all such fault lines led to a 15-year-long civil war, from 1975 to 1990, with as many as 150,000 people killed, and between 800,000 and one million displaced residents including "disappeared" residents and others kidnapped to Syria, and several billion dollars' worth of destruction to infrastructure and private property.[6] In short and tragically, identity- or sectarian-based politics fuelled civil war in Lebanon. That was a substantial reality in its different phases with other contributing factors including wars by others on Lebanese soil. That included the occupation by neighbouring countries, namely Syria and Israel. There were also other "crossroads" events over the decades including the Israeli-Palestinian conflict, Israel-Arab wars, Israel-Iran wars (with the Lebanese Hezbollah as an Iranian proxy), and the Syrian civil war.

The destruction of the Paris of the Middle East

The Lebanese civil war and all that occurred—shelling of urban neighbourhoods, hostage-takings, car bombings, along with the plethora of refugees—intensified the danger of belonging to the "wrong" tribe. Eventually, when kidnapped or stopped at militia checkpoints, Lebanese citizens could be killed just for being the "wrong" identity (i.e., religion).

There have been attempts at reform. The 1989 Taif Agreement, now blamed for fostering clientelism, at least put an end to the Lebanese civil war. It did so by reforming the balance of power: the total number of seats in Parliament was expanded to 128, with equal shares apportioned to Muslim and Christian political parties. An equally divided cabinet was also established. This changed the Christian-favoured power-sharing formula instituted by France to a 50/50 ratio. Furthermore, the powers of the prime minister were enhanced at the expense of those of the president of the republic (the prime minister being Sunni Muslim and the president Maronite Christian). In addition, the term for the Speaker of the Parliament (Shiite Muslim) was extended from one year to four years to try and deliver some continuity, and with it, stability. Lastly, the agreement resulted in a disarmament of national and non-national militias in Lebanon, except for the pro-Iranian Hezbollah.[7]

The Martyrs' Monument at Martyrs' Square in Beirut, riddled with shrapnel during the 1975-1990 Lebanese civil war. Martyrs' Square was part of the demarcation line that divided Beirut in half during the civil war.

Despite such reforms, the basis of Lebanon's political system is still defined by identity. It is why since 1989, Lebanon's citizens have been stuck in a rotting sectarian system according to which the following would *always* apply, as noted earlier (along with corrupt warlords at the helm): the President of the Republic must be Christian, the Prime Minister Sunni must be Muslim, and the Parliament Speaker must be Shiite Muslim. All other public posts are also divided according to religious quotas. Furthermore, there is a tacit "Anschluss" in governance between the corrupt (i.e., mafia) and military (i.e., militia), each of the latter covering for and protecting the other.[8]

In retrospect, it appears that the national honeymoon of modern Lebanon was short-lived and perhaps always built on a weak foundation, i.e., the divisive fault lines of religious identities. We can thus argue that the Lebanese project was a hopeless case from the start, a state artificially constructed on the jagged edges of identity politics instead of a nation united on the concrete surety that individuals matter more than sectarian identities. The latter approach has of course been the successful reform over the centuries in countries such as France, the United States, Canada (until recently), and elsewhere where the human tendency toward tribalism was checked by giving rights and power to the individual, not power-sharing for groups.

That liberal impulse is why, not incidentally, that for all the faults of the reforms, the wisest post-civil war gesture by the Lebanese government in 2009 was its decree to remove religious affiliations from citizens' identity cards.[9] That likely accords with the aspirations of ordinary Lebanese people, weary of hearing politicians speaking in their names as either Christians or Muslims, and so forth. My own experience as an expatriate in constant contact with family and friends leads me to conclude that Lebanese people want their politicians to speak in the name of Lebanon, and put that identity first, above all other sectarian identities and considerations. In other words, at least some people in this tiny Mediterranean country still dream of a country with one notion of citizenship and the rule of law equally applied to all.

Can Canada learn from Lebanon's sectarianism?

The tragedy of Lebanon was on my mind in recent years when I was invited to write an article on academic freedom for Nova Scotia's largest university union (CUPE 3912).[10] [11] In my published article, I stoutly defended common citizenship and all that that implies against the corrosive ideas of identity politics. An excerpt:

> When immigrants, newer or older ones including myself, flee their troubled countries of origin and arrive in their adoptive countries, they are grateful to the latter for safety, values, and opportunities. Indeed, when coming from fragmented and unstable birth countries, torn by civil war or other crises, where innocent people can be killed because of aspects of their identities, including religion, sexual orientation, or political opinion, it is natural to: (1) be lucid about the dangers of divisive identity-based politics, or modern forms of sectarianism, that are on the rise in countries like Canada; and (2) appreciate all what their adoptive countries offer them.[12]The danger and tragedy of identity politics is also clear to me because of my own immigration story. I landed in Montreal in 1990 at the age of seventeen, and although it took me two years to adjust completely to my new Canadian life, I felt soon thereafter that I was Canadian. I felt welcome in Montreal, Québec, first and foremost as a Canadian. I had the chance to visit almost all Québec's beautiful regions. I fell even more in love with Canada. Thus, it was natural for me to later partly dedicate my PhD dissertation to both the country of my birth and my adoptive country.

Fifteen years later, when I moved to Toronto, it took me all of two weeks to feel Torontonian, to feel at home. Later, when I left "Hogtown" after four years, I deliberately took the time to say goodbye to all those familiar faces whom I used to see daily, including those in the stores in the subway and on my street. Among those kind faces, there was a man whom I had the chance to meet again when I returned to Toronto many years later. I dropped by his store in the subway, and despite the huge number of people he sees daily, he recognized me—imagine this in a city of millions. He even asked about my spouse and if he found a job in New Brunswick (where we moved next). I left Toronto to accept a tenure-track position at Mount Allison University in Sackville, where it took me two days to feel "Sackvillian" and a proud New Brunswicker. Even the bad cook that I am managed to create a seafood chowder whereafter and I was told by my friends that I was officially a Maritimer.

Canada matters more than our tribes

The Canadians I have met over my three-plus decades have been unfailingly kind and good-hearted. When I walk in the streets of my university town, I am moved to see the town's taxi drivers honk their horns and wave hello. It always reminds me of my childhood neighbourhood in Beirut. When I visit the beautiful beaches, villages, and cities of New Brunswick, I meet good-hearted people who talk to strangers and make them feel welcome.

When I first arrived, local people in my town regularly asked my spouse: "Are you from far away?" And often when I would speak, they would ask me, "Are you from very far away?" For some in our easily-offended world, such questions themselves are supposed to be off-limits, as if they imply that the person and object of curiosity does not belong. I have never viewed such queries that way but instead as evidence of curiosity: "Are you from far away." Is there anything more benign and accurate than that? I am indeed originally from very far away... and yet I feel so rooted, connected, and welcomed.

Once, in a Tim Horton's in Moncton, a senior asked me if he could touch my curly hair. (Most people have straight hair around here.) My response: "Of course, why not? Go ahead sir!" with my spouse amused by the encounter. Conversely, when I visited the village of Bouctouche once, I bumped into a group of men speaking Chiac, a French-language dialect based on Acadian French mixed with English (like Yiddish or Creole). I was fascinated. I asked if I could record a snippet of their conversation to share with my sister abroad, a French writer and a journalist. They generously accepted. My spouse and I sat with them and chatted, comparing their French with the dialects of Lebanon and New Brunswick. As Canadians, we can be curious about one another's origins without being offended.

Every year pre-pandemic, I sent touristic-type videos to my loved ones abroad to show them scenes from New Brunswick and the Maritimes. At one point, a cousin jokingly asked if I was being paid by my government to promote my home province. I replied: "No, I just love it!" An insightful description of New Brunswick came from my spouse when we initially moved here: "New Brunswick," he said, "is like a mini-Canada." Indeed, it is, with those of First Nations, English and French ancestry present, "old" and new immigrant stock from other countries from around the world. I see such naturally occurring diversity even in semi-rural areas. New Brunswick is indeed a miniature Canada.

My ease of identifying and integrating with local communities has been possible precisely because the nation-state that is Canada was founded on the notion that individuals should be treated as equal before the law with neither favouritism nor prejudice shown based on irrelevant characteristics. That such an idea was not equally applied right away at Canada's conception does not take away from the fact that by the 1960s, and certainly by the time I arrived in 1990, discrimination based on ethnicity et al., had long been illegal. Such a conception of the nation state as anchored in the rights of the individual is in fact a core, critical part of the Canadian founding, its identity, and ought not be forgotten.

It is why, contrary to how Prime Minister Justin Trudeau described Canada as a "post-national state," i.e., one without "core identity" or "mainstream,"[13] he could not be more mistaken. A core identity where a few things are held sacred, the right to individual equality before the law and in everyday life first among them. It means that Canada is neither a hotel nor a large tent where tribes live next to each other, with favours bestowed or withheld by a powerful state and based upon unchangeable characteristics—ethnicity, colour, "race," ancestry and gender. It is why multiculturalism as envisioned by Trudeau lends itself to radical identity-based movements like wokeism.[14] The latter is a movement or a mindset highly aware of race and self-righteous in its obsession with diversity,[15] to the point of being close-minded like a cult. Sadly, despite any noble intention, the reality is that this state-endorsed wokeism acts as a modern form of sectarianism. Sectarianism or identity politics is the opposite of much-needed unity in Canada, which contrary to the oft-heard accusations of "systemic racism" has in fact been "systematically" welcoming to newcomers, not racist.

Indeed, my family, and many other older or newer immigrants dreamed of coming to the welcoming country of Canada, with its imperfections, stories, and histories. They love their adoptive country. They refuse to blindly follow trendy sectarian ideologies, which risk losing them, along with their fellow Canadians, common points of reference. When the latter are fully lost, the ultimate long-term risk would be to lose Canada's liberal democratic soul. This is actually easier lost than one might assume given that Canada is still in its historic infancy, not old in the grand scheme of history as is Lebanon.

My advice to "newcomers:" Do not upend Canada with anti-individual group preferences pushed upon you by those pretending to speak on your behalf. They act as if they know what is best for you and me. They impose their sectarian ideology on both of us while claiming to speak in our names, while obsessing about diversity. Is it not simpler, wiser, and safer for us as newcomers to celebrate our love for our adoptive country and love it back? That is far better than endorsing ideologies, which when pushed to the extreme, may risk weakening, paralyzing, or even potentially destroying the Canada we came to in order to escape the effect of such similar destructive ideas upon the countries of our birth.

Canada has opened its arms to welcome my family and me. It has offered us safety and dignity within the protection of a liberal democracy—at least up until now. In my case, after two years in Canada, I lucidly made the decision to stay and root myself in Canada. I kept my loyal love to my Lebanon while increasingly falling in love with "my" Canada. This is why I could never become suddenly ungrateful toward my host country, accusing it of "systemic racism" and "supremacy" against me or my family, at the urging of others. Not only that, it is also why I oppose efforts by politicians and elites to play with the fire of identity politics, recklessly taking us in a direction that could backfire on us all.

Indeed, the slippery slope of identity politics can take several increasingly dangerous forms. Some may be toxic and radical, ironically in the name of identity-based justice. It can also become absurd, losing contact with a compassionate or reasonable reality. Furthermore, it may even become authoritarian to the point of totalitarianism. No one wants to endure the latter even under the apparently noble cause of anti-racism as it may result in cases of intolerance, including but not limited to accusations and censorship sagas. The viciousness of those who wish to impose sectarianism on society is reminiscent of the "witch hunts" of yore, with shaming and professional or social cancellation. For me, intolerance of different opinions is not just a sign of small-mindedness, it is an attack on free thinking, academic freedom, and freedom of expression. Our beautiful Canada deserves better than the narrow-mindedness of identity politics.

When I moved from other parts of Canada to Sackville, I was asked a question often given to those who move from the "big city" to a small town: You come from a bigger place, how would you adjust to the smaller? Even my sister asked if the smallness of my new town, about 6,000 residents when full of Mount Allison university students (4,000 otherwise), bothers me. I replied that it is not the smallness of a place that would bother me, it is only small-mindedness.

CHAPTER 6

Is Canada systemically racist?

Matthew Lau

Much of what is said in the name of "social justice" implicitly assumes... the seemingly invincible fallacy that various groups would be equally successful in the absence of biased treatment by others.
—THOMAS SOWELL

It is accepted as fact in many quarters that Canada is a systemically or institutionally racist country. The federal government's Department of Canadian Heritage, for example, posits in its 2019-2022 anti-racism strategy that "we know that even today there are people and communities who experience systemic racism and discrimination. Racialized communities and indigenous peoples continue to face systemic barriers, notably in employment, justice, and social participation."[1] Likewise, the federal government echoes in its 2021-2024 anti-racism strategy the Prime Minister's assertion that there are in Canada "profound systemic inequities and disparities that remain present in the core fabric of our society, including our core institutions."[2]

Another government report, from the Ministry of Defence, claims that "white supremacy was first woven into the fabric of Canadian society with the colonization of Indigenous lands by European settlers," and since then, "government and institutional policies have exercised discriminatory control over the citizenship rights of Indigenous People, racialized people, religious minorities and LGBTQ2+ communities."[3] The institutionalization of racism, according to the report, causes worse health outcomes for the indigenous population, worse educational outcomes for blacks, and other harms towards racial minorities.

The federal government defines systemic or institutional racism as "patterns of behaviour, policies or practices that are part of the social or administrative structures of an organization, and which create or perpetuate a position of relative disadvantage for racialized persons."[4] Its claims that such racism is widespread in Canada today are echoed throughout other levels of government and their bureaucracies, in academia, much of the news media, and elsewhere.

The evidence does not bear this claim out.

To be sure, if the question is only as to whether personal prejudice or racism exists in Canadian institutions, then the answer is that there is some. Institutions are made of people, and as long as some people hold some prejudices (some always will) and reveal and act upon them (hopefully rarely), there will be racism in institutions. However, the *personal* prejudices of people within institutions does not constitute institutional racism in the classical sense, in which the rules or policies of the institution are discriminatory. Historical examples of real institutional racism include colleges and universities in decades past limiting the proportion of Jewish students on campus, or the minimum wage law implemented in British Columbia nearly a century ago, which had, as Thomas Sowell has written, "the intent and effect of pricing Japanese immigrants out of jobs in the lumbering industry."[5] But if the typical anti-racism activist today is looking for widespread institutional or systemic racism of the kind that existed before the mid-twentieth century, which was directed at minorities or women, they simply will not find it.

Ironically, the most socially accepted and likely most common form of institutional racism today is the discrimination practiced in the name of social justice or anti-racism. Below are four examples:

- In 2016, the University of Manitoba Senate approved a new admission policy for the Bachelor of Education Program in which only 55 per cent of admissions would be based on admissions scores, and 45 per cent on "diversity" categories that included racial preferences.[6]

- There are some government programs accessible only to people of a certain race or races. For example, in September 2020 the federal government announced up to $93 million in spending, expanded by another $52 million in Budget 2021, for a "Black Entrepreneurship Program."[7]
- A local bargaining unit of the Ontario Secondary School Teachers' Federation, representing 1,400 teachers and staff in the Halton region, adopted a new voting system in 2021 for decisions made by the board of local presidents. The new voting system weighed votes by skin colour: if visible minorities accounted for fewer than half the voters, their votes would be weighted more heavily.[8]
- The federal regulator requires the Canadian Broadcasting Corporation to apply racial preferences in its programming by dedicating at least 30 per cent of its spending on independent English programming to, as reported in the *National Post*, "producers who self-identify as Indigenous, official language minorities, visible minorities, disabled or LGBT."[9]

Such examples show that in Canada there are still institutional policies that outright discriminate based on race. Yet such examples clearly do not fit the governmental definition of systemic or institutional racism, in which "racialized persons" are put at relative disadvantage. That is not to say that visible minorities never suffer from racism, but as to the accusation made by progressives that Canada is a systemically racist country in which visible minorities suffer profound disadvantages, little evidence exists to support the fact.

Three observations

When it comes to progressives' charge of systemic racism in Canada, there are three major points of dispute. The first is that contrary to how the federal government defines systemic racism, it is not only visible minorities who are put into positions of relative disadvantage when institutional policies discriminate based on race. Most systemic racism in past generations certainly worked against visible minorities; yet today, modern examples of race-based policies seem to cut the other way. The teachers' union that weighs votes by skin colour, the University of Manitoba's admissions criteria, CBC's diversity requirements, and so on, are discriminatory toward Canada's white population.

The second point of dispute: pronouncements about systemic racism in Canada are overwhelmingly accompanied by prescriptions for top-down solutions; whether government regulations, federal programs, national strategies, or the like. Yet a great deal of unfair discrimination is done either by government itself or by institutions adjacent to government: public sector unions and universities, for example. It is therefore dubious that expanding top-down control would lessen the harmful effects of discrimination. On the contrary, reducing government control would likely help.

"It is a striking historical fact," Milton Friedman wrote in *Capitalism and Freedom*, first published in 1962, "that the development of capitalism has been accompanied by a major reduction in the extent to which particular religious, racial, or social groups have operated under special handicaps in respect to their economic activities; have, as the saying goes, been discriminated against."[10] More specifically, "the preserves of discrimination in any society are the areas that are the most monopolistic in character, whereas discrimination against groups of particular color or religion is least in those areas where there is the greatest freedom of competition." Much of the foundation of the economic study of discrimination was laid by Gary Becker, a student of Friedman's, and who like Friedman, was an economic Nobelist.

As the Concise Encyclopedia of Economics documents:

> Becker successfully challenged the Marxist view that discrimination helps the person who discriminates. Becker pointed out that if an employer refuses to hire a productive worker simply because of skin colour, that employer loses out on a valuable opportunity. In short, discrimination is costly to the person who discriminates. Becker showed that discrimination will be less pervasive in more competitive industries because companies that discriminate will lose market share to companies that do not. He also presented evidence that discrimination is more pervasive in more-regulated, and therefore less-competitive, industries. The idea that discrimination is costly to the discriminator is common sense among economists today, and that is due to Becker.[11]

Similarly to Friedman and contrary to the grand plans of progressives for top-down control Becker saw free markets as the antidote to discrimination. While it is in the interest of private enterprises to not discriminate based on race, governments operate based on different incentives and constraints. It is often in the interest of politicians, for example, to reflect societal biases and if they control the government, they have the power to discriminate. In the past, to the extent that white people were prejudiced, minorities suffered from institutional discrimination. Today, it is fashionable in some quarters to discriminate against the white population, largely to "correct" for past wrongs or perceived current wrongs.

The third point of dispute with the progressive narrative of a systemically racist country: the lack of convincing evidence that this is so. Certainly, there are specific instances of discrimination perpetrated by individuals towards other individuals, but this does not mean the country as a whole is rigged to disfavour certain people based on race. Even a government entrepreneurship program that disburses a hundred or so million dollars only to people of a certain race, however unfair and ill-advised, does not, in a country with a population of 38 million really rise to causing the level of harm so as to condemn the entire country as systemically racist. And while it is discriminatory, it is certainly not in the direction of the systemic discrimination defined by the federal government and progressive activists.

At bottom, there is no convincing case backed by direct evidence and statistical analysis to support the theory that Canada is today a systemically racist country in the manner that those who assert this usually mean.

What the statistics show—and what they do not

"Large disparities in the economic and other outcomes of individuals, groups and nations," Thomas Sowell has observed,

> have produced reactions ranging from puzzlement to outrage. Attempts to explain the causes of these disparities have likewise produced a wide range of responses. At one end of a spectrum of explanations is the belief that those who have been less fortunate in their outcomes are genetically less capable. At the other end of the spectrum is the belief that those less fortunate are victims of other people who are more fortunate.[12]

It is the second end of the spectrum from whence comes the narrative that worse outcomes for some Canadians, specifically visible minorities, are the result of discrimination by more fortunate Canadians.

Sowell has devoted multiple books to exploring the link between discrimination and disparate outcomes in the United States and worldwide, but a single example from Canadian data suffices to show that discrimination does not explain all, or even most of the disparities of outcomes between individuals or groups. In Canada, the life expectancy at birth for females exceeded that of males by 1.8 years in the year 1921 and rose steadily over the decades to 7.1 years by 1981. The trend then reversed, so that the disparity shrunk to 6.3 years by 1991, then to 4.3 years in 2011, since when it has remained relatively flat, according to data from 2019 (the latest year for which data are available) (see Figure 1).[13]

FIGURE 1

Difference in life expectancy at birth (female vs. male)

1921 to 2019

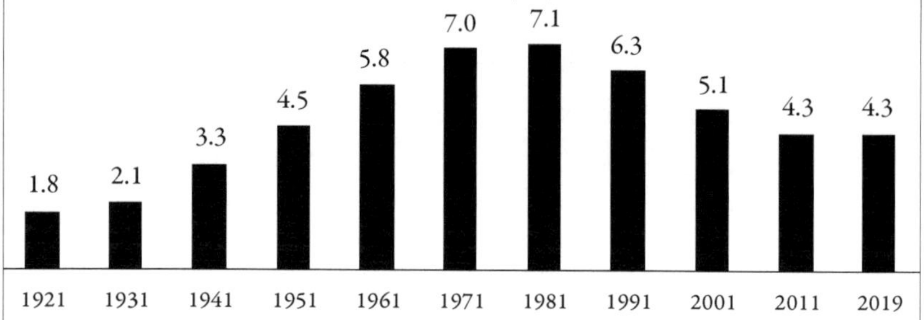

Source: Statistics Canada (2018), *Life Expectancy, 1920-1922 to 2009-2011*; Millar (1995); and Statistics Canada, "Table 13-10-0014-01: Life Expectancy and Other Elements."

Were we to attribute this disparity to unfair discrimination, we would have to conclude that Canadian men have suffered from over a century of misandry, which grew steadily more vicious from the six decades from 1921 to 1981 before abating somewhat over the past four decades, nevertheless today leaving men in the considerably disadvantaged position of living some 4.3 years less than their female counterparts on average. Few Canadians would buy that story. By parity of reasoning, no one should automatically conclude, without sufficient evidence, that disparities in outcomes between racial groups are the results of unfair discrimination.

Accusations of systemic racism in Canada are often made by pointing to disparities in labour market outcomes. However, a top-line look at the statistics does not support such accusations. Using data from the 2016 Census on the weekly earnings of Canadian-born individuals, a pair of Statistics Canada researchers compared the weekly earnings of 10 visible minority groups to those of the white population. Among men (see Figure 2), four had higher earnings than the white population (Chinese, Korean, Japanese, and South Asian), and among women (see Figure 3) seven had higher earnings than the white population (Korean, Chinese, South Asian, Japanese, Filipino, "Other," and Arab or West Asian).[14]

FIGURE 2

Average weekly earnings of Canadian-born men

By ancestry or race | 2015

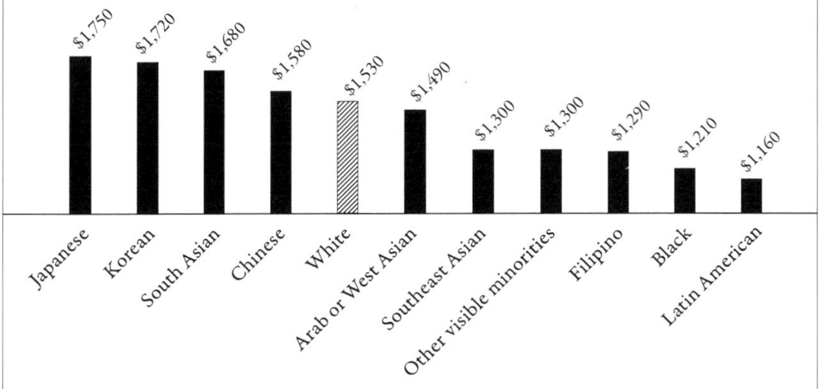

Source: Qiu and Schellenberg (2022), *The Weekly Earnings of Canadian-Born Individuals.*

FIGURE 3

Average weekly earnings of Canadian-born women

By ancestry or race | 2015

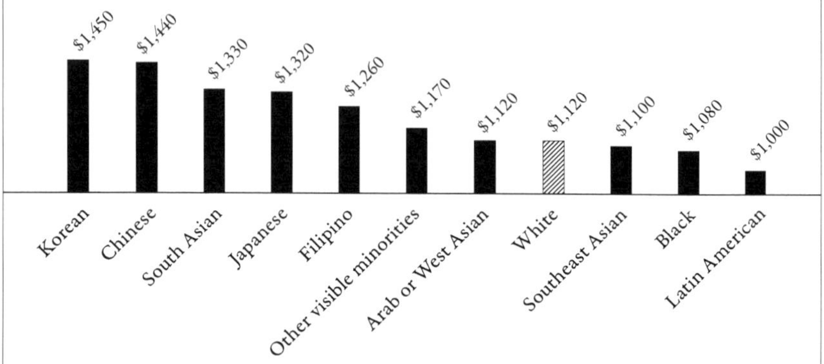

Source: Qiu and Schellenberg (2022), *The Weekly Earnings of Canadian-Born Individuals.*

The white cohort therefore finds itself somewhere in the middle of the pack, so the evidence in favour of the theory that Canada's institutions are rigged to disfavour visible minorities is indeed slight. Of course, the raw data alone may not mean much. It could be that, for example, Chinese men must be 25 per cent more productive than white men to earn three per cent more, and that black women earn 10 per cent less than white women despite being equally productive. In other words, an apples-to-apples comparison requires controlling for education, occupation, and other factors that affect earnings.

Importantly, the Statistics Canada report does attempt to control for such factors, again with results that dispel the notion that white Canadians have an unfair advantage over minorities. Segmenting the minority population into 10 racial groups and the two sexes yields 20 minority groups that can be compared against their white counterparts. Of these, five minority groups have earnings statistically higher than the white population after controlling for employment and sociodemographic factors (South Asian men, Chinese women, South Asian women, Filipino women, and Southeast Asian women), while only four (men from the Black, Latin American, Filipino, and "Other" racial backgrounds) have lower earnings, with the other 11 groups showing no statistically significant difference from whites.[15]

In other words, according to the Statistics Canada data, although the Korean and Japanese populations enjoy far higher weekly earnings than the white population, this is accounted for by differences in sociodemographic and employment characteristics (and thus we cannot infer from statistics that there is any discrimination that favours Koreans or the Japanese). Among the Chinese, however, relatively high earnings are explained by the sociodemographic and employment characteristics present among men, but not among women.

Thus, if we were to attribute to unfair discrimination earnings disparities not explained by the Statistics Canada's researchers' attempts to control for sociodemographic and employment characteristics, we would have to conclude that labour market discrimination favours Chinese women, but not Chinese men, and not Korean or Japanese women. We would likewise have to conclude that labour market discrimination favours Filipino women relative to white women, but white men relative to Filipino men. Moreover, the discrimination faced by Latin American and black workers singularly affects only men and not women. If this does not make any sense—which one must admit that it does not—then it must be allowed that unfair discrimination is a poor explanation for racial disparities in earnings.

To dig deeper into the data, another Statistics Canada report examined the differences in weekly earnings of workers by race, but categorized workers by sector: the non-commercial sector, large commercial sector, medium commercial sector, and small commercial sector. Large, medium, and small refer to the size of the employer, and the non-commercial sector includes health, education, social services, and public administration (see Table 1).[16]

Again, if we were to attribute to discrimination the earnings disparities not explained in this statistical analysis by sociodemographic and employment characteristics, we would have to conclude that the non-commercial sector very likely discriminates against the white population at the expense of visible minorities, since many visible minority groups earn more than whites, but none earn less. Moreover, racial discrimination by medium-sized commercial employers favours white men over Chinese men, but Chinese women over white women. Those same medium-sized commercial employers also favour

TABLE 1

Percent difference in weekly earnings relative to the white population (reference group) net of sociodemographic and employment characteristics among Canadian-born individuals aged 25 to 44

2015

Men	Non-commercial	Large Commercial	Medium Commercial	Small Commercial
White	0.0	0.0	0.0	0.0
Chinese	**5.1**	*-1.0*	*-3.9*	*-6.8*
Korean or Japanese	*-3.0*	*-2.0*	0.0	**1.0**
Southeast Asian	**3.0**	**2.0**	*-4.9*	*-7.7*
Filipino	**3.0**	*-7.7*	*-3.9*	**1.0**
South Asian	**7.3**	0.0	*-1.0*	*-4.9*
Arab or West Asian	**4.1**	**2.0**	**4.1**	*-9.5*
Latin American	**7.3**	*-9.5*	*-6.8*	*-14.9*
Black	*-2.0*	*-11.3*	*-15.6*	*-18.1*
Other visible minorities	**2.0**	*-7.7*	*-3.9*	*-8.6*

Women	Non-commercial	Large Commercial	Medium Commercial	Small Commercial
White	0.0	0.0	0.0	0.0
Chinese	**8.3**	**5.1**	**6.2**	**3.0**
Korean or Japanese	0.0	**3.0**	**8.3**	*-2.0*
Southeast Asian	**6.2**	0.0	**5.1**	**3.0**
Filipino	**9.4**	0.0	*-1.0*	*-2.0*
South Asian	**2.0**	**1.0**	0.0	*-1.0*
Arab or West Asian	*-1.0*	0.0	**3.0**	*-4.9*
Latin American	*-1.0*	*-4.9*	*-3.0*	1.0
Black	**2.0**	*-6.8*	*-10.4*	*-7.7*
Other visible minorities	**4.1**	*-3.9*	*-3.0*	*-2.0*

Differences relative to white men/women in **bold** if higher and *italics* if lower.
Source: Qiu and Schellenberg (2022), *The Relative Earnings of Individuals*.

Korean and Japanese women relative to white women, but for some reason that same discrimination is present neither in large nor small commercial employers.

Commercial employers seem to unfairly discriminate against visible minorities quite often, but only when it comes to men and not women (except for black women). And then even this discrimination against men follows a curious pattern: only small-sized commercial employers discriminate against Southeast Asian, South Asian, and Arab or West Asian men, while only medium and large-sized commercial employers discriminate against Filipino men. As before, the story reveals no pattern and makes no sense, so it must be that such conclusions—contrived by attributing disparities unexplained by sociodemographic and employment characteristics to unfair discrimination—are wrong.

Clearly, caution is needed when trying to draw inferences from statistics. It cannot be that disparities, even after researchers try to control for relevant factors (such as education, profession, and so on), can simply be put down to unfair discrimination. Other factors are always at play, and the reality is that the number of factors that affect earnings are innumerable and many of the material ones—such as individual preferences and family culture—are difficult or impossible for researchers to observe or measure.

Invariably, researchers cannot control for everything and so many find through statistical inference disparities that cannot be explained by the factors controlled for. There is no reason to suppose that the explanatory factor is unfair discrimination. Other possible explanations exist, and many are more plausible. This is particularly so in competitive industries, given, as Friedman and Becker wrote, the prophylactic effects of free markets and competition on discrimination.

Returning to the example of gender disparities, consider two studies. The first: published in 2021 in the Journal of Labor Economics on the gender wage gap among bus and train operators employed by the Massachusetts Bay Transportation Authority. "Female workers," the authors note, "earn $0.89 for each male-worker dollar even in a unionized workplace, where tasks, wages, and promotion schedules are identical for men and women by design." If tasks and wages are identical for men and women, why do women earn 11 per cent less? The researchers found "this earnings gap can be explained by female operators taking fewer hours of overtime and more hours of unpaid time off than male operators."[17]

In a second study, distributed by the National Bureau of Economic Research in 2018, researchers found the hourly wage gap between male and female Uber drivers to be seven per cent. This raises a pertinent question: how can women earn seven per cent less for doing the same work, where the algorithm that assigns work to drivers and determines pay is gender-blind? The researchers concluded that the disparity could be explained by three main factors. First, men had more experience on the platform and so knew better where and when to drive or accept trips to maximize income; second, men tended to drive faster; and third, men were more likely to drive in more profitable locations.[18]

An American study, therefore, that compared wage disparities between men and women by simply controlling for profession and hours worked, would find women earned 11 per cent less than men at the Massachusetts Bay Transportation Authority and seven per cent less than men when driving for Uber. Yet the disparity cannot be assigned to unfair discrimination. Other factors are at play—the willingness to taking overtime shifts on short notice in the first instance, and a combination of factors (including driving speed) in the second. These sorts of factors (among others) significantly affect earnings, but are difficult or even impossible to measure or observe in national studies.

What is true for gender is also true for racial disparities. Observed disparities in outcomes—whether life expectancy, earnings, or anything else—between individuals or groups, even after researchers have tried to control for the relevant factors, cannot simply be attributed to discrimination. Trying to do so results in stories that are inconsistent which make no logical sense, and in the Canadian context, the evidence simply does not support the idea that the country is systemically racist.

Conclusion: The evidence is lacking

Claims that Canada is a racist country in which the white population systemically oppresses visible minorities come from the highest quarters, including the federal government and academia, but evidence in favour of such claims is scant. Undoubtedly, anyone can suffer from individual instances of discrimination, but this does not constitute institutional discrimination in the classical sense, in which the rules or policies of the institution are discriminatory. Such cases of institutional discrimination today are thankfully rare—with, ironically, most exceptions taking the form of discrimination practiced in the name of anti-racism.

Another irony is that while those who claim Canada is systemically racist often call for top-down correction to whatever unfair discrimination that exists, the remaining institutional discrimination that exists is often instigated or enforced by government itself or government-backed institutions. This should come as no surprise, and is predicted by economic theory, as Friedman and Becker explained.

Lastly, a coherent story of Canada as a systemically racist country simply cannot be formed by statistical analysis and direct evidence. Assigning to discrimination differences in income (even after controlling for sociodemographic and employment characteristics) leads to conclusions that simply make no sense.

That does not mean that no personal prejudice or racism exists in Canadian institutions. It is only to say that the portrait of Canada as a systemically racist country painted by some is not supported by evidence.

PART II

It's complex: Canada's cancelled history

CHAPTER 7

Carving out a country: From Magna Carta to Confederation

John Robson

It is only in countries like England, enjoying constitutional liberty, and safe from the tyranny of a single despot, or of an unbridled democracy, that the rights of minorities are regarded.
—SIR JOHN A. MACDONALD to the Canadian Legislative Assembly February 2, 1865

The men who made Canada believed they were building a free country on the most solid foundation available, indeed the only one: Magna Carta's limitations on absolute power, and the institutions that had developed based on it. Following the Glorious Revolution of 1688 these institutions were adapted to local circumstances, including the 1763 Royal Proclamation which attempted to protect both indigenous and French rights including the *langue, loi et foi* in what would become Lower Canada and later Quebec. If such men could somehow be transported to the 21st century only to be told they and their creation were imperfect, they would be baffled that anyone should expect otherwise. They knew the limitations of human nature all too well, but which our modern utopians often disregard exactly that in planning the future or even in rewriting the past. And if told they could easily have done much better, Canada's founders would have been even more baffled at the presumption of their critics that perfect social justice could be had just for the asking.

Many of these critics seem to know nothing even about the immediate practical difficulties that forced Sir John A. Macdonald and his colleagues into a series of messy compromises, including creating a federal structure despite their devotion to the British unitary model because nothing else would have induced Quebec to join Confederation. This particular kluge turned out to be a brilliant innovation subsequently copied from Australia to India. But their default position was to the one system that had worked anywhere, ever, in protecting liberty under law. And rightly so.

Modern critics of our founders seem to think there was some readily available superior alternative to the structure of liberties that had arisen from Magna Carta and the successive pieces of legislation which followed it in England. But with their sober grasp of history and human nature, our Founders understood that their task was to adapt that irreplaceable model to the particular geographic, demographic and cultural realities of their fragile situation as much smaller neighbours of the American republic that had emerged from its Civil War as the strongest land power in the world and just acquired Alaska.

A history of people who knew history

They knew their history in ways contemporary politicians, citizens and pundits generally do not. In 2015 Prime Minister Stephen Harper recounted an anecdote where Macdonald, visiting England, "dined at the house of a gentleman whom he knew but slightly. Most of the company were entire strangers to him. The conversation turned on constitutional history, and Sir John happened to remark that he thought Bagehot the best authority on the British constitution. 'I am glad to hear you say that,' said his left-hand neighbour, 'for I am Mr. Bagehot.'"[1] It is difficult to think of a contemporary Canadian politician who could even pronounce the name Bagehot ("BADget"), let alone expound on his views.

This understanding included the once-familiar tale of Magna Carta; the Great Charter imposed on Bad King John at Runnymede in 1215 and the subsequent history of freedom in England and the Anglosphere. They knew of the dangerous rise of European absolutism during the Renaissance, and the bloody English Civil War in the 1640s to preserve Parliamentary restraints on the monarchy after Charles I tried to impose taxation without representation through dodges from forced loans to collecting "ship money" even from inland towns. They remembered the dangerous overreaction of the

Commonwealth in the 1650s in dispensing with any limits on the legislature, and the "Glorious Revolution" of 1688-89 that closed this turbulent chapter by ousting the block-headed King James II with minimal bloodshed when he tried to overturn the compromise settlement.

Our founders could easily recall that William and Mary replaced King James II on condition that they accepted the English Bill of Rights, exactly a century before the American one and full of similar constitutional protections including a ban on quartering troops inspired by Louis XIV's egregious practice of "dragooning" Protestants. And they remembered, and appreciated, stirring tales of the heroic defence of this parliamentary system against a list foreign tyrants; from Philip II of Spain and his Armada to Napoleon and his army, the latter defeated mere decades before Confederation.

Our founding debates, shamefully only published comprehensively in 1999,[2] do not reflect enthusiasm for big government, socialized medicine, and social engineering which too many Canadians wrongly assume is what the Canadian nation-state is all about. Instead, "British liberty" was the touchstone of proponents and opponents of Confederation alike. Legislatures rang with phrases like "I claim the rights and attributes of a free man, speaking in the presence of a British free assembly" (Stewart Campbell, February 23, 1869) and "... under the British Constitution we have far more freedom than any other people on the face of the earth," (William Lawrence, April 17, 1866) and "We have here a constitution for which the people nobly fought... and which was reluctantly wrung from the British government. We had the right of taxing ourselves, or legislating for ourselves" (George Hogsett, February 23, 1869).[3]

Why it matters: The founders' foundation for modern rights and responsibilities

These early debaters knew the key rights guaranteed in Magna Carta, from freedom of religion to a fair legal system; from security of the person to the protection of property; freedom from oppressive taxation; a say in how you, the citizen, are governed; even the rights of women, were timeless and universal. They knew that no other political culture had ever come close to guaranteeing such rights, even imperfectly, as Britain had over the centuries, including, it must be conceded, longstanding legal restrictions on Roman Catholics following Henry VIII's break with Rome, only properly lifted in the 19th century.

The Canadian founders, like those in Britain who finally removed restrictions on Catholics and belatedly banned slavery, also sought to identify and repair defects in political culture and institutions. It is often forgotten today that Macdonald himself was very enlightened for his times on aboriginal rights, was "the first leader in the Western world to advocate for granting women the right to vote"[4], and, like his colleagues deplored the American institution of slavery.

Nowadays it is habitual to ridicule Sir John for attempting to ensure that Canada's aboriginals were prepared to live in the modern world rather than being crushed by it. A professor of Native Studies at the University of Manitoba, Niigaan Sinclair, denounced him in 2015 as "a racist politician hell-bent on solving what he saw as an Indian problem. The problem, as it were, was Indians insisted on being treated as human beings." By which he meant refusing to become part of Western civilization, a circular argument if ever there was one because if Western civilization is good, helping people join indicates a favourable view of their humanity.

He added the canard that Macdonald deliberately starved aboriginals before winding up "Hey Johnny: me and a few million others aren't fit to change. Your assimilation project failed."[5] A more grown-up version is that Macdonald "worked to give the federal franchise to all adult male Indians in central and eastern Canada with the necessary property qualifications" and stood against other politicians who "unlike Macdonald, argued First Nations had no legal title to their lands at all."[6] He also tasked the North-West Mounted Police with impeding the ruinous American whiskey trade with aboriginals in the West, and was criticized by political adversaries for the generosity of his efforts to keep them from starving. In stark contrast to the infamous Sir Jeffrey Amherst a century earlier, Macdonald mounted determined campaigns to vaccinate aboriginals against smallpox before and after Confederation.[7]

Our Founders saw defects in their institutions. But they knew where Parliament, independent courts and individual rights came from and how dramatically they outperformed even French institutions, let alone those of

Russia or China. They valued the organic way such institutions had evolved rather than being handed down from Parnassus by advanced thinkers lacking practical experience. We should be so lucky to have their depth of historical recollection.

What every schoolchild and politician knew

Or any historical recollection at all, of a sort that was common not just in the 19th century but well into the 20th. A case in point is Josephine Tey's splendid 1951 "cold case" mystery novel *The Daughter of Time,*[8] in which a policeman immobilized by injury fends off boredom by investigating whether the last Yorkist monarch Richard III (reigned 1483-1485 and the last English king killed in battle) was really a monster who murdered his nephews as in Shakespeare's famous play with its infamous line "My kingdom for a horse."

In writing this book Tey took for granted that her mass audience would remember all kinds of details of a sort that Canada's founders certainly did. But how many Members of Parliament, in Canada or Britain, could now pass a quiz on them? At one point her hero reflects on a children's book containing iconic scenes from English history that stay in adults' memory "when tonnage and poundage, and ship money, and Laud's Liturgy, and the Rye House Plot, and the Triennial Acts, and all the long muddle of schism and shindy, treaty and treason, had faded from their consciousness." Scenes like Nelson dying on *HMS Victory* at Trafalgar that one suspects are totally forgotten today, and Canute, whose story we moderns dimly recall but usually get backward.[a] And Richard III murdering the princes in the tower.[9]

Such things were familiar to Canada's founders because they studied their history and knew where they came from, whereas today students struggle to recall what decade or even what century saw the world wars. And while we may topple statues of people whose careers we could not begin to describe, we are the fools for losing the details of liberty's story and the justified hope it inspires in the free institutions which were left to us, but which we are slowly letting slip away.

It may still be fairly widely remembered that Magna Carta was sealed under compulsion by Bad King John, villain of the Robin Hood stories, at

---

a) Canute did not believe he could stop the tide and staged his little demonstration to rebuke obsequious and impious courtiers.

Runnymede in 1215. When the BBC polled its audience about a "Britain Day" in 2006, its June 15 anniversary defeated even Remembrance Day. But who today understands that the rights it enumerated were not a wish list if only the government was not so wretched, let alone that its prime mover was the heroic Archbishop of Canterbury Stephen Langton?

Modern people generally assume any upholders of human rights before the 1960s, or in Canada 1982, were lonely rebels against callous, hypocritical tradition. So it is especially hard for them to grasp that the specific ones listed in Magna Carta, from trial by jury to property rights to due process of law, really were, by and large, upheld in England many centuries ago. (Even Magna Carta began as a revision of the 1100 Coronation Oath of John's great-grandfather Henry I, which in turn explicitly evoked the liberties of Anglo-Saxon England.) But it was a commonplace of English political discourse including at Court, before Magna Carta, that their ruler was subject to the law, not its source. No such thing can be said even of England's continental neighbours, let alone nations outside the Western tradition.

Moderns consequently also generally fail to appreciate the subsequent miracle that the protections affirmed at Runnymede in 1215 were not eroded or crushed with the passing of the years through the best, and worst, efforts of "modernizing" English monarchs from Richard II to Henry VIII to George III. Instead they were preserved and enhanced over 800 years, often in the face of appalling danger, making possible the kind of society we enjoy today, even as embryonic legislative assemblies in France, Spain and various Germany principalities were reduced to insignificance by the Renaissance rise of Absolutism. Macdonald and his colleagues knew much of this English story by heart, and were determined to play a constructive part in it.

The birth of our Parliament in 1265

If we read Magna Carta today, we find a surprising number of familiar important rights including trial by jury according to the law of the land, and courts accessible to the ordinary person because they sat locally rather than following the king. We also find within the Charter the protection of property, the right of widows not to be forcibly remarried or heiresses deprived of their inheritance, and perhaps most surprising, a pledge of no taxation without representation. The latter is expressed in the terminology of "neither scutage nor aid" which is archaic, but "by common counsel of our kingdom" which is not. And both ideas were neither obsolete nor obscure in 1867, as they had not been in previous crises from the American Revolution in 1776 to the revolt against Charles I in the 1640s, Parliament's defiance of Henry VIII over the Statute of Proclamations in 1539, or even in 1297 when Edward I consented to the principle of no taxation without the consent of the people's representatives.

Of course back in 1215 it was far from clear how this "common counsel" would work. Anglo-Saxon England had made frequent use of a "*witenagemot*" ("council") of leading citizens, but this body had lacked formal procedures, defined rights or a corporate identity. And the tangled tale of how an elected Parliament came into being, chosen by the people and with effective control over the actions of government, includes of course, the 1264 revolt of Simon de Montfort against King John's son (and Montfort's brother-in-law) Henry III, for incompetent extravagance rather than John's more efficient and effective malice.

Montfort is a distinctly imperfect hero, rightly condemned for vicious anti-Semitism. But also rightly praised for signal contributions to the institutions that made self-government and liberty under law a practical reality. After defeating the feeble Henry and his formidable son (later King Edward I, nicknamed "Longshanks"), instead of creating a pyramid of enemy skulls à la Tamurlane, he dragged the hapless monarch to Westminster Abbey and forced him to reissue Magna Carta before God and man. Montfort subsequently summoned a "model" Parliament, the first such assembly to include the common people as full participants, with two knights from every county and two burgesses from every major town (except the important Cinq Ports with four each), apparently freely chosen by local citizens in a vote without property qualifications.

In 1265 Edward escaped, ambushed, killed and mutilated Montfort. But when he became King in 1272, he cemented his legitimacy not by erasing the memory of Montfort but, rather, by summoning a Parliament that again included ordinary people. The commons were in, and nobody ever tried to expel them subsequently. Rather, as Longshanks himself put it, "what touches all shall be decided by all."[10] And as early as 1297, broke as usual, he assented to *De Tallagio non Concedendo* declaring that the king could not raise money without parliamentary assent. Those who study history can and should recognize how unusual and remarkable this moment is in the story of humanity which, for much of its duration, has consisted of the decisions of emperors, kings and other more "modern" tyrants, not those of legislatures chosen by the people all of which are modeled one way or another on the "Mother of Parliaments" in London.

When the American revolutionaries shouted "No taxation without representation" in 1776 they were not innovating. Nor were the Rebels of Upper Canada and the *Patriotes* of Lower Canada in the 1830s when they demanded "responsible government" where the executive depended for the revenue necessary to its program not on its own capacity to levy taxes, nor on subsidies from London, but on the consent of the elected representatives of the people.

For all free people

Some modern commentators insist that Magna Carta was an elite deal with no value to serfs or even free peasants and which lacked general statements of rights. But as the great jurist and statesman Edward Coke noted pointedly four centuries after Runnymede, brandishing the Great Charter against Stuart pretensions to absolute rule, Henry III's 1225 confirmation of Magna Carta "granted to all Archbishops, Bishops, Abbots, Priors, Earls, Barons, and to all Freemen of this our Realm, these Liberties following"[11] including, Coke added, "villeines (serfs), for they are accounted free against all men saving against the Lords." And to avoid a probable modern woke misreading, "men" here translates the Latin "*homo*" ("person") not "*vir*" ("male").

Moreover Magna Carta was, from Edward I's time, read aloud in all English cathedrals twice a year, in the vernacular, so even the illiterate would know their rights. But the proof of the pudding is in the eating, and every time this system was challenged, it ended up stronger and more solid rather than being gradually worn away.

As fits its organic evolution, we do not know how or when the single most vital development happened. But by 1346 the Commons were meeting as a separate chamber and by 1376 electing their own "Speaker" who crucially controlled procedure including counting votes at the command of the House, not the King (in a cynical motto plausibly attributed to Stalin, it does not matter who votes, just who counts votes[12]), and spoke for it in all dealings with monarch and Lords. It also seems important, looking back, that English clergy and nobles remained in a single upper house, whereas in the French *Parlement* or *États-Généraux* commons, secular nobles and churchmen sat in three separate houses whose ineffectual efforts aimed to safeguarding their own class interests, not the general good.[b]

The rise of Parliament

It is extraordinary how quickly Parliament, and the Commons within it, became decisive in England's government and constitutional order. Within 25 years of the first confirmed Commons election of its own Speaker, Longshanks' great-great-grand-son, Richard II, was deposed by the general consent of all classes for claiming "the law is in my mouth", that is, that he had unlimited power to rule by decree without any need for Parliamentary approval. In other countries such a claim was standard fare; even in France, which was relatively non-despotic by global standards, leading political theorist, Paris Parlement member and law professor Jean Bodin wrote in the 16th century that, "When edicts are ratified by Estates or Parlements, it is for the purpose of securing obedience to them, and not because otherwise a sovereign prince could not validly make law."[13]

In England those who deposed Richard II in 1399, like those who deposed Longshanks' son Edward II back in 1327, specifically cited Magna Carta. And Richard's would-be successor, Henry of Bolingbroke, then took a very revealing step: he brought his claim to become King Henry IV to Parliament for approval. Parliament's reaction was also revealing. Parliamentarians told the man who would be king that, in the past, monarchs had been wont to summon Parliaments, hear their grievances, then ask for money. Once they received the cash, however, the monarchs quickly lost interest in their subjects' concerns. So if Henry wished to be king, he must promise that henceforth, he would answer petitions before being granted revenue. Thus the modern system of royal assent to bills as a condition of "supply" was born.

---

b) The French parliament did not meet once between 1614 and 1789 and, when finally summoned, promptly shattered, with the strongest faction establishing a dictatorship disguised as a democracy.

Just seven years later, in 1407, the people's representatives confronted the Lords over a money bill, insisting that the Commons had primacy. King and Lords agreed that grants would be "made by the Commons and assented to by the Lords," which is why to this day in Britain, the United States and Canada, spending and tax bills must originate in the people's chamber. And then in 1414 the Commons forced Henry IV's son Henry V to agree that he could accept their bills, or reject them if he thought he could get by without any money. But he could not accept them then, after MPs went home, alter their text.

The long siege of Parliament

Those who made Canada could have recited in their sleep the long and convoluted story of subsequent monarchical assaults on the "power of the purse" including the famously six-wived Henry VIII (reigned 1509 to 1547), an outsized Renaissance man in every sense, who bullied and threatened Parliament to fund reckless borrowing to finance his wars.

In 1535, Henry summoned the influential Edward Montague over his stalled Suppression of Religious Houses Act. "'Ho man!' said he to the wretched Montague, kneeling before him. 'Will they not suffer my Bill to pass?' Then, taking Montague by the head, he added in the most peremptory tones: 'Get my Bill passed by to-morrow, or else to-morrow this head of yours will be off!' The Bill was passed."[14] But there were limits, vital ones.

In 1539 Henry took his most ominous step by sending Parliament a draft Statute of Proclamations saying his decrees had the force of law, precisely the hubris that had cost Richard II his throne and life 140 years and two dynasties earlier. But Parliamentarians defied him with resolute cheek, substituting a bill that supposedly let him make law by mere assertion, but then specifically exempted the "'inheritances, lawful possessions, offices, liberties, privileges, franchises, goods, or chattels' of subjects, and forbade the infringement of any 'acts, common laws... [or] lawful and laudable customs' of the realm."[15] Thus Henry was obliged to act through Parliament even when dispatching wives, stealing monasteries and making himself Pope of England so he could bed Anne Boleyn.

After the Tudors fizzled out when Elizabeth I died without issue, the next major threat to Parliament came with the Stuart monarchs from Scotland whose Parliament was an obsequious formality. The canny James I, descended from Henry VIII's sister (and James VI of Scotland 1567-1625) sailed close to the wind on many occasions between his English accession in 1603 and his death. But he avoided a direct showdown with Parliamentary leaders including the great jurist, statesman and at times political prisoner Edward Coke.[16] It is doubtful that any critic of our institutions today can recall his name (or pronounce it; it's "COOK").

James once barged into the Commons and tore from their journal a page recording speeches critical of his policy, still on display at Westminster. But he knew when to back down, unlike his timidly rigid son Charles I, whose attempted suppression of liberty prompted Coke's great Parliamentary remonstrance that "Magna Carta is such a fellow as he will have no sovereign." Charles' armed invasion of the Commons in 1642 led to the creation of a still-binding rule which bars agents of the Crown from the parliamentary chamber that is commemorated to this day when, for every throne speech, the "Black Rod" has the Commons door closed in his or her face.

Charles' aggressive actions triggered a disastrous Civil War that killed more English people per capita than World War I. The Parliamentary victory brought Charles' execution in 1649 and a "Commonwealth" interlude under Oliver Cromwell who mocked "Magna Farta" and whose own written constitution and other formalities only amounted, one wag said, to putting a wig on the point of a sword. But when Cromwell died in 1658 his son and putative heir belied his hapless nickname "Tumbledown Dick" by helping restore the monarchy in 1660 under Charles I's son Charles II before slipping quietly away. The "Merry Monarch" was cautiously devious like his grandfather James, but when he died in 1685 his brother and heir James II[c] roused the nation against himself so obtusely that in just four years the "Glorious Revolution" threw him out and brought in the English "Bill of Rights" whose guarantee of a right to arms preceded the American one by a century. Magna Carta was back this time and, apparently, to stay.

Magna Carta in the New World

Certainly British colonists took the Great Charter with them to the New World while founding the freest societies the world had ever seen. And also,

---

c) Apparently James once warned Charles against possible assassination only to be told something like "Ah, Jamie, they'll no kill me to make you king."

bafflingly, racial slavery, as complete and ghastly a denial of liberty as the world has ever seen. But Upper Canada also has the distinction of being the first British colony to ban the importation of slaves, in 1793 under Sir John Simcoe, a Christian opponent of slavery since his time as a British MP.[17] But we cannot determine exactly when the infamous institution was abolished here as courts exterminated it in a series of rulings some years before the formal ban throughout the British Empire in 1834.[18]

The British authorities in Canada even stamped it out among aboriginals, an aspect of their traditional culture habitually ignored rather than being either defended or confronted.[19] The Canadian Museum of Human Rights sweeps it away in a paragraph before pillorying the European version at great length.[20] But while there were more slaves in New France than the English Canadian colonies, including after 1763, the total seems to have been under 5,000 of whom, awkwardly, some two-thirds were aboriginals sold by other aboriginals to colonists.[21] And the flight of some 20,000 American blacks from slavery to Ontario alone in the decades before the U.S. Civil War testifies to the more enlightened, if far from satisfactory, racial situation in Canada at the time,[22] as does the service of many black Canadians in the War of 1812.

Despite gruesome failings on racial slavery, all the British colonists regarded liberty as their inheritance as Englishmen, as the American Revolutionaries would proudly repeat when push came to shove, which it did after the Stuarts fizzled out (like their Tudor predecessors) when James II's Protestant daughter Queen Anne died childless in 1714 and the crown passed to German Hanovers descended from James I's daughter. The first two Georges were mostly harmless, due in part to limited English. But George III undertook to undermine Parliament not by the failed method of brute force but through seduction. Perks, offices, flattery, even outright bribes, might have reduced the legislature to a quaint appendage of the executive had not George and his ministers overplayed their hand badly in the Thirteen Colonies.

When they did, the English in America rose up to defend their ancient liberties, right down to the 1775 Massachusetts great seal showing the New England Patriots mascot with drawn sword in one hand and in the other a scroll reading "Magna Charta." They were right, as the British Parliament conceded 200 years later by presenting Congress with a gold replica of Magna

Carta. In 1780, the Commons passed a motion saying "the influence of the Crown has increased, is increasing, and ought to be diminished."[23] In short, the executive was once again usurping its limits, precisely what the American rebels had complained of. After yet another Treaty of Paris granted American independence, the Revolutionaries made an explicit attempt to reestablish the ancient British constitution on even sounder foundations, whilst in Britain, the influence of the Crown was diminished, leading to the high noon of Victorian parliamentary self-government which would inform the vision of Sir John A. Macdonald and his colleagues for government in Canada.

Britain was, as "Land of Hope and Glory" would declare a decade after Macdonald died, "Mother of the Free." As the great British legal commentator William Blackstone in 1765 said, it was "[a] land, perhaps the only one in the universe, in which political or civil liberty is the very end and scope of the constitution,"[24] echoing John Milton who in 1649 called London "the mansion-house of liberty."[25] Macdonald and the Canadian founders wanted British institutions which guaranteed this civil liberty.

Obviously, this liberty was imperfect, including in its enforcement. But again, Macdonald and that great exponent of British liberty George-Étienne Cartier, with George Brown and many lesser lights, were well aware that human nature did not admit perfection. They knew that aiming too high brought disasters like that in France where the lofty and abstract sentiments of Declaration of the Rights of Man were accompanied by what Cartier called the "misery and shame"[26] of the French Revolution, from bloodthirsty terror at the outset to the eventual return of absolute monarchy with Napoleon.

Those who raised the vaguely comic-opera banner of revolt in Upper and Lower Canada in the latter 1830s admired the long struggle to uphold Parliamentary control over the power of the purse against an overbearing executive. Some of William Lyon Mackenzie's more extravagant enthusiasms lay outside even the American mainstream. But consider the unjustly forgotten Canadian *patriote* Pierre Bédard, editor of the first journal of political opinion in Quebec, *Le Canadien,* and first leader of the so-called French Party in the legislative assembly of Lower Canada, who Janet Ajzenstadt reminds us was such a fervent exponent of the British constitution that he drove colonial authorities to distraction by correctly accusing them of undermining it.

> Bédard, in upholding the right of legislators and journalists to speak freely, frequently quoted such acute and now discarded proponents of the British constitution as Blackstone and John Louis De Lolme, and insisted that the essence of responsible government was that the executive depend on the legislature for "supply," that is, for the revenue necessary to carry out its program. Precisely the rules imposed on Henry IV and Henry V in England in the early 15th century.[27]

In the same spirit, the father of responsible government in Nova Scotia,[28] Joseph Howe, presented "12 Resolutions" in 1837, the 11th of which said "the spirit of that [British] constitution — the genius of those Institutions is a complete responsibility to the people by whose resources and for whose benefit they are maintained." The 12th Resolution, in its entirety read:

> That as a remedy for these grievances His Majesty be implored to grant to this Province a Legislative Council, distinct from an Executive Council, whereby responsibility will be secured to the Commons; and, what they value above all other possessions, will be conferred upon the People of this Province, the blessings of the British Constitution.[29]

Such demands carried the day from New Brunswick to Ontario against token resistance. The pivotal Upper Canada Battle of Montgomery's Tavern was no Gettysburg, with just four killed and ten wounded, after which the losers fled in disarray and the victors promptly surrendered.

The revolt in Lower Canada was more protracted, bloodier and more culturally complex. But there was no nonsense of the chauvinistic and childish sort, such as that which Jean Chrétien regularly espoused, including in Northern Ireland in 2000: "I wish that the French had won the battle on the Plains of Abraham. But I was not there to wake up Montcalm."[30] Rather than defend Louis XIV-style absolutism, the *Patriotes* demanded British responsible self-government.

Skirmishing in Lower Canada lasted through 1838 and led to 100 battle deaths, 29 executions and 58 deportations to Australia. The British government sent Lord Durham, a.k.a. "Radical Jack," to Canada, knowing he would recommend self-government and they would grant it, with the Act of Union in 1840, the coming of responsible government in 1848, and the British North America Act in 1867.

In response to a bill to compensate for what were then French Canadians who had suffered losses during the rebellion, signed by the governor of the united Province of Canada despite misgivings, Tory rebels burned down the Parliament. But the legislature, and constitutional principle, prevailed against both the executive and the mob.[31] And there is surprisingly little to say on this point after 1867 because that principle was followed essentially without resistance or dispute.

Canadians were at one time justly proud of this legacy, even while struggling to secure it. Thirteen years before responsible government came to Nova Scotia, Joseph Howe was a journalist on trial for libeling the colonial authorities in 1835. The judge correctly told the jury truth was not a defense under current law. But Howe asked them "Will you permit the sacred fire of liberty, brought by your fathers from the venerable temples of Britain, to be quenched and trodden out on the simple altars they have raised?"[32] In response they acquitted him, thus nullifying the statute as obnoxious to liberty. No such story can be told in any other political tradition.

Our liberty was imperfect and still is. Our past contains events and habits that make us cringe, including legal procedures that winked at torture, and where defendants who could not call witnesses faced dreadful public execution. But it does not mean our predecessors were fools or hypocrites. It just means they were imperfect people, as we are, and who have not solved all the problems history bequeathed to us. Similarly, some of our efforts may also inspire baffled dismay in posterity.

For all their imperfections, Canada's founders handed down to us institutions that continue to permit and indeed require unrelenting efforts to improve. And nothing would surprise Sir John A. and his colleagues less than a claim that they had fallen short of perfection, except angry denunciations of them for having done so.

Postscript

It is not the purpose of this chapter to continue the story past 1867. But in two world wars and the Cold War the Anglosphere came together in defense of liberty. And while noting the efforts and losses of the Soviet Union in World War II, it was these free nations who furnished the key military, economic and moral strength to defeat those threats under the banner of liberty. No other standard could rally them, then or now. The claim that Canada is a genocidal settler state[33] is not a recipe for liberty but for a descent into bloody anarchy and the end of freedom. As Daniel Hannan wrote in *Inventing Freedom*:

> Magna Carta is a useful reminder of what freedom traditionally means. It defines our rights in essentially negative terms. If I have freedom of speech, you can't shut me up. If I have freedom of assembly, people aren't allowed to tell me who I'm allowed to congregate with or in what numbers. And it's worth reminding ourselves...in an age where freedom is used to mean pretty much the opposite... an entitlement, a claim – the freedom to work, the freedom to have affordable health care, the freedom from discrimination and so on. Freedom, if it means anything, means a guarantee against state coercion. That's the tradition that has set the Anglosphere apart from the radical tradition of Continental Europe.[34]

And as Winston Churchill wrote in his *History of the English Speaking Peoples* in 1956, Magna Carta raised the rule of law:

> into a doctrine for the national State. And when in subsequent ages, the State, swollen with its own authority, has attempted to ride roughshod over the rights or liberties of the subject, it is to this doctrine that appeal has again and again been made, and never as yet, without success.[35]

Certainly an appeal to Magna Carta was made in 1867 and, despite modern discontents, we Canadians can say some one hundred and fifty years later that it was made with great success.

CHAPTER 8

Sir John A. Macdonald saved more indigenous lives than any other prime minister

Greg Piasetzki

The only thing new in the world is the history you don't know.
—HARRY S. TRUMAN

Given that he died in 1891, the facts of Sir John A. Macdonald's life are unchangeable. The *story* of his life, however, has changed dramatically in recent years. During his life and for well over a century after his death, he was regarded as Canada's foremost founding father and one of this country's most colourful characters. Confederation was very much Macdonald's singular achievement—the product of his masterful skill at negotiation, plus plenty of patience and resolve. He was also noted for his sunny disposition and a lively sense of humour.[1] A fondness for the bottle and being caught in a serious political scandal may have tempered history's judgement, but only to the degree that such flaws revealed his humanity.

Lately, however, Macdonald has come to be defined by a completely different story. As a result of his participation in the Indian residential school system as well as the white settlement of the Prairies, it is now common to hear Macdonald's legacy described as a black stain on Canada's past. In 2018 Victoria removed a statue of him from in front of City Hall following an official statement that identified Canada's first prime minister as "the leader of violence against Indigenous peoples."[2] With similar motivation but somewhat less formality, in 2019, an angry mob tore down and decapitated a statue of Macdonald in Montreal, scrawling a profane slogan on his plinth.[3]

Queen's University in Kingston, Ontario, Macdonald's home for much of his political career, removed his name from the school's Faculty of Law building.[4] Sir John A. Macdonald High School near Halifax, Nova Scotia did the same thing.[5] "Our current name does not align with [the school's] values, nor does it reflect our school community," the school's principal told local media. Native rights activist Pam Palmater of Toronto Metropolitan University (formerly Ryerson University) goes much further in indicting Macdonald, claiming he was "responsible for genocide against Indigenous peoples."[6] It is now an open question whether Macdonald's name will remain on any of the innumerable other schools, buildings and landmarks christened in his honour.

For most of Canada's history, Macdonald was considered a nation-builder worthy of celebration and veneration. Today he is a war criminal, at least to hear some tell it. One storyline has given way to another. But a proper and balanced consideration of Macdonald's life as it was actually lived reveals that, through his own actions and policies, Canada's first prime minister was directly and deliberately responsible for *saving* the lives of untold numbers of indigenous people. It is easily argued, in fact, that no Canadian politician before or since has had such a salutary impact on Canada's native population. Given the temper of our times, this is not likely to be a popular notion. But that does not make it any less true.

Avoiding war and abiding by treaties

Canada's treatment of its indigenous people—and Macdonald's role in it—is best understood in comparison with that of the native population in the United States. Given the arbitrariness of the Canada/U.S. border, we can consider the divergent experiences on either side to constitute a natural (if, for some, tragic) experiment. The results very much favour Macdonald's Canada.

At Confederation, Canada was a small country of approximately four million people comprised of what is now southern Ontario and southern Quebec plus Nova Scotia and New Brunswick. The purchase of Rupert's Land from the Hudson's Bay Company in 1870 and the entry of British Columbia into Confederation a year later increased Canada's land mass tenfold; its indigenous population similarly grew from an estimated 20,000 to 100,000. Macdonald's plan was to turn Canada into a mighty nation befitting its new size by welcoming settlers from Europe and elsewhere to farm the largely empty Prairies. To do this would require a railway and the co-operation of the native people.

To the south lay the powerful United States. With a population ten times Canada's and better transportation links (including the Mississippi and Missouri rivers and a vast and growing web of railways), the U.S. had opened much of its western lands to settlement before Canada even existed. The westward progress of this unorganized torrent of trappers, buffalo hunters, goldminers, farmers, ranchers, sheepherders, merchants and assorted other fortune seekers was far from peaceful.

By and large, American settlers entered indigenous lands ahead of any formal government presence and without negotiation with the original inhabitants. What treaties were signed between native tribes and the government were often abrogated as soon as it was in the best interest of white settlers to do so. Forced migrations, as authorized by the Indian Removal Act of 1830, further contributed to the dislocation and grievous harm experienced by native Americans. The Trail of Tears, for example, uprooted 16,000 mostly Cherokee natives from Georgia and relocated them to Oklahoma, an area with an entirely different climate and geography. This process—what might be considered a "settlement first, negotiation second" approach—inevitably led to conflict and war. In 1890, as part of its regular census of the native population, the U.S. Congress requested a calculation of all lives lost in the more than 40 individual wars between indigenous tribes and American settlers or government troops since signing of the U.S. Constitution in 1789.[7] The government's best estimate for this hundred-year period put the death toll at 45,000 natives and 20,000 white soldiers and settlers. A more recent academic study using advanced statistical methods raises the native death toll to 60,000.[8]

Looking only at conflicts in the American West between 1850 and 1890—the period most relevant to the settling of Canada's Prairies—the Encyclopedia of Indian Wars calculates that 6,600 whites and 15,000 natives were killed or wounded in battles during this four-decade span.[9] It should be noted that the above figures do not include the loss of life caused by government policies carried out at gunpoint outside of war. The Trail of

Tears, for example, is estimated to have caused 4,000 to 8,000 native deaths, an astounding casualty rate of 25-50 percent.

Standing in stark and—from the Canadian perspective—greatly uplifting contrast to these appalling figures is a companion document to the 1890 U.S. Congress report, concerning the Canadian experience. Significantly, it makes no mention of any death toll arising from "Indian Wars" in this country. This was not an oversight. Since the British conquest of New France in 1761, there were no significant wars in what is now Canada prior to the Riel Rebellion of 1885. And this solitary armed conflict was a Métis uprising notable for its lack of large-scale native participation; the First Nation death toll from the entire conflagration was no more than a few dozen.[10]

Such a long and, it must be said, happy period of peaceful relations between indigenous and white populations in Canada was largely the result of British policy that sought to make and keep treaties with native communities. Recall that one of the American Revolution's underlying causes was the British colonial government's determination to prevent white settlement west of the Appalachian Mountains, a commitment made in the Royal Proclamation of 1763. The British approach is best characterized as "negotiation first, settlement second."

As Canada's first prime minister, Macdonald was extremely proud of this legacy of peaceful co-operation and co-habitation. And he was determined to maintain such a policy while overseeing the settlement of Canada's West. In 1870 Macdonald sent the Reverend Jean-Baptiste Thibault as his emissary to natives throughout the former Hudson's Bay Company lands. Thibault's instructions from Macdonald's Conservative government reveal the clear desire to avoid an American-style invasion of the Prairies:

> So far as you may have intercourse with the Indian chiefs and people, you will be good enough to remind them that while bloody and costly Indian wars have raged, often over long periods, in different sections of the United States, there has been no war with the Indians in any of the Provinces of British America since the conquest...Everywhere within the Canadas, the progress of settlement, while it furnished new employments to the Indians, was rendered practicable by treaties and arrangements mutually satisfactory, that have formed the secure basis of the sympathy and co-operation which have distinguished the Canadians and Indians...from the earliest exploration of the Country.

> It may fairly be assumed that the just and judicious treatment of the Indian Tribes forms the brightest page in the history of British America. Canadians cannot afford to sully it by any ungenerous treatment of the Indians in the North-West.[11]

This assessment of Canadian history was not simply a case of Macdonald's government flattering itself. That same year the U.S. Congress sent a commission to Canada to study native relations in this country. In his report, Commissioner F.N. Blake came to much the same conclusion, noting the remarkable lack of Indian Wars in this country, and the effect this had on the Indigenous population. "One of the most positive indicators on this point is their numerical increase during the last quarter century," Blake observed.[12] While native communities in the U.S. were in rapid decline as a result of war, forced removals, treaty violations and assorted other mistreatments, Canada's indigenous people were healthy and growing. As Blake noted, it was "an established rule with the British Canadian government to take no land from the Indians, except with the legal assent of the band, tribe or nation owning it."

To avoid repeating the violence associated with the settling of the American West, Macdonald appointed Treaty Commissioner Alexander Morris to negotiate with native tribes *before* widespread white settlement took place on the Canadian Prairies. This process consumed nearly a decade, but by 1877 seven numbered treaties had been signed covering all 30,000 natives residing in the southern portions of what is today Manitoba, Saskatchewan and Alberta. In exchange for relinquishing their broader land rights, the First Nations received reserves in their traditional territory and benefits including food, medicine, education and agricultural training. The native chiefs who signed these treaties were well aware of the alternative to British-style negotiation. This was not only because thousands of U.S. natives had fled across the "Medicine Line" into Canada to escape conflict with the U.S. Cavalry, but because many Canadian tribes traditionally roamed south of the border and had seen firsthand the violence.

While Macdonald is today frequently accused of perpetrating genocide against indigenous people, in his own time the prime minister was repeatedly rebuked by the Liberal Opposition for being overly generous in his native policy. In 1885, for example, he was criticized for placing native reserves on their traditional territories, which, in some cases, was prime farmland close to the Canadian Pacific Railway. Liberal MPs, such as New Brunswick's Peter Mitchell, felt this was a waste of good farmland and demanded Macdonald forcibly relocate the natives farther north so white settlers could more profitably take the land, a proposal disturbingly similar to the Trail of Tears. Macdonald opposed such a policy on moral grounds. As he said in the 1885 House of Commons Debates:

> The reserves they now hold were given them by treaty. They are on their property. We cannot deprive them of those reserves without another treaty. If it has happened that after these reserves were established near a railway, or another railway comes near them... we cannot help that. They live on their own property, they are free men.[13]

This is a clear expression of Macdonald's belief in the sanctity of treaties and his efforts to defend the best interests of Canada's native peoples. How many native lives were saved by his determination to sign and abide by indigenous treaties, even at the cost of delaying westward settlement or, in some instances, requiring white settlers to take lands farther from the new railway? It is obviously impossible to pick a precise number. But given the scale of bloodshed in the American West, it was clearly substantial.

The creation of the North-West Mounted Police

Another key piece of Macdonald's plan to avoid white/native conflict in Canada's new western territory was to create a police force to establish a system of law and order on the Prairies *ahead* of white settlement, again in contrast to the American experience. The North-West Mounted Police (NWMP), the precursor to today's Royal Canadian Mounted Police, was meant to deter incursions from the United States and protect the legal rights of both natives and settlers once settlement began. Despite claims that the modern-day RCMP is riven with racism and sexism, the force's very existence stands as testimony to the Canadian government's intention to protect the native population from depredation and genocide.

The design of the NWMP was deeply influenced by a report from Lt. William Francis Butler, a British soldier who toured the Canadian West at Macdonald's request in 1871. Butler had previous travelled the American

Plains and was outraged by the "terrible, heart-sickening deeds of cruelty and rapacious infamy" arising from the American "wars of extinction" waged against indigenous people. He was determined that Canada should avoid such a disaster, and proposed the creation of a mounted police force and system of travelling magistrates to protect the indigenous population and bring a formal process for justice to the Prairies. Macdonald wholly embraced this vision, as the following excerpt from the 1870 House of Commons debates explains:

> Hon. Sir John A. Macdonald said that it was intended to have a body of mounted rifles to protect the people from the chance of an Indian war. Under the beneficent rule of the Hudson's Bay Company there was peace in the Territory, while across the line there were frequent wars, and the Indians were shot down by emigrants going West—shot down ruthlessly. As the expectation was that there would be a large influx of emigrants from Europe or from Canada, and there was a fear that emigrants from the American States, accustomed to deal with the Indians as enemies, would be shooting them down and causing great disturbances, the necessity arose to have a small but active force of cavalry to act as mounted police.[14]

The most pressing issue facing the NWMP on its creation in 1873 was to counter the presence of American whiskey traders at Fort Whoop-Up, near present-day Lethbridge, Alberta. This was not only a threat to Canadian sovereignty but an immediate peril to local natives. "If left to ourselves we are gone. The whiskey brought among us by the Traders is fast killing us off and we are powerless before the evil," Blackfoot chief Isapo-Muxika said at the time. "A large number of our people have killed one another and perished in various ways under the influence, and now that we hear of our Great Mother sending her soldiers into our country for our good, we are glad."

The NWMP shut down the whiskey trade with relative ease, and afterwards natives and settlers alike came to trust the force to adjudicate conflicts in a neutral fashion. In 1873, NWMP Commissioner James Macleod and Reverend John McDougall met with leaders of the Blackfoot Confederacy to explain the intended role of the NWMP in maintaining peace. Chief Crowfoot, as cited in McDougall's book, *On Western Trails in the Early Seventies*, responded:

> My brother, your words make me glad. I listened to them not only with my ears but with my heart also. In the coming of the Long Knives [U.S. Cavalry], with their firewater and quick-shooting guns, we were weak, and our people have been woefully slain and impoverished. You say this will be stopped. We are glad to have it stopped. We want peace. What you tell us about this strong power which will govern good law and treat the Indian the same as the white man, makes us glad to hear. My brother, I believe you, and am thankful.[15]

Settlement of the Canadian West began in earnest in the early 1880s and led, as expected, to increased instances of conflict between settlers and natives on and off reserve lands. Considering the accusations made against Macdonald today, it is noteworthy that he was criticized in his time for instructing the NWMP *not* to show favouritism towards white settlers. Rather, he argued, it was their proper role to protect the rights of native and settler alike, as this speech in the 1885 House of Commons explains:

> The duty of the police is... a continuous one, and an increasing one, and the increase in the number of white settlers adds to the difficulty.... Settlers, as a rule, take a hostile position against the Indians, just as it has been in the experience of the United States all along the Western frontier. *The duty of the police is not only to protect the white man against the Indian, but the Indian against the white man*. (Emphasis added.)[16]

Macdonald wished to install a functioning justice system in the Canadian West prior to white settlement to protect native interests. Such an enlightened view will no doubt comes as a surprise to his many present-day detractors. But again, it is true. And in doing so, Macdonald undoubtedly saved many more native lives from American-style frontier justice.

Smallpox vaccination

The arrival of smallpox to North America was disastrous for native populations across the continent since they had no natural resistance to this deadly disease. In the 1830s, for example, an epidemic originating in the American West migrated north and killed three quarters of all Natives living in the Edmonton area.[17] The estimated death toll among indigenous people in pre-Confederation Canada runs to the tens of thousands. And while a vaccine for smallpox had existed since 1796, delivering it to remote indigenous communities was a logistical challenge that required a significant government commitment.

Prior to Confederation, the governments of Upper and Lower Canada under the joint leadership of Macdonald and George-Étienne Cartier had organized a vaccination campaign for provincial native populations as part of a comprehensive public health program. This was highly effective and quickly felt. In his 1868 Annual Report Federal Indian Affairs bureaucrat William Spragge remarked on the observed increase in the Indigenous population:

> One cause of this is that the contagious diseases such, as smallpox, which at times have swept off whole families, have, of late, been guarded against; and at periods sufficiently near to each other it is our practice to require professional men to make so general a vaccination as to leave little room for apprehension, of a repetition of such visitations.[18]

Once Canada took over the Hudson's Bay Company lands, smallpox vaccination was gradually expanded to include all native Canadians in the western territories as well. During the Liberal administration of Prime Minister Alexander Mackenzie, Dr. Daniel Hagarty was appointed medical superintendent for the Canadian West and given the huge responsibility of vaccinating the entire indigenous population. This objective was maintained following Macdonald's return to power in 1878. And it was again tremendously successful. In some native communities, the vaccination rate hit 100 percent, a remarkable feat that is rarely duplicated today. In the 1883 Annual Report of Indian Affairs local administrator E. McKay of the Birch River Reserve in Manitoba explained that:

> I distribute, according to instructions, the 1,000 points of vaccine matter received last summer, to the different Hudson Bay Company's officers, clergymen and school teachers to vaccinate all the Indians in their respective districts throughout this agency...The Indians universally expressed their unbounded gratitude for the generous consideration of the Government in protecting them from the dreaded ravages of small-pox, and in providing medicine chests at the different reserves for their sick.[19]

This nationwide policy was so successful that in 1885 when a particularly deadly smallpox outbreak killed 3,000 residents of Montreal, the Kahnewake native reserve across the river reported "but very few cases" of the disease.[20] Everyone on the reserve had already been vaccinated by the federal government. Untold numbers of indigenous people died throughout the Canadian West prior to the 1870s as a result of smallpox. Yet due to the commitment of Liberal and Conservative governments, the death toll among native Canadians from the disease by the 1880s and beyond was close to zero. As University of Saskatchewan historian and notable Macdonald critic James Daschuk wrote in his widely-cited 2013 book *Clearing the Plains*, the federal government "virtually eliminated smallpox as a major cause of mortality among First Nations."[21] Smallpox vaccination on the Prairies is one of Canada's great public health success stories and it saved many, many native lives. Macdonald deserves his share of the glory.

Famine relief for natives on the Prairies

The gravest charges against Macdonald's legacy involve his role in the famine among the indigenous population of the Prairies following the collapse of North America's buffalo herds in the late 1870s. The claim that Macdonald was responsible for a "state-sponsored attack on Indigenous communities" by denying food relief in order to open the Prairies to white settlement is forcefully made in *Clearing the Plains*. Perhaps the most stinging indictment comes from Macdonald's own words. Daschuk twice quotes Macdonald from 1882 saying his government was "doing all we can, by refusing food until the Indians are on the verge of starvation, to reduce the expense."[22] This line is also repeated in many current-day condemnations of Macdonald as evidence of his lack of compassion for indigenous people.

The near-extinction of the continental buffalo herds caused tremendous hardship for Canada's western indigenous communities, which depended on the meat, bones and hide of the buffalo for much of their sustenance and supplies. While this outcome was widely predicted in the late nineteenth century, it occurred much faster than anyone expected. Responsibility for this calamity cannot be laid at Macdonald's feet. Rather, it was the result of rampant American hunting aimed at the buffalo's eradication to facilitate settlement and farming, as well as United States military tactics to starve out certain native tribes, plus environmental changes.

The buffalo die-off occurred just as Macdonald's government was completing the numbered treaties process—deals Daschuk admits were largely fair and "reached from positions of mutual strength."[23] As a result, some treaties included explicit clauses for government aid. Treaty Six, for example, makes the following provision:

> That in the event hereafter of the Indians comprised within this treaty being overtaken by any pestilence, or by a general famine, the Queen, on being satisfied and certified thereof by Her Indian Agent or Agents, will grant to the Indians assistance of such character and to such extent as Her Chief Superintendent of Indian Affairs shall deem necessary and sufficient to relieve the Indians from the calamity that shall have befallen them.[24]

When the famine arrived with unexpected swiftness in 1878, the government reacted as its treaties dictated. Macdonald told the House of Commons that the "absolute failure of the usual food supply of the Indians in the North-West" created the "necessity of a large expenditure in order to save them from absolute starvation." A year later Macdonald announced a special council to investigate the food crisis and to "supply food to the Indians." Natives living on reserves were provided aid, mostly flour and bacon, as per the government's obligations. Recalcitrant tribes not on living on their reserve land, however, had their relief provisions withheld or reduced in order to induce them to move onto reserves as a negotiation tactic. Macdonald describes his policy in more detail in 1886 House of Commons debates:

> To the Indians who go upon their reserves we give food until they are able to support themselves, but we reduce them to half rations when they are simply wandering and demoralised Indians.... When these people are hanging about the Government stores and offices, we reduce them to as low a ration as is sufficient to keep life in their bodies; but we tell them: 'Go to your stations and we will give you food to take you there, and you will get full rations until you are able to support yourselves.'[25]

In making this statement, Macdonald is responding to criticism of excessive generosity made by the Liberal Opposition. And while half rations may sound draconian to modern ears, and is no doubt uncomfortable, it is not a death sentence. Keep in mind that no treaty obligated the federal government to provide rations to any natives living off-reserve. From this perspective, a diet of half rations should be seen as evidence of Macdonald's compassion rather than malice. Even Daschuk acknowledges that "Rations kept many from starving."[26] The reduction for some was meant to encourage those wandering natives to return to their reserves, where the treaties they signed required them to be. Recall that it was this strict and legalistic approach to treaties that distinguished Canada's native experience from the bloody and arbitrary American version.

Macdonald allocated considerable government resources to fulfilling its famine relief duties. In 1878 the federal budget for Indian Affairs was a rather modest $276,000. By the peak of the famine in 1884, this item had grown to $1.1 million, outweighing National Defence by a substantial margin. In 1884 Indian Affairs accounted for three per cent of the total federal budget and was the fourth-largest operating (non-debt) item, surpassed only by Public Buildings, the Post Office and Railways. Three per cent of the federal budget would be an impressive $11 billion in 2019.

This was the largest famine relief program Canada had provided up to that point. That it occurred in the midst of a severe economic recession in eastern Canada makes its scale all the more impressive. In fact, such a commitment to public aid in Canada would not be equaled until the Great Depression, nearly 50 years later. In his 1880 Annual Report of Indian Affairs, Edgar Dewdney, Indian Commissioner for the North-West reported that nearly all 30,000 natives under treaty in Western Canada were receiving some form of federal food aid.[27]

Acquiring a sufficient supply of food, shipping it across the continent and distributing it throughout the sparsely populated West, where there was as-yet no railway, was a daunting logistical task. Like many massive government programs implemented on short notice—including the recent response to the COVID pandemic—the famine relief program was bedevilled by allegations of incompetence and corruption, as Daschuk's book amply details.[28] And while corruption and incompetence are never acceptable, there is no evidence Macdonald personally or politically benefitted from these problems. Rather, Macdonald's famine relief program suffered from a constant barrage of political attacks regarding the overall cost to taxpayers. The Liberals wanted to spend *less* on the native file—much less.

Let us return to that damning quotation in which Macdonald appears to boast about keeping the native population "on the verge of starvation, to reduce the expense." While this appears callous and inhumane, that is not the whole story. Macdonald made these remarks during debate on the 1882 budget. Liberal MP David Mills, who later sat on the Supreme Court of Canada, was arguing that the $294,524 set aside for "Supplies for destitute Indians," was excessive and should be lowered. "I believe a barbarous population like the Indians may be made wholly dependent upon Government" through handouts, Mills asserted. He was, in essence, proposing that any money spent on native famine relief was money wasted because it would engender a culture of dependency. To this Macdonald retorted "When they fall into a state of destitution, we cannot allow them to die for want of food."[29]

Macdonald's statement about keeping natives "on the verge of starvation" was meant to acknowledge the Opposition's complaints about costs. But the full exchange reveals a deeper concern for the well-being of natives and their treaty rights. In a similar exchange, this one in the 1880 House of Commons debates Macdonald frames the issue as a moral one: "Public sentiment would not allow, and no Government would be worthy of their position, if they allowed the Indians to starve as long as we have the means to feed them. The Government adopted the best means for relieving them. We were obliged to find food for them."[30] Even Daschuk grudgingly acknowledged that the government's relief program prevented widespread death from hunger across the Prairies. "The Macdonald administration avoided," he wrote in *Clearing the Plains* "a region-wide mortality of the Indigenous population from famine, yet the quantity of rations was the absolute minimum to sustain life."[31] While he may have been parsimonious, Macdonald's famine relief policies clearly saved lives. This deserves recognition, not scorn.

It is also true that the collapse of their traditional way of life due to the disappearance of the buffalo led to many tragic outcomes for Western Canada's indigenous people, in particular an increased susceptibility to diseases such as tuberculosis. But eradicating this disease was far beyond

Macdonald's control; there would be no vaccine against tuberculosis (or "consumption" as it was usually called at the time) until 1921. In fact, tuberculosis was also a major killer of non-native Canadians in urban areas throughout Macdonald's time; between 1850 and 1900, for example, it was the leading cause of death among adults in Toronto.[32]

Residential schools

Residential schools also figure prominently in popular claims that Macdonald was responsible for a "genocide" of indigenous people. In fact, the first such schools appeared in Canada in 1695, long before Macdonald's tenure. And their application to western Canada cannot properly be regarded as a government plot to permanently eliminate native culture. Under the seven numbered treaties, the federal government was obligated to build and staff such schools only when requested to do so *by native leaders,* or, as Treaty Six clearly states, "whenever the Indians of the reserve shall desire it."

And they clearly did desire it: during Macdonald's tenure as prime minister no fewer than 185 on-reserve day schools and 20 residential schools were built. This reveals a strong interest among native leaders to have their children given a western-style education, as well as a preference for local over residential schools at this time. And attendance was entirely voluntary. Although the Progressive movement across North America at this time was pushing governments everywhere to make schooling universally compulsory, Macdonald resisted this for native children. Without parental support, he believed, native education would not succeed. Accordingly, it was left up to native parents to decide whether their offspring should go to school. This policy continued long after Macdonald's death. As late as 1920, attendance at all native schools in Canada was still entirely voluntary, as that year's Indian Affairs Annual Report makes plain:

- within day schools, the dropout rate from Grade 1 to Grade 2 was more than 70 percent;
- only 46 native students across Canada chose to continue to Grade 6 at on-reserve day schools.

Attendance in the residential school system was similar:

- In 1920 about half of all students in those schools returned home permanently after Grade 1;
- At Alberta's 19 residential schools, for example, native enrollment fell from 310 in Grade 1 to 171 in Grade 2 to 11 in Grade 6.[33]

These schools were not prison camps—anyone who wished to could leave. And many did.

It is a testament to Macdonald's enlightened leadership that he was able to persuade Canadians to build and staff native schools without enforcing compulsory attendance as was the case elsewhere in the country. Further, this policy continued for three decades after his death. Did this save directly native lives? Maybe not. But it was certainly a compassionate approach to the vexing problem of moving native Canadians from a pre-industrial to modern world. At the very least, it seems impossible to argue that Macdonald's voluntary attendance policy could be construed as "cultural genocide," as the Truth and Reconciliation Commission and many others have claimed.

Conclusion

Macdonald's legacy is complicated by the passage of time and changing perspectives. But through careful study of his own words and deeds, as well as the reports and actions of his officials, contemporaries, native chiefs and political opponents, what emerges is a clear and powerful picture of his enlightened view towards indigenous people and his strong sense of moral purpose.

Macdonald was determined to avoid the violence and dislocation that attended settlement of the American West. To prevent war, he relied on the time-honoured British tradition of signing and abiding by treaties. After this process was set in motion, Macdonald then created the NWMP to ensure law and order was established on the Prairies prior to large-scale white settlement. When smallpox threatened native populations, a comprehensive vaccination program was rolled out, similar to what he had overseen in Upper Canada. When the buffalo herds collapsed, Macdonald immediately initiated a massive relief effort and overcame enormous logistical and budgetary hurdles to provide food aid for the affected tribes.

And when indigenous tribes requested it, he offered western-style education—mostly in the form of day schools—on a non-compulsory basis. None of this can be construed as violence towards native people. It was, in fact, quite the opposite: an expression of genuine concern for their well-being. It should be considered deeply ironic that in his own time Macdonald's political opponents attacked him relentlessly for indulging Canada's "barbarous population" and fostering their dependency on government aid while today a new set of critics take the same facts and unfairly accuse him of genocide.

If Macdonald's story has changed, it is because Canadian society no longer understands its own history.

CHAPTER 9

How a "Maker of Canada" was framed: The unjust treatment of Egerton Ryerson

Lynn McDonald

I have now arrived at my charge among the Indians.
I feel an inexpressible joy in taking up my abode amongst them.
— EGERTON RYERSON, from his journal

In August 2021, the Board of Governors of Ryerson University announced that the university would drop the name Ryerson and permanently remove the statue of its namesake, Egerton Ryerson—the statue had by then been toppled and its head cut off and thrown into Toronto's harbour. The Board was acting on the apparently unanimous recommendations of a task force—"Standing Strong (Mash Koh Wee Kah Pooh Win),"commissioned by the university president in December 2020 to hold hearings, collect materials on Ryerson, and report. It did all of those, although it seems at least some members of the task force had already made up their minds.

We know this because when the Ryerson statue was toppled, the two task force co-chairs issued a statement saying there might be regrets among people who wanted the statue removed, given that they were not there to see it go down. It was hardly a neutral statement but an indication of what was to come: the rhetorical razing of Ryerson in the months ahead. The replacement name was to be the banal Toronto Metropolitan University.

The Task Force report included many positive comments about Ryerson and his relationship with the Ojibway, but with much bafflegab about principles of commemoration. It highlighted ten comments by unnamed "community members," not one of which was positive and some of which made unfounded accusations about Ryerson. Some were paeans of pain, such as: "We cannot continue to celebrate Ryerson in the faces of those who are wounded." The university's leaders should have addressed those hurts—a university has a "duty to care"—but they did not.

Ryerson: The founder of (free) public education

If Ryerson University's board of governors and statue-toppling vandals knew little about the man they wanted to erase from downtown Toronto, it is not because historical records are lacking. The first biography of Egerton Ryerson (1803-82) was published in a series called "The Makers of Canada" in 1906.[1] "Maker" was a particularly apt description for him for he pioneered free public education when the other provinces and the United Kingdom still only had fee-paying schools. Ryerson was instrumental also in the provision of teacher training and free public libraries. Ontario's system influenced the development of the school systems of the Western provinces and territories. Governor-general Lord Elgin was particularly complimentary about the institution of "normal schools," as these first teacher-training colleges were called, which had no precedent in the United Kingdom. Elgin pointed out that in England schools were built with little thought given to training the very people who would be required to staff them, i.e., teachers:

> It has often appeared to me that, within the whole range of human experience, it would be difficult to point out a more flagrant, a more instructive, instance of the error of putting the effect before the cause, than was exhibited in the course pursued by the friends of education in England and other countries, those, for a series of years busied themselves in building schools, and in endeavouring to induce children to attend those schools, without ever inquiring whether competent persons to conduct them could be procured, and without taking any sufficient and vigorous steps to supply the admitted want of competent teachers.[2]

Ryerson saw to these great achievements as a public servant, as Chief Superintendent of Education for Upper Canada (in effect the Deputy Minister of Education, the title given to his successor). When he was first appointed in 1844, few children attended school at all; schools all charged fees; and there were no trained teachers or teacher training. To formulate his recommendations, Ryerson began by embarking on an extended tour of schools and their administrations in the United States (he was especially impressed with New York and Massachusetts), Europe (where Switzerland, Prussia and Holland topped the list) and the British Isles (where, for textbooks, he liked Ireland).

Ryerson's commitment to a free, public system stemmed from his Christian beliefs. He was an ordained Methodist minister—a convert from the Anglicanism in which he was raised. He believed that, as God was the Creator and Redeemer of all, all God's children were equal. Methodism, for him, was no less than, "the precursor, the pioneer, the first and most effective promoter of civil and religious liberty for the entire country." He went on to celebrate:

> the glorious doctrines of the universal fatherhood of God, and the universal brotherhood of man, in the presence of which all earthly distinctions of title, of rank, of attainments, of age, of nations, disappear, and the universal equality of mankind—the foe of despotism and tyranny—stands forth as the basis and pledge of universal freedom.[3]

Ryerson buttressed his faith-based claim of education for all with what would now be called human resource theory. That is, he defended charging all ratepayers (residents with property) for schooling when they had no children themselves, on the grounds that everyone benefits from a better educated citizenry and workforce. He also thought that educated people were less likely to become criminals.

Free schools for all was a goal for Ryerson long before he had the formal appointment to achieve it. In an editorial in the *Christian Guardian in* 1831, he was unusually eloquent, calling education "as necessary as the light—it should be as common as water, and as free as air."[4] Ryerson was also eminently pragmatic when it came to education, promoting practical education. For example, he wanted "scientific agriculture" to be taught in schools, aware that agriculture was by far the largest industry in Upper Canada. He was also aware that industrialization was important, as can be seen in an address he gave to the Mechanics Institute.[5] In another speech, he stressed the great increase in productivity made with advances in machinery, as when he noted that with Arkwright's spinning jenny, 150,000 men could produce as much cotton as previously it took 40 million men.[6]

Ryerson's politics: democratic institutions, constitutional monarchy

Along with educational reform, Ryerson was a promoter of democratic institutions. He used the Methodist Church's magazine, the *Christian Guardian*—he was its founding editor in 1829—as a vehicle for reform. The promotion of democratic institutions was an uphill struggle in Upper Canada, which was dominated by the wealthy men of the Family Compact, and the established Anglican Church which was supported by public funds. There was an elected House of Assembly, but its decisions were subject to the unelected upper house dominated by the Family Compact. The appointed lieutenant-governor did not play a ceremonial role as they do now, but could and did refuse to sign bills. Ryerson had always to steer a steady course, for many reformers were supporters of "Yankee democracy" and even annexation. An intriguing letter by (then Mr.) John A. Macdonald to Ryerson denotes the choice among reformers as being between a "limited constitutional Monarchy or a Yankee democracy."[7]

Ryerson also used the *Christian Guardian* to promote other causes, notably the abolition of slavery where it yet existed in the United States and in the British Empire. He happened to be in London in 1833 when the last debate on abolition throughout the British Empire took place. The MP speaking was Edward Stanley, with whom Ryerson later connected on Canadian issues. Stanley argued that the time had gone by "when Parliament could decide the question whether slavery should or should not be perpetual," but now it was "the safest, the speediest, the most effectual mode procuring its final and entire abolition." He spoke about how conditions had recently worsened, and about the "frightful sacrifice of human life, by over-working the Negroes." He described measures for the religious instruction of the slaves, while pointing out that "religious instruction was inconsistent with the continuance of slavery."

Stanley closed with a tribute to the long-time leader of the abolition movement, William Wilberforce, and others who had "laboured in their generation strenuously and vigorously" for what they were "now about to accomplish." Wilberforce, then near death, was "the most religiously inspired, the most conscientiously-influenced [of] all who laboured in the dawn and the rising of this great and glorious cause." To great cheering he ended with: "Lord, now let thy servant depart in peace."[8] Emancipation took effect on 1 August, 1834.

Ryerson's Methodist commitment shaped his egalitarian, democratic views. His religious beliefs also anchored his views on the duty of citizens to support their lawful government. The clearest example of this commitment to the rule of law was his opposition to the Rebellion of 1837, in Upper Canada which was, for him, thoroughly wrong and perhaps even evil. The leader of the rebellion was William Lyon Mackenzie, (an ally to Ryerson on such reform campaigns as opposing the Clergy Reserves and the established church). On 7 December, 1837, a small number of men moved north on Yonge Street to Montgomery's Tavern, pursued by the militia. Mackenzie escaped to the United States, but a number of rebels were captured. The uprising was over in a few days, a deliverance Ryerson considered "providential." At year-end, on 31 December 1837, Ryerson gave a thundering sermon on the threat that the rebellion had posed to Upper Canada and the happy outcome that was its defeat.

In the sermon, Ryerson proclaimed that law and order were gifts of God. If the conspiracy "had not been crushed in the bud, [it] must have inevitably involved our country in the horrors of a civil war." He was uncategorical in his denunciation of such wars, calling them "the most ruinous kind of war...infusing poison of mistrust, jealousy and resentment," into "all of the enjoyments of life." He continued: "It arms neighbour against neighbour, and brother against brother, parents against children, children against parents."[9] He called the laws of duly constituted governments "the sacred fences of society," which when "thrown down," would open up avenues wide "to fraud, oppression and rapine." He continued to paint a grim picture of the outcomes of civil wars where people's "happiness, welfare and safety" were destroyed amid "scenes of blood, desolation and misery."[10]

Ryerson was not an unquestioning, blind loyalist to governments as if they could never be challenged, but the form of government mattered. He gave his support to a liberal social compact which necessitated a two-way obligation: subjects had the obligation to obey the sovereign, but the sovereign had an obligation to respect the constitution. He thus summarized his opposition to rebellions noting that, without civil government, there could be no security against "invasions and injuries" and "no man's property or life would be secure for half an hour."[11]

After stern admonitions about duties, Ryerson gave his hearers, and later readers, a stirring picture of events as they had unfolded during the rebellion. He noted how "the metropolis was defenceless [with] not an armed man in it,"[12] while the conspirators were armed and desperate and for them, "Defeat was ruin; success was power and plunder and booty."[13] Ryerson credited the saving of constitutional government and her citizens in Upper Canada as brought by no less than "the manifest interposition of the Divine hand, from the beginning to the end."[14] At conclusion of the affair, several months after Ryerson's sermon, of 31 December 1837, two men were convicted of sedition and hanged.

Ryerson as a friend and a "brother" to the Ojibway

While Ryerson's greatest contribution to Canada was the founding of a free, comprehensive, public school system—it would not have happened without him—his friendship with Indigenous people and promotion of their interests was another valuable contribution. This critical part of Ryerson's record makes the renaming of Ryerson university so egregious and wrong-headed.

In September 1826, Ryerson arrived at his post as a Methodist missionary to the Mississaugas of the Credit (i.e., near modern-day Mississauga). They, like other Indigenous people, had lost most of their territory and their numbers were also drastically reduced. The Mississaugas of the Credit were Ojibway or Chippeway-speaking, and Ryerson quickly began to learn their language. He loved his time with them. He was young and sturdy, lived in a wigwam at the start, and later moved into the home of a school teacher and his family. He was soon made a "brother" by a Chief, and given an Ojibway name, Cheehock, "Bird on a wing." His journal notes give us a glimpse of his relationship with the Ojibway.

On 16 September 1826, Ryerson reports how he "arrived at my charge among the Indians. I feel an inexpressible joy in taking up my abode amongst them. I must now acquire a new language, to teach a new people." One day later, he notes he has "commenced my labours amongst my Indian brethren. My heart feels one with them, as they seemed to be tenderly alive to their eternal interests. May I possess every necessary gift to suffer labour, and teach the truth as it is in Jesus." One week later, he reports with sadness the death of an Indigenous man who shot himself while intoxicated, and which Ryerson blames on "a wicked white man [who] persuaded them to drink cider which he mixed with whisky." Ryerson presided over the funeral.[15]

It is common in today's secular age to see nothing but evil in conversions to Christianity and from that starting point to condemn missionaries outright. That was not the view in the nineteenth century. In addition, the reality of proselytization was not simply "white" to "Indian" but more nuanced even by Ryerson's era. The first missionaries were European (Jesuits before the Methodists), but soon, Indigenous converts became missionaries themselves to their own community. Methodism, with its emphasis on "temperance," was particularly lauded. Alcohol, "fire water," was the scourge of Indigenous men, as with it was among many white settlers. Upon conversion, new Christians were expected to quit drinking—most did, and their lives immediately began to improve. Some Indigenous converts became eloquent orators and evangelists to their own peoples.

Historian Neil Semple described the ease of conversion for Indigenous people to Christianity, especially the Methodist version:

> In addition to the use of native preachers and a ministry that travelled to the natives, to a substantial degree Methodist success rested on the demand it made for a momentous, personal conversion experience and a profound commitment to Christ. The Methodist camp meetings, with their highly emotional release of spiritual energy struck an especially receptive chord among the Ojibwa and Iroquois. The forest setting, the similarity to traditional religious festivals, the mutual prayer, the powerful, uplifting hymns, and the creation of an often overwhelming psychological pressure were reminiscent of native quests for contact with the spirit world and the formation of a new persona.[16]

The Ojibway at the Credit had converted to Christianity before Ryerson's arrival but needed pastoral care and instruction. Yet he was able to give much of his time to economic development. Hunting and fishing could no longer sustain the Ojibway and if they were to survive the nineteenth century, they needed to learn farming. Ryerson enjoyed working the land with the

Ojibway; he also assisted them in their attempts to obtain clear title to their land. Unfortunately, he and they were unsuccessful. Ryerson also assisted the Ojibway, again unsuccessfully, with their quest for exclusive rights to their fishing grounds. His diary entry for December 16, 1826 recorded his efforts that week "to procure for the Indians the exclusive right of their salmon fishery, which I trust will be granted by the Legislature."[17] In practice, the Ojibway, when they could not get clear land title, moved, fearing that all the improvements they were making to their land would go to the benefit of white settlers.

Ryerson's support for his Indigenous friends can be readily seen in an introduction he made for an elected Ojibway chief, Kakewaquonaby, (English name Peter Jones). In Ryerson's letter to Lord Glenelg, colonial secretary, Ryerson called Kakewaquonaby:

> one of the first fruits of our Missionary labours among the aboriginal Indian tribes of the Chippewa nation, and whom I have known from the time of his conversion to Christianity, having myself been the first stationed missionary at the Credit River where Mr Jones and his tribe now reside.

Ryerson went on to explain that Kahkewaquonaby was a chief in his tribe and a "successful missionary to various tribes of his nation." He had been "deputed by his people to do all in his power to promote their religious and civil interests especially in procuring proper titles to reservations of land for their settlement," a subject Ryerson himself had already broached with Lord Glenelg. Ryerson explained the key point, that it would be "impractable to improve the civil condition of our much-injured aboriginal fellow countrymen unless the lands on which it is proposed for them to settle are properly and legally secured to them." He added that if Sir John Colborne had remained as lieutenant-governor in Upper Canada, he thought that the necessary title would have been granted.[18] But, with Sir Francis Bond Head in office, it was not, and Bond Head's letter to Lord Glenelg on Kahkewaquonaby shows what the Indigenous people were up against. Bond Head acknowledged Kahkewaquonaby's title as "*Chief* and *Missionary* of the Mississauga tribe of the Chippewa nation," but then labelled him "the son of an American surveyor who in open adultery had children by several Indian squaws."[19] Kahkewaquonaby, as a chief, was received by Queen Victoria in 1838, accompanied by Lord Glenelg, but this served no practical purpose.

The *Christian Guardian* published many reports about and by the Credit Mississaugas. Despite its name, the magazine was a general interest weekly publication with stories on international and national political affairs, the arts and sciences, in addition to reports on churches, missions (in many countries), Sunday Schools and temperance. A widely-read magazine, it was a forum for reporting the poor conditions experienced by Indigenous peoples, for example "their scanty supply of land, their poverty."[20] So also were the mission trips taken on by intrepid Indigenous missionaries. On one to the North-West Indians, John Sunday, original name Shawundais, ran out of food and was obliged to shoot crows and pick moss off rocks to survive. His journal was translated by John Jones, another Indigenous man, the school teacher at the Credit with whose family Ryerson had boarded.[21]

The framing of Ryerson and the failure of history at Ryerson

Given Ryerson's warm relationship with Indigenous people, it is staggering that he could be blamed for the residential schools established after his death. Yet a plaque placed next to his statue on the Ryerson campus in 2018 by the university president, Dr. Lachemi, states that Ryerson was "instrumental in the design and implementation of the Indian Residential School System." Yet there exists a long record—something that should be of crucial interest in a university—of scholarly publications about Ryerson by serious researchers, extending from 1906 to 2021, which yields no evidence with which to implicate Ryerson in this way. These include a two-volume *Life and Letters*,[22] three one-volume biographies,[23] and a biography of Ryerson's closest Ojibway friend.[24] Even the Truth and Reconciliation Commission, which reported in 2015, did not blame Ryerson for the residential schools; nor did its chair, Murray Sinclair, when he gave the Faculty Lecture at Ryerson a year later in 2016.

A substantial master's thesis and two papers based on it by Hope MacLean describe the voluntary, bilingual schools that Ryerson supported, which involved no forcible taking away of children from their parents. MacLean concluded: "How different the whole history of Native education in Canada might have been if [Ryerson's] experiment had continued."[25] Despite such plentiful evidence, accusations against Ryerson were uncritically repeated between 2010 and 2021, on social media and on television and in newspapers. The plaque placed next to his statue was to "contextualize" Ryerson's role, but it repeated baseless accusations as if they were true. In a university, academic standards and respect for primary sources should be paramount. But they were missing from action throughout the discussions held at Ryerson University about its namesake.

There is a great desire for "reconciliation" between Indigenous and non-Indigenous people, but it cannot happen without truth, which requires looking at facts—hard things to come by these days. Ryerson University failed utterly to acquaint its students with who Egerton Ryerson was and what he did that was so positive for Indigenous people. Nor did it address the distress described by Indigenous students evidently persuaded by false information that he was responsible for the school system that caused such pain.

Academics who do not accept the quasi-official narrative about Ryerson are terrified to speak out, especially the untenured, short-term instructors (of which Ryerson has many). To summarize, it is therefore not surprising that many Ryerson students, both Indigenous and non-Indigenous, are not aware that Egerton Ryerson:

- lived with Ojibway people and learned to speak Ojibway;
- assisted them with economic development, sharing his own farming skills learnt as a boy;
- actively supported their land and fishery claims;
- promoted the careers of Ojibway leaders who were both Methodist ministers and elected chiefs; and nominated one Indigenous leader, Dr Peter Edmund Jones, son of Chief Peter Jones, to be the Western superintendent of Indian Affairs in Canada West (Ontario).

If the Indigenous students, staff, and faculty at the university knew what Ryerson had done for and with the Ojibway of his time, they could have walked past the statue of him with a smile and a wave, grateful that at least he had supported them in an era when few others did.

Looking to the future at Toronto Metropolitan University

Ryerson really was a significant "Maker of Canada" and deserves to have his great contributions recognized again, at Toronto Metropolitan as elsewhere. This will take time, for large numbers of people will have to admit that they fell for false accusations, and that university officials themselves were responsible for much of the misinformation. I would not call for the name change to be reversed, but students, faculty and staff at Toronto Metropolitan University will have to live with that uninspired name. Ryerson's name, however, should, in time, be restored at the university on a prominent building. His Indigenous name, Cheehock, should also be acknowledged, perhaps by naming the central quad of the campus the "Cheehock Commons," given that the university strongly emphasizes its Indigenous roots. Lastly, a restored Ryerson statue, paid for by public subscription, should be erected in another central place, ideally on the grounds of Queen's Park, the provincial Legislature. A prominent public building in Toronto should also be named after him. The Toronto Reference Library, a fine building, would be a fitting tribute to the great advocate of free public libraries.

CHAPTER 10

A crime against Sir Matthew Begbie's humanity

Peter Shawn Taylor

I do not think the purpose of a government is to right the past.
It cannot rewrite history. It is our purpose to be just in our time.
—PRIME MINISTER PIERRE TRUDEAU to the
House of Commons, 1984

In March 2018, Prime Minister Justin Trudeau apologized for another in the apparently endless list of wrongs perpetrated by previous governments of Canada. This time the aggrieved party was the Tsilhqot'in Nation of British Columbia; their grievance was the pre-Confederation hanging of six chiefs for their role in what is now known as the Chilcotin War. Accused and convicted of mass murder at the time, today they are officially considered to have been warriors bravely defending their land against white invaders.

"We now understand that the treatment of the Tsilhqot'in chiefs represented a betrayal of trust and injustice that has been carried by the Tsilhqot'in people for more than 150 years," Trudeau told the House of Commons. And so these six native leaders, once convicted of murder, are fully exonerated of any crime or wrongdoing."[1] This follows a remarkably similar apology by former British Columbia premier Christy Clark from 2014, in which she said, "we confirm without reservation that these six Tsilhqot'in chiefs are fully exonerated of any crime or wrongdoing."[2]

As an exercise in political symbolism, Trudeau's ancient legal discharge was artfully executed, emotively delivered, and rewarded with maximum positive media coverage. And yet if it is a righteous and newsworthy act to hand out exonerations for injustices perpetrated upon historical figures associated with the Chilcotin War, there is no good reason to stop with these six war chiefs. Even the slightest nod to fair play or historical context should require us to acknowledge that the legacy of the presiding judge in this affair—the once-renowned and much-celebrated Sir Matthew Baillie Begbie—has also suffered a grave injustice. If Canada of 2018 is prepared to fully exonerate six war chiefs for horrific actions we now consider to have been honourable and reasoned, then we surely owe the same to Begbie, who was by colonial standards the most liberal, open-minded and minority-positive jurist of his day—and even by modern standards remains arguably the most impressive figure ever to wield a gavel in Canada.

When will Sir Matthew get his reputation back?

A long time ago—when colonialism was still a byword for high adventure and bravura—Sir Matthew Baillie Begbie stood at the vanguard of the Victorian ideal: born on a British troop ship on its way to Mauritius, educated in the classics at Cambridge and employed at the bar of the Chancery Courts of London. In 1858, thanks to political connections, he was named the sole colonial judge for the wild and woolly newly-created colony of British Columbia.[3]

As soon as he set foot on the West Coast, Begbie established a reputation as a hard-working and incorruptible purveyor of British common law tradition. He personally wrote the Gold Fields Act of 1859, legislation that was instrumental in establishing the crown's authority over the British Columbia gold rush—keeping in check many lawless American miners who made their way north. Begbie travelled extensively throughout his precinct to ensure the law was as fairly administered and easily accessible in the hinterland of the Cariboo as it was in the relative comfort of a courthouse in the colony's capital of New Westminster.

According to biographer David Williams, within a year of arriving in British Columbia, Begbie walked from New Westminster up the Fraser Canyon to Lillooet and back, a journey of over 560 kilometres, in four months. On horseback he established a regular judicial circuit: winter and spring along the coast, summer and fall in the interior.[4] In 1865, author Williams figures, Begbie travelled nearly 6,000 kilometres dispensing justice. During these trips, Begbie often lived off the land, establishing a reputation as a skilled frontiersman.

Begbie's golden reputation is further burnished by the fact he was not just an impeccably fair purveyor of law and order, but also an early proponent of native rights. He learned several native dialects in order to adjudicate without need of interpreters. He frequently refused to enforce culturally insensitive laws such as the infamous Potlatch ban, exhibited much sympathy for the damage done to natives by whisky-sellers and, in 1860 spoke in favour of the then-heretical notion of "Indian title" to the land. And despite his unfortunate nickname of "the Hanging Judge"—a term never applied in his lifetime—he was no friend of vigilantism and displayed no prejudice when handing out sentences. In his biography *The Man for a New Country,* Williams calculates that between 1859 and 1872 Begbie presided over 52 individual murder charges. Of these 38 resulted in guilty verdicts, of which he offered clemency to 11, including seven natives. "Interestingly," Williams writes, "he did not recommend clemency for any of the white men sentenced to be hanged."[5]

Begbie was equally tolerant of the Chinese community, another group victimized by widespread prejudice in early British Columbia. He repeatedly struck down discriminatory bylaws aimed at Chinese laundries and pawnshops, allowed elaborate oath-taking procedures for Chinese witnesses who refused to swear on a Bible, and openly spoke in their favour when surveyed by the federal government in advance of the now lamented (and dutifully apologized for) Chinese head tax. A questionnaire from the Royal Commission investigating the "Chinese question" in British Columbia asked: "Are they industrious, sober, economical and law-abiding, or are they lazy, drunken, extravagant or turbulent? Please answer the question fully." To which Begbie replied:

> Industry, economy, sobriety and law-abidingness are exactly the four prominent qualities of Chinamen... This is, I think, the real cause of their unpopularity. If Chinamen would only be less industrious and economical, if they would but occasionally get drunk, they would no longer be the formidable competitor with the white man which they prove to be in the labour market; there would be no longer a cry for their suppression.[6]

In recognition of his work ethic, duty and profound sense of morality, for most of British Columbia's first 100 or so years, Begbie was commonly paired with governor Sir James Douglas as the province's two most significant and revered forefathers. In further recognition of his contributions, Begbie was frequently commemorated in geography; his name graced streets, parks, mountains, lakes, schools and other public sites across the province.

But that was then. As a result of Begbie's involvement in the execution of those now-exonerated Tsilhqot'in war chiefs, his once-shining legacy is now steadily retreating into darkness. In 2001 the University of Victoria removed his name from the school's law building, and later a small statue of Begbie in front of that building later disappeared under mysterious circumstances.[7] A mural featuring Begbie dispensing justice that once graced the walls of the British Columbia Legislature was hidden from public view in 2008.[8]

In 2017, a much larger statue of Begbie—on horseback in the front lobby of the Law Society of British Columbia's building in Vancouver—was also purged. So was its plaque which read: "His 36 years of fearless and impartial service made a lasting contribution to the administration of justice in the Pacific region of Canada." But in capitulation to demands of modern Tsilhquot'in political war chiefs, the law society renounced the province's first chief justice and declared the statue "a reminder... of the province's colonial past and Justice Begbie's role in the hanging of six Tsilhqot'in Chiefs. The presence of the statue is offensive to them."[9]

Emboldened by this victory, the "Tsilhquot'in National Government" of Williams Lake, British Columbia subsequently demanded that the province should "remove Begbie's name from all public places" because he "wrongfully convicted six Tsilhqot'in war chiefs of murder and sentenced them to death."[10] Every testament to Begbie in every part of the province can now be considered under threat of removal to satisfy this demand. Once celebrated as a founding father, today he is considered *persona non grata* throughout much of the province. But if a review of the facts in light of modern-day sensitivities prompted the British Columbia and federal governments to declare the charges and punishment meted out against those six Tsilhqot'in chiefs to be unjust, surely we owe the same due process to Begbie.

The massacre that became a war

What we today call the Chilcotin War was once known as the "Waddington Massacre." In spring 1864 entrepreneur Alfred Waddington decided to build a private toll road into the area west of Williams Lake to take advantage of gold mining traffic, and possibly encourage permanent white settlement in the area. A road crew was sent up the Homathko River, chopping and carving its way into unceded Tsilhqot'in territory. In response, a Tsilhqot'in war party attacked. Over a period of a few days, 18 whites were killed, including most of the road crew, a nearby settler, ferry operator and wranglers from a pack train supplying the area.

The exact reason for the uprising remains unclear to this day. Some historians ascribe the violence to sexual interference with native women by the road crew. Others suggest desperation and starvation on the part of the Tsilhqot'in, in part because of a devastating recent smallpox epidemic. Plunder is another possibility. The explanation currently favoured by apologists for the killers is that the new road was seen by the Tsilhqot'in as a deliberate attempt to wipe them out via another bout of smallpox.

What we do know is that a handful of Tsilhqot'ins decided to engage in a campaign of bloodshed unrestricted by the formalities of modern, nation-to-nation warfare. The first killing took place at a ferry crossing, outside traditional Tsilhqot'in territory. Then the war party tore through the main camp of the road crew on the morning of April 30, 1864 in a surprise attack, made all the more surprising by the fact that many of the native attackers were employed as workers in the camp at the time. Most of the nine dead were killed as they slept, either shot or bludgeoned to death in their tents. The war party then moved upstream to an advance camp. There, reported a government party that surveyed the scene later, foreman Willy Brewster was found "shot, his head smashed in with an axe and his belly ripped up."[11] According to author Mel Rothenburger's vivid account in *The Chilcotin War,* Brewster's killers carved out his heart and ate it, and cut off his penis and stuck it in his mouth.[12] Other victims were also mutilated. One road worker threw himself into the river and drowned rather than allow himself to be captured alive. In Rothenburger's telling of the story, Brewster was a catalyst for the uprising because he had threatened the Tsilhqot'ins with smallpox after members of another local band had stolen 25 sacks of flour from the road builders' stores. The locals had good reason to be fearful and angry over the threat. In the previous two years an estimated 20,000 of the region's 60,000 aboriginal inhabitants had been killed by the disease. Half the Tsilhqot'ins had perished. Rothenburger writes of two American traders who had chanced upon a decimated village, gathered up blankets, and resold them to other natives who became infected and died (as did one of the traders).

Whatever the motive, such violence could not go unrebuked by the colonial government, and an armed party of 70 volunteers was promptly organized to bring the chiefs to justice. While it eventually succeeded, the circumstances surrounding the capture of Klatsassin, the ring-leader of the war party, are pivotal to present-day abjurations of Begbie, and require a closer look.

The disputed surrender

W.G. Cox, the gold commissioner for the province, led the Cariboo volunteer party. After several months on the run, Klatsassin's party was reduced to eating their horses and were on the verge of starvation. Cox sent word through an emissary that he would either accept the surrender of all guilty parties or continue pursuing the entire group and thus "kill all the men, women and children." This threat led to an exchange of gifts, and Klatsassin's appearance in Cox's camp to negotiations. Two days later the chief returned with seven other members of his band. "We are seven murderers who are here giving ourselves up, and I am another," Cox recorded Klatsassin as saying. Upon discovering that he had been made a prisoner by Cox, however, the chief declared "there is no murderer here." Later, he refined his argument: "We meant war, not murder."[13]

The meaning of the initial parley and subsequent surrender has been subject to much debate in the intervening century and a half. Cox's threat to kill Klatsassin's family clearly complicates his confession. And if we accept the modern interpretation of the killings as an act of war—and if the gifts exchanged were meant as a peace offering to establish a truce—then the circumstances of Klatsassin's capture appear to violate widely-accepted rules of warfare. Begbie, as trial judge for Klatsassin and the others, was very much attuned to the significance of the surrender. In a letter to British Columbia Governor Fredrick Seymour, he called the surrender a "very important topic."[14] He questioned Cox at length on the matter and even visited Klatsassin in his jail cell, a conversation reportedly conducted in the chief's native tongue. The judge concluded the accused had not expected to be imprisoned by Cox. Rather, Begbie suspected a rival chief who stood to gain from Klatsassin's removal may have deliberately mistranslated Cox's message and confused the purpose of the parley. Despite this murkiness, however, the judge concluded Klatsassin was about to give himself up regardless, due to a lack of supplies—something the chief did not dispute—and allowed the confessions to stand as evidence.

Biographer Williams, himself a lawyer, carefully considers Begbie's decision on the surrender and concludes that today, Klatsassin's self-incriminating statements would almost certainly be struck from the evidence. Yet the author admits application of this exclusionary principle was a very rare event in colonial-era courtrooms.[15] Besides, there were plenty of eyewitnesses who put Klatsassin and his co-accuseds at the scenes of the crimes, supporting guilty verdicts without any need for confessions. However the decision is viewed today, it is clear that Begbie showed a far greater concern for Klatsassin's legal rights than the chief had reason to expect from most other British colonial judges of his time. "It seems horrible to hang five men at once, especially under the circumstances of capitulation," Begbie wrote to Seymour of the verdict. "I do not envy you your task of coming to a decision."[16]

Indeed, it was not Begbie's decision that sealed Klatsassin's fate. A jury found five of the eight natives captured by Cox to be guilty of murder. Before Begbie pronounced upon them the mandatory sentence of death he asked, "What is your law against murderers?" "Death," they replied. "Our law is the same," Begbie said. "You are guilty of death."[17] While he had commuted sentences of capital punishment in other, less-politically sensitive trials involving natives, Begbie chose not to do so in this case. In any event, his was not the last word on the matter. First the province's Executive Council reviewed the trial, then Governor Frederick Seymour confirmed the death sentence, on October 18, 1864:

> After a most prolonged and careful enquiry and deliberation the Council were unanimously of opinion that no promise of any sort was made to any of these Indians by Mr. Cox on their surrender and that there was no reason why the justly deserved sentence of death imposed on five of them by the Law should not forthwith be carried out.[18]

If anyone should bear historical responsibility for hanging the five war chiefs (a sixth was captured, tried and hanged later that year), surely it is Seymour. So why has Begbie been made the villain of the piece?

The answer to that question, as well as why the Chilcotin killers deserve a public exoneration, can be traced to the 1993 report of the Cariboo-Chilcotin Justice Inquiry, a provincial investigation prompted by complaints about the administration of justice in native communities in the interior of British Columbia. While the bulk of this report deals with familiar modern issues such as high rates of native incarceration, treaty rights and conflict between natives and the RCMP, it made headlines for suggesting a posthumous pardon for the six war chiefs as a peace offering to improve local native/provincial relations. "Much has been written, but little is known with any certainty of the facts that led to the trial of those chiefs before Judge Matthew B. Begbie," the report notes. "Whatever the correct version, that episode of history has left a wound in the body of the Chilcotin society. It is time to heal that wound." Note how the inquiry takes no position on the killings, or Begbie's role in the final outcome; the facts are moot against the "healing" imperative.[19]

In the years that followed, the case for exoneration was built on the unsubstantiated assumption that the killings were an honourable act of war, not murder. In their recent apologies, for example, both ex-Premier Clark and Prime Minister Trudeau blandly state the native attackers removed "all settlers from their lands." What the law originally found to be a mass murder of 18 unsuspecting road workers and settlers is now officially recognized as a war between nations fully justified on the basis of a bio-terror threat, and which was lost only because of deception on the part of the white army.

The final requirement for this new narrative affirming the natives as victims is the transformation of Begbie into a villain. His punishment is to have his reputation rubbished and his name scrubbed from the province's road maps and lobbies.

Begbie, Macdonald, Langevin, Cornwallis...

This demand for scapegoats plucked from the pantheon of Canadian history has become a regular by-product of the "Truth and Reconciliation" movement. Begbie's fate is remarkably similar to that of Sir Hector-Louis Langevin, the influential French Catholic federalist and Father of Confederation who has lately been fingered as an "architect" of the Indian residential school system. In 2019, Trudeau removed Langevin's name from the building that houses his office in Ottawa after complaints from native leaders. Langevin was, in fact, the Minister of Public Works when Prime Minister Sir John A. Macdonald's government formalized its residential school program. Langevin was the program's "architect" in only the most literal sense of the word—he was responsible for putting up the buildings.[20] Laying the concept or creation of the residential school system at his feet is pure historical fiction. Another newly-minted villain is Edward Cornwallis, the first governor of Halifax, who responded to the practice of Mi'kmaq warriors scalping English settlers (for payment by the governor of New France) by establishing his own scalping bounty. In response to demands from descendants of the Mi'kmaq scalpers, Halifax City Council recently voted to remove a statue of the city's founder.[21] Historical context has no relevance in the nationwide effort to expiate Canada's collective colonial sins by taking the metaphorical scalps of as many prominent Canadian historical figures as possible.

Yet this villainization of Begbie is especially and ironically unjust. Casting his continued physical presence in the province as an impediment to reconciliation requires us to ignore his vast record of accomplishments in furtherance of law, liberalism and good governance during British Columbia's early days. It means wiping from popular history his impressive and laudatory record as defender of minority rights and native cultural traditions. Surely no representative of the British crown displayed a more enlightened view of indigenous traditions or interests throughout the province's colonial era. Removing his legacy in this way robs all Canadians of a fulsome understanding of the origin of minority rights in their own country. And it ignores the large and important role played by the British liberal, Christian and colonial traditions in the creation of a modern, diverse and tolerant Canada.

If we are intent on applying present-day standards of law and morality to adjudicate past actions—as is now apparently *de rigueur* in Canadian historical debates—it is true that Begbie's handling of the Tsilhqot'in killers falls short of a Charter-worthy regard for their legal rights. And if we accept that the Chilcotin War was in fact a proper war between nations, it is similarly true that Cox's inducements to Klatsassin look suspiciously like a trick that would be considered unethical today.

But such assumptions, if applied, must be fairly distributed. It is clear the activities of the Tsilhqot'in war party of 1864 also violate numerous contemporary standards of behaviour and ethics. Their declaration of war, for example, was not announced to anyone else in the colony. As such, the initial raid can only be seen as a sneak attack: a de facto act of terrorism. And the warriors who hired themselves out to the road crew and thus disguised themselves as friendly participants prior to the attack should similarly be considered guilty of acting as spies—conduct that has always been punishable by summary execution on the battlefield. Finally, the war party committed several horrific acts of ritualized mutilation on the dead, particularly in their bloodthirsty mauling of Brewster, that would be universally condemned as crimes against humanity if carried out today. Is this something that deserves exoneration? Or excused as something "many of us would have done," as Kamloops-Thompson-Cariboo Conservative MP Cathy McLeod said during bi-partisan parliamentary cheerleading for Trudeau's apology?[22]

The scales of justice have tilted decisively and unfairly against the reputation of Begbie. British Columbia's greatest judge deserves a fair trial of his own.

CHAPTER 11

Halifax cancels its founding father: The case of Edward Cornwallis

Leo J. Deveau

Faithfulness to the truth of history involves far more than research, however patient and scrupulous, into special facts. Such facts may be detailed with the most minute exactness, and yet the narrative as taken as a whole, may be unmeaning or untrue. The narrator must seek to imbue himself with the life and spirit of the time. He must study events in their bearings near and remote; in the character, habits, and manners of those who took part in them. He must himself be, as it were, a share or spectator of the action he describes.

—FRANCIS PARKMAN, historian and author of *Pioneers of France in the New World*, 1867

Anti-colonial activists waging war on Canada's history seek to impose a Manichean worldview where all historical figures are either good or bad, but never both. In the Canadian context, in blunt terms, that means "indigenous good and colonist bad." But let us pause on such a simplistic divide because informed history, nuance, facts, and then apologies are in order.

In Halifax, a lengthy campaign by activists has, since the 1990s, denigrated and demonized the city's founder, Governor Colonel Edward Cornwallis (1713-1776). In January 2018, they succeeded in having the commemorative statue of him removed from Cornwallis Park (ironically renamed the "Peace and Friendship Park" as of 2021), where it once stood since 1931. The new name of this park is Orwellian. There is neither peace nor friendship when one side attacks historical figures with misinformation, while the other attempts to defend the historical record. In the same instance, many leaders remain ignorant of their city's history, and many journalists who should know better, cheer from the sidelines with misleading sound bites.

One revisionist, Dr. Monica MacDonald, who has a doctorate in the field of "Communication and Culture," co-chaired a joint Task Force on the Commemoration of Edward Cornwallis and the Recognition and Commemoration of Indigenous History. Her co-chair was former Mi'kmaw Chief, Roderick Googoo. The task force came up with twenty recommendations in its final report submitted to the Halifax Regional Municipal Council (HRM) and Assembly of Nova Scotia Mi'kmaq Chiefs in April 2020, all of which were quickly accepted and passed in July that same year. Upon the release of their recommendations, MacDonald stated that, "colonization was inherently violent," a claim which endorsed the well-played, simple trope expecting residents of Halifax to believe that *nothing* good came out of colonizing Nova Scotia, a rather extreme statement given that without colonization, most of us, in Halifax and the rest of Canada, would not be here.

My response to the task force's recommendations appeared in the *Chronicle-Herald* shortly after the Task Force report was accepted by Council. I gave the report a "C+" because, far from being a balanced consideration of the debate surrounding Cornwallis, it was essentially a *mea culpa* to the Mi'kmaq community.[1] It offered little to non-indigenous residents—nothing of the spirit of reconciliation which is meant to be a collaborative process in mutual understanding and respect. Nor, regrettably, did the process have much to do with historical fact.

Historical facts matter including about colonial figures

In 1749, Colonel Edward Cornwallis, age 36, was commissioned by the British government to establish a settlement of over 2,500 colonists on the Atlantic coast of mainland Nova Scotia which the British initially called Chebucto (the Mi'kmaq called it Ki'jipuktuk—meaning "the great harbour"). Cornwallis later renamed the settlement *Halifax* in honour of George Dunk, the Earl of Halifax, who as President of the Board of Trade and Plantations coordinated the planning for establishing the settlement.

Over the last thirty years, it is clear that Cornwallis's name has become a political prop to support the local and national indigenous narrative of grievance, blame, and shame. In Cornwallis's case, the grievance also includes the charge of genocide against the Mi'kmaq, first espoused by a Mi'kmaw elder and author Daniel Paul in his 1993 book *We Were Not the Savages.*[a] His book provides an important contribution to the history of early settlement in Nova Scotia but in many sections, it is also a work of questionable historical assertions or outright misrepresentation of the context and era of Cornwallis. Worse, local journalists have long turned to it as a go-to source for easy headlines and quotations in any coverage of the controversy.

This media tendency has unfortunately further legitimized the misinformation that Paul has propagated. Indeed, Paul won an early victory in his previous grievance campaign in 2011, when the Halifax School Board drank what might best be labelled as his selective historical "Kool-Aid," and changed the name of "Cornwallis Junior High" to "Halifax Central." It was clear back then that in order to send historic names down an Orwellian, *1984*-like memory hole, the first task was to make people feel guilty. But that misbegotten name-change was just the beginning.

Paul's disdain for any historical nuance about the settlement of Nova Scotia has little to do with historical records and documents. Instead, his case relies on a great deal of circumstantial evidence and takes the form of socio-political analysis. In essence, it is an anti-colonialist rant masquerading as historical evidence. In Paul's non-history the indigenous were innocent of any violent actions as they were merely "fighting back to preserve their freedom and country..."[2] even though those lands (i.e., mainland Nova Scotia) had already been ceded in earlier treaties. Of course, all of this remains contentious, but that is the nature of history, which is why nuance is necessary in any historical account.

Let us explore the nuance of this claim. In the case of Cornwallis's *Bounty Proclamation* on 2 October 1749, British intelligence had determined that

---

a) Later in September 2017, then Dalhousie University President, Richard Florizone, issued a letter to students providing a free copy of Daniel Paul's book at the university's Killam library, stating that Paul's book had "... done much to raise public consciousness about Mi'kmaw history, identity and culture... We aim to provide all first-year students with their own copy which I hope will begin meaningful conversations both inside and outside of the classroom." He did not include a comprehensive reading list that reflected a range of historical perspectives necessary to have an informed historical understanding of the times Paul was writing about.

prior Mi'kmaq attacks at Canso (19 August) and Chignecto (6 September) and in Dartmouth (30 September) presented a clear and present danger to Halifax settlers. Thus, Cornwallis issued an order to construct five blockhouses connected by a palisade around the settlement (as seen in Moses Harris's 1750 illustration *View of Halifax Drawn from Ye Topmasthead*).[3] Further, as French authorities at Fortress Louisbourg were already paying bounties to the Mi'kmaq for British prisoners and/or their scalps, Cornwallis issued a proclamation offering a similar bounty for Mi'kmaq warriors, "... to be paid upon producing such Savage taken or his scalp." Women and children were to be taken prisoner.

Daniel Paul falsely defines Cornwallis's proclamation as an "extermination" order rather than an effort to remove Mi'kmaq warriors from the peninsula of Halifax and provide security to the settlement from attacks. Paul provides no context as to why the proclamation was deemed necessary—namely that the Mi'kmaq were close allies of the French based at Louisbourg, and as such had also been encouraged to attack the settlers in violation of signed treaties.[b] Paul also ignores the full wording of the *Proclamation*, which clearly states that the bounties to be paid were for the scalps of Mi'kmaq warriors only—not women and children. And yet, Paul deliberately states that the document calls for "the scalps of men, women and children." This misrepresentation—the use of the words "men, women and children" (which is not found in the *Proclamation*) is echoed by, among others, author Jon Tattrie in his entry in the Canadian Encyclopedia, which wrongly states that Cornwallis promised to "pay a bounty to anyone who killed a Mi'kmaw adult or child."

Paul's analysis ignored the wider context of the imperial wars of the period and the close alliance between the Mi'kmaq and the French in that struggle of empires. The history of that alliance records regular bounties paid for the delivery of scalps belonging to British soldiers and settlers obtained by Mi'kmaq warriors during numerous raids. As noted above, such bounties were paid by French officials at Louisbourg. and frequently also by the notorious Catholic missionary-cum-rabid nationalist, the Abbé Louis Le Loutre.

---

b) Mi'kmaq attacks were the most frequent and severe during Cornwallis's tenure (1749 to 1752) with four of the five raids occurring on the Dartmouth side of the harbour. The *London Magazine* later reported on the attacks. There was a reason why Cornwallis had to construct a series of forts and palisades around the settlement as seen in Moses Harris's 1750 sketch *View of Halifax Drawn from Ye Topmasthead.*

Adopting the familiar "good and evil" interpretation of history, Paul lays the charge of "genocide" against Cornwallis, feeling that the term genocide "aptly" described "the barbaric behaviour of the British in colonial Nova Scotia." This in turn is meant to justify his wild exaggeration that the statue of Cornwallis represented "white supremacist thinking."[4] For the author and his acolytes it seems everything comes down to genocide and white supremacy. This is grossly oversimplified history.

Paul's distorted mantra has now taken hold amongst many revisionists in Nova Scotia. Regrettably, no professional historians have come forward to publicly address Paul's charges. Though three historians sat on the previously-noted Task Force, their much needed and informed perspectives went missing. This is perhaps not surprising given that many academics have joined the revisionist bandwagon against Cornwallis. Perhaps they were cowed by fear, with the easier option to accept all grievance claims because the momentum of identity politics within the academic establishment seems mostly bereft of nuance and focused only on "lived history" based on the feelings of today versus the historical evidence (i.e., how people feel about what happened, rather than what actually happened). For those in the public square who attempted to better inform the public about the historical context surrounding Cornwallis and the origins of the Halifax settlement, it sometimes felt like Copernicus, trying to argue that the earth really revolves around the sun. No matter how much evidence one had, it was extremely difficult to change minds that were long ago made up.

Cancel culture on the east coast: How did we arrive here?

In the case of Halifax and Cornwallis, protestors first gathered in Cornwallis Park in May of 2014 calling for the park to be renamed and the statue of Cornwallis removed. They repeated the mantra that Cornwallis had "a very violent, genocidal past," and that "we have to stand against these kinds of things honouring people who represent that." Also, local city councillor Waye Mason, declared himself committed to "talking with Mi'kmaq and Acadian leaders to discuss possible solutions."[5] But it was clear even then that the solution was already a foregone conclusion. Mason made no mention of the majority of other citizens and taxpayers of Halifax, those who were routinely denigrated in these sessions as the "settler community."

In the spring of 2014, the regional municipality had already planned to give Cornwallis Park a new look with a multi-million-dollar "face-lift" so it is unlikely that the timing of the anti-Cornwall protest was a coincidence. Clues here appeared one year earlier, as when Mason reviewed plans for the park and rhetorically queried, "What do we do as a society with commemorative landscapes that are unrepresentative of present values?"[6]

Maybe Mason should have later consulted with the government of Quebec. When activists in Montreal pulled down the statue of Canada's first prime minister Sir John A. Macdonald, Premier Francois Legault commented that "We must fight racism, but destroying parts of our history is not the solution."[7] Heritage Montreal's policy director, Dinu Bumbaru also stated that his city "deserves an educated public discussion... not vandalism or similar executions. And Montreal deserves more monuments to add new voices. Not less."[8] In countries such as Great Britain, France, Italy, or Germany, communities take their sense of place and history seriously. In any case, it appeared that Mason wanted to be in front of the revisionist parade and adopted the pose of a leader dedicated to change for change's sake.

Another spur to the cancel-and-rename-it-all culture in Halifax came via the federal government, and the Truth and Reconciliation Commission, appointed by Prime Minister Stephen Harper and established in 2008. That Commission released its "call to action" recommendations in June 2015, by which time Halifax had already established an Office of Diversity and Inclusion whose work included plans to hire an urban indigenous community engagement advisor to write up an urban-aboriginal strategy. These actions were followed by a December 2015 Statement of Reconciliation by the regional council which declared its commitment to a new and equal partnership with Aboriginal peoples based on truth, dignity and mutual respect. As it turned out, that meant little in the way of respect, dignity, or equal treatment for historical figures such as Cornwallis, but rather, a one-way cancellation campaign against the founder of Halifax.

Just three days after regional council declared its Statement of Reconciliation at their December council meeting, Premier Stephen McNeil announced he was, with little advance warning to citizens, "ready to ask Halifax city hall to consider having a statue of the city founder Edward Cornwallis removed from a downtown park."[9] At the time, McNeil was also the then Minister of the Office of Aboriginal Affairs so this may have been a discussion already underway with the city. In addition, McNeil was responding to an earlier question from Progressive Conservative MLA Alan MacMaster who stated that the "statue of Cornwallis ... should come down."[10] By April 2016, the provincial and city musings were joined by the Halifax Mi'kmaw Native Friendship Centre which sent a letter to City Council asking that Cornwallis Street be renamed. "Since we opened [our Centre] ... we have suffered the humiliation [sic]. The argument that what Cornwallis did to the Mi'kmaq was the result of different times and values does not wash."[11]

In mid-May 2016, Councillor Mason introduced a motion to remove the name of Edward Cornwallis on *all* municipal "commemorations." Mayor Mike Savage, a former Liberal Member of Parliament, supported the motion. His late father, John Savage, had served as Premier of Nova Scotia from 1993 to 1997, and was, among other things, an honorary Mi'kmaw chief. Even with the Mayor's support, Mason's motion was initially defeated eight to seven in a council vote. Referring to the earlier protests demanding the removal of Cornwallis's name and statue, Mason seemed irked that he had not won yet and that further discussion and perhaps further opposition to such a cancellation might ensue: "Those residents, these citizens are going to want to continue to have that discussion and it's inevitable we're going to have discussion. We just haven't decided to have it at this point."[12] Shortly after Mason's motion was defeated the Cornwallis statue was ravaged by vandals with the now-familiar tactic of dousing it in red paint, this intended to symbolize the charge of genocide. It was another strategy in the constellation of activist actions to make it appear obvious and inevitable that the Cornwallis statue should be removed.

Local history down the memory hole

In October 2016, Halifax' municipal election returned Mayor Mike Savage with 68 per cent of the vote and Councillor Mason with 61 per cent. There were also new councillors elected who, as it would turn out, knew little about their city's history, and more specifically, as their later votes indicated, nothing at all about Edward Cornwallis. When City Council originally voted against Mason's motion in spring that year, Halifax's then-first Mi'kmaw poet laureate, Rebecca Thomas, wrote a lament poem called *Not Perfect.* Eleven months later, in April 2017, she was given a staged opportunity to read it aloud to the newly elected Council and called on them to reconsider the recognition given to Cornwallis in the city.

Thomas labelled Cornwallis a man "who prided himself on brutality" and used Mi'kmaq scalps "as currency." She then added a dose of guilt based on an incorrect feeling approach to history, pleading that, "I'm asking for your help to heal generations of spiritual welts because we were seen as animals only valued for our pelts."[13] It was an over-the-top display of moralism and an act of historical malfeasance. As for rationally debating the matter, Thomas stated, "[I]f the public isn't necessarily willing to listen and to have that conversation about a more inclusive history, another facet of history that makes them uncomfortable, then we have another conversation on our hands that we have to have."[14] Thus, inclusiveness to Thomas appeared to simply mean accepting a selective historical account devoid of context. The moralistic tone communicated the poet's view that only she knew the "truth" and this was the only truth to be tolerated. Unsurprisingly, such a stark statement coming from someone with an indigenous identity made even more citizens uncomfortable defending Cornwallis.

Halifax Councillor Shawn Cleary was so impressed by Thomas's presentation that he vowed to reintroduce Mason's earlier motion to remove the name of Cornwallis from all municipal properties. Just two weeks after Thomas read her poem, Mason's motion was reintroduced and this time it was a near shut-out, with councillors in favour by fifteen to one. They then directed that City staff create a report:

> with terms of reference and a recommended composition for an *expert panel* to review and advise Council regarding any changes to the commemoration of Edward Cornwallis on municipal assets, including Cornwallis Park and Cornwallis Street, and recommendations to recognize and commemorate the indigenous history in the lands now known as Halifax Regional Municipality.[15] (Emphasis added)

Four councillors (Hendsbee, Walker, Adams and Whitman) attempted to amend the motion to ensure that whatever recommendations might arise from the panel, would be "fact-based" or "evidence-based," rather than based on emotion. In an interesting display of the all-or-nothing, anti-nuance approach taken by the anti-history revisionists, this call for facts and evidence was felt by most councillors to be "already adopted as a core value, so its inclusion in the motion would be redundant."[16] Thus, the amendment was defeated—four in favour, twelve against, including Mayor Savage (with one councillor absent). Time would tell how evidence-based the panel's recommendations would be.

It should be noted that soon after the vote to cancel Cornwallis that spring, a CBC survey found that 58 per cent of Haligonians believed that Cornwallis's name should remain on public parks, buildings, and street signs.[17] It was an unusually strong majority, so strong that the CEO of the company that conducted the survey stated, "Quite often the silent majority is not represented in these kinds of debates. In fact, it's almost two to one against removing his (Cornwallis) name."[18] The strength of the poll result against cancelling Cornwallis perhaps revealed the public's natural presumption on the side of preserving traditional and familiar nomenclature, a healthy civic pride. After all, despite the events nearly 300 years earlier during colonial wars, this was still a question of how to treat historical figures. There could have been an educational opportunity to broaden historical contexts and deepen the narratives that represent both indigenous and colonial-offspring communities. But that was ever only possible if leaders took care to approach history and historical figures with caution, with attempts to understand the era in which these figures lived, or the "lived history" as one might put it today. This did not occur in Halifax.

Erasing the history of others

A case can be made and should be made that the indigenous, who for thousands of years resided on the lands in what is now known as Canada, have at times not been accorded deserved space in the historical record. In some cases, such omissions resulted from an ignorance on the part of later immigrants to indigenous oral tradition. In other instances, it would be fair to assert that some deliberate suppression of indigenous culture and history did occur. That is a wrong that always needed to be corrected. However, just as some earlier accounts ignored indigenous history, when an ideological or a "grievance" approach to history is in play, the same is possible today with other aspects of history. The danger is that all history could easily be erased if events and individuals are simply reduced to one-dimensional cardboard characters with both interpreted as only ever good or evil but never both. On 28 June, 2017 another report to the regional council concluded that:

> Ongoing engagement of the urban Indigenous Community will be instrumental in the success of any strategy. This engagement is complex and involved not only many levels within [Halifax Regional Municipality] but also many groups and individuals who represent the community.... Council is committed, through the expert panel, to recognize and commemorate the Indigenous history in the lands now known as Halifax Regional Municipality.[19]

There was no mention of other historical narratives that included the British, French, Acadians, or other cohorts involved in the founding of the British settlement, Halifax. It is almost as if many of the city councillors and activists wished to keep the general public ignorant of the origins of their own culture as settler descendants, who for the most part, hail from Europe.

In July 2017, protestors marched twice against the Cornwallis statue and in-between the two marches, Mayor Savage was tipped off about a plan to "forcibly remove the statue of Edward Cornwallis from the park."[20] He issued an official statement that such an action would not be condoned by the city or by Mi'kmaq chiefs. He pointed to the Council's goodwill effort to create an expert panel "inclusive of Mi'kmaq voices, to recommend an appropriate way forward," and concluded, "The municipality and its partners in policing will not stand in the way of legitimate public protest," but "nor will we condone violent action in the place of real dialogue."[21] In the interim, the civic authorities covered the statue with a shroud, presumably to dissuade protestors from taking it down. Mayor Savage explained that the "veil is a temporary measure, and will be removed after the demonstration."[22] However, once the protesters dispersed, with the shroud removed, a tarp was then placed over the statue.[c]

---

c) The shroud covering reminded me of my days as an altar-boy when all the statues in church were shrouded to deepen the penitential atmosphere for the Triduum in preparation for Easter. The tarp seemed to mimic the recent apologetic nature by HRM Council about all that came with Cornwallis and non-indigenous immigrants to North American shores.

In early October 2017, Halifax Regional Municipality's council voted fifteen to two to launch the expert panel that was proposed six months earlier with terms of reference provided in a September 2017 city staff recommendation report. The expert panel was to be called a "Special Advisory Committee."[23] Only then were city residents also informed that the committee would consist of a panel of eight with "equal representation from indigenous and non-indigenous backgrounds."[24] As it turned out, the Assembly of Nova Scotia Mi'kmaq Chiefs would eventually propose the Mi'kmaw representatives. But for reasons that remain unclear, the panel committee was slow to materialize, and when it did, it did not quite perform as intended.

What is clear in retrospect is that by early 2018, Savage and his then-deputy Waye Mason and two municipal staff travelled to Millbrook First Nation to consult with Mi'kmaq chiefs. The meeting appeared to be intended to address the chiefs' concerns about the panel. However, just two weeks after their consultation the Assembly declared that the "Chiefs unanimously agreed that this process has taken far too long and have therefore chosen to no longer participate in these panel discussions."[25] The panel had not yet even been formally established, the original purpose of which was precisely to try and sort through how to deal with competing historical claims and the figures therein, i.e., the legacy of Edward Cornwallis, and with the hope that facts and informed history would inform such deliberations. Instead, the chiefs demanded that the city "remove the statue of Edward Cornwallis immediately and deal with all commemorations of Cornwallis."[26] That was the end of the pretense that real dialogue was ever going to occur. Instead, the chiefs dictated policy and the end results to elected officials who already sent multiple signals that they were in full appeasement mode. No attempt was ever made by the elected regional municipality to express any other interpretation of the history of Halifax or the contributions of Cornwallis to the founding of a city where 439,000 people live today in a province of over one million residents.

Mayor Savage did respond later, noting that "The committee was meant to create the space to have challenging conversations about our shared history and future," and that "Reconciliation is a complex process, requiring the engagement of our community in its broadest form ... Regional Council remains committed to continued dialogue on our journey of reconciliation."[27] The words meant little. For just three days after the Assembly of Mi'kmaq Chiefs called for the removal of the Cornwallis statue, with only an hour's perfunctory "debate," on January 30, 2018, the Council took less than ten seconds to vote twelve to four in favour of "immediately" removing the statue of Edward Cornwallis and to place it in temporary storage "until Council makes a decision about the statue's long-term situation"—though it seemed clear that decision had just then already occurred.[28] At an estimated cost of $25,000, the statue was removed the next day. The motion to remove the statue also included a second item, for the "Mayor's office, to re-engage the Assembly of Nova Scotia Mi'kmaq Chiefs in establishing a special advisory committee...."[29]

Behind all this was a council and city staff fearful of more protests and a possible attack on the statue in early February. Senior staff and councillors had ostensibly anticipated "significant risk for damage to the statue, conflicts among protestors and counter-protestors and personal injury." Apparently, there was little desire to remind all Canadians that demonstrations that threaten municipal and federal property are a threat to all; given that, particularly in the instance of the Cornwallis statue, it has been implied that violence and lawlessness can deliver whatever a particular segment of society desires. Once the statue was gone, Mayor Savage offered a self-exculpatory explanation. "I feel strongly it's the right thing to do," he said. "Halifax is not the garrison town of Edward Cornwallis. It's a thriving, diverse, modern city that I believe will be largely shaped by those who've been here the longest and those who are finding it for the first time."[30] It was a curious expression of contempt for the city's founder and the context of that founding.

The mayor neglected the elected Council's earlier vote to create an expert panel before making any decision. He overlooked the Mi'kmaq chiefs refusing to participate in a panel discussion that might not recommend the result they wanted. Instead of respecting a democratic process, the preference of many Haligonians was subverted by an unelected body. Mayor Savage felt the removal of the Cornwallis statue was not in fact about cancelling yet another historical figure—even though it was: "This is not about re-writing history. This is about acknowledging that it is not cast in bronze... We can all be unshackled from what our history is, which sometimes holds us back from true reconciliation."[31] That may be, but the evidence was also clear that the mayor and his elected Council submitted to pressure and threats of violence. They failed to implement the legitimate process of civil discussion for which they themselves voted.

The mayor's rhetoric represented a denial of the historical fact that Halifax was established by Cornwallis and 2,500 dedicated settlers in 1749. Had Cornwallis not defended the British settlement in those critical years, there probably would not be a city called Halifax today, where peace, law and order, and eventually Canada's first representative government (1760), and later, elected responsible government (1849), would be born, where the fruits of the civilizing spirit of the Enlightenment would also take root and help shape the country that Canada has become.

The day after the statue was removed, a photo circulated on social media of Mayor Savage, Deputy Mayor Mason, then Councillor Lorelei Nicoll, then Mi'kmaq chief Morley Googoo, and Perry Bellegarde, then the National Chief of the Assembly of First Nations, as Bellegarde proclaims the removal of the Cornwallis statue as a "great step" towards "reconciliation." And yet, it does not appear to have reconciled indigenous peoples with the settler population. When surveyed for a second time in February of 2018, 62 per cent of Haligonians thought the statue should have remained where it was. By October 2018, regional council announced "an equal partnership between Halifax Regional Council and the Assembly of Nova Scotia Mi'kmaq Chiefs" in forming a "joint Task Force on the Commemoration of Edward Cornwallis and the Recognition and Commemoration of Indigenous History."[32] They would be responsible for their own determination of the process and procedures to fulfill its mandate, and the funding would be a joint and equal responsibility of HRM and the Assembly of Chiefs. The Task Force submitted their recommendations in April 2020.[33]

There were no surprises: Cornwallis was considered *persona non grata*. The formerly named Cornwallis Park, with the statue of Edward Cornwallis now permanently removed, was renamed the "Peace and Friendship Park,"[34] a vacuous entertainment space with an outdoor mini-amphitheatre that, symbolically, appears empty most of the time. Still to come was a change to the name of Cornwallis Street, planned for spring of 2023. As it turned out, the City was too impatient to wait even that long and just before Christmas 2022 the name was changed to Nora Bernard Street, this after a Mi'kmaw activist, murdered by her grandson in 2007.[35]

CHAPTER 12

Struggle and success: A balanced account of women in early Canada

Janice Fiamengo

I do not care about the platform, or woman's rights, or that kind of thing, but I believe women have as much intelligence as men, and that as civilization increases, the women are gradually and naturally coming to the fore.
– KATHLEEN (KIT) COLEMAN, *Toronto Mail columnist*, 1890-1911

Let us start with what we think we know about women in early English-Canadian society.[a]

The common narrative today is that Canadian women, like other women in the Anglophone world, were treated as second-class citizens: they lacked the right to vote, were confined to domestic drudgery, were barely even considered persons, and were generally excluded from the opportunities for free self-realization and participatory nation-building that their brothers, husbands, and sons possessed. Canadian men, in contrast, were allegedly privileged by a society that extended them many unearned sex-based advantages. As I will attempt to demonstrate, this formulation is not only simplistic but factually inaccurate, neglecting men's many hardships and sacrifices in early Canada, the successes that Canadian women achieved early on, and the remarkable willingness of a conservative society to support women's higher education, professional advancement, self-expression, and political participation.

---

a) The experience of women in French Canada was different enough from their English-speaking counterparts to require a separate account. This chapter will focus exclusively on Anglophone women.

Women achieved the right to vote federally in 1918. What is not generally known about suffrage rights in Canada is that both before and after Confederation, property and income qualifications restricted men's ability to vote at the provincial and federal levels, with the result that many poor men in late-nineteenth and early-twentieth century Canada—the same men, in many cases, who volunteered and died in World War I—also lacked the franchise. In his analysis of the gradual achievement of democratic governance in Canada, historian W. L. Morton explains that at the time universal suffrage was established, property qualifications for male suffrage were still in effect, meaning that full adult female suffrage came at the same time as full adult male suffrage.[1]

In the nineteenth century, the ability to vote was generally understood as both a privilege and a responsibility granted only to those who had proved their loyalty and fitness for decision-making. The male franchise carried with it the assumed duty to risk one's life in defence of country (and of the British Empire) at time of war. When women were granted the franchise, they were never assumed to pledge their lives in the same manner.

Though it is sometimes represented as a struggle, the female suffrage movement in Canada was not the incendiary issue it became in Great Britain, where members of the radical Women's Social and Political League engaged for years in vandalism, mass arson campaigns, and even targeted attacks (once with a thrown hatchet) on parliamentarians. Moreover, the Canadian movement for the franchise never attracted anywhere near a majority of support from women. Catherine Cleverdon, who has written Canada's primary study of the suffrage campaign, has noted that "The crowning argument of the opposition [to female suffrage] right down to the day of final surrender was that women did not want the vote and would not use it if they had it. There was considerable evidence to support this contention, particularly in the Maritime Provinces and Quebec."[2]

Cleverdon quotes a suffrage activist from British Columbia, Rose Henderson, admitting that the vote was extended to women with little demand on the part of women, most of whom never even passively supported it. "Certainly a few women put up a determined fight," she conceded, "but the masses of women at no time and in no place were with them, so that it would be wrong to conclude that women's political emancipation came about solely through their own efforts and desire for freedom."[3]

Early Canadian women did not see themselves as victims

Such assertions make uneasy reading for anyone attempting to use the franchise as a major marker of female exclusion. The fact is that most women in Canada did not express anger at men or a conviction of female victimhood. Some, such as skeptical feminist and writer Sara Jeannette Duncan, who as a young woman seems never to have had to struggle to find appreciative outlets for her witty opinions and social commentary, were not at all certain that most women had the political knowledge or interest to make effective use of a ballot. In an 1885 article written under her pseudonym Garth Grafton for the Toronto *Globe* newspaper, Duncan was not unsympathetic to the women's movement, but most definitely was not a zealous supporter, giving her opinion that "Nothing is more unconsciously dramatic than a woman's outcry against suffering which is often hers through no fault of her own; nothing more beautiful in all the dim world of abstractions than the intuitions with which she guards the hearth stone she has made sacred. But if she asks the ballot by virtue of her ability to sorrow eloquently or to know what is best for the baby, it seems to me that she will be sorely puzzled to know what to do with it when it is hers."[4]

Duncan admonished female readers that in order to become responsible voters, they would need to inform themselves far more thoroughly about national, international, and economic affairs than most women had so far done. The well-worn claim of female moral superiority was insufficient: "In the political field as everywhere, women will need all their moral superiority; but to ardour they must add acumen, and to sincerity sagacity, and to disgust with the present conditions the ability to improve them before they can hope greatly to influence the political situation."[5]

As Duncan intimated, most women had their hands full looking after their homes and families in the years before World War I. Outside of the country's few urban centres, colonial and Confederation-era Canada was still largely rural. In much of Ontario and the west, in fact, the land was still in the process of being won from the wilderness. Men's work in subsistence farming and fishing was so arduous, and family interdependence so vital for survival, that few women would have imagined complaining. Accounts of the settlement period in Canadian history by both men and women (though it was primarily women who had the leisure time to write and the incentive to keep in touch with family in the Old World) stressed the equivalence of the sacrifices of men and women at a time when life expectancy was about half what it is today.

The division of labour: Not due to sexism

Under pioneering conditions, the traditional division of labor between outdoor (male) and indoor (female) was not a matter of sexism, but of practical reality. Men did the harshly physical work that pregnant or nursing women could not attempt without danger to their health and that of their unborn or young children. It was all too common for men to die felling trees, burning agricultural fields, or in storms at sea. An injury from accident or repetitive strain, especially in situations where it was impossible to rest or consult medical professionals, could maim a man for life. In *Roughing It in the Bush* (1852), her lively chronicle of life in the Ontario bush from 1832-39, British immigrant Susanna Moodie could not spend much time commiserating with her husband when he dragged himself home one afternoon with a broken leg from an accident with an agricultural implement. Love for her partner was inseparable from an awareness of his material indispensability to their growing family as she related how "When I saw him on whom we all depended for subsistence, and whose kindly voice ever cheered us under the pressure of calamity, smitten down helpless, all my courage and faith [...] seemed to forsake me, and I wept long and bitterly."[6] When the doctor failed to arrive from Peterborough, Moodie did what she could for her husband, recording that "the dear sufferer contrived, with assistance, to bandage his leg" and carry on.[7]

Women's domestic work was also exhausting and seemingly endless: bearing and tending to children (often without medical attendance, as in Moodie's case), dealing with constant illness from ague (malaria), baking bread, cooking meals, making and mending clothes, washing bedding, making soap and candles, and supervising household projects. Writing in the early 1830s from a farm in Thornhill, just north of York (later Toronto), immigrant Mary O'Brien reported matter-of-factly and with satisfaction to her sister in England that "It yet wants a day of a fortnight since my confinement and I have been all day superintending not only the household affairs but the labours of seven or eight men, besides nursing my babies."[8]

Many of O'Brien's letters, as in her description of the birth of her second child, emphasize pride in her own and her family's resilience as well as the ability of genteel men and women to perform what they had never before imagined:

> After dinner I went into mama's room to get out of [the family's] way and from thence I did not very immediately return, for a few minutes made me the mother of another son. The nurse had not arrived, but Mama was so completely taken by surprise that she had no time to be alarmed. With Edward's [Mary's husband's] assistance and Flora's ministrations, she did all that was requisite for me and the baby [....] Such is the way we manage things in the bush.[9]

It is difficult not to marvel at the hard-won pride.

Written in the same decade, the letters of Lucy Peel in Sherbrooke County, Lower Canada, to her parents in England also emphasized the exigencies and triumphs of managing in the bush, making clear the inter-dependence of husband and wife and the emotional and practical strength thereby gained. Like Edward O'Brien, Edmund Peel attended his wife during childbirth, writing to Lucy's parents shortly after that he considered it "nothing more than false delicacy which would make a man absent himself" at such a time, though confessing that he was "quite distracted" by his wife's sufferings. "As soon as the child was born," he related, "I staggered into an adjoining room and cried like a child until I again saw Lucy smiling and free from pain."[10] When their beloved little girl died just a few weeks short of her first birthday, the couple consoled one another in their heartbreak and looked forward with shared trepidation and longing to the birth of their next child. Accounts like theirs, at once engrossing and sobering, reveal the deep bond sometimes forged by the back-breaking work and emotional endurance required for bush survival.

Not all immigrants did survive. In *Roughing It in the Bush,* Moodie tells of a winter journey of mercy to a woman and her children who were nearly starving after having been deserted by the woman's alcoholic husband; she also wrote of a former gentleman who, maddened by the loneliness and rigors of frontier life, ultimately committed suicide. Moodie's own immigrant sister, Catharine Parr Traill, though writing with cheerful zest of her determination to "cultivate all the mental resources"[11] necessary to make a happy home in the wilderness "for the sake of [her] beloved partner,"[12] was all too sadly aware of her husband Thomas's severe depressions. Mental illness and addictions were common in an unforgiving land but difficult to treat or acknowledge; most men and women lived with exhaustion and pain.

In the second half of the nineteenth century, it was mainly in the cities and amongst the prosperous middle and upper-middle classes that some women sought increased political rights and took advantage of the educational and professional opportunities available to them. The rapidity with which determined and talented women obtained university degrees and forged careers for themselves as doctors, lawyers, public speakers, journalists, authors, and politicians demonstrates that a significant number of men welcomed the entry of women into formerly male domains. On the occasions when the women were not welcomed, they had powerful allies and organizations to aid their cause.

Higher education for women had been uncontroversial since well before Confederation, with many women attending Normal Schools and Ladies' Colleges to prepare for careers as teachers, nurses, and office personnel. Later in the century, university co-education opened more doors, as Mount Allison University in Nova Scotia became the first to admit women in 1862. Acadia followed in 1880, Dalhousie in 1881. Queen's University in Ontario accepted female students in 1872, with Victoria College, Cobourg following in 1877. The pattern was thus set for the rest of the country.

As women began to study and earn degrees alongside their male peers, they moved also into the prestigious professions of law and medicine. Emily Howard Stowe was one of Canada's first female medical doctors. Raised by devoutly egalitarian Quaker parents and tutored from a young age in herbal healing, Stowe studied medicine first in the United States, at the New York Medical College for Women, before being accepted to the Toronto School of Medicine in 1871, where she and Jennie Trout were the first Canadian women to work towards a medical degree. Though it does not appear that Stowe ever took the medical licensing exam, she openly practiced as a doctor in Toronto for over a decade and was admitted to the Ontario College of Physicians and Surgeons in 1880.

19th century women were not shrinking violets

A determined feminist advocate, Stowe also founded Canada's first suffrage association in 1876 and became a tireless supporter of women's professional advancement. In the last decade of the nineteenth century, she campaigned successfully on behalf of Clara Brett Martin when Martin sought to obtain a law degree. Martin had graduated with a Bachelor's in Mathematics from the University of Toronto in 1890 but was initially refused entry to the Law Society of Upper Canada, which claimed that women were legally excluded. Only after a member of the Ontario parliament (with the energetic encouragement of Ontario Premier Oliver Mowat) introduced a bill giving the Society power to admit women—and even then, not without resistance—was she grudgingly allowed to study (at Osgoode Law School). With the ongoing advocacy of the National Council of Women of Canada, including Lady Ishbel Aberdeen, wife of Canada's Governor General, Martin was at last called to the Bar in 1897, whereafter she established a successful law practice in Toronto and worked to address women's legal issues, including child custody rights.

Few women faced the direct opposition that Martin had encountered, and the relative ease with which many talented women integrated themselves into Canadian public life testified to an Anglophone inheritance that valued women's diverse roles and intellectual capacities. Protestantism had long stressed the importance of education for both sexes while Enlightenment ideals promoted rational argumentation in the pursuit of truth. From mid-century on, women had been contributing their voices to public debates as novelists, poets, and essayists, and they gained particular prominence as journalists with the advent of mass circulation daily newspapers in the late 1870s and 1880s.

Fierce intellectual integrity and compassion were embodied in the life and writing of Kingston resident Agnes Maule Machar, daughter of a Presbyterian clergyman whose home was a gathering place for Canadian intellectuals. Machar, a popular novelist and poet, was an impassioned advocate of the Social Gospel—the application of Christian principles to social problems—and published prolifically in the most prestigious Canadian periodicals of her day, impressing readers with her wide range of theological and philosophical reference. Writing under the pen-name Fidelis not to hide her female identity—it was well known—but to stress her abiding faith, she championed higher education for women, mandatory schooling for poor children, and factory legislation to protect workers amongst many other causes. In the 1870s, she garnered acclaim in an extended debate in the pages of the *Canadian Monthly and National Review* with well-known Canadian public intellectual William Dawson LeSueur, nicknamed the Sage of Ottawa, on the implications of Darwinian science for the continuing relevance and truth claims of Christianity. Though always scrupulously civil, Machar was unafraid to sharply chastise her learned opponent for what she saw as his sometimes sloppy and bad-faith arguments. Ultimately LeSueur admitted that of the three writers who had attempted to answer his anti-theist arguments, Fidelis's responses were the strongest. In 1892, Machar published a well received novel about industrial conditions, *Roland Graeme, Knight,* in which her epigraph, "To ride abroad, redressing human wrongs" was an apt description of her own life's work.

Many women followed in Machar's footsteps over the next half century, carving out respected and, in some cases, remunerative roles for themselves while advancing new possibilities for women through their vibrant personalities and points of view. The aforementioned Sara Jeannette Duncan, who declared her era "a golden age for girls, full of new interests and new opportunities,"[13] earned her literary start at the precocious age of 24 when she covered the New Orleans Cotton Centennial for her hometown paper, the *Brantford Expositor*, began contributing articles to the *Globe* newspaper, and eventually secured a regular column there called "Woman's World," where she wrote on everything from recipes to reviews of serious literature to jaunty tirades. She also found regular work at the *Washington Post, The Week,* and the *Montreal Star*, where she reported on suffrage conventions and parliamentary debates, opined on Canadian copyright law, decried Canadian cultural complacency, interviewed professional women (including a high school friend who had become a professor at the Kingston Women's Medical College), and generally observed the social scene in prose notable for its buoyant self-confidence and wit.

On one occasion, Duncan wrote an adroit article, "W.D. Howells at Washington"[14] mainly about the exhilarating experience of encountering the soiled boots of the acclaimed American novelist; she saw the boots on the landing of the fashionable Washington boarding house where Duncan herself was staying at the time, and the footwear (as well as Howells' appearance the next morning at breakfast) became the occasion for a bravura literary excursion by a woman whose imaginative resourcefulness never failed. A few years later, Duncan became internationally celebrated when she and another journalist, Lily Lewis, toured around the world to find material for humorous dispatches home; the experience was eventually published to acclaim in 1890 as *A Social Departure: How Orthodocia and I Went round the World by Ourselves.*

No name was better known at the turn of the twentieth century than that of Kathleen Blake (Kit) Coleman, who spent decades, from 1890-1911, writing an internationally-known Saturday column, "Woman's Kingdom," for the Toronto *Daily Mail* (later the *Mail and Empire*) as an editorialist, book and theater reviewer, social commentator, and much-sought-after advice-giver. Dubbed "Queen of Hearts" (by Jean Blewett, a rival *Globe* journalist turned admirer), she engaged readers with her tart yet empathetic, often extraordinarily detailed, answers on everything from courtship and marital problems to religious doubts and questions of moral conduct, as well as more mundane matters such as how to grow a thick mustache or care for perspiring feet. If she occasionally startled readers with her brusqueness and willingness to tackle taboo subjects such as domestic abuse and abortion, she also enthralled them with her evident commitment to readers. "Never mind his telling you that if you do not marry him his life will be ruined. Better he should ruin one life than two,"[15] was a typical brief zinger.

Coleman also expressed moderate but assertive views on the much-canvassed Woman Question. Responding to one inquirer, she expressed faith in the gradual evolution of women's social position: "I do not care about the platform, or woman's rights, or that kind of thing, but I believe women have as much intelligence as men, and that as civilization increases, the women are gradually and naturally coming to the fore."[16] On another occasion, she was skeptical about the rhetoric of equality, telling her correspondent that "The new woman movement—a fine one in moderation—has overshot the mark in the vain effort to equalize the sexes; the chief charm of which is that they never can be equalized."[17] When the paper offered her the chance to travel, Kit documented journeys to California, Jamaica, and London in lively accounts that included some then-popular stunt journalism, in which Kit disguised herself as a man to walk the slums of London. Ultimately, she established her fame as the first woman war correspondent when she was sent to Cuba to cover the Spanish American War of 1898. Though fiercely protective of her privacy and not averse to scolding importunate readers who asked for personal details, Kit's compassionate wisdom and the glimpses she offered of a self who suffered and understood gave piquancy and authenticity to all that she wrote.

Some newspaper writers, such as the *Sunday World's* feisty Flora McDonald Denison (leader of the Canadian Suffrage Association from 1911-1914), chose a more defiantly partisan perspective, explaining in an early column, "To the questions of an interested admirer, 'Are you a socialist, a Christian, a spiritualist, a freethinker, an Ibsenite,' I would simply reply: 'I am a suffragist.'"[18] Unabashed in her support for the militant British suffragettes in their nationwide bombing and arson campaigns, Toronto-based Denison rhapsodized about the gloriously compassionate and crime-free new world that would come into being when feminist women held power. For Denison, the suffragettes were holy warriors who in their willingness to go to prison for their lawbreaking were "displaying more heroism than was ever displayed in any war that was ever waged."[19] She expressed deep admiration for suffragette leader Emmeline Pankhurst, "a woman willing to give her freedom or her life for the sake of principle"[20] and reported with breathless admiration of a former imprisoned hunger-striker who, when a jug of milk was brought to her in her cell, reportedly "took up the jug in her hands and then [...] rose in all her fine heroism, put it down, and was not tempted again."[21] Denison's only expressed disappointment was in the lack of radical activism in Canada; she admitted, tellingly, that "Possibly the worst thing about the movement here is that there is no opposition."[22]

Poet and travelling performer E. Pauline Johnson, or Tekahionwake, chose racial conflict and potential reconciliation as the primary themes of her writing and activism, exploring Indigenous and Euro-Canadian relations in the late nineteenth century. Daughter of a Quaker mother and Mohawk father who had grown up on the Six Nations Reserve in southern Ontario, Johnson embodied in her literary style and mixed-race heritage the complex loyalties that she sought to reconcile. She became the most popular travelling performer in turn-of-the-century Canada. From her debut at the age of thirty in 1892 until she retired in 1908, Johnson toured North America to promote respect for Indigenous peoples mainly through recitations of her verse; but she also relied upon the erotic thrill evoked by her romantic costume, a buckskin outfit she purchased through the Hudson's Bay Company and embellished with a fur pelt on one sleeve, a bear-claw necklace, and a Sioux scalp. Some of her most popular performance pieces were angry denunciations of injustice, such as "A Cry from an Indian Wife" (1885) about the Northwest Rebellion, and "The Cattle Thief" (1894) about starvation and land loss on the prairies. Such poems, targeting the "greed of white men's hands"[23] and exhorting whites to "give back our land and our country"[24] were often singled out by reviewers as some of her most discomfiting political challenges; her message about indigenous rights was taken seriously by many in her audience.

Canada primed for the political reception of women

The success of Canadian women as journalists, public speakers, and social commentators suggests that both men and women were willing to turn to them for both practical advice and visions of social flourishing. This willingness to take women seriously was nowhere more clearly illustrated than in the political sphere, where a number of women not only made significant contributions in the early twentieth century but also attracted national and international admiration.

Nellie L. McClung, raised on a homestead farm in Manitoba, became Canada's best known social reformer and politician. As a writer and political campaigner, she used her attractive personality and eloquence to demand a leading role for women in national affairs. Newspapers reported her words in detail when she campaigned, in the late spring of 1914, on behalf of the Manitoba Liberal Party, which had officially declared itself in favor of woman suffrage. McClung spoke at close to one hundred venues, winning converts to the feminist cause through her vivid analogies, home-spun aphorisms, droll mimicry, and ability to joust effectively with hecklers. She drew on a deep well of belief in female moral superiority in her arguments, promising her audiences that when women ruled the world, "human life would be held dearer [...] than it is now."[25] "Men make wounds," she quipped, "and women bind them up."[26]

A good deal of the power of McClung's formulations came from the fact that she did not contest widely held associations between women and the home, but cleverly extended the association so that the home came to encompass the entire sphere of human activity, which she alleged was in dire need of a good "clean-up": "Women have cleaned up things since time began," she pledged, "and if women ever get into politics there will be a cleaning-out of pigeon-holes and forgotten corners, on which the dust of years has fallen, and the sound of the political carpet-beater will be heard in the land."[27]

No one could doubt the paradigm-shifting import of McClung's jubilant assertion of superior female competence, and her positive reception proved her appeal. Ultimately, McClung was elected as a member of the Alberta legislature, serving for the Liberal Party (though often voting with the United Farmers of Alberta government) from 1921-26. A few years later, she made history again when, as part of the Famous Five, she petitioned the British Privy Council on the question of whether women were qualified to serve in the Canadian senate. The other women who added their names to the appeal had similar achievements and public recognition: Louise McKinney had been the first woman elected to the Legislative Assembly of Alberta. Henrietta Muir Edwards was expert in law, and had joined forces with Lady Ishbel Aberdeen to establish the Victorian Order of Nurses and the National Council of Women of Canada. Irene Parlby was a long-serving MLA in Alberta and the first Canadian woman to be appointed to a cabinet position. Emily Murphy was Canada's first female magistrate.

Their case, which became known as the Persons Case, is sometimes falsely invoked to suggest that there was some doubt in the late 1920s as to whether women actually were persons. In fact, the question referred narrowly to whether the word "persons" in the British North America Act included women in its definition of those eligible for senate appointments, and it was answered in the affirmative, with the earlier ruling by the Canadian Supreme Court overturned. For McClung and her feminist allies, it was one in a triumphant sequence of affirmations.

It is possible to tell the story of nineteenth- and early-twentieth-century Canadian women as one of struggle for rights in a male-dominated society. But responsible scholars and the women themselves attest that the struggle, where it existed, was a relatively short one. Over the past one hundred fifty years, women in Canada have had most of the same opportunities for self-determination and self-expression as their brothers. Women worked hard and were rewarded for it: few of them saw men as their adversaries, and the vast majority of men were sympathetic to women's desires for equal opportunities. In order to be fair to the past, we should acknowledge the many firsts of Canadian women and the many men who supported them in their bold ventures.

CHAPTER 13

The British colonial achievement and its deniers

C.P. Champion

The Mounted Police have protected us as the feathers of the bird protect it from the frosts of winter.
—CHIEF CROWFOOT on securing Treaty 7 for his people, 1877

The Gandhis and the De Valeras would have long since entered heaven had they been born in one of the French colonies.
—HO CHI MINH on the British Empire, 1922

When Steven Spielberg's anti-slavery epic *Amistad* was released in 1997, I saw it in the World Exchange Plaza in downtown Ottawa (long since closed). It was not bad, but what I remember most was the reaction of a good-looking couple in their early thirties in the row in front of me, perhaps Somali or Ethiopian, during a climactic scene when frigates of the Royal Navy's West Africa Squadron blasted a Spanish slave post onshore at Sierra Leone. Enforcing Britain's 1807 *Slave Trade Act* across the Atlantic World, the Royal Navy and Royal Marines freed 150,000 Africans at the cost of 17,000 British servicemen's lives.[1] But as the frigates' shells sang and the stone and mortar of Lomboko tumbled into the sea, the nice couple in front looked at each other sceptically. He said, "Yeah, right!" and she smiled back. More bemused than outraged, they must have thought Hollywood was up to its usual tricks. More likely, like almost everyone else, they believed that colonialism could only ever be an unmitigated evil, and all colonial powers equally terrible.

Scepticism is perhaps well-advised for the historical moviegoer. Any representation of the past is liable to distortion, accidental or deliberate.

But it is typical for such misrepresentations to project modern usages and mores onto historical figures. Kevin Costner's *Dances with Wolves* is absurd, demonizing the Pawnee and ennobling the Sioux.[2] The pro-IRA film *In the Name of the Father* tells "so many lies that it makes the central proposition of a miscarriage of justice questionable."[3] And any audience that can watch *The Woman King* (I cannot) will refuse to believe that the British Empire, thalassocracy of the long 19th century, whose builders and planters had used slave labour (like every empire since the Kings of Sumer and Akkad), could have developed within itself an abolitionist conscience no previous empire ever exhibited, and embraced a multi-ethnic movement to end the trade. That the same colonial power would then expend military resources and manpower to implement its anti-slavery policy must be even harder to believe. Yet that is what the British did. Even if the academic debate continues today around the economic and political motives behind it, there can be no doubt of Britain's early and decisive role in ending slavery and the transatlantic slave trade.[4]

The abolition movement stands out in world history because the persistent horrors of slavery, including sexual slavery, were ubiquitous from the dawn of time into the 20th century. The Ottoman Turks bought and sold captive women shamelessly, including even aristocratic girls kidnapped from Europe, for their harems and the Imperial Seraglio,[5] and made sex slaves of Armenian genocide survivors as recently as 1915.[6] Of course this has occurred in the 21st century too. It is an uncomfortable thought that slavery and slaving have been near-universal practice at one time or another on every continent. Slavery, albeit with cultural variations, is the historical norm.

Abolition, on the other hand, is an aberration that originated in the Anglosphere and which, had it not, showed few signs of appearing anywhere else. Even Marxist historians do not deny this fact, though many have belittled the religious and humane motives for abolition to insist instead that slavery was abolished for economic reasons such as the decline of profit.[7] It irks progressives terribly that the heroes of anti-slavery, champions of freedom and natural rights, were 18th century small-c conservatives: liberals, Whigs, Tories, Baptists, and evangelical Christians like William Wilberforce, who is quite deservedly lionized in another good film, *Amazing Grace*.

Wilberforce was but a schoolboy when in 1772 the Chief Justice of the King's Bench, Lord Mansfield, ruled slavery "odious" and illegal in

England.[8] By the 1780s, having grown into a fashionable rake, Wilberforce was elected to Parliament, underwent an evangelical conversion, and joined the movement to abolish the trade and reform the morals of his nation.

The abolitionists of 1807 were part of a worldwide movement across the English-speaking diaspora. Upper Canada had abolished slave importation in 1793, as had every former British colony in the Northern United States shortly after declaring Independence in 1776, while most moved quickly to abolish slavery entirely. The impetus in Upper Canada came from the Colony's first Lieutenant-Governor, the Eton-educated High Church Anglican, freemason, and veteran of the Revolutionary War, Colonel John Graves Simcoe.

Biographical history and historical facts are today rejected by education experts seeding our collective doom in pursuit of their social justice utopia. People seem to believe that it will be possible to build a brighter, more equitable future if we just treat history with contempt. That is because, as G.K. Chesterton observed, "all feeble spirits naturally live in the future, because it is featureless; it is a soft job; you can make it what you like. The next age is blank, and I can paint it freely with my favourite colour." By contrast, he wrote, "It requires real courage to face the past, because the past is full of facts which cannot be got over; of men certainly wiser than we and of things done which we could not do."[9]

Centre-left governments appear to be content to let the cultural forest fires burn, sometimes piling on the fuel. On the other hand, conservatives lack the courage and strategic and tactical agility to resist. When I briefly assisted the Alberta government in assembling knowledge-based elementary social studies curricula in 2021, their communications experts refused to defend it, saying, Reaganesquely, "we don't negotiate with the terrorists." By the latter they meant egregious left-wing experts and their CBC chorus. But the correct metaphor for the tenured charlatans of Gramscian unwisdom is not terrorists but agents of Soviet *maskirovka* and active measures. Alberta's spin-doctors misjudged their enemy. To confront the Soviet-style deception, lies, negative history, and character assassination emanating from the vicious "woke" activists who have infected parts of the Canadian Left, the only method that could possibly succeed would have been an overwhelming proactive factual information campaign to promote understanding and knowledge of the good and great foundations of our society, using every instrument available. But they refused. Hence their feckless and ignominious failure.

To return to abolition history, it is a stumbling block to the liberal-left because it contradicts their ambition to impose a dreary, divisive, negative hegemonic narrative.[a] They deploy destructive scare-words ("racism," "settler colonialism," "white supremacism," *ad nauseam*) to obviate the need to confront inconvenient complexity and basic facts, and the fundamental goodness and greatness of Western Civilization. Their scare-words are an easy tool to demonize anyone who questions their dogmas, let alone commends the extraordinary accomplishments of Europe and even the liberal Enlightenment.[b] And, possibly without realizing it, they commit one of the most fundamental intellectual errors: they fail to draw distinctions between different sorts of things—in this case, they fail to distinguish between progressive and regressive expressions of imperialism.

Progressive and regressive imperialism

British colonialism should be differentiated from its rivals as a progressive species. As the sociologist Lewis S. Feuer sought to demonstrate in his study, *Imperialism and the Anti-Imperialist Mind*, British colonialism stands in contrast to the regressive systems of Mongolia or Spain and the more recent Communist imperialism.[10] Most regressive colonialisms were based on conquest and brutal exploitation, while the British Empire was assembled to some extent by force and for profit, but also by consent and mutual arrangement with local rulers and, as J.R. Seeley famously put it, "in a fit of absence of mind."[11] By the second half of the 19th century the British Empire was already emerging as the free association of states that was to be the British Commonwealth of Nations. That is why Canada's longest-serving prime minister, W.L. Mackenzie King, distanced himself from rabid anti-imperialists, "which I am not," he wrote: "I believe in the larger whole, with complete independence of the parts united by cooperation

a) On the politically "useful" past, though from a liberal perspective, see J.H. Plumb, *The Death of the Past*. Palgrave Macmillan UK, 1989.

b) Dr. Christopher Shannon critiques the Enlightenment from a Roman Catholic viewpoint in *The Catholic World's* "Rethinking the Enlightenment from Within the Catholic Intellectual Traditions" (2021), but progressives would surely dismiss his perspective, stemming from such an "oppressive" institution <bit.ly/3U5fVw5>.

in all common ends."[12] In King's lifetime that meant a Commonwealth "united" in defeating Nazi Germany and Imperial Japan and later, in resisting Communist expansion.

The noble struggle of anti-Communism included by any measure the most successful portion of the former Chinese Empire, the island colony of Hong Kong, because it remained outside the Communist orbit until 1997. It was literally a sea-swept "barren rock" when the British acquired it in 1841, so that two generations later the great leader of the Chinese Revolution, Dr. Sun Yat-Sen, "began to wonder how it was that... Englishmen could do such things as they had done, for example, with the barren rock of Hong Kong, within 70 or 80 years, while China, in 4,000 years, had no places like Hong Kong."[13] British colonialism meant order, peace, progress, and prosperity for the people of Hong Kong, who transformed the rock into one of the great cities of the world.

The regressive type of colonialism features prominently in Adam Hochschild's bestseller, *King Leopold's Ghost*, which describes the rape of the Congo under Belgian rule. The Belgian colony that inspired Conrad's *Heart of Darkness* was not the paradise of the King's dreams, "with gigantic trees, exotic animals" and "grateful inhabitants." Rather, the Congo was a place of "starving porters, raped hostages, emaciated rubber slaves, and severed hands."[14] Yet even Hochschild refuses to blame colonialism for Africa's problems today. With the sense of proportion that seems to be lacking in much academic discourse today, Hochschild wrote: "Much of history consists of peoples conquering or colonizing each other. Yet, from Ireland to South Korea, countries that were once ruthlessly colonized have nonetheless managed to build reasonably just, prosperous, and democratic societies."[15] Why, he asks, has most of Africa "not done so"?

The reasons, Hochschild suggests, "go far beyond the colonial heritage." He cites "the abysmal position of women" and "the violence, repression, and prejudices that go with that." He cites "deep seated cultural tolerance" in African societies "of strongmen" such as Mobutu, the long-time dictator of Zaire, successor state of the Belgian Congo. Notably, Hochschild cites the way "the long history of indigenous slavery is still deeply and disastrously woven into the African social fabric"—that is to say, African slave-trading that predated the advent of colonial empires. "Despite the thievery of Leopold and his successors," Hochschild concludes, "it is wrong to blame the problems of today's Africa entirely on colonialism."[16] Hochschild has a B.A. in history from Harvard, and was for many years a left-wing activist; he later taught journalism at the University of California Berkeley. But these passages from his bestseller, which might not survive the review process of an academic press today, are more reasonable and sane than anything written about the colonial experience by some of the more narrow-minded and politicized of our university teachers in recent times who either misconstrue or fear viewpoint diversity.

The horrors of the Congo are not only a reminder of this contrast between 19th century imperialisms but also, as Lewis Feuer pointed out, among other conquerors and empires of history: the Romans, Greeks, Venetians, Ottomans, Portuguese, Spanish, French, Chinese, Aztecs, Zulus, and so on. The goal of a true educator is to equip students to draw intelligent distinctions, but how many students or educators would be able to do that now? The tendency today instead is to foreground a feeble and oversimplified conception of "white settler colonialism" whose "inherent violence" is stated rather than proven, often without context or nuance.[c] In their preconceived ideas about deconstructing white "superiority" or "supremacism," "inherent violence," and "gender," they overlook fundamental facts such as the long history of conquests by (to use their ugly race language) "non-white" peoples or the captive-taking and slave-holding of non-European peoples.

African tribes acquired and bartered humans amongst each other, who could be "sold, killed or pawned," or sold to Arabs and Turks, a phenomenon covered in the 1977 study, *Slavery in Africa*,[17] but hardly anywhere else. There was slavery too, in China and among First Nations of North America, about which there are few books.[18] Some have pretended that slavery in non-European societies was benign because, for example, African and North American indigenous slavery involved assimilation, kinship, and adoption.[19] The elephant in that particular room is that "kinship and adoption" meant essentially cultural genocide for the captives, their own culture and identity being erased as they were forced to become members of the captor society.

---

c) Katie Pickles and Myra Rutherdale (2014), *Contact Zones: Aboriginal and Settler Women in Canada's Colonial Past* (UBC Press),; and Mark Anderson and Carmen Robertson (2011), *Seeing Red: A History of Natives in Canadian Newspapers* (University of Manitoba Press): 84-85. One can pick almost any academic publisher's catalogue and find examples *ad infinitum* of this dreary taxpayer-funded quasi-scholarship.

Try telling the Huron-Wendat that Iroquois adoption was benign; or the victims of the *Mfecane*, the forced migration and massacres of other Africans caused by Zulu imperialism; or Coast Salish victims of the Haida, put to death during raids or as captive chattels during the Potlatch.[20]

That sort of selective anti-scholarship has become endemic among our younger academics, who are incapable of assimilating conflicting and contradictory information. This makes their publications largely worthless but also in a nihilistic way destructive, a kind of intellectual sabotage, as anti-Western civilization (or perhaps even more accurately given the wide differences between empires, anti-*English* civilization) activists delude themselves that they, and the underdog of the month, will benefit from the destruction of their own society.

Unfortunately, while there are imperfections, I would suggest that there is no society in the world in which visible minorities and indigenous people would have been better off than in the North American societies of recent decades. That is because modern economic prosperity, which results from the gradual unshackling of capitalist potential first discovered in the Middle Ages and the Italian Renaissance,[21] is the only system in the world capable of generating the vast surplus wealth necessary for low-productivity sectors of society to siphon off their existence, either through private charitable actions or by means of confiscatory taxation by incontinent governments. Yet like the proletarian victims of Communist propaganda in the past, some people actually seem to believe that if you were to destroy our present patriarchal capital-based order, then present-day under-achievers would somehow emerge as top dog! Personally, I would not bet on that outcome.

That colonial empires contained elements of greed, "othering," "gendering," and so on, is in a sense banally true; obvious insofar as these elements are part of the human make-up and are and always have been present everywhere and presumably always will be. There can be no *tabula rasa*, no blank slate.[22] No one can pretend that Mongol, Zulu, Chinese, Haida, or Haudenosaunee aggression, conquest, and captivity were bereft of racial and sexual components. We should be surprised instead at the mitigation and comparative *absence* of these traits in history.

What is remarkable about the British Empire is not that injustices were present on many occasions, but that they were *opposed* vehemently, and often successfully, from within. Can anyone seriously maintain, if the

Europeans had never colonized North America or Africa, with Christianity in their wake, that indigenous peoples would have abolished the slaving practices that were endemic to their cultures? Or that the Aztecs would have ended their ritual cannibalism and human sacrifice? What of the Aztecs' neighbours, the Chimú, whose recently-excavated mass grave contained more than 140 child victims found with their hearts removed, having been sacrificed "to stop bad weather"?[23] It is at least unlikely that such practices would have been stopped without the influence of European colonialism. For if all colonialisms were the same and left only an evil legacy, the British and Canadian governments could not have marked the bicentenaries of the Abolition of the Slave Trade and Slavery in a manner at once solemn and festive, in a nuanced acknowledgement of past wrongdoing together with a celebration of the rectification of social ills, as the federal government of Stephen Harper did with Black History Month in 2007 and 2008.[d]

In contrast, the typical academic response to the Black Lives Matter fracas of 2020 was not to provide a disinterested analysis of how much racial prejudice really remains in Western societies or to propose useful avenues for improving the lives of citizens of African descent; it was not to weigh one set of ideas against another. It was to join in a Gadarene media and social media stampede linking a narrative of police excess with a bogeyman called "legacies of racism, slavery and colonialism today." It was as if abolition should not be celebrated at all because to do so undermines their grievance-based polemic.

Julia Gaffield, associate professor of history at Georgia State University, claimed that BLM had "put many on the defensive. White people [sic] are quick to tout stories of abolition, emphasizing the path bravely forged by imperial powers," and in so doing, "They diminish the realities and consequences of slavery and colonialism by demanding gratitude for ending the same violent systems they had previously implemented." But if there was evidence that anyone was trying to "diminish" slavery or "demand" gratitude for abolition, she did not provide it, nor did she acknowledge that in fact the United States fought a Civil War in which over 334,000 soldiers from the

---

d) Former Alberta Premier Jason Kenney, when federal Minister for Multiculturalism and Canadian Identity in 2007-08, twice dedicated Black History Month to abolition themes, proposed and curated by a talented Guyanese-Canadian official in the Department of Canadian Heritage, John Dennison (1947-2014), who later served as a Citizenship Judge in Ottawa.

Union, white and black, died from battle or disease while serving[e] so that black slaves could be emancipated.[24] President Lincoln's policy is of course another example of free citizens in an English-speaking society acting to isolate and remove an evil within.[25]

Indigenous refugees flee to Canada

The Empire on which the sun never set has never lacked detractors. In Canada the first British-bashers were, naturally, the French. Their dreams of empire were interrupted by the Hudson's Bay Company in 1670, as were French ambitions in India by England's East India Company (the world's first joint stock company, established in 1600, two years before the Dutch East India Company), and finally vanquished in the British-French-Indian War that ended with the French defeat at Plassey in 1757 and the surrender of Montreal in 1760. One recorded indigenous reaction, that of Minavavana, a Chippewa chief, showed little warmth for the conqueror: "Englishman, you know that the French king is our father.... It is you that have made war with this, our father."[26]

Later the tables turned. With the French subdued and the Americans claiming the frontier, more than one indigenous group realized there was a reasonable prospect of refuge and protection under the Crown—beginning in 1784 with Joseph Brant (Thayendanegea), who migrated north with his Mohawk people, who had lost their lands in New York State.[27] There are shades of meaning in the term "Loyalist,"[28] but the Six Nations broadly merited the full meaning, repeatedly volunteering to fight for the Empire in Upper Canada: in the War of 1812; in support of the Colonial Government in the upheavals of 1837-39; in the British Government's Nile Expedition in Egypt and Sudan (1884); and in the British Empire's forces in Flanders and France (1914-18), when the Six Nations of Grand River declared war separately on Kaiser Wilhelm II as Allies of King-Emperor George V but were obliged by Ottawa to enlist in the Canadian Expeditionary Force.[29] In short, the experience of the relative merits of British rule made some First Nations so loyal that they fought repeatedly on the Empire's behalf (and they were not doing it for the money).

---

e) The National Parks Service notes that total Union casualties were 642,427 and are divided accordingly: 110,100 killed in battle; 224,580 from diseases; 275,174 wounded in action; and 30,192 prisoners of war.

In the meantime, another band of Indian fugitives, Sitting Bull and his Sioux/Lakota, sought protection from the Crown north of the U.S. boundary in 1877 after they and their Cheyenne allies had wiped out Lt. Col. George A. Custer and the 7th U.S. Cavalry at Little Big Horn. They remained refugees in Canada until their return and surrender to the U.S. in 1881. Also, too often forgotten are the words of the Blackfoot/Siksika chief Crowfoot who, after securing Treaty 7 for his people, said in 1877: "If the police had not come to this country, where would we all be now? Bad men and whiskey were killing us so fast that very few of us would have been alive today. The Mounted Police have protected us as the feathers of the bird protect it from the frosts of winter."[30]

As it happens the Blackfoot-Kainai were themselves migrants from further east. As they pushed westward to occupy new territories, their long-standing economic and military rivals, the Upper Kootenay/Ktunaxa, were driven out of their own traditional grounds east of the Rockies to the Lower Kootenay lands between the Rockies and the Selkirks in the B.C. Interior. Such First Nations migrations are another awkward problem for progressives whose accepted narrative—based on a mystical faith in unreliable oral tradition—is that First Nations were present "from time immemorial" on whatever traditional and supposedly "unceded" lands they happened to occupy at the time of European contact.

In reality all humans have migrated from somewhere and many have displaced someone else, including aboriginals whose migrations and ethnic replacement of other aboriginals were prehistoric but have left archaeological evidence. Others, like the Iroquois/Haudenosaunee, fought and drove their indigenous enemies out of traditional lands, to which they then laid claim.[31] True scholars can only reject the prevailing charlatanism that constitutes oral history, indigenous knowledge, and "ways of knowing" that are essentially similar to folkloric and invented traditions.[32] Such real and imagined claims to land and wealth are limited only by the extent of the supine cooperation of those in authority who purport to recognize and validate such claims.[f]

---

f) See for example M. Bruchac, "Indigenous Knowledge and Traditional Knowledge," in C. Smith (ed.) (2014), *Encyclopedia of Global Archaeology*: 3814-3824, who praises "distinctive understandings, rooted in cultural experience, that guide relations among human, non-human, and other-than human beings in specific ecosystems… a system broadly identified as Indigenous knowledge, also called traditional knowledge or aboriginal knowledge."

As with humans everywhere, Canada's indigenous people were obliged to share the land, flora, and fauna they claimed for themselves. It is not well enough known that most aboriginal nations were ethnocentric and referred to their own groupings as "The People," "the good people," or "the good humans," and the like, privileging their own *Volk* over lesser mortals at the other end of the lake.[33] And if this or that land enjoyed by them until some of it was settled by French, British, and British-American colonists, consider what would have happened to indigenous peoples had Canada been reached first by Spanish Conquistadors.

Or consider what might have happened had the Chinese pursued world exploration and conquest following the Chinese-Muslim explorer Zheng He's 15th century voyages.[34] The Qing Dynasty dominated China by a series of brutal wars to quash local and regional rebellions and to crush minority peoples and tribes, some of whose languages and cultures were lost in various Manchu and Han onslaughts. There is nothing in Canadian history to compare with China's conquest of its frontiers, unless one perversely distorts indigenous smallpox epidemics (which killed many, but which were accidental) into something they were not. Alternatively had the Ottoman Turks managed to cross the Atlantic, outflanking the West Europeans, great numbers of Canadian indigenes might have ended up slaves of Suleiman the Magnificent, or become the targets of deliberate extermination like the Armenians. Consider again what the results would have been for Canada's less advanced indigenous peoples had the more advanced Aztecs possessed rudimentary seafaring technology, and used it to conquer and sacrifice their way up the St. Lawrence and into the Great Lakes, or into the Strait of Georgia and up the Fraser. One could speculate on the numbers of Canadian indigenous whose corpses would have been sent tumbling down the bloodied slopes of pyramids as priests clad in human skin held their victims' beating hearts aloft to the god Huitzilopochtli, their skulls incorporated into sacred towers.[35] Novelist David Malouf put the case somewhat differently in the case of Australia: "Aboriginal people have no reason to rejoice that it was a British style of invasion and displacement that destroyed their way of life and savagely reduced their numbers," Malouf opines, "but when we look at what happened to the Caribs, or in Guatemala and Brazil, one wonders if they would have had less to endure under an occupation [of Australia] by the Spanish or Portuguese."[36] Malouf's example sounds oddly like a reason to celebrate the "British style of invasion" rather than lament it.

In spite of all the overwhelming anti-colonial propaganda we hear now, Canadian indigenous were fortunate to be British subjects rather than subjects of the Sultan or the Middle Kingdom. When Captain James Cook arrived at Nootka Sound in 1778, local Nuu-chah-nulth warriors reported to their chief that the sailors must be "fish come alive into people" on "that floating thing out there." Did the sailors have fish-like faces or did the indigenes really believed they were shape-shifters? We will never know for sure. The Spanish had traded with the Nuu-chah-nulth only four years earlier.[37] If some of Cook's crew resembled fish, at least they were *British* fish, representing a land of open-minded men expanding new vistas of science and in the process of ending slavery worldwide.

There *were* in fact slave raiders who continually attacked the Nootka and other West Coast indigenous peoples including the Nanaimo (Snuneymuxw) and Cowichan (Quw'utsun) but the attackers were not Europeans but the notorious Haida. Indeed, "Slaves were a common outcome of [indigenous] Northwest Coast warfare," writes anthropologist Leland Donald.[38] In turn it was the Royal Navy and the Colonial Governor, the great Sir James Douglas, who in the 1860s phased out indigenous slavery gradually by "discouraging intertribal marauding."[39] There are eye-witness accounts by Snuneymuxw telling of Haida or Bella Coola raiders from the north still attempting to steal sheep (and children), for example, on early 20th-century Gabriola Island.[g]

For better or for worse, indigenous people in Canada ended up as "wards or children of the State," a complex legacy that is beyond the scope of this chapter. But overall, Canadian indigenous people fared better in the British Empire than they might have otherwise. That is not to say there were not egregious failures, but around the same time Canada was negotiating Treaties 8, 9, and 10, the German Empire was undertaking the extermination of the Herero people in South West Africa.[40]

The experience of Canadian indigenous people included Indian Residential Schools—for a minority of children. The schools have become a great national scapegoat but only one-third of indigenous children ever attended

g) I have notes of these accounts from the records of the Gabriola Museum and Archives, Gabriola Island, B.C.

one, and even then, for an average of only 4.5 years. Most students were from families that were already Christian, already went to church on Sundays, and wore modern clothing before their parents or guardians sent them to school. Chiefs and parents in many cases *asked* for schools, applied for their children's admission, and visited the schools regularly. Two-thirds of indigenous children either attended day schools or no school at all.[41] It is well-attested that some of the schools actually taught some Cree and Blackfoot as well as French or English. Alumni of residential schools and their descendants have been found to be more likely to *retain* indigenous languages.[42] Local white children sometimes attended residential schools because they were the best option. To date, there is no evidence that any child went missing or was murdered at any residential school. Any graves near the schools, sometimes located right on the reserve, in fact lie in cemeteries well-known but neglected by indigenous people themselves. A truly balanced and factual account of residential schooling has yet to be written. The Truth and Reconciliation Commission Report has been an intellectual, academic, and moral failure. It must be said that the self-flagellating Canadian response has been a degrading misadventure in virtue-signalling and national masochism.

The French experience

In Quebec, the traditional view that British rule after the Conquest of 1760 was in most respects benign has long been challenged. But some elements of it remain persuasive, so long as the standard of historical measurement is not absolute perfection. It is true that during the Seven Years' war Major-General James Wolfe permitted British troops to use indigenous methods of warfare, and to burn down many farmsteads, in pursuit of victory in 1759. The British after 1760 also cut off communications between the *Habitants* and their metropolises in France and Rome. There was much economic disruption including the displacement of commerce, as the old economy of New France was superseded. Still, much was left intact—French traders enjoyed seniority in the Beaver Club, for example, and British engineers rebuilt old Quebec and continued to restore it in the 19th century. It was Frederick Temple Blackwood, Lord Dufferin, from 1872 to 1878 one of the best Governors General of Canada, who insisted that the city's walls, gates, and other fortifications be preserved,[43] and they are what visitors see today.

Also left intact were the French language and a broad freedom of Roman Catholic religion for both French and Indian subjects, despite the contemporary English conviction that Popery was the enemy of liberty. Seigneurial landholding, civil law, local and autonomous religious institutions, and a vibrant town and village culture and way of life all survived and flourished. Indeed in Quebec, the British were more than tolerant of their subjects' differences. If someone had been there to "wake up Montcalm and tell him the English were coming," as Jean Chrétien lamented in one of his memoirs, it is arguable that French inhabitants of Quebec would not be as free, as prosperous, or even as numerous as they are today.[44]

Why not? Is it not likely that a triumphant France, had the Revolution of 1789 still ensued, would have put the Québecois through the horrors of the Terror, with New France resembling the Vendée? Instead, as we know from history, in the Province of Quebec under British rule a new, more political and dynamic francophone society was born. Newspapers appeared for the first time in the 1760s, and the *Quebec Gazette* and *Gazette de Montréal* began discussing emerging ideas of liberty in both French and English.[45] The first synagogue opened in Montreal in 1760, where Jews previously had no standing because the French authorities permitted only Roman Catholics to enter the Colony.

It is true that the "loyalty" of the populace was by no means dependable, as Guy Carleton lamented. In turn their political awakening would take time, but members of the clergy, seigneurs, and military officers (French and Canadian-born) became consultants in the Governor's circle. Accommodation of the French majority was codified in the *Quebec Act* of 1774, which the British Parliament passed to secure a wide degree of religious liberty for the French and Indian Catholics. Clearly the *Act* stemmed from Machiavellian motives: the preservation of order in the Province and a certain subornment of the clergy, militia, and landowning element to the Crown, with the far-fetched hope of eventually converting the *Canadiens* to Protestantism and Enlightenment by precept and example, but it was not envisioned that the French would become more British through any use of force.[46]

Thus as the historian A.P. Thornton described it, imperialists of the late 19th century, by which time many more thousands of square miles and millions of subject peoples had been added to the pink portions of the map, could assume a noble vocation:

> Maintaining the *pax Britannica* was maintaining also civilized conditions among a fifth of the human race. But true imperialism involved something more than this task of maintenance. It was not by what it took away, but by what it gave—not by depriving alien races of their own character, language, and traditions, but by ensuring them that the retention of all these things, and at the same time opening new vistas of culture and advancement—that Imperialism sought and should always seek to win these races to itself.[47]

The original multiculturalists: British Quebec

If historians of pluralism and accommodation are in search of a founding charter for multiculturalism, they may have it in Guy Carleton's 18th century *Quebec Act*. This British legislation "marked a moment when truly imperial subjecthood was imagined and realized" for non-Protestants, as "a subjecthood that could accommodate the many peoples and the many laws of the British Empire," as one historian of the "bonds of belonging" in the British Empire, Hannah Weiss Muller, put it.[48] When the first elected assemblies in Upper and Lower Canada were convened in 1792, French Canadian participants were delighted to discover a uniquely English creation, the "Loyal Opposition," a concept whereby defeated parties and their supporters are not completely vanquished and shut out of the political process. The French and English-speaking elected members in Lower Canada expressed their "very high satisfaction" with their new assembly, as Michel Ducharme has shown, praising the British system which, they wrote, "gives to [England] so decided a superiority and advantage over other nations."[49]

Thus began the political tutelage of the Québecois. There had been no parties or elections in New France nor were any on the horizon—though there were town and parish meetings and grassroots consultations with the local *Capitaine de milice*.[50] Once given British liberty, Lower Canadians developed a movement for reform in the early 1800s. Liberal papers like *Quebec Mercury* opened in 1805 followed by *Le Canadien* in 1806. Press freedom as yet remained imperfect: Sir James Craig shut down *Le Canadien* in 1810 and jailed its owner over a poem recommending his overthrow. Nevertheless, criticism, tension, and advocacy over responsible government continued.

The more radical elements of Lower Canadian nationalism finally exploded, having been demagogued by Papineau and his English-speaking peers, in the Rebellions of 1837-38 in some areas roughly suppressed by Sir John Colborne. The bombardment and village-burning of the "*Vieux brûlot*" ("the old firebrand") have duly entered the anti-British annals. Even so, mainstream French Canadian nationalism included pro-British opinion, not least because after restoring order the British sped up overdue reforms and granted responsible government. "Our Loyalty is not one of speculation, of pounds, shillings, and pence," said doctor and 1812 war veteran Sir Étienne-Paschal Taché, a future Father of Confederation, in the 1840s. "We do not carry it on our lips, we do not make a traffic of it. But we are in our habits, by our laws, and by our religion ... monarchists and conservatives." And Taché added that, "the last cannon which is shot on this continent in defence of Great Britain will be fired by the hand of a French Canadian." Nationalists to the left of Taché called this treasonous, but Taché's remarks have been described as "an excellent expression of French-Canadian nationalism of the time, which fought the dominance of the British in America without questioning the colonial tie."[51]

It was Taché's son, Eugène-Étienne, who coined Quebec's motto, "Je me souviens." To this the composer and teacher, Eugène Gagnon, added the words: "*né dans les lys, je grandis dans les roses*" ("born among lilies, I grew up among roses"), which led to an entwining of French lilies, English roses, and French Canadian maple leaves in the architecture of the provincial assembly, today's National Assembly of Quebec.[52] (Incidentally the façade of the main Assembly building has one of the most admirably comprehensive and inclusive collections of historical statuary anywhere, illustrating the ecumenical nationalist spirit of the time.[53])

As Quebec nationalism narrowed and erupted again in the second half of the 20th century, this "French Canadian Loyalism" faded.[54] But it did so not in response to *British* repression but to a *Canadian* (which is to say, Ontario-dominated) government that was seen to be betraying the principles of federalism.[55] The British role in the Patriation story of the 1980s was to support the ancient rights of Provinces formed in the 1700s before a "confederated" Canada existed, meaning their right to be properly consulted in the constitutional revisions that Pierre E. Trudeau attempted to impose unilaterally and underhandedly in 1980-82.[56]

Comparative colonialisms—including Communist imperialism

The virtues and vices of Empires are relative things. Yet as the old school German Social Democrat Eduard Bernstein once wrote: "No nation has exercised in its colonies a sense of fairness, of live and let live, in such a degree as has the English."[57]

In India, the British government, which took over from the East India Company in 1858, set up the Indian National Congress, an embryo parliament, in 1885, with 73 mostly Hindu delegates representing all parts of India. Mohandas K. Gandhi became its leader in 1921, launching a campaign for *swaraj*, Indian self-rule. While Indian nationalists were divided over the best way to achieve independence and democracy, Gandhi raised the banner of civil disobedience, *satyagraha*, with non-violent protests like the Salt March (1930) and the Quit India movement (1942).

The Vietnamese nationalist-turned-Communist, Ho Chi Minh, was flabbergasted at what Gandhi and Irish statesman Eamon De Valera got away with in open opposition to British rule. In developing his own Viet Minh independence movement under Socialist and Soviet influences, Ho Chi Minh wrote that the French in their colonies were:

> [M]asters in the art of savage repression and the manufacture of loyalty made to measure. *The Gandhis and the De Valeras would have long since entered heaven had they been born in one of the French colonies.* Surrounded by all the refinements of courts martial and special courts, a native militant cannot educate his oppressed and ignorant brothers without the risk of falling into the clutches of his civilizers.[58] (Emphasis added.)

By contrast, some Indian nationalists praised the virtues of the Raj. Even if "educated and thoughtful Indians" resented British control, wrote Nirad Chaudhuri, "intellectually not one of them denied that British rule had rescued India from anarchy and brought peace and prosperity to the Indian people."[59] Chaudhuri was by origins an Untouchable, from the lowest caste in the Hindu system, which might explain why he was so struck by the benign aspects of a relatively progressive Empire on a sub-continent whose pre-British cultures harboured so much inequality and injustice. In his autobiography, which he dedicated "to the British Empire," Chaudhuri recorded that the Raj "conferred subjecthood on us but withheld citizenship," a limitation "to which yet every one of us threw out the challenge: '*Civis Britannicus Sum*' because all that was good and living within us was made, shaped, and quickened by the same British rule."[60] If that distinction is too subtle for today's humanities professors, they may be less intellectually astute than a 19th century Untouchable. Simply put, some of the most disadvantaged Indian subjects were proud to call themselves "British citizens."

The cruellest, most destructive empires in modern times were Hitler's Third Reich (1933-1945) and, on a greater scale, the Communist empires of the U.S.S.R. (1917-1989) and the People's Republic of China (1949-present), plus assorted client states like North Korea, Vietnam, Cambodia, and Cuba. These regimes made the 20th century "the Age of the 'G'—guillotines, genocide, gaols, gallows, gas chambers and Gulags," wrote the great Austrian Catholic reactionary, Erik von Kuehnelt-Leddihn, a perceptive critic of the horrors of Leftism.[61] The origin of Communist evil lies in utopian ideology, with the self-entitlement of a party vanguard to obtain power and impose a perfectly just and equitable society on the masses by any means necessary. Those means typically require stifling, and even murdering, dissident voices. Never in human history were more people persecuted, deprived of natural rights, starved, tortured, gassed, shot, or worked to death than by Party-controlled totalitarian atheist regimes. The societies repressed by the Communist empires are still struggling today to overcome their brutal legacies, including, at the time of writing, the unresolved fate of Ukraine.

By the standard of these regimes, it is difficult to understand the degree of condemnation that has been heaped on the colonial empires whose closing phase was marked by a valiant resistance to the spread of Communism in Asia and Africa, a case where colonialism was the lesser evil to Marxism-Leninism. But as repeatedly mentioned above, history has seen many examples of conquering empires and squalid chiefdoms whose conquests were characterized by shocking brutality and annihilation of people without remorse and matched only by Communism itself. For people sympathetic to left-wing ideas to single out Britain for condemnation is hypocrisy and ignores Britain's progressive role in the history of the modern world.

What other empire, when its strength dwindled, left behind a free, organic association of states like the British Empire-Commonwealth over which the late Queen Elizabeth II elegantly presided? Known today as the Commonwealth of Nations, it is an entirely voluntary organization of countries that have chosen to maintain British ties long after the tide of Empire subsided. Some members that left the Commonwealth even came back: South Africa quit the Commonwealth in 1961 but re-joined in 1994. Pakistan quit in 1972 but re-joined in 1979. Mozambique joined the Commonwealth in 1995 and Rwanda in 2009 though neither had been a British colony; nor had Togo and Gabon, which joined in 2022. This is not to overlook the important Francophonie Organization, an imitator of the Commonwealth cobbled together much later, in 1970, whose worldwide membership presents a similar case: an allegiance to French language and culture that transcends differences over the past that Communists for decades sought to aggravate in the hope of dividing people and sowing enmity.

More than half the former British colonies and protectorates are republics that remain members of the Commonwealth headed by the British Monarch. That fact lends a totally absurd and anachronistic, as well as formulaic, air to contrived headlines at outlets like *The Guardian* in September 2022 such as "Queen's death intensifies criticism of British Empire's violent atrocities."[62] It is an ugly tribute to British liberty that such things can be said in the heart of the former Empire.

One of the strangest recent manifestations of British-bashing was the tendency to attack the Queen, immediately after she died, as the symbol of an Empire over which she herself had scarcely ruled. Elizabeth II came to the throne in 1952. By the mid-1960s, Britain had let go of the remnants of the white-ruled Empire. India and Pakistan were already long gone (1947). Independent states were born in Ghana and Malaysia (1957), Nigeria (1960), Jamaica (1962), Guyana (1966), and on the list goes; almost all via peaceful transfers of power. Never before in history has power been handed over by an empire so stably. The million dead in India at Independence were the result of conceding to Muslim nationalists that the British consolidation of a unified Indian state could be split up to give birth to East and West Pakistan, much to the anger of critics like Raj civil servant Penderel Moon, who excoriated partition in his classic account, *Divide and Quit*.[63] If anything, decolonization was done more quickly in some places than it should have been, but successive Labour and Tory governments were both intellectually, morally, and militarily weak and influenced to too great an extent by Socialism and its attendant failure of moral integrity.[64]

The fashionable attack on late British colonial policy is typified by the attempt of Harvard's Caroline Elkins to equate the British and native Kenyans' repression of the terrorist Mau Mau organization with the Soviet Gulag,[65] a ludicrous misapprehension. Mau Mau was not a people's movement for justice but a terrorist organization whose victory would have been worse than any British-Kenyan repression to stop them, just as in the Malayan Emergency of 1948-60 British Commonwealth forces fought back and defeated a Communist takeover. "Mau Mau has spoiled the country," said the first President of independent Kenya, Jomo Kenyatta, "Let Mau Mau perish forever. All people should search for Mau Mau and kill it."[66]

Modern Malaysia is a majority-Muslim elective monarchy which the British helped set up and remains a member of the Commonwealth. Recently the island province of Penang rejected calls to rename its capital of 200 years, George Town, named after King George III, which a professor at the International Islamic University of Malaysia had criticized as "a legacy of British colonialism." Penang legislators rebuffed the silly professor because, they said, "George Town is famous world over and everyone already knows and accepts the name."[67] The latter is true of many things in Canada too, and yet here, elected officials are too cowardly to resist anti-history activists who demand the erasure of illustrious *Canadian* leaders from streetscapes, let alone British ones.

Critics of Britain's empire ensnare themselves in a contradiction. They denounce the British legacy for various wrongs. They allude to excesses carried out, for example, by military authorities in India, Africa, or the Far East such as "massacres" in Hola, or Batang Kalin, or Jallianwallah Bagh. In the case of all, there were mitigating circumstances. By contrast, truly large-scale massacres which were ideologically-driven, and for which there are no defensible mitigating circumstances, were carried out by the Ottomans and the Soviets in the 20th century, and yet these atrocities go unmentioned. The contradiction is that where such historical events were concerned—massacre, famine, and the like—the British Empire was the least offender. People of every hue under British rule were less oppressed, less subject to arbitrary abuse and murder, more free, more prosperous, and more likely to live in a successful future state than people under any other 20th century regime and perhaps most empires in history. By contrast, India's greatest rival today in size and population, mainland China, was never directly ruled by Great Britain and is today lumbered with a corrupt and decrepit totalitarian Communist Party oligarchy.[68] Indian nationalists may have their criticisms but they can hardly deny that today they benefit from the world's largest Parliamentary and common law system, and a market economy that is one of the world's fastest-growing; much of this owing directly to the British legacy and what the free Indian people have done with it.

A recent example of the contradiction is William Dalrymple's "Empire" podcast, which presents old left-wing arguments and resentments as something new and, of course, humanely liberal (because liberals desperately need to believe they are the good guys in every encounter).[69] In the first episode, Dalrymple and his BBC co-host, Anita Anand, bitterly deplored the formation of the world's first "joint stock company," the future East India Company, and its depredations, claiming that India was a paradise before the 18th century British spoiled it. But as the English naval historian C. Northcote Parkinson, best known for Parkinson's Law (that "work expands to fill the time available"), wrote:

> It is futile to look back in anger at all the Company achieved.... [W]e are ourselves the product, steeped in a tradition which has fashioned our lives from the wearing of pajamas to the drinking of tea. We cannot turn our backs on a past which is also the present, on fathers who were so like ourselves.[70]

To quote an American historian who uses similar language, "To hate the British Empire is to hate ourselves."[71] Besides, it would seem that Dalrymple and Anand's real bugbear is capitalism itself, or as Anand sneeringly put it, those "nouveaux riches" who made money in the East India Company—another example of a contradiction since *nouveau riche* describes her own family, who sent Anand to a posh British public school which today would cost at least $20,000 Canadian dollars per year to attend.[h]

---

h) Bancroft's was founded in 1737 and charged £4,396 per term in 2012. At three terms per academic year, that would be at least $20,000 a year in Canadian dollars in 2022, cf. archived page from *Guide to Independent Schools* <http://bit.ly/3AHQkCl>.

There is something very fishy about all the caterwauling about racism and legacies of slavery and genocide, cultural appropriation and intergenerational trauma—especially when the slogans happen to coincide with calls for large amounts of cash. The same themes seem to be cropping up everywhere, whether with regard to slave history in the Anglo-American world or the various misfortunes of indigenous peoples in Canada and Australia. In each case there are calls for historical "reparations." Can it be a coincidence that the modern Left's catchphrases and demands for unearned and unwarranted compensation on false pretences are everywhere the same? On one level it is the old syllogism of the envious under-achiever: "That capitalist has money; I did nothing to earn that money; give me that money."

Fundamentally the History War that the contemporary Left inflicted on unsuspecting populations in the Western world is a replay, or extension, of the Cold War. Lenin's notion that imperialism was "the highest stage of capitalism" was supposed to signal the doom of free market economics, Parliamentary systems, and especially the British colonial achievement because it was the most successful at improving the lives of its subjects. The old order, just like today's free market model, was supposed to be replaced by the socialist Utopia—a dangerous dream that has soaked deep into the leftist mind.

What Lenin caricatured as "exploitation of oppressed nations" and "parasitism" by the "civilized world" (his use of the term "civilized" is, of course, ironic, just as it is when "woke" and/or left-wing academics use it today) echoes in the words of revolutionaries like Fidel Castro, who said "powerful nations... blackmail, extort, pressure, attack, and strangle small nations." That may be true, by and large, of some colonial powers and it was certainly true of what Lewis Feuer accurately called "Communist imperialism."[72] But it is not true, in the main, of the British. If Castro had ever headed a great empire one shudders to think of the added horrors he would have inflicted.[73] Even with limited means his troops committed atrocities in Angola, and propped up Ethiopia's Colonel Mengistu, whose "Red Terror" (his own term) starved at least 400,000 victims.[74]

Contemporary people too easily fall into what they assume is good progressive thinking but whose origin is actually Leninist dogma: namely that colonialism was a "moribund" phase of capitalist exploitation, the last-ditch attempt of the rich to cheat the poor and of the white to oppress the non-white. In reality, some empires—French, Spanish, Portuguese and others in the Middle East, Africa, and Asia in previous centuries—took a spoils approach, while others, like the British, progressively developed their colonies economically and politically. Ideological opportunists, reflexive activists and other advocates of a purely negative view of history currently have the upper hand. Governments at the federal and provincial levels have not been courageous or effective in the History War that has been foisted upon us. In many cases people have no idea there is an ideological war going on and are unwilling to do what is necessary to fight it.

There is today "a huge tide of scum rising," as British M.P. Alan Clark described the ambient vulgarity and class warfare of the 1990s.[75] If sensible and patriotic people are to resist the tide, then leaders must become better-informed and must seek to educate the public about the fraud and hollowness of hateful activists' simplistic but effective anti-historical themes. Modern education technocrats and their simpleton curricula must be called out, resisted, and defeated by using effective communications, rallying well-informed parents and teachers, and replacing poisonous ideas with rich, engaging, and high-quality knowledge-based curricula such as that promoted by E.D. Hirsch's Core Knowledge Foundation.[76] That is not to say Hirsch's is the only commendable approach, but it should not be the only approach that is excluded in a supposedly diverse society.

And so, for many, if not all, let the cheer be, "Rule Britannia!" Spielberg was right: British naval forces really did shell that slave post in Sierra Leone, and others like it. British officers supported abolishing the practice in India of burning widows alive on the funeral pyres of their deceased husbands, known as *suttee* or *sati*. And they passed the *Female Infanticide Prevention Act* in 1870 to criminalize the murder of baby girls by Indian parents who valued baby boys more highly (as, alas, many there still do today[77]). The list could go on. But to paraphrase the famous Monty Python scene in "The Life of Brian," apart from those and many other enlightened actions that make up the Empire's largely positive legacy today, we may well ask: "What have the British ever done for us?" [78]

PART III

Renewing Canada

CHAPTER 14

A new challenge for Canadians of any colour: Remixed racism

Jamil Jivani

The segregationists now face some hard alternatives. They can continue to seek or maintain segregated facilities. In this event, they must live with discord... Or finally, they can accept the principle of equality.
—MARTIN LUTHER KING JR.

For centuries, black Canadians have been part of inspiring political and social movements aimed at pushing Canada to live up to its ideals. When black men and women pressed for equality of opportunity, we challenged Canada to truly be a land where the rule of law reigns supreme and individuals are not defined by what they look like or where their parents come from. But today's "chattering classes"—academics, journalists, politicians, and increasingly, too many CEOs—do not encourage Canadians to recognize the success of previous generations of black Canadians who fought hard for a better life. Rather, they advance a worldview that suggests little has changed and that black victimhood has remained a constant throughout the decades, with blacks ostensibly held down by abstract ideas like "systemic racism" and "white privilege."

For a black Canadian to be accepted by those who advance this anti-history narrative often requires blacks to play the role of a long-suffering minority in need of a well-intentioned white liberal saviour. It means parroting their preferred political talking points and social values. Even where the majority of black people might disagree with elite liberal consensus, black men and women who seek acceptance in such circles will feel pressured to downplay genuine, diverse community perspectives in favour of a narrow range of "acceptable" opinions. Consequently, some of the most important issues in black communities tend to receive little attention because they are not a priority for those who believe racism can explain human success and failure, or who believe that government-as-parent is akin to real parenting.

The result is that pressing issues such as the role of fathers and family formation, the role of churches and faith, or the importance of wealth creation, educational attainment, the negative influence of popular culture, and the ripple effects of violent crime are mostly ignored in the analyses by academics and other elites who talk only to each other, not to most people in the black community. It is why black Canadians who want to genuinely help our communities often risk having our authenticity attacked by people who believe black men and women should only think and speak in one way. It is far easier to remove oneself from the public square than to be verbally assaulted by those who believe a black person's ideology should mirror the *Toronto Star* editorial page or the CBC newsroom. But the continued pursuit of justice, which black Canadians have contributed immensely to, requires perseverance.

The rise of remixed racism via "anti-racism"

Modern self-described anti-racism borrows from the racism of the past and reintroduces it to modern audiences with a new, *faux*-progressive style. It is increasingly obvious in government departments, media companies, school boards, universities, and corporations, all of which focus on race and whether one is "black enough" (or "enough" of some other identity). This trendy new phenomenon goes by many names: anti-racism, neo-racism, the elect, critical race theory, identity politics, wokeness. It is difficult to pin down a term that adequately describes precisely what is going on but I will propose one: remixed racism. Like a top forty single that samples a golden oldie, remixed racism changes the tempo, speeds up the chorus, and maybe even introduces a rapper to spit a hot sixteen bars. But in the end, remixes are always another variation of the same tune.

For example, Canada's federal government made remixed racism official policy at Global Affairs Canada (formerly the department of Foreign

Affairs) under the guise of anti-racism training. That is not the only federal government department engaged in modern-day racial profiling. Workshop materials obtained by the *Toronto Sun* in 2021 showed that federal government officials are taught that perfectionism, feeling a sense of urgency about some matter or task, individualism, fealty to the written word, and objectivity are all characteristics of white supremacist culture.[1] In other words, the federal government uses taxpayer dollars to teach that race and culture are one in the same, and certain cultural ideas or useful practices associated with hard work, science, and democracy are incompatible with non-white cultures.

If the racism sounds familiar, it is because Social Darwinism was based on similar notions that some races were of a lower "intellectual standard" because of cultural differences. Government of Canada anti-racism training also reflects the paternalism found in colonial writings, such as British politician Thomas Macaulay's 1835 memo titled *Minute on Indian Education*. This memo argued that Indians were in need of white saviours because they were culturally incompatible with science, due to their "monstrous superstitions" and "false history, false astronomy, false medicine."[2]

It takes little imagination to grasp what might happen when Global Affairs Canada and its diplomats and officials carry this paternalistic attitude with them overseas; negative ramifications will inevitably follow the labelling of core civil rights and useful liberal democratic practices as inherently racist. Picture Canadian representatives telling African and Asian nations that the foundational idea underlying civil rights and individualism is white supremacy. Or imagine Canada's trading partners being informed that they might be white supremacists if they demonstrate a fondness for objective reasoning. And what might the world's Christians, Muslims, and Jews who believe in holy scriptures think of the government of Canada labelling worship of the written word as "white"?

We have also seen what remixed racism does to domestic policy-making. In early 2021, the federal government announced a program entitled "Support for Black Canadian Communities Initiative." However, after the program was announced, federal officials sent an email rejecting hundreds of organizations that applied for funding. Their email informed some black community leaders that their organizations were not black enough to qualify. Specifically, the initiative disqualified some black groups on the grounds that they were not satisfactorily "led and governed by people who self-identify as Black." According to the *Toronto Star*, the pool of rejected applicants includes Operation Black Vote, which is operated by a team of black Canadians and also supports the election of black people.[3]

Department officials retracted the initial rejection letter a day later, but community leaders were not persuaded by a second letter's alternative explanation that applications were rejected because of missing information. Operation Black Vote's chair, Velma Morgan, told the Canadian Press, "As if we're incompetent or foolish and we're going to believe the second email over the original email."[4] The federal minister of Family, Children and Social Development, Ahmed Hussen, was reportedly "furious" about the initial rejection letter. And for good reason. The letter revealed that federal civil servants were unfamiliar with the black community groups being evaluated for grant opportunities. More importantly, having government officials measure "blackness" feels like a throwback to colonialism. The dehumanizing act of questioning a black person's blackness is unfortunately far too common. No one should be surprised that the individuals who received the rejection letter took offence. Amidst the controversy, a thoughtful observer might have asked: Was the federal government interested in having a measurable impact with public dollars? The rejection letter said nothing about selecting grant recipients based on who can best support black youth and families. Neither Employment and Social Development Canada, the department behind the program, nor its critics commented on grants going to black Canadians most in need. Instead, the focus in that controversy has been on the racial identity of leaders applying for funding.

Canada's struggle with remixed racism does not stop in Ottawa. The City of Hamilton brought us back to the "anti-miscegenation" era of pre-1967 United States with its 2021 decision to distribute COVID-19 vaccines in a manner that would divide families and households by race, as when the city offered vaccine appointments to residents in five postal code areas, but specified that only "Black and other racialized populations/people of colour ages 18+" could receive the vaccine (i.e., no white people).[5] These municipal officials showed absolutely no concern for what their approach would mean for multi-racial families that include white people living in the same home with people of colour. Hamilton's disregard for such families is a remix of Jim Crow-era hostility toward multi-racial families.

Remixed racism in the media

Too many in the media and in corporations are also guilty of anti-Martin Luther King Jr. advocacy, i.e., treating people as different based on their skin colour as opposed to focusing on their character and competence. In the United States, consider how the *New Yorker* also got in on the remixing in the magazine's 2021 attack on Christianity. Quoting a sociologist from the University of Oklahoma, the *New Yorker* went so far as to argue that "the greatest ethnic dog whistle the right has ever come up with is 'Christian,' because it means 'people like us,' it means white."[6] Subordinating Christianity to racial politics is a familiar theme from the 1800s and prior. Conflating the Christian identity with white identity is something you would expect from colonial forces and slave owners but regardless of how the argument has been tried in the past, it has never been true. It harkens back to 20th century racism, but when you remix it for today's woke audiences, one of the world's largest magazines has no problem peddling prejudice.

Canadian media companies are also no strangers to remixed racism. This became obvious in 2020 when Canada's "progressive" journalists were exposed as evading their responsibility to cover stories that might cast doubt on their own judgment concerning the far-left. For years, organizations like the CBC, the *Toronto Star* and the *Globe and Mail* relied on a small, unrepresentative group of voices to speak on behalf of minority communities. As with the game of musical chairs where the losers are those who cannot find a chair when the music stops, the same few activists and academics appear in social justice-themed stories, parroting the same old talking points that list myriad problems but lack practical solutions while actual, useful voices are nowhere to be found in such news stories and opinion columns. Since the rise of social media activism against police brutality in the mid 2010s, these voices are increasingly and problematically chosen based on their Twitter clout. The news is still a business, after all, and those with large Twitter followings help drive traffic to stories they are featured in, which means more clicks and more advertising revenue for news outlets. A shift to social media-centred reporting accompanied the rise of wokeness in newsrooms, and the embrace of woke tenets, such as privilege, victimhood, and cancel culture.

Although 2020 was a unique year in some ways, nothing really changed with respect to how journalists used their power against people of colour. Led by newspaper and broadcast executives like Phillip Crawley (*Globe and Mail*), John Boynton (*Toronto Star*) and Brodie Fenlon (CBC News), journalists took the heightened interest in racism that year as a chance to double down on playing the role of factitious kingmakers. Unfortunately, minority communities generally lack the resources and platforms to push back.

But truth does prevail, eventually. By the end of 2020, the ethical and methodological flaws in media decision-making were exposed in a series of activist attacks on an upstanding Ontario judge who was deemed not "woke" enough. To understand the significance of the judge's ordeal, consider his background: Imagine you grew up seeing some of the harshest conditions in your city including public housing and poverty. Like many of your peers, you struggled in school, but a dream to attend university was realized thanks to God's grace, mom's love, hard work, and student loans. After exceeding all expectations to become a lawyer, you chose to represent clients in the neighbourhoods you once called home, eventually starting a criminal defence and human-rights law practice.

After such an improbable rise, consider how you would feel when given the opportunity to serve on the judiciary, the institution that adjudicates on matters of inequality with which you are intimately familiar. You bring your unique insights into the courtroom and you are an exemplary member of the judiciary. But because you are a highly regarded member of a beleaguered community, you feel compelled to do more. Everywhere you turn, you are reminded of the many problems in need of solutions: drive-by shootings that put parents and children in danger of stray bullets; failing schools that allow high-potential children to slip through the cracks; viral videos of police misconduct that erode trust between police and communities in need of ethical law enforcement. You are left to wonder if you should be a voice for change outside of the courtroom, too, and what exactly that entails.

This dilemma has been the life of Ontario Court Justice Donald McLeod. And there was no precedent that he could turn to for guidance. A unique trailblazer, Justice McLeod is a first of sorts: a black Canadian judge whose intellect and spirit for the downtrodden was forged on Toronto's toughest street corners. Moreover, he accepted that he did have a responsibility outside of the courtroom. In May 2016, after a Rexdale drive-by shooting killed Candice Rochelle Bobb, a pregnant black woman whose child soon after succumbed to his premature birth, Justice McLeod called for an emergency town-hall meeting to interrogate the many challenges that afflict low-income black families. In 2017, he launched the Federation of Black Canadians, which set out to advocate for solutions to social and economic challenges that disproportionately affect black communities across the country. However, by February 2018, the non-partisan federation was in a manufactured controversy due in part to its advocacy to federal government and Liberal party officials. In November 2018, Justice McLeod was forced to appear before the Ontario Judicial Council on allegations of impermissible advocacy and other misconduct. Although he successfully defended himself at that first disciplinary hearing, the judge was subsequently suspended for almost two years, as he was forced to face a second hearing starting in late 2020.

Justice McLeod's persecution was driven primarily by two entities. First, Twitter activists affiliated with Black Lives Matter's Toronto chapter targeted Justice McLeod because he did not share their Marxist approach to social change. Complaints heard by the Ontario Judicial Council cite statements from these Twitter activists, who were hell-bent on proving that a Marxist revolution is necessary for the suffering of impoverished black communities to cease. Their myopic worldview threatened the Justice McLeods of the world: individuals who are beloved and respected by ordinary black people for remembering where they came from after achieving improbable success. And far too many corporate media outlets helped undermine black communities by promoting the rantings of Twitter activists whose sentiments are not widely shared. Second, the complaints against Justice McLeod needlessly politicized his behaviour and interactions as a black man in his community. For instance, he was accused of providing improper legal advice because he shared his personal opinion on how a pair of black youth should respond to a racial profiling incident at Parliament Hill in 2019. Another complaint argued that the judge engaged in lobbying because he delivered a speech at a community event where politicians were present.

In late 2020, the Ontario Judicial Council heard this and other sworn testimony in the disciplinary hearing against McLeod. That testimony made clear the authoritarian impulses from individuals affiliated with Black Lives Matter's Toronto chapter and others who targeted Justice McLeod because he did not share their far-left politics. According to testimony, these imitation-authoritarians secretly recorded at least one conversation with the judge and shared it without his knowledge; asked the judge to set up a meeting and then used evidence of that meeting to conspire against him; and drove a wedge between Justice McLeod and young members of his community by misrepresenting his mentorship as legal advice or intimidation. Also, activists and academics affiliated with Black Lives Matter's Toronto chapter targeted Justice Macleod because he dared advocate for black communities without bowing to the regressive political agenda promoted by the likes of BLM. This led to accusations that his work with community organizations such as the Federation of Black Canadians, which he helped found, prevented him from being an impartial arbiter. BLM-affiliated activists and academics also accused him of lying about his work serving black communities, which led to accusations of perjury based on his statements in a previous disciplinary hearing. As to the consequences of such rhetorical attacks, on the final day of testimony before the disciplinary hearing recessed for Christmas 2020, the Ontario Judicial Council heard from a black Muslim community leader who was part of Justice McLeod's volunteer organization. With tears running down her cheeks, this highly-regarded woman recounted the harassment she received from social media activists who targeted Justice McLeod. The activists tried to sabotage her career, too, by sending letters to her employer and even posting her personal information online. At one point, she feared for her safety and was concerned about living alone.

The saboteurs who drove this black Muslim community leader to tears are the same far-left voices amplified by reporters, editors, and columnists. Consider the backgrounds of the individuals in the troubling group that targeted Justice McLeod and his colleague. It included: a then-Ryerson University (now "Metropolitan University") professor quoted as an authority on race and gender issues by the *Toronto Star*; an author who was shamelessly promoted by CBC's "Being Black in Canada" project; a poet regularly interviewed on CBC platforms and websites; and a University of Toronto professor treated by the *Globe and Mail* as an "anti-racism" expert.

Problematically for such agenda-driven media and its benighted spokespeople from BLM, the self-described Marxist organization ended up embarrassed in June 2021 after the Ontario Judicial Council (OJC) *finally* dismissed a misconduct complaint against Judge McLeod.[7] In its decision, the OJC saw no merit in the complaint that McLeod's advocacy efforts damaged his standing as an impartial member of the Ontario court. "We are not satisfied... [that McLeod's transgressions] were such as to diminish public confidence in Justice McLeod's ability to carry out the duties of his office or the administration of justice generally," read the OJC decision.[8] Given how these media-anointed representatives tried to ruin the lives of black Canadians who refused to bow down to the far-left, it was of little surprise that none of these progressive news outlets published anything substantive about Justice McLeod's disciplinary hearing when it began in late 2020. Neither at any point did they acknowledge what BLM-affiliated activists and academics did to him and his colleagues.

Perhaps the most clarifying example of media narratives insisting on black victimization can be found in coverage of local policing. For example, in 2022, Toronto's police chief James Ramer offered an apology for what he called systemic racism, and the *Toronto Star* went to work to reaffirm racial grievances about law enforcement. Such reporting was a revealing case study on how media-driven race politics are created and sustained, and the ways that news media might attempt to manipulate black communities. It matters because such narratives are influencing policymaking at every level of government.

The first part of media-driven race politics is when journalists claim authority to speak on behalf of an entire race of people. The *Star's* 2022 reporting began with just such an audacious assumption. One article in June that year, shortly after the police chief's apology, asserted that "Black Toronto voices reject police chief's apology,"[9] as if there is such a collective as "Black Toronto." Another June 2022 article stated that the chief's apology "fell flat for so many Black Torontonians,"[10] again making the same collectivist assumption. It was bizarre that the *Star* would feel entitled to arrogate to itself such omniscient knowledge of what all blacks think and to have determined that we all think the same things. Moreover, neither of the two reporters who wrote these stories were black, the newspaper did not commission a poll of black Torontonians to gauge the opinions of community members, and the *Star* provided no evidence to persuade readers that it possessed some secret knowledge of how the masses of any demographic group think or feel.

This brings us to part two: journalists who select sources that echo a victimhood narrative that originates with elites. The majority of sources quoted in the *Star's* articles were academics, including three from the University of Toronto. It is hard to imagine any community that university professors are a representative sample of, aside from university professors. And yet reporters often quote academics as though they are official representatives of black people, despite 40 per cent of black youth believing universities are inaccessible to them, according to Statistics Canada.[11] These professors were not elected by anyone or chosen by members of a local community organization to speak on their behalf. The public was asked to simply assume that people with doctorate degrees can channel the priorities of parents in working-class neighbourhoods or middle-class business owners, whose lives are markedly different from professors with generous public-sector salaries and benefits.

One possible explanation for this trend is that some professors simply say whatever the journalists want to hear. Take the University of Toronto's Akwasi Owusu-Bempah as a clear example. The *Star* quoted Owusu-Bempah as one of the "Black voices" that rejected Chief Ramer's apology. He complained in one article that "there's nothing new in this news." However, one year previous, in May 2021, Owusu-Bempah told CTV News that an apology for racism is exactly what he wanted. When asked by CTV News, "what do you think the government should be doing at this stage to address some of the concerns that some of these communities may have?" Owusu-Bempah answered:

> First and foremost, I'd like to see a formal apology from the Government of Canada for the historical and contemporary treatment of Black people... An apology would go a long way to help us understand and come to grips with the reality of what's got us to this place, to this position in the first place.[12]

Owusu-Bempah's ever-changing opinion underscored the third and final part of media-driven race politics: the need to keep media coverage and Canadians on the "racism treadmill." That is the term coined by the online journal *Quillette* to describe the phenomenon of institutions and individuals that refuse to acknowledge progress on matters of racial inequality,[13] i.e., that there has been little or no progress on racism as a threat to our communities, even after decades of activism, and policy and legal changes. In addition, an economy has been built on this racism treadmill: Media companies generate revenue from polemics or professors who think media hits can strengthen their push for tenure—they have an economic incentive to encourage racial grievances and downplay narratives that could give power to working- and middle-class families to speak for themselves.

The *Toronto Star's* reporting was an example of the racism treadmill in action; it separated the two fundamental components of law enforcement: fighting crime and respecting rights. In none of its 2022 reporting on Chief Ramer's apology did the *Star* discuss crime, nor did it mention that the chief might consider apologizing for the racial disparity of black people being disproportionately victimized by violent crime. Nor did it appear to put much effort into speaking to black people with alternate points of view. An honest attempt to move the conversation from identifying problems to finding solutions must acknowledge all racial disparities, not just the ones that align with a chosen media narrative. But honest reporting did not appear to be the *Toronto Star's* objective.

Woke corporations

The spread of remixed racism has been accelerated by the trend of corporations going woke. This requires some analysis of why and how this has happened before getting into what can be done about it.

An example: Larry Fink, the CEO of the investment management firm BlackRock, is one of the most influential business leaders in the world. He once rejected the term "woke,"[14] but nonetheless, Fink champions a brand of capitalism known as "stakeholder capitalism," which insists that big businesses ought to engage in social activism and not be limited to the traditional purpose that corporations have served: earning profits for shareholders. Meanwhile, former Unilever CEO Paul Polman also once urged us to accept that stakeholder capitalism is a sign of the times, saying that, "Today, staff and customers believe [that business leaders] should embody the company's values and speak out on big, touchstone issues, from race to fake news and climate change."[15] The World Economic Forum is all-in on this approach to using corporate power for political ends, as are the CEOs of some of the world's largest businesses.

Some Canadians are supportive of corporations with a "social purpose" or those that believe in "social responsibility." It sounds nice, especially if it means businesses are being mindful of pollution or environmental degradation. But it becomes detrimental for our democracies when the richest people in the world use corporate power to pursue an unelected and unaccountable political agenda. A useful, thoughtful counter-punch to this dangerous trend comes from Vivek Ramaswamy, founder of the biopharmaceutical company Roivant Sciences, who in recent years has begun ringing the alarm bells about stakeholder capitalism's consequences for democracy. As Ramaswamy wrote in 2020:

> Speaking as a CEO and a citizen, I don't want American capitalists to play a larger role in defining and implementing the country's political and social values. I think the answers to these questions should be determined by the citizenry—publicly through debate and privately at the ballot box.[16]

On this point, *National Review*'s Andrew Stuttaford agreed. He believes that when corporations pursue political objectives that are unconnected to "the economic objectives of those businesses," it poses "a threat to the democratic order."[17] With regard to stakeholder capitalism; it is not obvious what the distinction is between a connected and an unconnected political objective. Stakeholder capitalism essentially gives businesses a blank slate to define who their "stakeholders" are and what the company's responsibility is to those groups. A business could define its stakeholders as the local community and take action to support local food banks and homeless shelters, for example. But helping your neighbour is distinct from the coercive type of capitalism that leaders like Fink and Polman advocate for, which includes using corporate power to influence how the populace thinks about key issues like race, identity, and patriotism. Supporters of shareholder capitalism would likely treat both sets of objectives the same way, yet Fink and Polman's approach to "social purpose" is much more political in nature because it stands to affect how our democracies function (or will cease to, as the case may be).

Relative to Canada, BlackRock is a significant shareholder in BCE Inc., the parent company of my former employer, Bell Media. In 2021, BCE was listed as one of BlackRock Canada's "top holdings."[18] A read through BCE's 2021 proxy circular (a communication to shareholders) suggests that the company practices a form of stakeholder capitalism that resembles what Fink publicly champions. Interestingly, the proxy circular included a withdrawn shareholder proposal that inquired about BCE's "social purpose." BCE's response to the withdrawn proposal focused on the business activities of the company and their social relevance. However, elsewhere in the document, BCE alludes to a social purpose that is worth examining closely.

Consider BCE's message to its shareholders stated in its 2020 circular. It claimed that Bell took "meaningful actions to address the impacts of systemic racism on Blacks, Indigenous and people of colour at our company and in our communities."[19] This section of the company's proxy circular, titled "Why Diversity and Inclusion Matters," is revealing: Systemic racism is one of the most loaded political terms in western democracies today. It sharply divides countries on racial, partisan, cultural, and ideological lines, because many readings of the term insist that western democracies are racist. BCE did not just apply the term to its own business practices, which would be within its right, but went so far as to commit to addressing systemic racism in its "communities."[20] This can easily be perceived as BCE calling Canada a racist country. Similarly, in 2022, the company again followed up with a circular lecturing its shareholders, employees, and customers about how racist Canada was and is.

BCE committed itself, its shareholders, and its staff to a broad and undefined social purpose with no specific definitions or scope. In the proxy circular, Bell included some specific human resources and philanthropic goals, but was unclear how deep this commitment went. If I were a shareholder, I would wonder how BCE's commitment to fighting systemic racism conflicts with maximizing shareholder profits. And I also wonder what, exactly, BCE meant by "systemic racism" in the first place. As a former Bell employee, I would offer that it is worthwhile for shareholders to inquire about how BCE's political agenda affects its employment practices. My experience with Bell indicates that BCE's political position on systemic racism may have some trickle-down impact on management's willingness to pressure employees to embrace certain liberal political views or potentially risk termination. That would be an ill-advised strategy to retain the best talent, but it can work if the goal is to emphasize politics, not profits.

Few people are naive enough to think that BCE puts its profit motive aside entirely and there is no reason to doubt that BCE's CEO and board chair do value profits for BlackRock Canada and their other shareholders. But one must recognize just how political some corporations have become, and why using terms like "woke capital" to describe their social activism is necessary: Corporations like BCE are not traditional businesses that just want to sell a good or service. They want to have an impact on the public's views on race, identity, and patriotism. Their understanding of race and capital is not informed by economists with a long record of work on race, culture, and community outcomes (e.g., economist Thomas Sowell or other thoughtful academic analysts such as Glenn Loury or John McWhorter). Instead, leaning on a loaded term like "systemic racism," too many corporations practice "stakeholder capitalism" fed to them by non-experts who misunderstand basic concepts, statistics, and capitalism itself.

My own stance: No one gets to tell me what kind of black man to be

After Black Lives Matter zoomed into the public consciousness following the murder of George Floyd in 2020, there was a renewed enthusiasm to confront anti-black racism. There is still a long way to go, in part because, ironically, anti-black racism now takes the form of *remixed* racism combined with stereotyped notions of what a black man should be, usually with reference to one's ideology or politics. Thus, in 2020, one of Canada's oldest newspapers, the *Globe and Mail*, published an article about me that purported to be concerned with anti-black racism, but actually pitted black people who are conservative (like me) against those who are radical or progressive. The article suggested that blackness is measured by one's political views, and the article's headline underscored this message. According to the article, I must have failed an ideological racial purity test that black people, especially those in leadership positions, must pass. How Canada's supposed paper of record in 2020 could be so blind to ideological diversity in any racial community is shocking and reprehensible.

After I presented my concerns to the *Globe*; the newspaper made a factual correction and adjusted its headline, but even with these changes, the newspaper's inflammatory, intellectually incurious article accused me of "anti-blackness"—bizarre unless you believe black men are only permitted to hold particular views. Thus "anti-blackness" means I do not possess the political views that some people believe black people should have. Insofar as I could tell, there were three particular opinions I held that my detractors pointed to as "anti-blackness":

- I did not and do not support Black Lives Matter, which received hundreds of millions of dollars from donors, yet was unrepresentative of and unaccountable to black communities. I disagree with this political organization's support for Marxism and opposition to the nuclear family (even though the unjust killings of black men made BLM a conduit for a movement against police brutality).[21]
- I believe a politically motivated defunding of police without community consultations will leave some neighbourhoods vulnerable to violent crime, such as what has occurred in New York City, Portland, and Seattle among others.
- I believe hip-hop and social media conflicts are some of the reasons why gun violence plagues our cities; subcultures (as well as socio-economic structures) matter when trying to solve any social problem. Billion-dollar corporations promoting a violent form of masculinity to vulnerable black boys and young men is a disastrous cocktail. Many peer-reviewed articles and violence intervention programs support these beliefs, which I discuss in my book, *Why Young Men*. I also listen to the youth workers and police officers who tell me that social media conflict is contributing to violence in their neighbourhoods.

Among black people, as in any other part of our society, I am far from alone in my views. Enter any church, community centre, WhatsApp group, school, or workplace and you can find healthy debates on these topics. There is no racial consensus, and the idea that such a thing exists is both preposterous and demeaning. On many social issues there are as many conservative black Americans as there are liberal ones. Even on the issue of policing, which the *Globe and Mail* attacked me over, black Democrats poll more in favour of increasing police budgets (38%) than white Democrats (32%).[22] (No comparable data exists for black Canadians, unfortunately.)

But some in the media too often present a racial consensus on these topics by assuming a plethora of Twitter voices are somehow representative of "blackness." The *Globe and Mail* and other outlets allow a small, vocal fraction of black activists on Twitter to yield disproportionate power over an entire demographic. This practice is undeniably elitist when you factor in who uses the platform. Twitter users tend to be less diverse, university-educated, and hyper-progressive in their politics when compared to the broader population. And only a very small percentage of Twitter users account for most political discussion on the platform, as just six per cent of users in the United States make up 75 per cent of political content on Twitter.[23]

Imposing an ideological racial purity test on black men and women is wrong. It is censure. It is divide-and-conquer. It is colonial. But news media companies who purport to be anti-racist are often blind to this reality. Consider, for example, that the *Globe and Mail* has decided to capitalize the letter "b" in black and invites black writers to contribute to its opinion pages. But how much does any of that matter if your paper is going to insist that black people are supposed to think and say the same things? What kind of agenda is a news outlet supporting if it is narrowly defining an entire demographic by what Twitter activists say?

So let me be clear: My blackness was not given to me by the *Globe and Mail*. God did that. No newspaper can take my blackness from me. We can address anti-black racism and provide hope to black communities without demanding that black people in positions of leadership parrot the left's unhelpful ideological talking points.

The core problems: Detached academic theories, victim narratives, and politicized history

If Canadians are to understand how remixed racism arose in recent years, we must grapple with the assumptions and objectives of critical race theory (CRT). One might think of CRT as an American idea. And it did start out that way. The theory's two primary architects are Columbia University law professor Kimberlé Crenshaw and former New York University law professor Derrick Bell. But CRT's central premises will sound familiar to any Canadian who has paid close attention to our federal and provincial governments or the multinational corporations that do business in our markets. Critical race theorists have accumulated a significant amount of influence in Canada, as evidenced by the pervasiveness of such terms as "systemic racism" and "white privilege."

Let us first establish what CRT is. Crenshaw defined her theory as a world view focused on "the ways that racial inequality is facilitated, and the ways that our history has created these inequalities that now can be almost effortlessly reproduced unless we attend to the existence of these inequalities."[24] The phrase "almost effortlessly" is key to understanding CRT's central premise that racism lives inside our laws and policies independently of our intentions. In the *Capital University Law Review*, Bell wrote that "racism is an integral, permanent, and indestructible component of this society." He concluded that "Black people will never gain full equality in this country."[25]

Proponents of these ideas do not think highly of countries such as Canada given that their ideology demands radical, destabilizing change to our institutions. Also, CRT disempowers people of colour by defining us as perennial victims. Examples of Canadian governments and businesses embracing CRT are countless. They include the already-noted Global Affairs Canada which incorporated the ideology into its training of government officials. In 2022, it also included almost every member of Ontario's provincial parliament who voted in favour of Bill 67, which, had it made it into law after being sent to committee, would have mandated the practice of CRT in the administration of public education.[26] In the spring of 2022, even Home Depot found itself in hot water after passing around a controversial flyer that informed its employees about "privilege."[27]

Of all the parts of Canadian life where CRT advocates and practitioners have established power, the most troubling place to find such divisive race politics is in our public schools. Parents in particular ought to be alarmed.

- In Calgary, the Alberta Teachers' Association has started an Antiracist Teachers Network Newsletter that pushes CRT material onto teachers who work with students as young as kindergarteners.

- In southwestern Ontario, the Waterloo Region District School Board has censured its only black school board trustee, Mike Ramsay, who has raised concerns about CRT in Waterloo public schools.
- In Toronto, CRT is promoted to community members by administrators, such as the principal of Victoria Park Elementary School in the city's east end. In her weekly email updates to parents, Victoria Park's principal has distributed content from critical race theorist Robin DiAngelo, who was embroiled in controversy for telling Coca Cola workers to be "less white."
- One university in Alberta has also evidently fallen victim to CRT dogma. Just after the Derek Chauvin verdict in 2021 when the former police officer was convicted of murdering George Floyd, many black Canadians weighed in on the debates prompted by the Chauvin verdict. Ghanaian-Canadian blogger Samuel Sey was one of the conservative voices among the crowd. He noted the high stakes to the conversations then occurring about policing, arguing that, "What's happening in America isn't necessarily hatred for police officers. And it's surely not about love for black people."[28] Sey argued that what was happening could be summed up as: "critical race theorists want to end liberal democracy to establish a postmodernist, Marxist, 'antiracist' system." [29]

What was telling in a Canadian context, though, was Sey's encounter with Calgary's Ambrose University that year, which was a revealing example of how black conservatives in Canada are silenced on important issues of race and justice, and just how deep the damaging assumptions inherent in critical race theory have sunk into our academic institutions. In February 2021, Ambrose's vice-president of student life issued a public apology after the university hosted an unnamed guest speaker who, according to the (white) vice-president of student life and (white) president of the student council, "dismissed the ways that bias and prejudice build systems that hurt and oppress."[30] The student council also initially characterized Sey as causing "severe harm" to students.[31] According to Sey, he was the guest speaker the vice-president was referring to but refused to name. In other words, Ambrose University apologized for hosting a black man who did not parrot the predictable talking points that the school's administrators believed black people should say. As Sey later wrote:

> Their statement of apology said, "in February 2021, a guest speaker at The Well event denied the existence of systemic racism and caused severe harm to those who were in attendance." They said I "denigrated" the students and suggested I oppose "Black, Indigenous, and People of Colour" They also insinuated I didn't "take racism seriously."
>
> The entire basis for the statement is cowardly. However, the most cowardly thing about the statement isn't what they said—it's actually what they didn't say.
>
> Ambrose didn't mention my name. That's probably because they didn't want to make it known they were hating a black man while they were virtue signalling about their love for black people. They probably didn't mention my name because they didn't want to make it known they were suggesting I was a self-hating black man for choosing to disagree with their agenda.

Sey noted that his apparently controversial talk on racism for Ambrose University was titled, "What Is Racism?" He referenced several scriptures and argued that "The Bible is the best book on racism." He also argued that "the biblical definition of racism is incompatible with Robin DiAngelo's and Ibram Kendi's definitions of racism." Sey's point and the assumptions within critical race theory are clear: Critical Race Theorists actively pit communities against each other on the basis of their skin colour. But people of colour are not a monolith, which is why he ended his talk with what was once a classic definition of racism: judging a person by their skin colour. As Rey put it, "If you assume the worst of a black person because of their skin colour, that's racism. And if you assume the worst of a white person because of their skin colour, that's racism."[32]

No amount of political correctness can replace the father

There are multiple problems with Critical Race Theory that hollow it out as a presumed explanatory theory for outcomes: It is simplistic in attributing all or most disparities to racism, a monocausal approach that neglects a variety of important factors that shape our lives, including the role of fathers. On this matter in particular, we must wonder how many more children have to skip another Father's Day before it becomes possible to note that no amount of political correctness will change this fact: a good father can do more for kids than any government program. Fathers are a solution to many of the social ills that plague our communities and we should not be afraid to say so, even if that means offending ivory tower sensibilities.

Some politicians in the United States are honest about this. Following the May 2022 school shooting in Uvalde, Texas, Utah Senator Mike Lee argued that part of America's gun violence problem can be attributed to fatherlessness. His point was overshadowed by a debate over gun control, but his argument still has merit. That same month, American journalist Timothy Carney cited studies from the United States Department of Justice, the academic journal *Psychology, Crime and Law,* and Princeton University's Public Policy School to back up Senator Lee's concerns.[33] Research shows that when a father is missing in a child's life, the odds of that child being exposed to violent behaviour increase significantly. Adam Coleman, author of *Black Victim to Black Victor*, offered similar insights in the *New York Post* after the Uvalde tragedy, writing that, "Your father is supposed to be your source of security, a builder of confidence and a teacher for how to regulate your emotions in stressful situations. Most crucial, the father is the son's purpose compass as he helps guide him throughout the trials of adolescence towards purposeful adulthood."[34]

To address such realities, Florida governor Ron DeSantis signed legislation in 2022 to "encourage responsible and involved fatherhood" through "educational programs, mentorship programs and one-on-one support."[35] When retired football coach Tony Dungy appeared alongside DeSantis to endorse the bill, Dungy faced a storm of criticism over his pro-fatherhood comments. Indeed, the criticism was so widespread on social media that Dungy felt the need to respond. Dungy stood up for himself by rightly pointing out that President Barack Obama once tackled the problem of fatherlessness, too.[36] In fact, the former coach's comments at DeSantis' press conference were similar to comments President Obama made in 2008. It is progressives, not Dungy, who have changed since Obama was in the White House.

There was a time — not too long ago — when people across the political spectrum would openly recognize these truths. Recall, for instance, when Justin Trudeau was first running for prime minister in 2015. Journalist

Francine Pelletier asked him about the prevalence of misogyny among young men. The Liberal leader included a dose of reality in his answer: "There's a lot of communities in which fathers are less present than they have been, or might have been, in the past and there's a need for engaged, positive role models."[37] Much has changed since then and the prime minister is a helpful barometer for measuring just how abruptly our culture has shifted. His reasonable and accurate comments on fatherhood in 2015 received blowback from legacy and social media, and it appears as though the woke mob left him rattled. Just three years later, in 2018, Trudeau settled in among the social justice warriors, as he made obvious when adding words like "peoplekind" to his vocabulary to replace "mankind."[38] Today's version of Trudeau is unlikely to advocate for fathers as a solution to any social ills, but that does not make fathers any less important. Mass shootings in the United States, which Prime Minister Justin Trudeau has exploited to increase Canadian gun control, have underscored the value of an involved and responsible father in people's lives.

Trudeau's late-career dodge notwithstanding, his earlier 2015 comments that recognized the importance of fathers is why Canadians could use legislation that encourages fathers. In Canada almost one in five Canadian kids lives in a single-parent household and in over 80 per cent of those single-family homes, it is the father who is missing.[39] There is no clearer example of blatant elitism than refusing to help these struggling families out of some desire to appease politically correct watchdogs. We should expect institutions to not only acknowledge these truths, but to act on them. Public policy and community initiatives can keep more families intact, yet in today's political environment in Canada, supporting fathers is a route to controversy. Except that getting to potential solutions first requires open dialogue about the problem: A good father can make a world of difference in the life of a child, just as can a good mother.

A superior model: The vision of Martin Luther King Jr.

It is easy to feel discouraged when thinking about the degree to which Canadian institutions have absorbed an activist agenda that does not make life better for the people these institutions claim to help. But giving up is not an option as it is hard to imagine nurturing strong character traits in Canada's next generation of leaders without healthy and intact families, schools that value academics over activism, and community pillars like churches and other places of worship. The traditional institutions under attack today still hold the promise of a better future for all communities. Besides, our communities deserve better. That means that courage and strength matters as does a principled stand, and few have demonstrated this better than Martin Luther King Jr. and his call for attention to character, not colour.

Character *does* matter and critical race theory and identity politics have strayed far from some of the ideas that King lived and died for. Not too long ago, Canadians openly and unapologetically shared King's vision for a united nation made up of upstanding individuals of strong character. A *Toronto Star* op-ed from 2007 borrowed from King's famous "I Have A Dream" speech. The published headline reads: "Character, not colour, matters."[40] It is hard to imagine a mainstream newspaper publishing a headline emphasizing character over colour today. After observing how journalists and editors have behaved in recent years, any mainstream newspaper publishing a headline inspired by King's dream today would likely need to hold an emergency Zoom town hall for their staff to express sadness and anger. Twitter mobs would demand an apology, too.

Regrettably, in the third decade of the 21st century we rarely, if ever, see public figures acknowledge that the fight to overcome racial division is partly a spiritual battle. King's message of racial reconciliation was as religious as it was political. Although King was clear about the need for public policy to address racial inequalities, he did hope for a future in which race would be less important in human interactions. King's firm belief in the importance of character is timeless, and we could all learn something from the civil rights icon. If government officials are solely fixated on the colour of the leaders who are applying for grants, then they will not appropriately weigh the character of the leaders entrusted with public dollars to support communities with urgent needs. Canada should strive to realize King's dream of a world where people are judged by the content of their character, not the colour of their skin.

CHAPTER 15

How the Yukon Court of Appeal denied Charter rights to an Aboriginal Canadian

Peter Best

It is not in the power of the present generation to dispose of the birthright of its descendants. Liberty and self-government are inalienable rights.
—T.L. WOOD, Legislative Council (British Columbia), March 10, 1870

Travellers driving to Yukon Territory can expect a variety of novel road signs alerting them to their upcoming destinations. At the outskirts of Whitehorse, for example, sits a large carved wooden sign welcoming visitors to the "Capital of the Yukon" emblazoned with a paddle steamer and sunny mountain vista. Dawson City's sign pays homage to its Gold Rush glory days with a Belle in a fancy dress waving from the second-floor balcony of a dance hall. As for Old Crow, a remote native community about 800 kilometres north of Whitehorse, there is no road in at all. But if there was, recent legal battles suggest a proper road sign would contain the warning "Charter-Free Zone Ahead."

Old Crow is the hub community of the sprawling Vuntut Gwitchin First Nation, covering nearly 8,000 square kilometres in northern Yukon. It is also the focus of a set of recent court rulings undermining the bedrock concept that all Canadians share the same core rights as guaranteed by the Canadian Charter of Rights and Freedoms. In place of this fundamental doctrine of equality for all, Canada's courts seem bent on installing a doctrine of race-based laws. Ironically, in this case, such rulings increasingly deny Aboriginal

Canadians on reserves rights that other Canadians take for granted.[a] It is now up to the Supreme Court of Canada to decide if such a legal caste system is compatible with a modern, *liberal* Canada.

Running for office in Old Crow

Set along the meandering Porcupine River near the Alaskan border, Old Crow is accessible for most of the year only by plane. As a result, approximately 300 of Vuntut Gwitchin's 560 members choose to live off-reserve. Such is the case for Cindy Dickson, who makes Whitehorse her home because of her son's health needs and her job as executive director of the Arctic Athabaskan Council, an intergovernmental forum representing indigenous people of Athabaskan descent in Canada and the United States. "I consider Old Crow to be my home—I grew up there," Dickson said in a 2022 interview with C2C Journal.[1] "But I moved out to further my education." In an effort to improve representation for that majority of band members who live outside Old Crow and having in mind the Aboriginal cultural value that citizenship does not depend primarily on physical residence, in 2018 Dickson put her name forward for election on the Vuntut Gwitchin council. "There is a real need for leadership to reach out to our members wherever they live. I see a lot of our citizens here in Whitehorse and they have struggles," she explained, "We need someone to advocate at the political level for all those citizens that live outside Old Crow."

As a trustee of the Vuntut Gwitchin Business Trust and an active member of her local community, she is eminently qualified to serve that role. But the Vuntut Gwitchin First Nation's constitution states that only residents living in Old Crow can serve on council. Since Dickson observed past council members meet the residency requirement by claiming an empty cabin in Old Crow as their permanent residence, she figured the rule was not a significant barrier. But after her nomination papers were accepted by the clerk, Dickson was told that her name had been removed from the ballot by the Vuntut Gwitchin leadership. When Dickson requested a meeting to make her case, she was stonewalled. "I was shocked and upset. I sent letters

---

a) In this chapter, I use the word "Aboriginal" and not Indigenous as did the justice in this case.

and texts and no one got back to me," Dickson recalled. Out of options, she filed a legal petition in 2019, arguing the residency requirement violated her Charter rights as a Canadian citizen to be free from discrimination. She lost both at trial and on appeal; her case is now headed to the Supreme Court of Canada.[2]

The Dickson decision

Section 15(1) of the Charter states that "every individual is equal before and under the law and has the right to the equal protection and equal benefit of the law without discrimination." This guarantee provides much of the legal foundation and overall force to the traditional rights and freedoms that are separately expressed in the Charter and that Canadians enjoy on a daily basis: freedom of religion, freedom of expression, freedom of the press, freedom of association and assembly, the right to life, liberty and security of the person, and the right not to be deprived of same without due process. Some other rights, however, do not apply to *all* Canadians. Section 25, which covers "Aboriginal rights," states that, "The guarantee in this Charter of certain rights and freedoms shall not be construed so as to abrogate or derogate from any aboriginal, treaty or other rights or freedoms that pertain to the aboriginal peoples of Canada." It goes on to list various treaties, royal proclamations and land claim agreements that may offer additional rights or privileges exclusively for the benefit of native peoples. Among these are a right to self-government. Section 35 explains that any future rights will be given equivalent protection.

My view is that the Charter's framers intended sections 25 and 35 to protect the additional rights Aboriginal peoples may enjoy without disrupting the other rights they hold in common with all other Canadians, a legal notion sometimes promoted as "Citizens Plus."[3] While this may violate the universalist notion of strict equality among all Canadians, what has happened to Dickson seems far more damaging to her core civil rights: she was essentially stripped of her full panoply of rights in her chosen nation of Canada due to her status as a member of an aboriginal community. How could this happen? Aboriginal affairs analyst, expert and former British Columbia Liberal leader Gordon Gibson wrote of the deliberations around section 35 that it was "constitution-making by inattention," and "the nature of the last-minute negotiations—complex, occasionally bitter, and hurried—militated against any consideration of aboriginal rights."[4] He also cites the late Melvin Smith, a senior constitutional advisor from British Columbia: "Nothing has been written that suggests there was any serious example of what the words meant."[5] It therefore seems unlikely the framers conceived that section 35 would ever be interpreted in a manner that deprives an Aboriginal Canadian of her full Charter rights and protections.

In defending its power to limit council eligibility to Old Crow residents, Vuntut Gwitchin leadership argued that section 25's protection of "Aboriginal rights" allows it to set aside Dickson's individual equality rights in favour of the collective rights of the band itself. The band council claimed that section 25 and the self-government agreement VGFN signed with Ottawa in the 1990s gave it a free hand to discriminate against its members as it sees fit, without regard to Canadian norms. "Vuntut Gwitchin practices, customs and traditions related to leadership and governance are...rooted in the land itself," Chief Dana Tizya-Tramm testified at trial.[6] Another witness affirmed, "Most VGFN cultural and political values...are collective in nature."[7] In 2021 the Yukon Court of Appeal sided with the Vuntut Gwitchin First Nation. The result seems a perversion of the original intent of section 25; Dickson now has *fewer* rights than other Canadians, not more.

The case turns on a clash between Dickson's individual rights as a Canadian citizen to be free from discrimination in pursuing lawful activities such as running for elected office, and the Vuntut Gwitchin's collectivist claim that as an Aboriginal government it is allowed to ignore such obligations because of its historic customs and connection to the land. Such a collision of rights left Yukon's courts twisted in knots. As Madam Justice Mary Newbury noted in her judgment upholding the trial decision, the *Dickson* case is "particularly difficult" because it raises "issues that have never been dealt with by a Canadian court...regarding s. 25 and how it relates to personal Charter rights held by citizens of self-governing first nations."

It is "difficult" partly because of the courts' expansive habit of imaginatively reinterpreting Canadians' individual Charter rights into areas not previously imagined. Justices have thus frequently ordered elected governments to abide by strict timelines or meet ambitious funding requirements in order to correct policies they themselves find to have violated Canadians' individual rights as reinterpreted by the justices. In some cases—assisted suicide and the right to strike as examples—these "rights" have simply been invented by justices reading between the lines of the Charter rather than ruling on its text as written.[8] Now, however, this urge for individual rights-expanding, court-made law has crashed headlong into "a collective right...being exercised by a self-governing first nation," as Justice Newbury put it.

The lower court ruled that Old Crow's residency requirement did not breach Dickson's Charter right to equal treatment. And even if it had, the judge said, the Vuntut Gwitchin government was fully insulated against Charter challenges by section 25. The Yukon Court of Appeal essentially upheld the lower court ruling. When individual rights come into conflict with the collective rights of Aboriginal self-government, the collective wins. Such a finding requires creating a distinction between laws for Aboriginal Canadians and those that apply to the rest of us. As Justice Newbury wrote, "The kinds of considerations relevant to the determination of which rights 'pertain to' Aboriginal persons are obviously not the same as those normally examined... [for non-Aboriginal people]. Where the 'collective' is a first nation that has survived years of paternalism and the suppression of its culture, the better view seems to be that under s. 25 the collective right should prevail undiminished."

In arriving at her momentous conclusion, Justice Newbury accepted the Vuntut Gwitchin First Nation's argument that there are "inherent differences between the liberal Enlightenment concept of individual rights and the collective nature of Indigenous rights." She also gave credence to the many Canadian legal academics who agreed it was acceptable for First Nations to sacrifice the civil liberties of their "citizens" in this way. Previously, academia championed activists such as Nelson Mandela and the Reverend Martin Luther King, Jr. in fighting for the principle of race-blind laws applied equally to all individuals in their respective countries. Today, some Canadians who self-describe as liberals argue against efforts to do the same in our country.

A sword and shield to create a *Charter*-free zone

Given this result, Dickson sought and was granted leave to appeal to the Supreme Court of Canada. Ten intervenors have been approved for the case, including the Canadian Constitution Foundation, which intended to speak on her behalf.[b] The organization's director of litigation, Christine Van Geyn, made clear what was and is at stake: "We will argue that the purpose of section 25, when read in context, is to ensure the Charter is not used as a sword by non-Indigenous peoples to deny the special status of, or a benefit for, Indigenous peoples. Its purpose is not to shield all Indigenous government conduct from Charter scrutiny."[9] All the other intended intervenors were aboriginal groups, including the Teslin Tlinglit Council, Council of Yukon First Nations and Carcross/Tagish First Nation. Many intended to speak on behalf of the Vuntut Gwitchen First Nation which itself launched a cross-appeal to also overturn Newbury's decision. At issue for this Aboriginal coalition is that, unlike the lower court, Yukon's Court of Appeal ruled that the residency requirement actually *does* violate Dickson's Charter rights, but only in a theoretical way. Justice Newbury declared that Dickson's "inability to serve on the Council without moving to... [Old Crow] is an incursion on her equality rights. For those brought up in the Western democratic tradition, this incursion is indeed a serious one." Despite such a threat, however, Justice Newbury agreed with the lower court that section 25 acts as a shield against all efforts to defend such rights. It is therefore impossible to enforce Dickson's right to stand for office with the Vuntut Gwitchin, even when it involves a serious matter such as democratic participation.

Yet it does Dickson no good to discover she has a right if she cannot act upon it. "Growing up, I just took it for granted that I was part of the Canadian Charter," Dickson recalled in her 2022 interview. "Nobody ever told me it didn't apply." This sense of inequality is what has mobilized her to action including her appeal to the Supreme Court of Canada: "I felt I could not just leave it with section 25 being used as a shield against our own people. If I did, I would always regret it." Dickson added that her actions should not be seen as an effort to diminish the concept of self-government. Rather, she says, "it strengthens self-government by adding clarity. And it acknowledges our individual right to challenge." But the mere possibility that Charter rights could have a presence in the Vuntut Gwitchin community has also mobilized the Aboriginal lobbyist industry into action. It is their goal to convince the

---

b) At the time of writing in January 2023.

Supreme Court of Canada that section 25 means the Charter is always and everywhere off-limits, eliminating any legal flights of fancy that it could even be *theoretically* in effect on reserves. The native intervenors, in other words, want the Vuntut Gwitchin First Nation, and presumably all other First Nations territories in Canada, declared Charter-free zones, full-stop.

As it stands, the *Dickson* decision is a troubling rejection of the principles upon which Canada was founded and which serve as the foundation for our continuing liberal democracy. If the Supreme Court does not categorically reject the lower court decisions, Aboriginal Canadians will be deprived of their birthright civil liberties on their "nations" or reserves and will be further set apart from the rest of the country. In opposition to such moves, encouragingly, native self-government agreements signed subsequent to the Vuntut Gwitchin First Nation agreement, such as the 2000 Nisga'a Final Agreement specifically declare Charter rights to be in effect on native lands.[10] However, if Dickson loses her appeal, there would appear to be nothing stopping the Nisga'a from similarly denying the Charter rights of any of their citizens because constitutional law takes precedence over such agreements. This further highlights the error in Old Crow that the Supreme Court now has the opportunity to correct. As Dickson put it, "I am a proud Canadian and I am proud to be a First Nations person." She should not have to pick between the two.

National implications

Supreme Court of Canada decisions apply across the country, as the Dickson decision certainly will. For example, in 2018 the Quebec Superior Court ruled that the Mohawk reserve of Kahnawake's by-law prohibiting mixed-race couples from residing on the reserve was unconstitutional under the Charter on the ground that it discriminated against individuals on the basis of family and civil status.[11] One of the Aboriginal plaintiffs was Waneek Horn Miller, who competed for Canada in the 2000 Summer Olympics. She met her future non-Aboriginal husband there, and in 2002 they married and have lived on the reserve since that year and now have three children. If the Supreme Court of Canada upholds the decision of the Yukon Court of Appeal then conceivably Horn Miller and her family could be legally evicted from the Mohawk reserve. The result would be to create a Canada in which the disgraceful application of a blatantly racist but now perfectly legal marriage miscegenation law echoes the Jim Crow era in the American South. Other similar Charter violating examples on reserves and self-governing nations across the country could then pop out into Canadian constitutional jurisprudence and into daily lives, akin to stars in an increasingly darkening night sky.

The big problem of small governments

Beyond the obvious unfairness of denying Dickson her full rights as a Canadian, it is also necessary to grapple with how the interests of Aboriginal Canadians are to be protected if the decision is not overturned. In its ruling in 2021, the Yukon Court of Appeal declared that the intent of section 25 was to "allow Aboriginal governments to protect, preserve and promote the identity of their citizens through unique institutions, norms and government practices." If so, where can we find these unique Aboriginal judicial bodies? The Yukon Court of Appeal considered evidence from Dave Joe, the Vuntut Gwitchin's lead negotiator for the 1993 self-government agreement, that the Vuntut Gwitchin constitution was intended to replace the Charter, since the Charter "was not developed with any consideration of Vuntut Gwitchin legal and political traditions or governance."[12] Yet this concept of the VGFN's "legal traditions" seems more mythological than substantive.

The 1993 agreement called for the establishment of a "Vuntut Gwitchin Court... [which would] have power to hear and decide all cases of alleged violation of Vuntut Gwitchin Laws." Thirty years later, no such court exists. Rather, the current case about the legality of local band council rules was litigated in a Yukon courtroom by lawyers and judges using traditional British-based procedural and substantive laws. Indeed, it seems a stretch to imagine there could ever be a unique court system for a community of 560 people, of whom only 260 live in Old Crow. Even if one was created, it would be unlikely to act as a bulwark in defence of Dickson's individual rights. As Aboriginal writer Rob Louie pointed out in a 2022 *Lawyer's Daily* article, the odds are stacked against any band member trying to challenge the reserve establishment:

> A First Nation election appeal typically looks like this. An electoral appeal body is comprised of a lawyer hand-picked by the band manager, or a few band staff and a hand-picked lawyer; the First Nation is named as a nominal party and represented in the electoral appeal by another hand-picked lawyer; the incumbent chief and council pay their lawyers out of band funds; and the incumbents that ran in the election are at the centre of the election appeal.[13]

It is difficult to imagine the individual rights of any resident being properly defended in a system prone to such self-dealing and reinforced by familial ties. As Louie asked rhetorically:

> What realistic chance do band members have against chief and council who control their money and resources? For many band members in Canada, the battle is not just with the Crown, it is also with their own leadership. Perhaps reconciliation within Indigenous communities needs to take place before reconciliation can happen with Canada.

A similar theme runs through Dickson's personal experiences: "Many people are upset with me, not just in my community, but Yukon-wide. They say that if someone is elected chief, you have to support them. I feel like the Black Sheep—all eyes are on me." Dickson reported having heard from lots of supporters as well, but they're not as easy to spot:

> I have been receiving a lot of support from regular people at other First Nations. But it is not always public because it is tough to challenge a First Nations government. We often talk about the need for an Ombudsman or another neutral process that would allow people to bring up grievances. We need a stronger voice so that First Nations governments have to look at their policies to make sure all their citizens are treated equally and fairly.

Despite the popular romantic image of Aboriginal governance as a dreamy exercise in pastoral collectivism, life on the reserve is more often akin to the crony capitalism familiar in other less-advantaged parts of the world. The predominant reason has nothing to do with race or culture. As Tom

Flanagan, professor emeritus of Political Science at the University of Calgary, has noted, it is the eternal problem of small democracies typical of First Nations communities.[14] As Gordon Gibson wrote in 2014, "The reserve system is the centre of this...Indians are human beings just like the rest of us. But most are burdened by the system."[15] Indigenous writer Calvin Helin's *Dances with Dependency: Out of Poverty Through Self-Reliance* echoes Gibson's observation.[16] Helin wrote of band chiefs who were "colonizers of their own people" and how life on most reserves was "a situation not unlike many banana republics." Dickson's individual right to be free from discrimination cannot be protected by the "unique legal traditions" of a tiny remote northern outpost comprising several hundred residents. As with anywhere else in Canada, a proper defence of her rights requires the institutional power of a large and depersonalized legal system.

As history and human nature have demonstrated repeatedly, classical liberal values and a cosmopolitan ethos focussed on the sanctity of the individual over any kind of collective right that infringes on the individual are the best guarantees of a life free from unjust rule or authoritarian *diktat*. "The individual human being is the ultimate unit of all law...[and his or her] well-being is the ultimate object of all law," wrote Hersch Lauterpacht, a British professor of international law whose work on genocide and crimes against humanity laid the foundation for the 1946 Nuremburg Trials against officials of Germany's National Socialist regime.[17] We should heed Lauterpacht's trenchant, wise observation. The prospect of quasi-apartheid laws that distinguish between the race of the individual in order to advance retrograde collective goals is not only socially and economically divisive, it should be morally toxic to any thoughtful Canadian. Amidst endless talk of reconciliation, the most obvious benefit Canadians can offer their Aboriginal compatriots is full access to the entire suite of legal protections the rest of us take for granted daily.

CHAPTER 16

Indigenous peoples have a chance—if they grasp it

Joseph Quesnel

While Aboriginal people are not responsible for the conditions that have created the welfare trap, much of the currently prevailing mindset and the actions of the "Indian Industry" and a handful of leaders are contributing to keep Aboriginal people caught in the trap.
—CALVIN HELIN, *Dances With Dependency: Indigenous Success Through Self-Reliance*

First Nations people have both a choice and a chance. It is clear that they seek the same good life and avenues to the same as do other Canadians and despite any rhetoric to the contrary: greater opportunity for themselves and their children, and honest, transparent governance in their communities. Although most are committed to addressing past struggles, such as unresolved land claims and recognition of indigenous rights—no easy task given different views about what those terms mean—many are more concerned about economic independence for their communities and jobs for themselves and their family members. Rather critically, and whether they like it or not, some indigenous leaders need to respond to these changing priorities just as mainstream Canada must grasp that positive change will not occur overnight.

Some context. The past decade has seen an increase in financial transparency from First Nation governments and organizations, which is precisely what First Nations people on reserve desire: transparency and accountability from their leaders. Evidence for this exists in the high number of First Nation communities that still post financial information online despite the federal Liberal government's decision to stop enforcing a previous Conservative law requiring that they do so. Not coincidentally, the more this occurs, the more such reforms will help lay the groundwork for future opportunities and prosperity. This is positive as it means ever-fewer indigenous people would accept a return to past obfuscation. In addition, an increasing number of indigenous communities now demand that they be equipped with the vast array of economic tools that are critical to improve their communities, including the property rights that mainstream Canadians take for granted as a foundation for flourishing individuals, families, and communities. Further, indigenous Canadians have embraced the development of the natural resources that lie within their territories, including how some First Nations are now equity partners on major projects. This is another important development. It means that despite the rhetoric about decarbonization, many indigenous communities see their future entwined with Canada's resource economy. They see it as offering one significant path to prosperity.

The historical context: Over-governed then; over-governed now

Reflecting on the evolution of federal policy, it should be obvious in the third decade of the 21st century that one significant mistake made by the federal government in history was to federalize every issue involving indigenous peoples.[a] For better or worse, the British set out on the federalizing policy path starting with the Royal Proclamation of 1763 which determined that the indigenous inhabitants of this land would be treated as collectivities and negotiated with through signed treaties that set out rights and responsibilities. From the start, though, it was the central government and it alone that dealt with First Nation communities.

As with most top-down approaches that exist far from local conditions, indigenous policy in Ottawa became rigid and inflexible in meeting changing needs and circumstances. It forced onto indigenous people a "one-size fits all" system of governance. Not only this, but the Indian Act did not keep up with the rapidly evolving changes taking place in Canada. For example, as

---

a) There is one exception: In one respect, we should celebrate the original policy relationship with Canada's First peoples in 1867 because it protected indigenous lands and peoples; something that did not happen in other democratic countries of that era.

provinces began to create education and health care systems, First Nations on reserve found themselves islands of federal jurisdiction within the provinces. Programs and services delivered by local or provincial governments to other Canadians were instead delivered by distant federal civil servants to First Nations. Whereas provinces were able to tailor policies to suit their populations, indigenous people had to contend with an inflexible federal Indian Act regime that denied them full access to their own lands and required them to sign off with far-away Ottawa on most aspects of public life.

In the 21st century, First Nations people on reserves find themselves facing the same problems they dealt with at the start of Confederation: an inflexible federal regime that demands oversight for basic economic transactions, band governance that is more accountable to the federal government than its own membership, and land restrictions that were intended to protect the indigenous land base but that now prevent indigenous entrepreneurs and governments from accessing capital. In other words, First Nations still have 19th century tools in a 21st century world, which explains the slow progress out of poverty on many reserves.

A mostly positive revolution from within

Still, there are signs of an economic spring. First Nations have changed in recent decades because a growing urban middle class formed from members exposed to the way in which the rest of Canada lives. They support certain constitutional rights for their communities but are much more open to voluntary change and want democratic governance and prosperity. As a journalist and indigenous policy analyst for over 15 years, I have witnessed and documented this shift within the indigenous populace. In addition, indigenous leaders have emerged who have galvanized indigenous support for change. They have challenged the so-called Aboriginal orthodoxy. British Columbia indigenous businessman and lawyer Calvin Helin, whose 2008 book *Dances with Dependency* documented the problems of dependency within First Nations communities, is an example. So, too, are reformist political leaders such as Kamloops Chief Manny Jules,[b] Chief Clarence Louie of the Osoyoos Indian Band, and Ellis Ross, now a Liberal member of the British

---

b) I worked for a brief time with the First Nations Tax Commission where Jules is the chief commissioner.

Columbia legislature but who previously was the elected chief councilor for the Haisla First Nation on the coast of British Columbia. It was Ross who, in attracting natural gas investment to that territory, was the main force behind its drive from poverty to prosperity. There are also now many pro-business, pro-reform indigenous voices, and many pro-development indigenous organizations such as the Indian Resource Council and others.

The best way to understand the dynamic now underway in indigenous Canada is its parallel to a previous revolution in Quebec. In July 2022, Diane Francis wrote in the *Financial Post* of how indigenous peoples in Canada were undergoing a "Quiet Revolution."[1] This was a reference, of course, to the period in Quebec's history when that province, and the society therein, underwent profound social and political upheaval, including calls for modernization. The indigenous version of the Quiet Revolution Francis was referring to involved revelations of alleged corruption and scandal related to internal politics within the Assembly of First Nations (AFN). Francis was on to something: Change within the Assembly could indeed lead to a wider democratization within indigenous public life. That said, the societal changes or Quiet Revolution within indigenous communities have been occurring for some time and transcend the headlines about the AFN. Indigenous people—through their exposure to city life and the norms and values of Canadian democracy—have changed and now demand middle class prosperity and a life free of corruption and nepotism, the latter of which remains common on reserves.

This desire for reform and prosperity became obvious to me between 2007 and 2013 when I was lead researcher on a project called the Aboriginal Governance Index (AGI) at the Frontier Centre for Public Policy, a Winnipeg-based think tank. The project involved asking average First Nations people living on reserve what they felt about the quality of governance and services in their community. As far as we were aware, we were the first organization to attempt this type of survey. The project eventually grew to include all Prairie provinces.

One key observation from the Index we developed was that some First Nations operating under the Indian Act adopted policies that created a clear separation between band politics and service delivery. Establishing this so-called "firewall" between politics and administration ensured that nepotism and corruption were kept to a minimum. Bands that created this firewall could also easily adopt transparency rules and post financial statements and electoral information on band websites. Fast-forward to today and it would help if the federal government were to give band governments the incentive to adopt such policies, i.e., to link policies for lending funds and other policies that are beneficial for reserves with consistent transparency and financial controls. For example, when a First Nation applies for a loan through the First Nations Finance authority, the federal government requires that they adopt certain financial administration practices. This is not just a "stick" but a "carrot" as a commitment to good financial standards will also open up the First Nation to other lending options.

Reasonable First Nations leaders have long recognized that the governance proffered under the auspices of the Indian Act was prone to centralization and ripe for nepotism and corruption. This form of governance allowed a few families on small reserves to succeed while most languished. Band governments offered jobs and other benefits to their family members and supporters. Band politicians held disproportionate power because they were able to control government benefits and certain aspects of reserve life such as education and social assistance. Public policy expert, former British Columbia Liberal leader, and one-time aide to Pierre Trudeau, Gordon Gibson, called this the problem of "small governments with large powers."[2] The lack of independent media and band government scrutiny meant that band governments could run their operations with little regard for transparency and accountability to members. Over the years, First Nation citizens have frequently complained to the federal department of Indian Affairs about these abuses.[3]

Basic governance is one reason to enact better financial controls. Another is that a growing number of First Nations already realize that such transparent and accountable governance is required when they engage in joint ventures or perform other off-reserve business activities. It is essential, then, that the federal government ensure that all First Nations have the level of accountability and transparency that mainstream Canada takes for granted. This might seem like interference to some, but it is the minimum necessary to ensure that the rules are uniform and fair for all First Nations.

Aboriginal Governance Index respondents also expressed a desire for financial transparency from band governments. Reformers got their wish when the federal Conservative government (2006 to 2015) introduced the First Nations Financial Transparency Act, a law that required the publication of audited statements and chief and councilor salaries. The law stirred controversy when it revealed the exorbitant salaries of some chiefs, but it was popular with rank-and-file members. Unfortunately, after 2015, the successor Liberal government stopped enforcing the law and allowed some communities to stop posting this information. The federal government must return to enforcing this law—the requirement is appropriate and should not be dismissed as illegitimate interference given that First Nations residents themselves demand just this level of accountability. Such a requirement is not unreasonable: First Nation communities are governed with public/taxpayer funds—their own and transfers from others—and are thus required to operate accordingly; for now, the federal government should intervene where necessary with selected First Nations until their members can ensure accountability on their own.

Herein lies the apparent contradiction. Although indigenous communities say they do not want any interference, there must be *some* to ensure that First Nations residents receive fair treatment and a level of accountability for the money spent. Just as mainstream Canada needs to recognize the value of incrementalism, indigenous leaders and the indigenous public must accept that the process towards reformed governance necessarily involves the federal government, for now. That is realistic both from a constitutional perspective and practically: The federal government plays a critical role in ensuring that local leaders and political organizations with a narrow agenda do not dominate governance and decision-making, and do not crowd out necessary systemic reform across communities and for Canada as whole.

Reforms here will require looking at progress incrementally and also avoiding mistakes of the past on both sides, i.e., by First Nations and by mainstream Canada. For example, the most prominent ongoing example of an "Ottawa knows best" mentality is the Indian Act itself, which requires federal oversight of band elections, membership issues, and myriad other areas. The second example is the White Paper of 1969 which unilaterally proposed to change the relationship between First Nations and Canada with little indigenous input. A more recent example was the debacle over the First Nations Governance Act where indigenous communities opposed changes to First Nations governance systems, though some of those changes such as published financial statements were in the interests of their members. This was contentious because it also included provisions, beyond financial ones, that many First Nation communities saw as interfering in their governance systems.

Replacing the Indian Act with some other form of devolved governance is the end goal, but it will not happen quickly. A far better and wiser approach is for a First Nation community to make incremental changes to the Indian Act, negotiating away parts of it that are particularly egregious, and then continuing to remove more and more of it until one day the community wakes up to its complete absence. This is already happening on many reserves through sectoral and negotiated self-government and devolution agreements. But the Indian Act and its various intrusions will not disappear overnight. While it may be correct to describe some indigenous societal views as undergoing a revolution, that does not mean that in practical terms the Indian Act, for example, can be abolished in one step. Other Canadians need to respect how deeply ingrained the legislation is to First Nations and allow them to remove elements only when they are ready. A cautious, conservative, and incremental approach will work best. With the foregoing in mind, here are three practical ways First Nations can move ahead by choosing to grasp the chance in front of them.

Reform One: Embrace property rights

According to the Public Policy Forum, indigenous entrepreneurs invariably report that the main barrier to their success is access to capital, and that access is hampered by on-reserve land restrictions.[4] First Nation governments also say they lack capital to pursue initiatives or ventures. As a result, government becomes the default lender and funder of indigenous ventures. But this is unsustainable. Even in the case of on-reserve housing, the federal government and band governments became default loan guarantors. This places both parties at tremendous risk by placing liability for the debt on both sides. Fortunately, some First Nations have sought ways to move around this barrier and worked with the federal government where needed to foment useful reforms:

- In 1951, the Indian Act was amended to allow for certificates of possession, a quasi-private property instrument that allowed residents to own their homes, though they could only transfer them to other band members, thus diminishing the reform's economic value.
- Over the past few decades, the federal government has introduced institutions such as the First Nation Finance Authority to provide low-interest loans to First Nations by giving them access to the bond market. First Nations collateralize revenue streams to secure these loans. While this is an effective and helpful way for First Nations to secure capital despite their limitations, it deals mainly with the symptoms and not the cause, which are the land restrictions.
- Long-term leasing on reserves also provides some form of property rights but, as the name suggests, is limited in duration and value.

Some First Nations sought to address the cause of poverty, which was the lack of capital caused by unique land restrictions. In July 2009, I wrote an editorial in *The Globe and Mail* documenting[5] a historic conversation going on in northwestern British Columbia. The Nisga'a Nation was moving to pass legislation that would grant individual property rights to Nisga'a members on a voluntary basis. The First Nation could use its self-government powers to do this, since when its treaty was signed the Nisga'a Nation received all its land in collective fee simple. In the end, the proposal only affected a small minority of Nisga'a lands that were zoned residential. In 2016, I wrote another column in the *National Post* where I provided an update on the Nisga'a experiment.[6] Sure enough, no economic or personal catastrophes had followed the 2009 legislation, and there had been no foreclosures. Some Nisga'a who took advantage of the new rules were able to start small businesses.

At the time, some First Nations still under the Indian Act also began to express an interest in full private property rights. One report from the Senate Committee on Aboriginal Peoples made this observation:

> The Committee heard that there is a growing middle class among First Nations people, and that, in some communities, there appears to be a generational shift toward embracing the possibility of private home ownership. Stewart Breaker, Service Area Manager, Siksika Housing Administration suggested that "[t]he older members hold that treaty right to housing. Those under age 40 want to have something to own rather than just having hand-outs. The environment is changing... Several witnesses expressed the conviction that if people own their own housing, they are more likely to take responsibility for maintaining their homes. Chief Duncan Michano in Pic River First Nation in Ontario told the Committee that "when people own their houses, they have a stake in it, they are proud of it, they care." [7]

The closest the federal government came to introducing property rights on reserves was under the Conservative government (2006 to 2015) when it proposed a First Nations Property Ownership Act that would allow willing First Nations to opt into the legislation, and which when in effect would transfer title from the Crown to that First Nation.[8] Legislation of this type would expose the disconnect between indigenous leaders, activists, and academics from everyday First Nation people who are eager for the positive change this could bring. This Act should be reintroduced under the current Liberal government, with the proviso that the best the federal government could expect is a voluntary buy-in from First Nations who desire to opt in. Such an Act could serve as a "demonstration effect" for other bands to participate as previous bands become more successful. That approach also has the benefit of being observed over time and being tweaked.

A caveat: Location matters

Frank assessments in the 21st century of the failures and potential successes of First Nations includes looking honestly at the problem of location. It is a problem for many bands, as resource wealth alone cannot save all First Nation communities. Many First Nations do not have access to natural resources at all and never will, given their location, while many other communities are also in less desirable locations in general. Many fly-in communities in particular lack a natural economic base. Thus, to have any hope of adjusting to market realities, they will need to view their land in market terms. Some remote reserves will need to be "divvied up" with Certificates of Possession or leased long-term to others, while their residents move and seek education and employment opportunities near towns and cities where opportunities for prosperity do exist. This is why First Nations must have an honest conversation with themselves and then the federal government about the viability of some reserves.[9]

Property rights are not a panacea for First Nations and would mainly benefit those bands situated in commercially viable locations, but it is a start on the path to unshackling First Nations from federal interference. To achieve this goal, indigenous businesspeople and leaders need to push for property rights.

Reform Two: Commit to transparent reporting

The First Nations Financial Transparency Act is useful beyond just the posted audited financial statements of individual First Nations communities, though that is critical: First Nations governments are public entities and their governments are largely funded by taxpayers so this information should be available to the public. But there is another reason to adopt transparency in practice as well as in spirit. The public and First Nations members could learn about own-source revenues that First Nations communities are generating, revenue streams that are separate from federal and provincial government transfers. This would be useful for reasons of accountability but also, positively, to enable other First Nations communities to see what works on the path to more financial independence.

In 2016 the Fraser Institute released a study on own-source revenues for First Nations in Canada.[10] Due in large part to data available via the First Nations Financial Transparency Act, the study revealed that a growing number of First Nations are receiving revenues from a multitude of sources and that for some, own-source revenues exceed government transfers. This means that financial independence is achievable for many communities and the federal government should use this knowledge to help other communities achieve self-sufficiency.

The federal government could thus help First Nations identify and cultivate independent revenue streams where they exist and should give these communities an incentive to find these sources. Own-source revenues provide communities with more money to spend on their own priorities. Financial independence from government transfers is the most important goal for indigenous communities, the holy grail of indigenous politics.

Whether it is band governments, the Assembly of First Nations, or any of the multitude of indigenous political organizations, all are financed by federal and provincial governments. This single funding source creates an accountability mismatch. For band governments, if revenues are generated off-reserve, members do not see such monies as their own. There is thus a temptation to waste the money or use it for patronage purposes. If monies are generated directly from business ventures or members, there is a direct accountability relationship. More broadly, First Nations know they cannot truly call themselves independent when they are largely dependent on other governments.

Over time, the federal government can help communities develop their own-source revenues and, as much as possible, wean them off federal transfers. Of course, finding new sources means giving indigenous communities the economic tools that other Canadians take for granted, such as the individual property rights mentioned in the first point that will enable them to secure access to capital and less top-down economic control from Ottawa.

Reform Three: Explore resource wealth possibilities

A few decades ago, few people would have thought that an indigenous consortium could realistically consider taking ownership of a major pipeline expansion project. But it has occurred with the Trans Mountain Pipeline and similar ownership possibilities are in play for other major projects.[c] Critically, a significant number of First Nations are located close to natural resources and thus potential projects.[11] Critically, for communities in remote locations, these projects are likely their only path to prosperity. It is why the more sophisticated bands have increasingly sought to work with private partners to develop such resources to advance their communities. Those include impact benefit agreements with tens of millions of dollars for indigenous

---

c) "Indigenous Groups Still Aim to Buy Trans Mountain Pipeline, Even as Costs Soar," CBC News (March 7, 2022) <https://bit.ly/3S0CZNd>.

communities in the form of employment, training dollars, contracts for indigenous firms, and other revenues. Such agreements are why, over the last few decades, First Nations, Inuit, and Métis communities have increasingly become strategic partners in resource and energy business ventures. In 2019, a Macdonald-Laurier Institute study articulated the success of First Nations as they sought access to capital.[12] The picture in that report was much more optimistic than one might have expected: It revealed that in recent years, First Nations have witnessed a steady and impressive expansion in access to capital. Contrary to public perceptions, for the first time in Canadian history conventional market sources of capital have overtaken government transfers as the main source of indigenous economic development capital. In fact, the level of capital accessed and at work supporting indigenous businesses activity more than doubled between 2003 and 2013.

A growing indigenous middle class open to reform is the exact constituency that can use resource wealth on or near their own traditional territories to help those communities prosper. These players have not waited for First Nations politicians or the federal government to give them permission. They have instead defied the Hollywood- and activist-induced stereotypes of First Nations as opposed to natural resource development. They instead support such development where it aligns with their interests and where it is on their terms.

In summary, in an example of complementary policy, the ability of First Nations to engage in the resource economy will require selected changes to the Indian Act, but will bring with it an improved investment climate on reserves. First Nations themselves must embrace property rights and demand the same financial tools that other Canadians have if they are to be successful in attracting capital. Further, First Nations leaders must insist that the federal government abandon its "net zero" ambitions and anti-energy policies which are reflexive and ideological and not pragmatic. To keep natural resources in the ground poses the greatest threat to potential indigenous prosperity.[d]

---

d) The federal government and the provinces must improve and harmonize indigenous consultation policies to ensure they have clear language and identify which indigenous parties need to be consulted on any given resource development project. Meanwhile, indigenous communities must ensure they have protocols in place to deal fairly and practically with resource investors. First Nations must also expel foreign-funded environmentalists that have infiltrated reserves and tacitly support indigenous communities only so they can oppose development.

Finding a grand compromise in First Nations-mainstream understanding

One last frank truth must be acknowledged: The real division in the 21st century is not necessarily between "indigenous" and "settlers" as many vested interests, too many academics, and some indigenous ideologues claim. Instead, the division is between middle-class, pro-reform indigenous leaders, grassroots indigenous peoples, and businesspeople, versus the indigenous political organizations and scholars who are overly invested in the status quo including reflexive, unproductive activism. That status quo includes an attachment to ongoing government-granted preferences including, ironically, for the continued isolation of indigenous peoples, but this time justified with reference to protecting an assumed "pure" culture. This opposition to needed change is why reformists in government and elsewhere must find common cause with the indigenous reformist voices who are already pushing for change, and marginalize those too invested in the status quo.

Here, yet more frankness is required. While indigenous communities crave change to match the reality of the 21st century and how prosperity is created, they are not interested in rolling back some hard-won rights. Also, the Indian Act, the residential schools experience, and the White Paper[e] have hardened them to radical change, especially coming from the top. At the same time, while governments and the Canadian public are generally aware that First Nations do not want change imposed upon them, First Nations communities need to accept the position of the Canadian public: Canadians have collectively provided benefits above and beyond what was strictly required by treaties or the Constitution and have done so for decades, and want to see positive, concrete results.[13] The mainstream population wants to see justice for First Nations but most Canadians are also pragmatic. Ultimately, the Canadian public wants First Nations to strive for economic self-sufficiency and a more equal relationship between themselves and the rest of Canada. So as First Nations have their concerns recognized, it would

---

e) In 1969, Prime Minister Pierre Trudeau and his minister of Indian Affairs, Jean Chrétien, unveiled a policy paper that proposed ending the special legal relationship between Aboriginal peoples and the Canadian state and dismantling the Indian Act. Although some aspects of the White Paper were positive, such as the abolition of the Act, the dismantling of the Indian Affairs bureaucracy, and the introduction of more private property, the paper called for ending the treaty relationship and pushed for changes that many communities were simply not ready for.

help if First Nations also recognized the general public's concerns over financial sustainability, and how the Canadian public has been generous in offering benefits that they did not have to provide, including preferential tax treatment (only Treaty 8 mentions taxation at all, as one example). Or how Canadians have supplied indigenous governments with their dollars and how indigenous communities enjoy the benefits of tax exemptions. The Canadian public has grown weary of endless land claims and constant litigation. Most Canadians desire for First Nations to be self-sufficient and also desire finality on all land claims and settlements. It would thus be reasonable for First Nations to recognize the good-faith attempts of successive generations of other Canadians.

If First Nations people desire a government that abandons top-down politics and imposed changes, then it would be helpful if Canada's indigenous peoples grasp positive change by demanding progress of their leaders in several important areas—accountability and transparency, financial independence, support for property rights, and embracing resource wealth creation—and even recognizing that some reserves will never be viable. By grasping at all these opportunities, indigenous people can prospershould they so choose; or they can also choose to languish, but the choice will be theirs alone as will the consequences be they positive or negative.

This goes both ways: If politics is the art of the possible, mainstream politicians and some in the public need to shift their approach and meet indigenous people where they are at. Concurrently, First Nations must become self-sufficient, become full members of Canadian nation-state, and meet the Canadian public where they are at including adopting realistic and mainstream positions and policies. This is the compromise worth seeking. It would represent a grand compromise of the best kind, towards a flourishing Canada for all.

CHAPTER 17

How teaching the full history of world slavery frees us from selective guilt

Marjorie Gann

The British taxpayer paid a hefty price for the abolition of the slave trade for almost half a century... British taxpayers spent almost as much suppressing the slave trade for forty-seven years as the country profited from it in the half-century before slavery was abolished.
—DOUGLAS MURRAY

In March of 1803, the English ship the *Boston* anchored in an inlet of Nootka Sound in British Columbia. On the morning of March 13, according to an account of these events by the twenty-year-old ship's armourer, John R. Jewitt, "several of the natives came on board in a canoe from the village of Nootka with their king, called Maquinna, who appeared much pleased on seeing us and, with great seeming cordiality, welcomed Captain Salter and his officers to his country."[1]

Over the next nine days, a spirit of conviviality prevailed: the Nootka and their king revisited the ship regularly, dining with the crew, drinking the Englishmen's rum and contributing delicious salmon to their meals. But soon the Nootka and the sailors had a falling out. Maquinna's men massacred all the crew except for Jewitt and John Thompson, a sailmaker. As a skilled metalworker, Jewitt was valuable to the Nootka because he could repair their weapons and fashion hooks and ornaments; when Jewitt convinced his captors that Thompson was his father, they spared his life as well. Jewitt and Thompson were enslaved by Maquinna for more than two years, until they escaped onto another British ship that pulled into Nootka Sound.

Jewitt and Thompson's gripping adventure is retold in my book for young readers, *Five Thousand Years of Slavery*.[2] Whenever I introduce the book to middle and high school students, I open with a collage of five photographs: a ragged Chinese child, an escaped African-American slave, a tall African in modern dress, a ragged Indian child standing behind the Canadian antislavery campaigner Craig Kielburger, and an eighteenth-century English gentleman in a trim waistcoat and frilled white collar—the John Jewitt who spent two years in Nootka captivity. When I ask my young audience, "Can you point to someone who is *not* a slave in this collage?" everyone of course points to the two people with white skin: Kielburger and Jewitt.

To most of us, the word "slave" conjures up a picture of a black man picking cotton in the American South or cutting sugar cane on a Caribbean plantation. But slavery has been around for as long as human beings. It has been practised on every continent, by people of every skin colour, against people of every skin colour, and by virtually every culture. Because the book *Five Thousand Years of Slavery* is written for a North American market, fully half of it tells the story of slavery in the United States and the Caribbean, concentrating on the Middle Passage, the brutality of plantation slavery, and cruel domestic slavery. It corrects common misconceptions: that American slavery happened only in the American South (the enslaved Sojourner Truth, for example, was born in upstate New York), or that all abolitionists were white men (Olaudah Equiano in Britain and Frederick Douglass and Harriet Tubman in the U.S. are just the most famous of many black abolitionists). The book analyzes other forms of slave resistance, including rebellions (Nat Turner in Virginia, Samuel Sharpe in Jamaica), flight (especially along the Underground Railroad to Canada) and subtler forms of resistance, like work slowdowns and the often-cryptic messages in the spirituals composed by black slaves.

Beyond local to global understanding

But the local story is only half the story. And it is critical, today, for young Canadians to learn the other half.

Western culture is at a pivotal moment in its self-understanding. In the wake of the May 2020 George Floyd murder, an event which captured Canadians' imagination, though it did not happen here, a wave of self-criticism pushed a pernicious educational movement to the forefront: Critical Race Theory (CRT). In its original configuration, CRT uncovered ways in which systemic racism continued to disadvantage black people despite the passage of the 1965 Civil Rights Act in the U.S. However, the simplified version which has trickled down into classrooms singles out people of European heritage as oppressors and those classified as "visible minorities" as victims. This distortion of history has been implemented in schools across the United States and is making inroads in school boards in Canada.[a]

For example, the Elementary Teachers' Federation of Ontario (ETFO) has produced twelve lesson plans for three levels of education (Primary, Junior and Intermediate Divisions)[b] promoting the Critical Race Theory ideology with students as young as Grade 1. A lesson for Grades 4-6 is designed to show how "the ongoing process of colonization has resulted in the under-representation of First Nations, Metis and Inuit, and racialized peoples at all three levels of government." It asserts that students must learn in school "to re-imagine a more equitable distribution of power [and] disrupt the individual and institutional barriers that contribute to the economic and political systems of White power and privilege." Students are to discuss "how privilege and inequality is reinforced by the economic system of capitalism."[3] A lesson for Grades 7-8 has students think about who is the "Best Person in the World." It assumes students will produce a list that is preponderately

---

a) In Ontario, the Ministry of Education mandated a "robust, comprehensive and strategic professional learning plan for senior staff on equity, human rights, anti-bias and anti-black racism" for Peel District School Board (PDSB). This "Senior Team Learning Plan," as outlined by a submission to the board on February 23, 2021, is infused with recommendations for training in Critical Race Theory, with segments on "settler colonialism," "intersectionality," and "power and privilege." If this ideological bias is inculcated in senior staff, it will inevitably infiltrate curriculum. See <https://bit.ly/3VwO7CP>.

b) These lesson plans can be accessed at the bottom of Samuel Sey's article, "Critical Race Theory in Canadian Schools," on his Slow to Write website, <https://bit.ly/3MBowVi>. The purpose of these lessons (which ask the students to do very little reading or writing) is to turn them into activists; each lesson includes a "Call for Action." For parents who think that the purpose of schooling is to teach their children to read, write, and calculate, this must come as quite a surprise.

white and male; if they produce a list with more balance, they are to "discuss why their list differs so greatly from other classrooms where this lesson has been used." The lesson of white male privilege is not to be lost.[4]

Rather than a history of Western guilt, students deserve a more comprehensive history. Learning about world slavery offers an education with breadth and depth, posing probing questions within many disciplines:

- Geography: Since slavery is universal, where outside North America has it been practised? Why did it take different forms depending on location?
- Sociology: How is chattel slavery different from serfdom? How was serfdom in Western Europe different from serfdom in Russia? What is debt bondage, and where and why is it practised to this day? What were elite slaves (like the educated administrators in the Ottoman Empire) and how were they employed?
- Political science: How did (and do) totalitarian regimes like Russia, China, and Cuba employ punitive slavery to stay in power?
- History: In what ways was slavery as practised in the ancient Near East, classical Greece and Rome, and medieval Europe alike and different?
- Women's history: Where were female slaves preferred to male slaves, and why?
- Military history: Where and why were slave armies (Janissaries, Mamluks) recruited?
- Art history: In what cultures were gifted slave musicians, singers and dancers trained, and how were they employed?

A complete history of slavery would transcend finger-pointing, examine the growth of antislavery sentiment in the West, and ask:

- What were the religious and intellectual roots of abolitionism (for example, Christianity and the Enlightenment)?
- Why did the two significant abolition movements in history (in Britain and in the United States) arise only in these countries?
- What was the role of women in the antislavery movement, and how did this influence the later movement for women's suffrage?

Teaching slavery in a global context

The facts of slavery in early Canada—*panis* (indigenous) and black enslavement in New France, the arrival of black slaves with the Loyalists, and the gradualist antislavery legislation crafted by Lieutenant-Governor John Graves Simcoe for Upper Canada in 1793—arise naturally from the study of early Canadian history; they should be taught in a global context, so that Canadian slavery is not presented as mirroring a uniquely Western sin.

The saga of human enslavement is one of the saddest in the history of humanity; the saga of abolition is one of the noblest. To even begin to understand these phenomena, students need to hear the voices of slaves and bear witness to the courage of abolitionists. Here, then, are stories that will speak to Canadian students. Multicultural in the best sense of the word, they span the globe and examine the social structures and customs of our fellow human beings with honesty, nuance and subtlety.

Captured by the Maliseet of New Brunswick, 1689

In August of 1689, English settlers living near Pemaquid Falls, New Brunswick, were gathering in the harvest when they were attacked by thirty to forty Maliseet natives. Young John Gyles, with several members of his family, was captured. He retold the story of his capture and subsequent enslavement in *Memoirs of Odd Adventures, Strange Deliverances, etc., in the Captivity of John Gyles, published in 1735.*[5]

Gyles recounts the death of his father from gunshot wounds, the escape of his brother, and the brutal torture of captives he witnessed. He explains, "A captive among the Indians is exposed to all manner of abuses and to the extremest torture, unless their master, or some of their master's relations, lays down a ransom; such as a bag of corn, a blanket, or the like, which redeems them from their cruelty for that dance." He goes on to describe torture by an old native woman, who "will take up a shovel of hot embers and throw them into a captive's bosom. If he cry out, the Indians will laugh and shout, and say, 'What a brave action our old grandmother has done.' Sometimes they torture them with whips [etcetera]."

"Indian captivity" stories became increasingly popular in the eighteenth century; some were first-hand accounts, others fictional, so the details of

Gyles's account, published almost half a century after his capture, must be treated with circumspection. But there is no reason that Gyles's slavery narrative should be treated with any less respect than the slave narrative of Solomon Northup (the free black man in New York sold into slavery in the American South in 1841) or of Mahommah Gardo Baquaqua, an African enslaved in Benin, on the West Coast of Africa, whose story was told to Englishman Samuel Moore, and published in 1854.[6]

Chief Joseph Brant, British ally and slave owner

With the end of the American Revolution, Haudenosaunee Mohawk Chief Joseph Brant (Thayendanegea), Chief of the Six Nations, arrived in Upper Canada with his warriors in 1784, having sided with the British during the Revolution. They were settled on land that Governor-General Frederick Haldimand had purchased on the Grand River from the Mississauga people. Brant did not arrive empty-handed. Back in America, he had owned as many as thirty slaves, some black, some indigenous. He arrived with a young black slave girl named Sophia Pooley, whom he had bought, together with her sister, when she was seven years old. He sold her when she was twelve.

Sophia told her story late in her life to abolitionist Benjamin Drew, who included it in his 1856 collection of slave narratives, *The Refugee: or the Narratives of Fugitive Slaves in Canada, Related by Themselves.*[7] Sophia's memories of life with Brant were mixed. Though enslaved, she was also included in family activities, and remembers hunting deer with Brant's children ("When I lived with old Brant we caught the deer... Peggy and Mary, and Katy, Brant's daughters and I") but also recalls being mistreated by Brant's wife, whom she called a "barbarous creature" who beat her and scarred her brow when she cut her with a knife. Brant, says Sophia, defended her to his wife, with the words, "You know I adopted her as one of the family, and now you are trying to put all the work on her."[8] That a venerated indigenous Canadian like Brant kept slaves contradicts the stereotype of unrelieved indigenous victimhood.

From African slave traders to Caribbean slaves—and back again

In 2010, when the question of reparations to black American descendants of slaves was being hotly debated, the eminent African studies scholar Henry

Louis Gates Jr. outlined the complexities of the issue in a *New York Times* column. It was, Gates explained, not *white* slave traders who went upriver to capture black Africans for the transatlantic slave trade. It is estimated that "90 percent of those shipped to the New World were enslaved by Africans and then sold to European traders."[9] Two of these West African slave traders were members of the ruling family of Old Town, a settlement in Old Calabar on the Calabar River at the Bight of Biafra. Little Ephraim and Ancona Robin John were cosmopolitan Africans who could speak English and even took European-sounding names. Their story reveals the values of these African middlemen and the Europeans who traded with them.[10]

In 1767, faced with a stalemate in the lucrative slave trade along the Calabar River caused by rivalry between the Robin John family of Old Town and the Duke Family of New Town, further down the river, frustrated English traders contrived to trick the Robin Johns into boarding one of their ships, where they were put in chains and taken to Dominica, to be enslaved by a British captain for five years. They found another captain who promised to release them, but instead sent them to Virginia for sale. Because they were literate, they were able to appeal to successive American courts for their release, ultimately making their way back to Britain. There, they were taken under the wings of antislavery Methodist Charles Wesley, who converted them to Christianity and facilitated their return to their families and former elite status in the trading port of Calabar. By this point, they were deeply indebted to a friend of Wesley for their passage to Africa, which troubled Little Ephraim, who made this plea in a letter to Wesley: "[H]ow shall I pay My good friend Mr. Jones who has been so kind in Laying out so much money to save us [?] ... if we must not sell slaves, I know not how we shall pay[,] which I have a great desire to doe."[11]

The modern reader may be shocked that Little Ephraim, having experienced the harshness of slavery, would even consider inflicting such misery on others. But this must be understood in the context of the Calabar milieu, in which the Robin Johns were aristocrats. Theirs was a society whose wealth was rooted in the slave trade—in their world, slavery was not opposed in principle, as it was in the Wesleyan circle.

19th century slavery in America, Egypt, Nigeria, and East Africa

When the supply of American cotton to British textile mills declined during the American Civil War, Ottoman-ruled Egypt rose to the occasion, importing additional black slaves from Sudan to work the fields of Egyptian cotton plantations and keep the British mills supplied.[12] Starting in the mid-eighteenth century with the birth of Wahhabist Islam, Fulani jihadists from Masina along the Niger River conquered Hausaland and moved on to the Bornu and Adamamba states, creating the Sokoto Caliphate, which by the end of the nineteenth century held as many as 2.5 million slaves. (The Sokoto Caliphate is today's northern Nigeria, where Fulani extremists continue to attack non-Muslims, in this case black Nigerian Christians, as they did a century ago.)[13] Thus, the nineteenth century saw high numbers of slaves in *both* the United States (where four million black Americans were freed at the end of the Civil War) and in Africa.

When people hear the words "the slave trade," they usually think of the transatlantic slave trade, which has been extensively documented. Relying on primary source documents like abolitionists' pamphlets, shipping records, and drawings of slave ships, scholars paint a detailed picture of how slaves from the west coast of Africa were packed into ships and made the crossing to the Caribbean, South America, and ports like Charleston in the United States.

But slaves were widely traded in North, Central and East Africa as well. Scholars date the trade in these regions from at least a millennium before the beginning of the transatlantic trade.[14] The Arab-controlled trans-Saharan trade carried slaves in caravans across the desert to North Africa and to the eastern Mediterranean coast. Slave routes in southern and eastern Africa delivered slaves along the Red Sea, the Arabian Sea, and the Indian Ocean to Arabia, to Zanzibar's clove plantations, to Madagascar, and even as far east as India. There was considerable internal African trade as well.[c] The voices of slaves in Africa are difficult to access, as, unlike in the United States, Britain and Canada, nineteenth-century Africa birthed no indigenous antislavery

---

c) *In Slavery in the Arab World*, Murray Gordon calls attention to the relative paucity of research and writing about slave trading in North, East and Central Africa. He explains: "As many as eleven million Africans, approximately the same number estimated to have been taken from Africa's West Coast in the European-controlled triangular slave trade, were forcibly removed from their families and communities to do service in Arab households, harems and armies. Despite the long history of slavery in the Arab world and in other Muslim lands, little has been written about this human tragedy" (Introduction to the American edition, unpaginated). The estimate of eleven million in both cases may be low.

campaigns that saw abolitionists transcribing and publishing the narratives of freed slaves to arouse public indignation over their treatment. However, some freed slaves, late in life, told their stories to sympathetic missionaries or to their families. The life story of Meli shows how persistent the practice of slavery in Africa was, well after it had ended in the Caribbean and the United States.[15]

Meli was first captured by slave traders in what is now Zambia at the age of five.[d] Harshly treated by a man and his wife who put her to work and starved her, she was repeatedly sold until she ended up in a strange village. She began to hear rumours that white people were attempting to wipe out slavery in the region, but was sold to Arab traders and marched away with them. It was on this march that white colonials patrolling the slave trade attacked the Arab traders, and Meli and the other children in the slave coffle were saved:

> After a short while we heard gunshots. Everybody was scared and jumped and scattered into the bush... I went to the anthill where I found a little boy, hidden. He said, "Hide your head in the elephant grass. Get down. Don't let them see us."

The children did not realize that the white men were targeting the Arab traders, not them, but when the sound of gunshots stopped, Meli made her way to a Christian mission, where she was taken in. The missionaries educated her and enabled her to marry.

King Leopold II of Belgium's slave kingdom

As in East Africa, in Congo, too, it was Christian missionaries who played a significant role in protecting the locals against abuse. For example, in the late nineteenth century, two British missionaries made a heroic contribution to ending the brutal colonial reign of King Leopold II of Belgium over the

---

d) Historian Marcia Wright calls her "Meli" or, on occasion, "Mama Meli." She does not provide a last name. Meli's story was written down by her son and edited for publication by a grandson. During the years of enslavement, her name was changed by successive owners. When she arrived at the mission in Kawimbe, the missionaries gave her the name "Mary," which became "Meli." She was later baptized and married to Jones Changolo, so it is possible she took her husband's name, though this is not indicated in Wright's account.

so-called "Congo Free State," where the Belgians enslaved anything-but-free Congolese to harvest rubber and personally enrich the Belgian King.

Greedy for a colony of his own, Leopold had joined other European powers in the "Scramble for Africa," acquiring the Congo as a Belgian colony. He then made cynical use of European antislavery sentiment, convening a series of purportedly antislavery conferences starting in 1889 on the specious grounds that developing roads and railroads in this colony would hasten the end of the internal slave trade. His agents then set up rubber-trading stations along the Congo River. With a bicycle craze sweeping Europe, there was a demand for rubber for tires, and the slave-harvested rubber sap made Leopold fabulously rich. The Congolese rubber slaves were victims of unspeakable atrocities—held as hostages, beaten, burned, and starved, their hands or legs amputated as punishment for failure to harvest their rubber quotas.

In 1898, Alice Seeley Harris and her husband arrived in the Congo as British missionaries, hoping to convert the Congolese to Christianity. Upon witnessing the brutality of Leopold's Belgian agents, the couple found another calling: to publicize these atrocities in Britain and America, through pamphlets, photographs, and speaking tours that included lantern slides of Alice's chilling photographs of victims of the atrocities of Leopold's lackeys. By 1908, Leopold was in disgrace and his personal Congo fiefdom had been turned over to the management of the Belgian government.[16] When Alice and John Harris returned from a trip to the Congo in 1912, they reported "immense improvement." However, reports of forced labour and brutal treatment of workers persisted into the 1920s.[17]

Mui-Tsai: Girl slaves in China

It is widely known that, traditionally in China, daughters were valued less than sons. In cases of extreme poverty, when whole families were at risk of dying of starvation, parents often sold their daughters. Though the term *mui-tsai* literally means "little younger sister," being a *mui-tsai* did not mean being a beloved adopted daughter. It meant that a girl was bound to a family as a servant, and in some cases as a sexual servant to the master. This is what happened to Janet Lim (her Chinese name was Chiu Mei, meaning "Autumn Beauty"), born in 1923 and sold into slavery six years later, after the death of her beloved father. A convert to Christianity, Chiu

Mei's father had progressive ideas for his time, and had promised her an education. Unfortunately, he died before he could keep that promise. Her mother remarried, and when hard times hit, her stepfather decided to sell his stepdaughter to a dealer. Desperate to find her mother, Chiu Mei attempted to escape, but was found and returned to the woman who had purchased her. This is how she describes what happened next:

> I had never seen the mistress so savage before; she was like a tigress, she sprang at me and shouted that I was an ungrateful dog. She got hold of my hair and flung me to the floor. She sat on my stomach and pinched my body between her great long fingernails. They sank deeply into my flesh... I must have fainted, for the next thing I remember is waking up to find myself chained to a door and there I remained chained for a month.[18]

The cruel mistress later took Chiu-Mei to the British colony of Singapore, where she was sold again. The head of her new family was a lecherous old man who pursued her persistently. His intention was to make her his concubine. However, the British Colonial Office saw the *mui-tsai* system as a form of slavery and put pressure on the Singapore government to control it. As of January 1, 1933, no new *mui-tsai* were to be imported and all existing *mui-tsai* were to be registered with the authorities, who would investigate their treatment. The penalties for violating these laws were strict, so Chiu Mei's mistress took her to a government office to register her. Now Chiu-Mei knew what to do. When an Englishwoman from that office visited the home where she was enslaved, she escaped with her. Her owner was required to pay her for all her work, and Chiu-Mei was enrolled in a school where she was educated. She became a nurse, and after the Second World War, met and married an Australian doctor. Many years later she told her story in a book, *Sold for Silver,*[19] written under her English name, Janet Lim.

"Blackbirding" in the southern Pacific

Slavery was common in the southern Pacific. In what is now New Zealand, the indigenous Maori both sacrificed and cannibalized their captives.[20] In Hawaii there was a separate slave class known as *kauwa*, marked off on their foreheads by distinctive tattoos. They were sacrificed to the god Ku.[21]

Slavery in the south Pacific was not just indigenous. When the British colonized Australia and Fiji, labourers were needed to work Fiji's cotton and sugar plantations. An Australian doctor and adventurer named James Patrick Murray fitted out a ship and plied the coasts of islands, luring natives from their villages and transporting his human cargo to Fiji. Men like Murray were known as "blackbirders" because they dressed in black and made their way at night, kidnapping young, healthy men to provide unpaid labor. (The islanders left behind lost their strongest workers.)

Murray was breaking the law. Decades before, in 1807, Great Britain passed a law ending the transatlantic slave trade, and ever since, the Royal Navy, at the behest of the British government, policed the slave trade on the high seas, creating the West Africa Squadron which, between 1808 and 1860, captured 1600 slave ships and freed 150,000 African slaves.[e] Though the policing efforts initially targeted the transatlantic trade, blackbirding by British citizens such as Murray, or by sailors, was equally illegal after 1807. Thus in 1869, the British sent Captain George Palmer, already experienced in West Africa, to intercept the *Daphne,* a blackbirding ship making for Fiji. His description of the hundred-plus men from the New Hebrides on that ship makes for chilling reading: "They were stark naked, and had not even a mat to lie upon; the shelves were just the same as might be knocked up for a lot of pigs,—no bunks or partitions of any sort being fitted."[22]

Palmer tried to have the ship's American skipper and Australian owner convicted in a Sydney court, but without success. However, his book *Kidnapping in the South Seas* exposed the crime of blackbirding to the public.

The role of religion

Students in our increasingly secular country, taught in secular schools, learn little about one of the most powerful forces for abolition in Western history: religion. Yet from its inception, the abolitionist movement was rooted in Christianity. The first to conclude, as early as the 1670s, that holding slaves was against God's will were Quakers, who began to urge their coreligionists

---

e) In his 2022 book, *The War on the West*, Douglas Murray noted that "the British taxpayer paid a hefty price for the abolition of the slave trade for almost half a century.... British taxpayers spent almost as much suppressing the slave trade for forty-seven years as the country profited from it in the half-century before slavery was abolished" (145).

not to keep slaves. Deeply immersed in the Hebrew Scriptures, Protestant abolitionists in Britain and the United States filled their antislavery tracts with biblical references. Here are some examples:[f]

- Samuel Sewall's *The Selling of Joseph*, published in Massachusetts in 1700, states unequivocally that "all Men, as they are the sons of *Adam*, ... have equal right unto Liberty ... So that Originally, and Naturally, there is no such thing as slavery." He interprets Exodus 21:16 ("He that Stealeth a man and selleth him, or if he be found in his hand, he shall surely be put to death,") as forbidding slave capture and slave trading.[23]
- In *An Epistle to the Clergy of the Southern States*, Sarah Moore Grimké wrote, "What an appalling spectacle do we now present! With one hand we clasp the cross of Christ, and with the other we grasp the neck of the down-trodden slave!"[24]
- In *The Bible Against Slavery* (1837), Theodore Dwight Weld quotes all the verses he can muster to bolster his argument that the Bible opposes slavery and to refute those who cite Canaan's curse as biblical sanction for slavery.[25]

Among the staunchest opponents of slavery and the ongoing slave trade in Africa in the late nineteenth century were Christian missionaries. Often stereotyped exclusively as "Bible thumpers" who imposed the Scriptures on Africans, many were nonetheless selfless people who, often at great risk, committed themselves to saving African lives. After Alice Harris photographed a bereaved father staring dolefully at his child's dismembered hand and foot, her husband John remarked in a letter, "I think great credit is due to my wife for the promptness and courage she shewed [sic] in getting such a picture under such circumstances, as every minute might have brought the traders to the Spot."[26] And it was Moravian missionaries whom Meli trusted to keep her safe when faced with the threat of re-enslavement in Zambia.

---

f) The Devil, of course, can also quote Scripture, and pro-slavery advocates found verses in the Bible to justify slavery: God's curse of Ham was read as an endorsement of black slavery; slavery was regulated, but not banned, in Leviticus 25; and Paul in his *Epistle to Philemon* tells the runaway slave Onesimus to return to his master.

Teaching about our shared humanity

If this brief survey of slavery on six continents teaches us anything, it is that, when it comes to enslaving our fellow human beings, there are no ethnic saints and no racial sinners—just human beings. Europeans enslaved Africans, but they purchased them from Africans who captured them upriver. The Nootka of the west coast of Canada and the Maliseet of the east massacred, tortured, and enslaved Europeans. Haudenosaunee chief Joseph Brant enslaved blacks. As Americans were enslaving Africans to pick cotton on southern plantations, the Ottoman rulers of Egypt were importing slaves from Nubia for the same work. The list, as we have seen, goes on and on.

Teaching that slavery was universally practised immerses students in factual—not romanticized—history. Eschewing selective finger-pointing, it acknowledges that all peoples have been capable of committing an evil that, until recently in human history, was not even recognized as such.

Unfortunately, current trends in education risk dividing, rather than uniting, Canadian students. As we saw earlier, Critical Race Theory (CRT), which attributes collective guilt to only one (the white) skin colour, has been adopted by several Canadian school boards. Consider, for example, these angry tweets (March 15, 2020) from "educator, scholar and activist" (her words) Vidya Shah, assistant professor in the Faculty of Education at York University. Shah takes aim at a white school principal in Toronto for his frustration with his board's obsession with white privilege: "White 'bystanders': Your silence perpetuates racism. So does 'choosing' to disengage, giving your white peers the benefit of the doubt... again, waiting until you're a ________ to speak up, and taking issue with white ppl who talk about white privilege. Your complicity is violent."[27] In an article published in October of that year, Shah went further, questioning Canada's right to exist: "White supremacy and settler colonialism have existed in this place that some refer to as Canada."[28]

In contrast to this divisive thinking, we would do well to consider the observation of the late Chief Rabbi of the Commonwealth Lord Jonathan Sacks on how victim thinking plays into a cycle of revenge. When you are obsessed with hatred for those you believe mistreated you or your ancestors, Sacks explains, you are not free. He asks us to listen to the words of Moses addressing the Israelites poised to enter the Promised Land: "Do not hate an Egyptian, because you were a stranger in his land."[29]

As descendants of Egyptian slaves, the Hebrews had good reason to despise the Egyptians, but Moses knew that vengefulness was not the answer. Hate, he understood, would re-enslave the people who had escaped enslavement to Pharaoh: "Hate makes us slaves. Therefore, let it go. Do not wage war on the children of darkness. Make sure that you and your children are sources of light."[30]

If Canadian children are to be "sources of light," they require enlightened instruction. A universal history of slavery is not only historically accurate, which is important enough. In a country as diverse as Canada, it also sheds light on our common humanity—with all the good and all the evil that entails. Giving students a nuanced understanding of our shared past will be critical in forming the next generation of Canadian citizens.

CHAPTER 18

The problem with Canada's "woke" self-loathing: A view from abroad

Gourav Jaswal

As an immigrant myself in Canada for more than 38 years, I cannot believe the level of self-loathing and fake guilt the so called "woke" liberals have. As a "coloured" person and humanist, I dislike this prevalent conversation.
—An Iranian immigrant to Canada, writing to the author in 2021

I have spent my entire life living beyond a 10,000-kilometre radius of Canada, so readers will need to forgive me if I never cared too much about what Canadians were up to. However, a few years ago, my sons started school in Canada and I began to ping Google News Canada (and read the *National Post*) as avidly as I consumed the media in Goa—the sleepy, tropical beach-side state where I live in India. And what I read every other day about Canada repeatedly strikes me as puzzling and often outright absurd.

One such curious item caught my attention in May 2021, when then mayor of Vancouver, Kennedy Stewart, apologized for the brief handcuffing of a black retired B.C Supreme Court justice, due to what was subsequently discovered to be a case of mistaken identity. A *mea culpa* for any mistake is wonderful. But the mayor immediately declared without investigation that it was clearly the result of "systemic racism". And then added the astonishing statement that, "As someone who continues to benefit from colonialism, I recognize my privilege."[1]

My home country of India has a long history of colonization; over two hundred years by the British, in addition to the French and the Portuguese, the latter being the ones who colonized the state where I live. The Portuguese left only in 1961 following military action, over 14 years after the rest of India had been liberated from the British. What I have discovered, however, living in the middle of the remnants of their buildings, their cuisine, their bridges and causeways and their language, is that the legacy of colonialism is impossible to paint in a singular shade unless one is willing to sacrifice truth for ideology.

As a citizen of a previously colonized country and colonized province, I am bemused at the attempts to derive declarative certainties where facts lead to nuanced possibilities. And Indians understand this. Even when the English team beats India in cricket (which happens rarely, I should note), none of the half a billion Indian fans complain that it is because the English "continue to benefit from colonialism," despite our history of subjugation.

Yet the now-former Vancouver mayor asserted that he "continue[d] to benefit from colonialism"? This is a man whose life-story tells me that he came from a family that lost their home and went bankrupt, yet who still managed to get a degree at Acadia University. He moved from Nova Scotia to British Columbia in 1989 with only $100 in his pocket and worked his way up, becoming an academic, a member of Parliament, and then mayor of one of Canada's largest cities. He appears to have done this through hard work and determination, not by exploiting colonialism. Of course, if the mayor indeed intended to erase his self-declared unearned privilege, instead of vacuously signalling, then he would have resigned and given over his position to the purported victims of this colonialism he cites.

Canada as a racist haven?

If Vancouver's mayor was engaged in an odd modern form of self-flagellation, other Canadians also seem convinced they live in a racist state—including those who are actually the living repudiation of the "Canada is racist" trope. I have a personal example. A few years back, a delightfully warm-hearted woman I have known since she was a teenager, and who immigrated to Canada from India in her 30s, started complaining about racism in Canada. It was especially perplexing given the fact that she is currently an elected representative in a provincial government. It is staggering to claim that a country which you moved to as an adult and have no ethnic connection to, where you do not belong to the majority religion or race, and where your first language is not either of the national languages of that country—is racist, when it has allowed you to frictionlessly rise to the highest levels of society and government.

My friend's claim of systemic racism is even more absurd when I contrast Canada's laws with those of the state in India where I currently live: Goa. There is absolutely no chance that I could be elected to the legislature of Goa despite my being Indian by birth, because my family's ethnicity is originally from the different state of Himachal Pradesh. And despite the significant blurring of boundaries of class, caste, language and religion in past decades, such differences still matter in India. That is why no one from outside Goa has any chance of getting elected to our state legislature, which is why no one in the past 20 years *has*. Yet my friend—a woman who lived a majority of her life in India—and within a decade of her immigrating was elected to a provincial legislature, believes and declares that Canada is racist?

Canada as a petri dish for idea-viruses

Ever since my older son started university in Canada, it is claims such as these which have made me increasingly worried that Canadian culture has become a petri dish for dangerous and virulent thinking: Where the dominant discourse asserts that every claim of repression should be acknowledged as fact and every culture treated as if it were equally important to the Canadian mosaic and indistinguishable from the foundational beliefs of the majority that created Canada's original story and institutions.

For example, I chanced upon the holiday calendar issued by a School Board in Ontario and noticed that a remarkable number of days were marked with esoteric religious holidays.[2] The Ninth Day of Ridvan of the Baha'i faith is listed, as is Farvadegan of Zoroastrianism. Since there are only about 100,000 adherents of Zoroastrianism in the world (of which 61,000 are in India)[3] I am skeptical on how many have found their way to Canada, but at any rate, I cannot imagine there are too many adherents in this particular school district. It is odd then, to me, that a few Canadians at a public schoolboard in a secular country that is 63 per cent Christian feel the need to mark holidays associated with religions that a miniscule number of residents in the country adhere to.[4] At the same time, it has become increasingly insensitive to cheerily wish people a "Merry Christmas."

I am proud of the richness of the 2,000-year-old Indian civilization, including its languages, history, culture, literature and cuisine, and I never aspired to send my sons to Canada for their education. But since that is the way the dominoes of fate fell, I embraced the reality and began to eagerly anticipate what they would learn in Canada. My hope was that they would imbibe the rugged sportiness, the quiet sense of civic pride and social service, as well as the cheery optimism that Canadians are rightfully renowned for. In short, I was looking forward to my sons becoming a little more 'Canadian' in Canada. But every week seems to bring a new episode in the unending TV series that should be called 'Canada's Got Stupid!' Now I worry that they have become distanced from all that is wonderful in India, and instead are immersed in the worst of Canada.

Canada's chattering classes to Canadian history: Drop dead

I first wrote of these concerns in a *National Post* column in 2021, a column prompted by yet another apology by yet another Canadian politician. And the feedback from that column led me to a bemusing realization: Canada is a rare country where its majority seems to be constantly shushed. After a mere 48 hours of publication, the blizzard of online comments on my column exceeded 800, and the real wonder for me: the emails; dozens and dozens of which filled my Inbox, that eventually totalled over 28,000 words.

The voices I heard through these emails moved me, for they appeared entirely authentic: anguished voices, anxious voices, angry voices, tired voices. A wounded army veteran, a renowned chef, a refugee, a young dairy farmer in British Columbia, a provincial government minister, and émigré Canadians, living in Italy, Costa Rica and Florida. Most of what they had to say was surprisingly resonant with my own views. (Of course, a few were strident in their opposition; one commenter succinctly reviewed my work in ten words: "This is the stupidest article I have ever read. Congratulations!")

However, no matter what they wrote, every email seemed more authentic than the progressive drivel that dominates social media, politics, and universities where new theories keep many professors out of touch with average people and with average struggles. The voices tweeting cacophonously online are not the largest in number or the wisest, but they are definitely the loudest, shrillest and most combative. The letters I received made me realize how so many people (overwhelmingly, native-born Canadians) feel silenced. And how happy they were that someone with my ethnicity spoke out, because they would be crushed under social opprobrium if they voiced what they felt. As a result, I thought that some of the voices who speak for Canada, but which usually go unheard, should have a chance to be listened to in their own words.

The myth of a past, privileged generation

I was touched deepest by stories from people whose families over generations built the Canada that much of the world admires today and that millions of Canadians still love. Consider the retired schoolteacher who wrote:

> My grandparents came over just after the Irish Ghost ships over a century ago. A full 1/3 of the 200,000 immigrants were dead within a year. And in the early 1900's, orphans from Ireland were adopted by prairie families to work the farms. I guess colonialism ain't [as] cracked up [as] what some say.
>
> I have the "privilege" of [having] grandparents and parents who fought in both world wars, and [who] lived through a depression. Living in an immigrant-majority area myself for [two] decades, I taught here for a dozen years. I met a number of wonderful neighbours, parents, and students. Of course, there were troubled and sometimes misguided individuals, but no race or culture was exempt.
>
> But in our new post-modern era, you are either right or wrong, oppressor or oppressed, victim or success. Rarely an opportunity for respectful discussion, in a world of believed absolutes. Sadly, I no longer have a voice.

A reader of Polish descent shared:

> I am in Canada because when my father was released from a Nazi slave labor camp, he wanted to get out of Europe. So, what's the point of telling you this? In a strange repetition of history, I have discovered that I am now part of the great guilty white tribe and my tax dollars and contrition are required.

An Albertan touchingly said:

> My Dad was a World War II veteran and was a very proud Canadian. If Dad was alive, he would shake your hand for this article. [After his name he added,] From Canada. One of the best countries in the world, but for how long?

An 88-year-old woman shared her moving family history:

> My two grandmothers came to this country more than 100 years ago with eight children between them and without husbands, both of whom had died during wars. They took menial jobs to survive and feed their children, all of whom received a Grade Eight education before leaving school and going to work to help support themselves and the family.
>
> I was born during the Great Depression and can recall my father's desperate attempts to find work. He was too proud to take what the government called "Relief Payments." I recall how my unmarried uncles hopped on freight cars in search of work. I can recall my brother losing his hearing because his ear-drum burst due to an infection. We could not afford doctors.
>
> It was only during the war when my father found steady employment in the armed forces that our circumstances improved. Then my parents began to save. I completed high school, trained as a nurse, worked for a couple of years in that profession, returned to school to obtain a degree [in] Nursing, married a physician, had four children, returned to school again and received a Master's degree in Education, and finally a Ph.D. in Psychology.
>
> This is why I feel so strongly about this county and the opportunities it has presented to the impoverished and persecuted.

From mainstream to supressed minority

Suppression of dissenting minorities is unfortunately common around the world. Not just in dictatorial regimes like China and North Korea, but even in democracies run by heavy-handed elected leaders, such as in India, the Philippines or Brazil. Incredibly, in Canada it is people from the majority—in terms of race and religion—who seem to feel that expressing even a mildly dissenting opinion will get them denounced as "racist." The typical result is social ostracism or damage (sometimes outright destruction) to their businesses and careers. A lifelong resident of Vancouver who has travelled extensively wrote:

> I have seen extreme poverty and suffering in Africa and India, extreme government surveillance in China and Russia, I've been robbed and beaten in Thailand and Belgium, seen drugs and crime in Eastern Europe and Mexico. Yet all of those countries have something beautiful; their people... don't wallow in pity and whine because they don't get anywhere doing so. You need to pick yourself up, learn your lesson and don't make the same mistake twice.
>
> Canada used to be like that. Now we're too busy apologizing and throwing out the red carpet for the weakest, unstable and incapable people in society to give them a platform to criticize our nation and systems. To speak out is social suicide. I am a business owner and I risk losing my livelihood and life's savings if my company goes under. So, the good people remain quiet, the sick people go unchallenged, the politicians apologize and Canada is sinking off into the sunset.

A Regina resident who grew up in Toronto wrote to me to note the extreme apology culture that represses reasonable dissent from the extremist view that Canada's history necessitates shame and endless apologies:

> I enjoy meeting immigrants to this once great country. I want to learn why they left their homes and families and moved here and [I] never tire of hearing their stories. I'm 67 so have heard a few.
>
> If we look through the history of most countries, each was taken over, invaded, colonized or otherwise subjugated by another race or culture. Yet it seems that Western democracies are the only ones feeling such guilt that we continually apologize for the past. The past is past, we acknowledge it, vow not to repeat it and move on.
>
> The sad thing is that while many people in Canada feel as you and I do, we cannot speak openly about it as we are immediately labelled a "racist," a "white supremacist" or "denier" and all conversation screeches to a halt.

A reader with a doctorate in Philosophy who has had a distinguished career said:

> I want to retire and travel while I still can. Poor countries are my goal. Where the people are real, because they have to be. First World problems are mostly self-created. It's almost like people need a certain amount of adversity in their lives, and if it doesn't come naturally then they have to make it up.

One father from Calgary even feared a stampede of disdain in his own home should he have shared my 2021 column with his offspring:

> We have four children and, of course, we love them dearly. But at least two of them seem unwilling to read, reflect and then have a discussion that doesn't devolve into irrational comments and name calling. Thanks for your article. I'd pass it on to our kids, except they'd accuse me of being racist!

A mother of five children noted the lack of appreciation for what in fact allowed Canada to become one of the more educated, prosperous nations in the world:

> Lack of knowledge of history and of other cultures has destroyed us. In schools, they cannot teach about the downfalls of any other culture, for fear of offending people. All they do here is criticize our OWN culture. The culture which helped bring about industrialization, innovation, exploration, and education! That's why we home-school our kids. We want them to learn the truth.

Facts are now racist?

A common sore point among respondents to my public defense of Canada was the reluctance within institutions to confront empirical evidence about the origins of social ailments, despite this being an obvious pre-condition for any remedy. The American economist Thomas Sowell has done this in the United States since the 1960s—analyses of how education, or cultural and religious beliefs, or family dynamics affect people's chance of failure, success and crime rates—but there is little such research performed in Canada, because such analysis is presumed *de facto* racist. As one example, a Toronto resident mentioned:

> I find it especially hilarious that in Ontario, collecting crime statistics that include the ethnic origins of the perpetrator... was abolished at least 20 years ago if not earlier. Why? Because the statistics show that in certain areas, certain ethnic groups are shown to produce a higher amount of crime than others. The underlying reasons are never addressed, as that too would be racist. But collection of that is branded racist and allowed to be prevented. So much for actually dealing in facts.

Many readers discussed the sharp edges of guilt they are constantly made to feel, for events that happened decades before they were born. But one reader pointed out an unexpected and insidious effect of the constant drum-beat about "white privilege":

> As a white male, I've become so accustomed to being labelled privileged that I've simply accepted that is the case. I have therefore been a most willing apologist for my ancestor's colonial ways. But one of the drawbacks to this continual portrayal... is that it perpetuates an unconscious racism whereby you feel you truly do have some advantages. Perhaps a little smarter. A bit more industrious. More capable... it's difficult for me to articulate this exactly.

Other readers shared helpful perspectives about keeping racism in context, even as Canada strives to improve:

> Some Canadians are mildly racist in some small ways. It consists of the odd snarky comment made somewhere to someone. That isn't going away.... All sorts of tribes diss other tribes... Anglicans make jokes about Catholics and Priests make snarky cracks about Bishops.

A retired public servant added:

> Were Canadians racist in the past? Yes, along with pretty much the rest of the white world. Did we learn from the campaigns to eradicate racism, sexism et al. that have swept over us in the last 60 years? In my opinion, yes. Canada still contains racists, but I think an indicator of their non-existent influence is that they have to huddle in corners talking to each other.

The new Canadian patriots: immigrants and minorities

Emails from readers are of course not a statistically representative sample. But among my correspondents, the group that most fiercely disputed the view that minorities in Canada are subject to indignities were minorities themselves. The most vocal and heartfelt defence of Canada came from almost every first-generation immigrant who wrote in—whether they arrived in Canada 50 years ago or just five years previous.

Consider one thoughtful response from an immigrant who arrived to Canada just four years ago:

> I'm an immigrant from Brazil, arrived here in 2018 at 35 years of age. During this entire time, I have never felt the slightest racism from anyone. I have had four jobs and worked my way up to the same level I had back home. It only took me two years, with no connections or friends. I continue hearing about systemic racism, white privilege and colonialism, but I really cannot see this personally.

A Sikh Canadian wrote:

> [Prime Minister Justin] Trudeau has been apologizing for things that occurred in Canada even before it became a nation. Canadian Universities now have "black only" graduation ceremonies. Kids cannot say "Merry Christmas" in school...

Another reader, whose ethnic origins are in Iran, was equally frank:

> As an immigrant myself in Canada for more than 38 years, I cannot believe the level of self-loathing and fake guilt the so called "woke" liberals have. As a "coloured" person and humanist, I dislike this prevalent conversation.

Another, from a twice-immigrated family, said:

> I've lived in Canada for forty-five years, migrating from Jamaica, where my ancestors came from northern India. Our self-pity comes from our leaders' desire to accommodate the world instead of building a country for Canadians.

Another added to the criticism of the country's leadership for pushing a divisive, identity politics narrative:

> I came to Canada at the age of 21 with $10 from then-communist Czechoslovakia after Russian invasion. I struggled, learned English, got a university degree....

He started a company that was eventually sold for considerable value. Here is how he saw the process unfolding:

> The slow Canadian decline probably started in the late 60's with the election of Pierre Trudeau. The son's only credential is his father's pedigree. His father began the destruction of Canada, but at least he was a professor and thinker. This guy is a former drama teacher that thinks he can a run a country of some 30 million people.

At turns moving, fascinating, intriguing, thought-provoking and tough-minded, all of these notes were sincere, real, and deeply felt. A few, however, were of a decidedly lighter variety. Like the one from a renowned television personality, who offered a helpful idea: "Mr. Jaswal, could you please move to Canada and run for Prime Minister. You'd probably win." While that is an attractive thought, I think I should set my sights a tad lower and take up another idea offered by one correspondent: "I think you have a gold mine with your reference to a 'Canada's Got Stupid' TV show. If it became a YouTube channel..."

Despite the unhinged beliefs that Canadians are forced to endure in social discourse and that are increasingly becoming legislated as state policy; it appears that Canadians have not lost their tradition of self-deprecating humour. That may be exactly where everyone in Canada should start: to re-embrace the foundational values that created this wonderful country that millions of people in the world aspire to live in.

CHAPTER 19

Ideas, immigrants, and the future of Canada

Ven Venkatachalam and Mark Milke

The vast migrations of peoples over the centuries have left many racial and cultural groups in settings radically different from the settings in which their own cultures evolved, facing challenges and opportunities undreamed of by their ancestors.
—THOMAS SOWELL, *Race and Culture: A World View*

Ideas can change the trajectory of individuals and entire nations. From Adam Smith's notion of the "invisible hand" which helped spread free market ideas and prosperity, to the opposite notions of Karl Marx which spurred revolutions, repression, and entrenched poverty, to religious conceptions of any variety which have anchored cultures, ideas affect how people see and govern themselves and each other. Ideas have impacts that outlast armies and empires.

Immigrants, likewise, can have a profound effect upon the culture and direction of any nation-state, given they are "carriers" of ideas and can actualize them by changing societal assumptions and, in liberal democracies, voting patterns. It is significant, for example, that early Chinese immigrants to the west coast of North America in the mid-nineteenth century came from an entrepreneurial region of China and carried a penchant for starting businesses with them to California and British Columbia.[1] Similarly, it is significant that refugees to Florida who fled Cuba after Fidel Castro's 1959 revolution were staunch anti-communists, an orientation that has had an effect on the idea culture and politics of that state ever since.[2]

Given the importance of ideas and immigration, it is worthwhile to examine the flow of both. In the case of Canada that examination will reveal how the most positive aspects of ideas and immigration can fuse together to create a free, flourishing future for all within the project that officially began at Confederation in 1867 but which has been underway since the first settlers crossed the Bering Plains 20,000 years ago.

That first migration and all the others since then are not unique. Since the start of human civilization, men, women, and their children have been on the move—across hard and soft borders and in some cases literally halfway around the world. They did so for reasons that ranged from better economic opportunities to the need to flee tyrants to the chance to be closer to family. The rise of mass transportation in the later nineteenth century has only accelerated the trend: passenger ships, trains, automobiles, buses, and airplanes have all aided the great movement of people who find a home elsewhere. The result is that in the twenty-first century a greater proportion of the world's population now lives in a country other than the one in which they were born than at any time in history. As of 2019, there were approximately 272 million international migrants[3] or roughly 3.5 percent of the global population.

These migration trends are relevant to Canada. Canada's current high immigration levels combined with internal turmoil over what ideas matter now and in the future. Canada thus might well be a test case revealing how the interaction between ideas and immigration will play out in the coming decades. Whether one's ancestors arrived 20,000 years ago, or were from mainly European "stock" and arrived in the last 500 years, or have come from any other part of the globe since the 1970s, the origins and changes in Canada's demographic make-up matter, as do the reactions of other Canadians to that mix, because a nation-state must unite diverse people around a conception of the "good life" and must agree on a way to govern itself. Making such decisions necessitates some minimum agreement on what the "good life" and "good government" means and how it is actualized in policy. With that preface in mind, let us now turn to the changing makeup of modern-day Canada.

Overview of immigration to Canada and changing identities

The global migration patterns noted above have been visible in most developed countries, Canada included. Immigration to Canada has been relatively high in recent decades and especially in recent years. With rare exceptions, such as in the late 1970s or during recessions in the early 1980s and during the COVID pandemic, immigration to Canada has steadily increased, tripling since 1972 (see Figure 1).

For example, between 2016 and 2021, over 1.8 million immigrants settled permanently in Canada. In 2021 alone, more than 406,000 people immigrated to Canada (with similar or higher numbers expected for 2022 when the final numbers are calculated). That was more than triple the 122,006 who arrived in 1972.[4] As a result of such migration flows, by 2021, nearly 23 per cent of Canada's population was composed of landed immigrants or permanent residents, the highest proportion among G7 countries[5] (see Figure 2). In other words, more than one-fifth of Canadians are now foreign-born, a level last reached in the 1920s.[6] Similar flows are projected in future years,[7] with the share of landed immigrants or permanent residents forecast to reach a high of 34 per cent of Canada's population by 2041.[8]

FIGURE 1

Number of immigrants to Canada

1972–2021

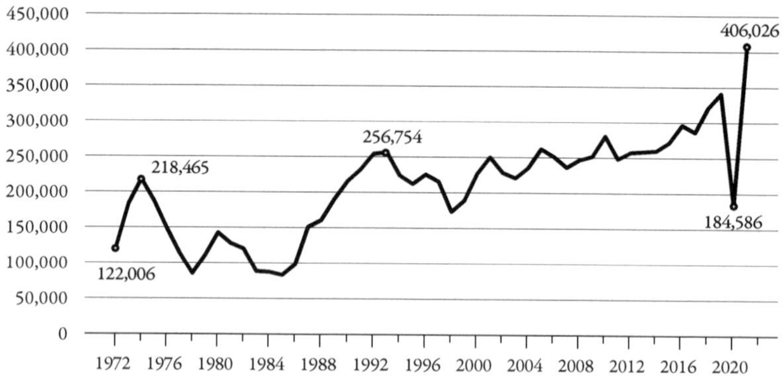

Source: Statistics Canada, Table 17-10-0014-01.

FIGURE 2

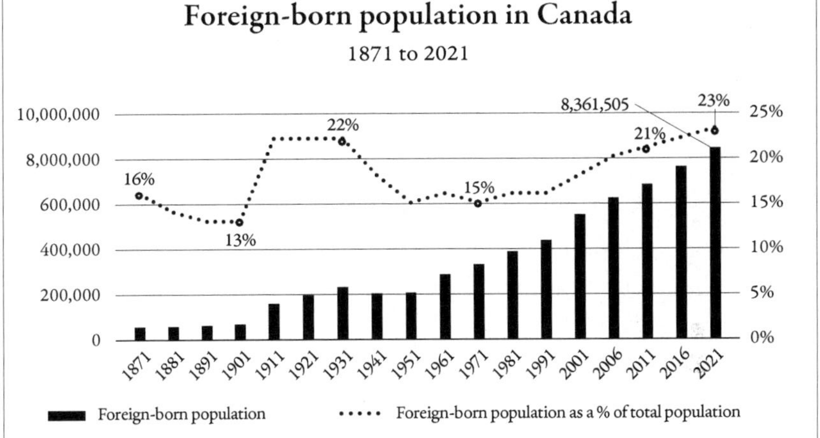

Statistics Canada, 2021 Census of Population.

Increasing ethnic and religious diversity

During the first few decades after Confederation, the overwhelming share of Canada's foreign-born population came from the British Isles, Europe, and Scandinavia. Those regions accounted for over 88 per cent of Canada's foreign-born population in 1871. A full century later, that proportion had declined only marginally, to just under 80 per cent as of 1971. However, starting in the early 1970s, the composition of the immigrant population changed significantly. The growth of non-European immigration source countries since 1971 has transformed the ethnic origins of the foreign-born population in Canada, as well as the overall population mix. By 2016, the traditional source of immigrant stock, i.e., mainly European and British, declined to just under 28 per cent.[9]

As a proportion of all immigrants, those from Europe, Australia, Great Britain, South Africa, and the United States form a smaller share of all foreign-born immigrants than at any time in Canada's history, while the proportion from Asian countries is noticeably higher (see Table 1). Immigrants from Asia alone accounted for over 48 per cent of Canada's foreign-born population as of 2016. By 2036, the forecast is that Asian-born immigrants will comprise 57 per cent of Canada's foreign-born population.[10] Before 1971, just over 12 per cent of immigrants[11] were a visible minority but as of 2021, 83 per cent of recent immigrants were projected to be in that cohort. In 2021, the most common country of birth for recent immigrants[12] was India followed by the Philippines and then China. Those three countries alone account for about 38 per cent of Canada's recent immigrants.[13]

The religious composition of immigrants has also changed. Prior to 1971, 78 per cent of those who immigrated to Canada identified themselves as Christian. That proportion has declined ever since.[14] After 2001, over 36 per cent of immigrants between the ages of 25 and 54 (the available data subset) were of a non-Christian faith, just over 38 per cent identified as Christian, and nearly 26 per cent said they had no religious affiliation.

Immigrants are integrating into the workforce

The most widely recognized indicator of successful socialization is the participation of immigrants in the labour market (the proportion of that cohort working or searching for a job). The closer that level is to the overall level for a native-born population, the more successfully are immigrants integrated into the society. For example, in France, the labour force participation rate for the foreign-born population stood at 67 per cent in 2019, a low compared with other countries. In Canada, the labour force participation rate for the foreign-born cohort was higher than in most G7 countries at just over 79 per cent, 12 points higher than France.

The positive rates are also clear in higher employment rates and lower unemployment rates for foreign-born persons in Canada when compared with other G7 countries. For example, the unemployment rate for foreign-born people in Canada was 6.3 per cent in 2019 compared with 5.5 per cent for native-born Canadians. That is a marginal difference and can be explained by language difficulties, accreditation for skills, adjustments to a new country, and differing average education levels, among other factors. The difference in unemployment rates between foreign-born and native-born in Canada is small particularly when compared with Germany, where the unemployment rate for those born outside the country is more than double that for native-born Germans (see Table 2).

TABLE 1

Percentage distribution of the place of birth of Canada's foreign-born population

1871 to 2011

	British Isles	Europe (excluding the British Isles)	United States	Caribbean, Bermuda, Central and South America	Africa	Asia (including the Middle East)	Oceania and others
Observed							
1871	83.6	4.8	10.9	0.0	0.0	0.0	0.7
1971	29.5	50.2	9.4	3.2	1.4	5.0	1.3
1981	23.3	43.4	7.8	7.3	2.6	14.1	1.5
1986	21.0	41.6	7.2	8.7	2.9	17.5	1.1
1991	17.2	37.2	5.7	10.4	3.8	24.6	1.1
1996	13.8	33.1	4.9	11.1	4.6	31.4	1.0
2001	11.6	30.4	4.4	11.0	5.2	36.5	1.0
2006	9.7	27.1	4.0	11.3	6.1	40.8	1.0
2011	8.3	23.1	3.9	11.7	7.3	44.9	0.8
2016	7.0	20.7	3.4	11.6	8.5	48.1	0.8
2017 projections							
2021	6.0	17.2	3.4	11.6	9.7	51.3	0.8
2026	5.1	15.1	3.3	11.5	10.5	53.8	0.7
2031	4.5	13.4	3.1	11.4	11.2	55.8	0.7
2036	3.9	12.0	3.0	11.3	11.7	57.4	0.7

Source: Statistics Canada (2017).

TABLE 2

Employment, unemployment, and participation rates by place of birth in G7 Countries

% | 2019

	Employment Rate		Unemployment rate		Participation rate	
	Place of birth		*Place of birth*		*Place of birth*	
	Foreign-born	Native-born	Foreign-born	Native-born	Foreign-born	Native-born
Canada	**73.2**	**74.9**	**6.3**	**5.5**	**78.1**	**79.3**
France	58.9	66.6	13.1	7.8	67.8	72.3
Germany	70.8	78.2	5.6	2.6	75.0	80.3
Italy	61.4	58.7	13.1	9.6	70.7	64.9
Japan	N/A	N/A	N/A	N/A	N/A	N/A
UK	74.7	75.3	4.3	3.7	78.0	78.2
United States	72.2	69.8	3.1	3.9	74.6	72.7

Source: OECD Database

Educational attainment among visible minorities

One critical measurement of success is education. In Canada, visible minorities were far more likely to have a university bachelor's degree or above than were white Canadians. In 2015, among people employed across various sectors who were between the ages 25 to 44, 24 per cent of white men and 38 per cent of white women possessed a university degree. Meanwhile, 49 per cent of men and 62 per cent of women of South Asian descent possessed a university degree. The percentage rose further, to 65 and 61 per cent for men and 73 and 71 per cent for women of Korean and Chinese ancestry (see Figure 3).

Visible minorities have always been part of Canada's population, though in much smaller numbers and as a proportion before 1971. The higher education levels among many visible minorities is relevant for two reasons: It calls into question assertions from those who oppose immigration on the grounds that low-skilled immigrants may become dependent on social services. It also calls into question a claim from others that Canada is systemically racist. The high levels of education for visible minorities—native-born or foreign-born—combined with high labour force participation rates and low unemployment rates for immigrants, together with Matthew Lau's findings in a previous chapter on ethnicities and incomes, all cast doubt on both assertions. Instead, that many of the foreign-born arrivals to Canada and many native-born visible minorities have higher education levels than white Canadians is clear evidence of their success despite claims made to the contrary.

FIGURE 3

University degree compositional characteristics of Canadian-born men and women by ethnicity, ancestral origin, or colour

2015 | Ages 25-44 | Bachelor's degree or higher

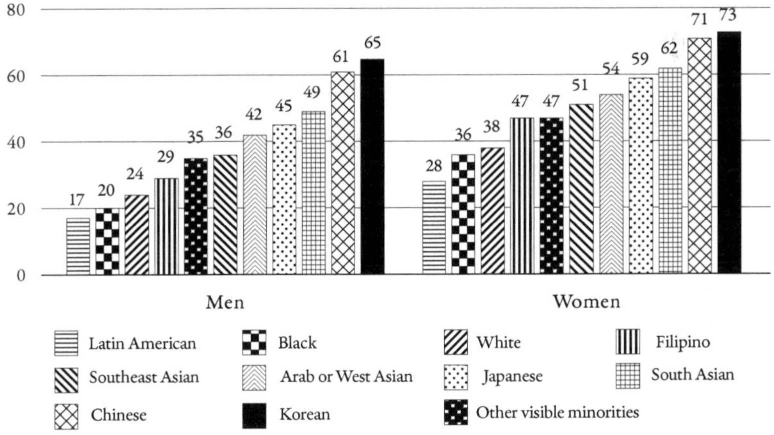

Source: Statistics Canada, 2016 Census of Population.

The response to immigration: Mostly positive

The data are clear that that immigrants to Canada in the last five decades, but increasingly in the twenty-first century, have mostly emigrated from different nations than those where "old stock" Canadians or their ancestors originated, i.e., the British Isles or Europe. Increasingly, the most recent immigrants are visible minorities and of a faith other than Christian or Jewish, or have no faith at all. The labour participation rates for immigrants closely parallels those for native-born Canadians. More broadly, Canadians of a visible minority (both native-born and newcomers) generally have higher average education levels than white Canadians, depending on the immigrant cohort. This integration success for immigrants and visible minorities is supported by acceptance data on migrants from a 2019 poll. It found that that among 145 countries,[15] Canada ranks as the most accepting country for migrants, at about five times the acceptance rate of the least welcoming countries for immigrants worldwide (see Figure 4).[a] That, too, is another measure of success, of social harmony among most Canadians.

FIGURE 4

Countries most and least accepting of migrants

Migrant Acceptance Index, out of 9

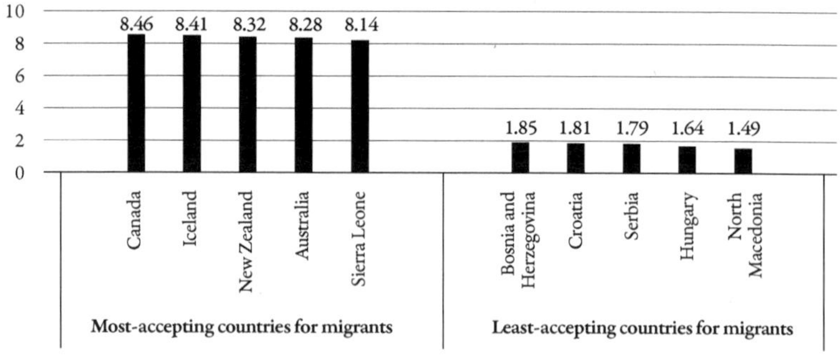

Source: Gallup (2019).

---

a) The index is based on three questions that Gallup asked in 140 countries in 2016 and 2017 and updated again in 145 countries in 2019. The questions ask whether people think migrants living in their country, becoming their neighbors and marrying into their families are "good things" or "bad things".

Culture and beliefs are critical because they are idea- and assumption-rich

The foregoing is positive. But now, back to question of how to unite people with diverse origins around a shared set of positive ideas. Historically, native-born citizens or older immigrants might have wondered if newer arrivals would hew to the common assumptions that might have attracted arrivals in the first place. For example, in the twentieth century it was common for those fleeing tyrannies and autocracies to emigrate to Canada precisely because it was mostly free in areas such as expression, the economy, association, religion, and other areas and thus unlike the Soviet Union, China under Mao, Germany under Adolf Hitler, Vietnam under communism, and multiple other examples. Canada was and is also peaceful, which was attractive to those fleeing civil wars or genocidal governments. Canada is also relatively free of corruption, another attractive facet of Canadian life when compared with countries where bribery is expected as cost of doing business or carrying on everyday life.[16]

Given that Canada's population will be increasingly ethnically dissimilar to that of the past and, depending on the assumptions of new immigrants, traditional Canadian mores could be weakened or strengthened. There is certainly the potential for illiberal ideas to take hold and thrive as not all ideas and cultures are alike in their core assumptions, for example, about the role and rights of women. We began this chapter with a quotation from the American economist Thomas Sowell on the threats and opportunities for migrant populations the world over. In his six decades of economic work on race, culture, and outcomes, Sowell has also made clear that ideas among cohorts and culture vary enormously and that no one should assume every idea has equal value—some are indeed superior to others. Instead, as Sowell points out, the history of humanity has been one of testing and sharing ideas over time. He notes that a critical factor in economic and other aspects of a successful cohort or country is "the cultural receptivity of different peoples"[17] to tried, true, and successful ideas both on a grand, country-wide scale and on an individual scale.

It is critical for present and future Canadians to unite around ideas which make possible human freedom and flourishing and discard poor ones that can lead to the opposite ends. That imperative makes an implicit and positive case for all Canadians to focus not on identities that are unchangeable, but on laudable ideas that can be shared by all. The attention to ideas matters because every culture brings with it different assumptions of what the "good life" looks like and how society should be organized. Still, despite the reality of these differing assumptions, diverse people can fuse together cohesively when they find a new or common goal to which they can aspire.

One of the authors of this chapter is an immigrant and the other is a third-generation descendant of immigrants. As we continue to build Canada, it will be useful for Canadians to ponder our diversity and our differences, and to consider what divides us and what potentially unites us. Rather useful to remember, every Canadian ultimately has a shared evolutionary origin which speaks to our common origins. It is why the 1867 project known as Canada should be infused both with reality and goodwill as we incorporate new immigrants who, if the data are correct about their mostly successful integration, could help successive waves of arrivals build upon the accomplishments of previous generations.

CHAPTER 20

Renewing the peaceable kingdom: Why ideas and not identities should matter

Mark Milke

Your rights take priority over those of the state... The collectivity is not the bearer of rights: it receives the rights it exercises from the citizens.
—PIERRE TRUDEAU, Cité Libre dinner speech,
Montreal, October 1992

It is time to debunk a nonsensical myth that has metastasized in Canada in recent years: That any attempt to rank ideas and values as preferable or civilized is intolerant at best, racist at worst, and a sign of a misplaced cultural superiority complex.

The concept that no idea or value should trump any other became a point of contention during the tenure of the federal Conservative government between 2006 and 2015. That government implemented reforms to the citizenship guide given to new Canadians. The most famous revision was the 2011 version which referred to "barbaric cultural practices," specifically female genital mutilation and "honour" violence and killings in which a girl or woman is subject to violence or murder by the men in her life because she is seen to disrespect, dishonour, or disobey those men. The guide noted that Canada's immigration policy was open and generous but under the section entitled "The Equality of Women," the guide was clear that "Canada's openness and generosity do not extend to barbaric cultural practices that tolerate spousal abuse, 'honour killings,' female genital mutilation, forced marriage or other gender-based violence."[1]

Justin Trudeau, the then-Liberal critic for Immigration, Refugees and Citizenship, was scornful of the wording. In a Toronto radio station interview in March that year, Trudeau asserted that using the word "barbaric" was "pejorative." He noted that "I think that's part of the tone that I'm uncomfortable with."[2] After being accused of moral relativism by then Immigration Minister Jason Kenney, who said the term "barbaric" was *meant* to be a pejorative, Trudeau defended his reaction. He argued that:

> My problem with the use of the word barbaric is that it was chosen to reassure Canadians rather than actually change unacceptable behaviours. The subjective value loaded into that word makes it easy to dismiss as an insult, rather than a statement of basic, simple fact.

While noting that he himself would use the word "barbaric" in a personal conversation to describe female genital mutilation, he mused that "in an official Government of Canada publication, there needs to be a little bit of an attempt at responsible neutrality."[3] (He later backed away from those last two words.) Trudeau argued that such acts should instead be described as "totally unacceptable," which he asserted would still be "clear, strong, and objective, without being 'us civilized, you not.'"[4]

Trudeau's 2011 response is an example of the confusion or even opposition to the notion of a necessary hierarchy of ideas with some superior to others and which should rightly and openly be labelled as civilized or the opposite. Those superior ideas include core Western liberal values such as the rights of individual women and have been a hallmark of Western thought and, beginning in the 19th century, increasingly actualized in policy and law. Additional comments Justin Trudeau made shortly after he was sworn in as prime minister in 2015 illustrate two related problems: His reluctance to clearly articulate a minimum standard necessary to be a contributing member of the "peaceable kingdom"[a] and his hollowing out of Canadian history. In

---

a) The phrase has its origin in the Old Testament book of Isaiah, where in the eleventh chapter a reference is made to the "peaceable kingdome of the branch out of the root of Jesse…." Literary critic Norththrop Frye popularized the phrase as applied to Canada in a discussion about the 1834 painting by Edward Hicks with the same name. Frye's thoughts were noted in the 1965 book *Literary History of Canada: Canadian Literature in English* (see https://bit.ly/3QSUwGe).

a 2015 year-end interview with the *New York Times*, Trudeau described his view of Canada this way:

> There is no core identity, no mainstream in Canada. There are shared values — openness, respect, compassion, willingness to work hard, to be there for each other, to search for equality and justice. Those qualities are what make us the first post-national state.[5]

Trudeau's comments can be deconstructed any number of ways. The prime minister contradicted his own claim that Canada has no "mainstream" or "core identity" by going on in the same interview to trumpet the "shared values" of Canadians. He listed what he thought those were, another way of saying that Canadians *do* have a core identity and that there is a dominant, i.e., mainstream view. Beyond the prime minister's contradictory conceptual confusion, there was a practical reason to articulate a standard of beliefs and behaviour: any country that wishes to survive as a functioning entity and avoid cracking up into a broken, dysfunctional set of competing tribal clans needs agreement on the basics of what citizens should rally around.

Canada's identity: British liberalism and French ideology

In addition to Trudeau's confusion, he also made an historical error: Canada does have an identity and one would think that Trudeau, himself the biological product of French and English coupling, would have been aware of it. Canada, as with other nations, is a fusion of battles and ideas and political compromises mostly, though not exclusively, between the English and the French.[b] In general historical terms, one can reference the pre-1759 history of French Canada or the decisive victory of the English over the French on the Plains of Abraham in that year[6] and the Royal Proclamation of 1763; the inflow of United Empire Loyalists during and after the American Revolution; the 1840 Act of Union that fused together the colonies of Upper and Lower Canada into the Province of Canada;[7] 1867 and Confederation; or even the 1982 Constitution courtesy of Prime Minister Pierre Trudeau and willing premiers of the day who recognized the English and French dominance of British North America and enshrined both languages into the Constitution.

---

b) Both the British and the French had indigenous allies.

As well, ponder the ideas that bound Canada together. They assume the worth of the individual and were directly inherited from the United Kingdom, but which are also the product of Jewish and Christian intellectual history,[c] as well as the Renaissance, the Reformation, and the Enlightenment. These ideas and developments include: the Magna Carta of 1215 and its enunciation of rights including to property and on the limits on rulers and the implicit assumption of the rule of law; the Enlightenment writings of John Locke on the social contract and his overall contribution to liberal thought; the 1688 Glorious Revolution which limited the power of the monarchy; the economic works of Adam Smith and others on the usefulness of free markets; the value of political and societal evolution rather than revolution written about by Edmund Burke; the public and parliamentary anti-slavery advocacy of abolitionists, most chiefly the initial efforts of British parliamentarian William Wilberforce that led to millions more converted to that cause; John Stuart Mill on the "why" of liberty; and Mary Wollstonecraft on the rights of women—among many others.

It is precisely because such concepts are ideas and not connected to ethnicity, race, or gender, that they can and are adopted by peoples the world over regardless of whether they share the Christian faith of William Wilberforce, or the skin colour of Adam Smith and John Stuart Mill, or the gender of Mary Wollstonecraft. Anyone can adopt preferences for a free nation, a free economy, and equal opportunity. The most recent example has been Hong Kong residents who, while they obviously share the culture, history, and ethnicity of those in mainland China, have been in near-constant protest against the regime in Beijing for withdrawing freedoms first tasted under British colonial rule. Also, many among the older generations in Hong Kong deliberately fled communist China earlier for just such freedoms.

---

c) For more on this, see Larry Siedentop (2014), *Inventing the Individual: The Origins of Western Liberalism* (Penguin Books). For a more specific Canadian book on the history of liberal thought in Canada, see James M. Forbes (2022). *Protestant Liberty: Religion and the Making of Canadian Liberalism, 1828-1878*, McGill-Queen's University Press. Forbes makes the case that Lockean, liberal thought in Canada had its origins in the religious and cultural assumptions of Protestantism, and specifically Protestant Dissenters. The existence of Protestant dissenters such as Baptists, Congregationalists, Methodists and others had an interest in freedom to worship and belief vis-à-vis the powerful Anglican establishment. The religious freedoms carved out by and for them later to led to other freedoms, even unintendedly, for Catholics who even Dissenting Protestants might think were incompatible with a liberal order, and then tolerance and political freedoms which today we label as "liberal."

The example of Hong Kong shows the attractive power of superior ideas—freedom to flourish in this instance—over mere identities, and how one's ethnicity, colour, and gender are irrelevant to the transmission of ideas.

All this matters to a proper understanding of Canada including the rights and responsibilities assumed "normal" today. All of the foregoing and more were critical to those who shaped a liberal democratic country on the northern half of the North American continent pre- and post- Confederation. As an example, the members of the Constitutional Association of Quebec, formed in 1834 and which historian Michel Ducharme categorizes as "one of the modern pillars of the defence of liberty" in its day, were fully versed in their British-inspired rights: "Freedom for our persons, opinions, property and industry... are the common rights of British Subjects," asserted that early Quebec association. Following on such an understanding, early Canadian statesmen conceived of Canada's core identity in much the same way. William Lawrence, speaking in the House of Assembly in the pre-Confederation debates in March 1867 remarked that "We are a free people, prosperous beyond doubt, advancing cautiously in wealth, under the protection of our good old flag.... Under the British Constitution we have far more freedom than any other country on the face of the earth."[8] Or consider a former Liberal prime minister, then opposition leader Wilfrid Laurier, in an 1894 speech in Winnipeg in which he attacked the Conservative government of the day for its protectionist policies. In so doing, Laurier referenced a list of freedoms which he thought were self-evident and which the Tory government should not injure. The list is a recitation of the essential freedoms that any classical liberal would hold dear and which came from across the Atlantic: "The good Saxon word, freedom; freedom in every sense of the term, freedom of speech, freedom of action, freedom in religious life and civil life and last but not least, freedom in commercial life."[9]

All of the foregoing bears witness to a core Canadian identity that remains constant, one that prizes freedom and values responsibility and which is derived from historic British understandings and interpretations of liberalism. It was that classical liberal approach, today often called small-c conservative or libertarian, that served as the dominant Canadian approach to its institutions—reform not revolution—and to daily life; freedom to associate, speak, create, of religion and of the press, and to be entrepreneurial; favouring home and hearth over the incessant politics of European coffee houses and wild-eyed continental fanaticisms. That identity was obvious in laws and policy and also in selected constitutional anchors put in place in 1867 and 1982, as well as a parliamentary articulation of the same in 1960 with a Bill of Rights passed under Prime Minister John Diefenbaker.

Ideas—not your identity—matter

One can note all such historical developments that informed and fused modern Canada, any and all of which contradict the Trudeau notion that Canada has no core identity. It is here where the most egregious part of Trudeau's thinking on Canadian nationhood emerges and should be critiqued—that Canada thus is the "first post-national state." Canadians should hope not because, historically, there are two distinct types of nation-states with regards to citizenship. The first is based on unchangeable characteristics such as ethnicity or race, i.e., states based in and defined by ethnic nationalism—tribalism writ large. The other, second type of nationalism, revolves around shared ideas, the civic nationalism that exists in Canada, France, Australia, New Zealand, the United States, and the United Kingdom, among others.

States founded on civic nationalism are based on an idea with rights and responsibilities attached to the individual.[d] Thus, one can be Protestant, Jewish, an atheist, Buddhist, or a Muslim, or a thousand more varieties and one's rights and responsibilities are constant without reference to one's identity. In states based on civic nationalism, one is not, for example, normally taxed at a different rate or given a lesser or harsher sentence based on whether one is white, black, indigenous, or part of a specific religious

d) This ensures that the ground rules of interaction are agreed upon by citizens, be it the rule of law and equal treatment before the law, the necessity of fair, free, and periodic elections in the peaceful transfer of power, or other fundamental rights and responsibilities. These have been hallmarks of Western liberal democracies but have been assumed by multiple non-Western nations as well, including South Korea, South Africa, and a plethora of other nation-states.

group.[e] (Moreover, when countries such as Canada have departed from the equal treatment of citizens and newcomers—the denial of the vote to indigenous Canadians or the Chinese head tax—such departures have usually been condemned by fair-minded thinkers.)

Thus, traditionally in the West and increasingly in selected other countries, the civic model of citizenship includes nation-states based on a shared set of ideas and ideals. In France, those ideals are captured by the motto "liberty, equality, and fraternity"; in the United States it is "life, liberty, and the pursuit of happiness"; in Canada it is "peace, order, and good government." While Canada's credo is not as robustly "idea obvious" as are the other two, it is derived from British and French influences and thus includes assumptions about freedom, the rule of law, the necessary division of powers, and so forth.

Of course, as with any nation composed of human beings, all such nations often fell short of the ideals and founding ideas, but that does not take away from the fact that, for example, the American Republic was founded upon an idea: Freedom as an individual's birthright. That idea is what eventually compelled Americans to expand civil rights to black Americans, women, and others after they were finally and properly considered full persons—

---

e) This notion of equality before the law and in other spheres has been eroded in recent decades in part by policy and in part due to court judgements. In the 1980s, the federal government under Brian Mulroney's Conservatives began to imitate the American policy of racial and general preferences, known as "affirmative action" in the United States and as "employment equity" in Canada. The Canadian policy was and is illiberal, anti-individual, and unnecessary. As Martin Loney chronicled in his 1998 book, *The Pursuit of Division: Race, Gender and Preferential Hiring in Canada*, there was no statistical case for illiberal hiring by race or gender, not when one understood that differences in outcomes observed in the data in Canada in the 1970s and 1980s resulted from a variety of factors ranging from the average educational levels of a cohort to culture and much else. On another matter, differences in sentencing, the 1999 Supreme Court of Canada's Gladue decision gave the green light for judges to award lesser sentences to indigenous offenders on the justification that they came from disadvantaged backgrounds (*R. v. Gladue*, (1999) 1 S.C.R. 688, *Judgments of the Supreme Court of Canada*, Lexum (October 23)). The Court ignored both a relevant fact and an unfortunate consequence: Almost every person faces some disadvantage in their own life or perhaps a "slow start" due to their ancestors or the ancestors of others. Critically, to sentence an indigenous male, for example, convicted of sexual assault (against an indigenous woman) to a lesser sentence based on his ancestry means the woman he attacked has received less justice than a woman of a different ancestry, a fundamentally illiberal result.

individuals.[f] In contrast, if inequality had been assumed as natural as per ancient Greece or Rome or in most other civilizations in history, movement towards individual equality of opportunity and rights would have been stillborn because it never would have even been conceptualized.

Likewise, after 1789, however imperfectly the French Revolution brought it off, the French solidified their concept of the nation-state: that liberty, fraternity, and equality are the ideas that should be cherished in common. The United Kingdom and Canada have also shown that they value ideas: From the Magna Carta onward, each nation's core ideas are of the sort enunciated by Laurier and others: classical liberal freedoms, assumed responsibilities in tandem, and limited government as the foundation for our nation states. As with the United States, that not all peoples were initially granted citizenship or full rights in Canada, France, or Great Britain does not change the fact that the ideals and ideas of equal treatment of the individual in law and policy were and are the basis for our political self-organization. The assumption that the individual mattered and that liberty mattered is precisely what drove reforms when existing laws and policies were injurious to individuals and/or selectively applied to persons of one colour or religion but not equally to all.

That attachment to a liberal ideal of equality of the individual and, ultimately, freedom *for* the individual and her chosen beliefs is at the heart of our core identity as Canadians. It is something that modern politicians such as Justin Trudeau forget, or deliberately omit, at their—and our—peril. It is precisely because most Western countries do not ground their citizenship and systems of government on ethnicity or religious adherence, or have long since abandoned such requirements due in part to a conflict with equal treatment of the individual, that care must be taken to preserve the founding or adopted civic ideals and ideas. After all, most Westerners and certainly most Canadians likely disdain ethnic and religious nationalism; we see it as too limiting for the type of nation in which we wish to live. But the reason such nationalism is constricted and discriminatory is for the opposite of

---

f) The attention to the rights of the individual is why American slaveholders and even the American Supreme Court battled the notion of full personhood for blacks for much of the 19th century: Because to recognize black Americans as full persons would have meant that the state would have had to treat blacks as individuals with the full panoply of rights to which they would be entitled. It would also have required such slaveholders and justices to recognize their own racism.

what Trudeau assumes—that Canada has been emptied of all content, of all ideas, and is now a free-for-all *potpourri* of cultures and ideas, none superior to any other. The reason countries such as Canada mostly "work" is not because citizens live in a relativistic vacuum, but because states built on civic nationalism of the liberal democratic variety, either at the start or during their development, rallied around the idea that the *individual* should be at the center of law and policy, not some artificial collective.[g]

Expressed differently, the fundamental unity in nation-states such as Canada results not from an absence of belief, an absence of unifying ideas, or from a void inside our heads. If that were true, there would exist no agreement on constitutional and political organizational fundamentals such as one-person-one-vote elections, or the necessity for the rule of law, or the British-Canadian model of accountable government. To be sure, nations can unite around harmful or evil ideas. A plethora of Germans in the 1930s did just that when they rallied around the anti-scientific notion of "race purity" and all that that entailed under National Socialism and Adolf Hitler. But whether a harmful idea or ones that have been prevalent in liberal democratic nation-states, absent unity on the basics, a nation-state would expose itself to something akin to what happens in an atomic explosion—the atom splits apart and destruction spreads outward. When nations suffer a severe internal crisis over what constitutes a minimum core set of beliefs and unity necessarily observed by all, the result is anarchical dysfunction at best, or civil war at worst. France in 1789, Spain in the 1930s, Yugoslavia in the 1990s, and the American Civil War in the 19th century are all examples. In the latter case, disagreement over the basics from the South—that no state shall secede and that no man should enslave each other and this on the presumption that human beings were made in the image of God—is

---

g) The collective—however defined by race, class, ethnicity, gender, or one's attachment to a favourite sports team—is artificial because the collective is not the entity that is born, bleeds, hurts, loves, and dies. Only the individual does that. While we often speak of collectives as if they were living organisms, the reality is that the family, neighbourhood associations, a tennis club, environmental group, or a country are composed of individuals but are not "an individual." The difference is critical because giving collectives power over the individual means giving specific individuals *within* that collective power over other individuals—governments led by politicians, for example. This is why the exercise of such power can only be justified if all individuals are subject to the same rules and responsibilities. This is core to the notion of the rule of law—that it applies equally to all.

an example of a disagreement over the fundamentals of the nation-state. It took a civil war to resolve that disagreement over the basics and, positively, the abolitionist North won.

Some ideas *are* better than others

In contrast to Justin Trudeau's conceptual confusion and his notion of a hollowed-out nation-state with "no core identity," his father, Pierre Trudeau, prime minister of Canada between 1968 and 1979 and again from 1980 to 1984, was clear about Canada's core identity and its historic commitment to classical notions of individual liberty. Unlike many of today's politicians, this equal treatment of the individual in law and policy is something that Pierre Trudeau grasped and argued for in 1992 in debates over the Charlottetown Accord. That referendum which, if passed as an amendment to the Constitution, would have granted special status to Quebec and have allowed its government to treat citizens differently based on their identity and language preference (anglophones, francophones, or others). That accord would have constitutionalized the allowance of such discriminatory treatment. It was why Trudeau was clear that to recognize Quebec as a distinct society and constitutionalize its "collective" right to discriminate against individuals was wrongheaded. That was because to give collectives *defined by language, ethnicity, religion, or race, power over fundamental liberties* creates the potential for clashes between such collectives, in addition to being illiberal. As Trudeau remarked:

> And that is why the theory of collective rights is a dangerous one. Larger and smaller collectives confront each other in the heart of one and the same country, and that can eventually lead to civil wars.... And that's why the French Revolution established liberty as a fundamental right . No-one is subject in his fundamental rights to the state: that is *liberalism* —which says that the individual in the exercise of his fundamental rights precedes the state, and all individuals are equal—that's the American Constitution, that's the Universal Declaration of Human Rights.[10]

Unlike his son, Pierre Trudeau grasped that tribalism based in unchangeable characteristics has been the norm in human history, which is why citizens must instead consciously think of each other as individuals first and define each other that way in law and policy if they are to avoid the unresolvable conflicts that arise between collectives.[h]

It is not that collectives do not exist or that collective action is always invalid. By definition, a nation is a collective where governments ostensibly act in the interest of all citizens. Trudeau argued as much in his 1992 Montréal speech. But the point of such collective action in a liberal state is that when a government passes a law or creates a policy, or when a court imposes a sanction or a sentence, such measures should apply equally to all regardless of whether one is black, white, or indigenous; rich or poor; a woman or a man; French or English; and a thousand other possible ways in which people can be defined. If the goal is a liberal, colour/ethnic/race-blind society, one should not be rewarded, punished, or exempted from the rules based on one's identity. As Trudeau well understood, conflict will be the inevitable result when people are elevated or oppressed by the state based on unchangeable traits, or due to rarely-changed characteristics such as language or religion.

This attention to individual rights is why Pierre Trudeau was opposed to Quebec nationalists who used the power of government to restrict the rights of the linguistic minority, i.e., the English. This is also why the concept of "citizens plus" is nonsensical. One is either an equal citizen under the law and in policy, or not. Differing legal regimes or policies based on unchangeable characteristics, or even freely chosen attachments such as language, are *de facto* discriminatory and illiberal to the individual not in the favoured group. Trudeau's attention to the individual and to necessary of equality under the law is why he opposed the Charlottetown Accord in 1992—he believed it would have further balkanized Canada. He saw the individual and the equal treatment of individuals as paramount: "Citizens, you are all first of all *equal among yourselves....*"[11]

Pierre Trudeau's battle against Quebec's illiberal nationalists came from that conception of individuals as core to civic nationalism and was critical then and now if citizens are to think of themselves as civic equals. It is also necessary because a collective writ large, such as governments, possess

---

h) I hasten to point out that while Pierre Trudeau was correct in his valuing of individual equality when it came to ethnocentric Quebec nationalists, he was in error and a collectivist on almost every other policy matter. Trudeau was a collectivist on economic matters and in foreign affairs catered to collectivist regimes which greatly infringed upon civil liberties, as his ongoing support of repressive regimes in China and Cuba demonstrated.

substantial powers and can make life exceedingly difficult for an individual citizen. Such a collective can even become tyrannical. This why in the same rhetorical breath when he emphasized the need for equality among citizens, Trudeau also emphasized that rights ultimately flow from *citizens* and not the state "[Y]our rights take priority over those of the state... The collectivity is not the bearer of rights: it receives the rights it exercises from the citizens."[12]

This, then, is why equal treatment under the law is such a critical policy: Individuals "hand" power to the state and in turn the state must not treat one individual as inherently more privileged or more punishable based on one's identity. To do otherwise is to break the bargain between the state and the individual: I allow the state to engage in certain actions with power transferred from me as a citizen, and in activities that only a government can do—set up courts, arrest those who break laws, tax me for some good that presumably only a collective can provide—and in turn, the state promises not to prefer another citizen over me but to treat us as moral and legal equals.[i]

To place that idea at the pinnacle of a country's self-understanding means anyone is potentially welcome provided they commit to that idea and others that allow for a free and flourishing nation. Anyone can rally to such notions; it matters little whether one was born in Buffalo, Beijing, Beirut, or Barrie.

Back to Justin Trudeau. Embracing these concepts *also* assumes a robust defence of desirable norms and a frank hostility to those that do not pass muster, such as ideas and practices that subjugate women. The attachment to an idea, and a sensibly grounded one at that, is at the heart of our core identity as Canadians. While our idea culture is often taken for granted, or wrongly blamed for this or that historical ill, Canada's core identity is

---

i) There are exceptions to this rule of equal treatment of the individual, but those exceptions have never been problematic for liberal thinkers. Lawmakers do not allow those under age sixteen to possess a drivers' license. They also often set differing tax rates based on income. These laws and policies do treat individuals differently, but they are common-sense defensible: The point of denying a fifteen-year-old a license is because a vehicle can be dangerous and the young have yet to develop some of the mental and physical capabilities necessary for operating one safely. They would be indefensible if, for example, lawmakers decreed that a white sixteen-year-old could drive but a black sixteen-year-old would have to wait to drive until age eighteen. Or if a government allocated different tax rates to people earning the same income based upon their skin colour. This is why so-called "affirmative action" or "employment equity" programs are illiberal: They do take into account unchangeable characteristics such as ethnicity and colour.

based on ideas and institutions that ultimately allowed for the equality of the individual and for human flourishing.

Linking the past to the future

Drawing on the work in previous chapters in this volume, it is clear that the integration and socialization of many immigrants in Canada has been largely successful. However, continued success for new arrivals and everyone else already "here" depends on all Canadians holding fast to and cherishing the ideas pointed to by Bruce Pardy in the first chapter: "[R]eason... the rule of law, individual liberty, private property, and capitalism." It was indeed this combination which produced a cornucopia of higher living standards and freer peoples in the societies which embraced the same in the last two centuries. Further, all such notions should be attached to the rights of the individual precisely because that is the only way to avoid the unhealthy fracturing that occurs when ethnic, racial, linguistic, or religious collectives are given institutional power and where potentially deadly clashes can result.

As the data in the previous chapter reveal, within two decades over one-third of the people who call Canada home will have had no natural-born connection to it. Nor will they necessarily be aware of the founding ideas that anchored Canada in peace, order, good government, and prosperity, and which over time led to greater opportunities for increasing numbers of people. The ideas that created Canada may be unknown to future Canadians despite the fact that such sentiments and founding principles may be the reason that many sought to emigrate to Canada in the first place. That makes the case for an even stronger idea culture that unites Canadians around laudable propositions, not identities.

Nations anchored in a shared set of ideas and ideals will always need to insist that anyone wishing to join must subscribe to the same. Positively, once people unite around laudable ideas, citizens are less likely to fall into the abyss of division created by irreconcilable and unchangeable identities. The idea of ordered liberty—Canada's idea culture for centuries—should be renewed. It can be the basis for a country that can be free and in which everyone can potentially flourish.

Editor acknowledgments

Book projects are even more work than solo ventures and there are multiple people who brought *The 1867 Project* to fruition. The first "thank you" is to the board of the Foundation and to donors to the Aristotle Foundation for Public Policy. My sincere thank you to Sheri MacMillan, David Hood, Jack Mintz, and Kim Moody, as well as Roy Ratnavel and Patrick Ward. As a new educational and public policy think tank—an ideas factory—early supporters are critical to such a venture. Generous support came from the Gwyn Morgan and Patricia Trottier Foundation, "anonymous," the Hunter Family Foundation, and other donors as well as board members who generously donated time, financially, and with their advice.

I also wish to credit a friend for the title for the book. Shannon Joseph offered up *The 1867 Project* as the name for the new think tank now known as the Aristotle Foundation for Public Policy. I demurred and stuck with my preference for the dead white male from Greece given his connections to ancient discussions about the good life and initial stirrings of democracy. Nevertheless, the 1867 idea had much merit, so it seemed only fitting to adopt it as the title of the Foundation's first book. As I explain in the foreword, Canada has always been an ongoing project and that is how foibles, failures, and successes in Canada pre- and post-Confederation should be viewed.

I offered fame but not much fortune to every author whose work appears in this book. Readers will benefit from their generosity in providing chapters that articulate the concerns many of us have about Canada and their belief (and mine) that telling the truth is a start to reforming the errors abounding daily in discourse, policy, education, media, culture, and in government in Canada. Thank you to all nineteen authors who contributed and for humouring me on the multiple edits, usually without much notice.

As well, I am grateful to the various editors and proofreaders who helped polish various chapters in addition to my own efforts. Thanks to Peter Shawn Taylor, Danny Randell, and Kristin McMahon, and a shout-out to Gordon Clark who not only wrote his own chapter but at the last moment stepped in and used his decades-long newspaper editing eye to offer advice on another chapter. Milan Szabo designed the book and its cover. Milan has been the designer on my last few books and his design eye is superb. As always, if there are errors in what you hold in your hand, it may be due to the author but as the editor it is more likely that any error or omission is mine.

—Mark Milke

Acknowledgments and credits

Some chapters in *The 1867 Project* contain text that has appeared elsewhere. All such work was revised before inclusion and the editor and the Aristotle Foundation for Public Policy gratefully acknowledge and thank the publications and the authors including *C2C Journal* (Peter Best, Gourav Jaswal, David Millard Haskell, Greg Piasetzki, and Peter Shawn Taylor), *Dorchester Review* (Leo Deveau), and the *National Post* (Gourav Jaswal and Jamil Jivani). Gordon Clark's chapter was based on a longer essay he published previously on medium.com. Bruce Gilley's chapter was first published as a shorter version by the online magazine *Minding The Campus*. Bruce Pardy's chapter contains material adopted and/or adapted from a number of previously published pieces, including: "Substantive Equality: Some People Are More Equal Than Others," Advocates for the Rule of Law (February 2019); "Apocalyptic Science: How the West Is Destroying Itself," *Financial Post* (June 26, 2020); "In Critical Race Theory, White Self-Flagellation is the Only Choice," *The Epoch Times* (July 24, 2020); "In Universities, the Revolution is Now Complete," *National Post* (October 14, 2020); "2020 Hindsight: Our Year of Bowing Down to 'The Science,'" *Financial Post* (December 23, 2020); "Covid Is the Virus, Wokeness Is the Disease," The *Epoch Times* (December 19, 2021); "On Speech and Conduct, Repressive Tolerance Is a Feature, Not a Bug," Macdonald-Laurier Institute and The Epoch Times (June 3/4, 2022); "Classical Liberalism Versus Equity: Review of Wanjiru Njoya's 'Economic Freedom and Social Justice: The Classical Ideal of Equality in Contexts of Racial Diversity,'" *Cosmos + Taxis* (forthcoming 2023).

Endnotes

Foreword: Canada: The centuries-long project

1 Will Durant (1953), *The Story of Civilization, Volume 5: The Renaissance: A History of Civilization in Italy from 1304-1576 A.D.*, Simon and Schuster: 145.

2 Durant (1953): 145-156.

3 Durant (1953): 161.

4 Canada (undated a), "10 Quick Facts on... the First World War" <https://bit.ly/3leeJv2>.

5 Canada (undated b), "Indigenous People in the Second World War" <https://bit.ly/402WG9J>.

6 Canada (undated c), "Second World War: 1939-1945" <https://bit.ly/3FgCbOL>.

Chapter 1: The four doctrines of the Apocalypse: Critical Theory and our compromised institutions

1 Karl Marx (1888), *The Eleventh Thesis on Feuerbach.*

2 James Lindsay (2020), "Critical Theory," *New Discourses* (July 8) <https://bit.ly/3AqAqeR>.

3 Max Horkheimer (1982), "Traditional and Critical Theory," *Critical Theory: Selected Essays*, Matthew J. O'Connell (trans.) (Continuum): 188-243 <https://bit.ly/3PWQgUn>.

4 Brian Duignan (2022), "Postmodernism," *Britannica Encyclopedia* <https://bit.ly/3cthO60>.

5 Ozlem Sensoy and Robin J DiAngelo (2017), *Is Everyone Really Equal? An Introduction to Key Concepts in Social Justice Education* (Teachers College Press).

6 Arica L. Coleman (2019), "What's Intersectionality? Let These Scholars Explain the Theory and Its History," *Time* (March 28) <https://bit.ly/2IrRt5Q>.

7 Rebecca Bodenheimer (2021), "What Is Critical Race Theory? Definition, Principles, and Applications," *ThoughtCo* (June 11) <https://bit.ly/3Tnwa8p>.

8 James A. Lindsay, Peter Boghossian, and Helen Pluckrose (2018), "Academic Grievance Studies and the Corruption of Scholarship," *Areo Magazine* (February 10) <https://bit.ly/2zObwaX>; Lindsay, "Critical Theory"; and James Lindsay (2020), "Social Justice," *New Discourses* (February 24) <https://bit.ly/3jSGXdY>.

9 Antonio Gramsci (1971), *Selections from the Prison Notebooks of Antonio Gramsci, edited and translated by Quintin Hoare and Geoffrey Nowell Smith, International Publishers, 235.*

10 Nicholas T. Parsons (2020), "The Long March Through the Institutions—Douglas Murray's Book on Our Civilization and Its Discontents," *Hungarian Review* XI, 3 (May 7) <https://bit.ly/3AUGe1q>.

11 Bill C-5, *An Act to amend the Criminal Code and the Controlled Drugs and Substances Act*, 1st Session, 44th Parliament, 70-71 Elizabeth II, 2021-2022 <https://bit.ly/3e59gCQ>.

12 Herbert Marcuse (1970), "Repressive Tolerance," *A Critique of Pure Tolerance* (Beacon Press): 81-123; James Lindsay (2021), "How Not to Resolve the Paradox of Tolerance," *New Discourses* (January 26) <https://bit.ly/3AluAeI>.

13 Marcuse, "Repressive Tolerance," 109-110.

14 Liberal Party of Canada (2021), "Protecting Canadians from Online Harms," *Forward for Everyone* <https://bit.ly/3Kpxaos>.

15 *Law Society of British Columbia v Andrews*, [1989] 1 SCR 143, para 34; *Fraser v Canada (Attorney General)*, 2020 SCC 28.

16 William Whewell (1840), *The Philosophy of the Inductive Sciences,* Volume II (John W. Parker): 318 <https://bit.ly/3PYOQbP>.

17 Bryan Benham and Charles Shimp (2005), "Falsification in Social Science Method and Theory," in Kimberly Kempf-Leonard (ed.), *Encyclopedia of Social Measurement* (Elsevier).

18 @sammiking70 [Samantha King] (2022), Twitter post (February 24) <https://bit.ly/3ARVBrr>.

19 Eugyppius (2021), "There Isn't One Plan, There Are Fifty Thousand, and Nobody Is in Charge," *A Plague Chronicle* (November 30) <https://bit.ly/3e6IdXT>.

20 Greg Piasetzki (2020), "Sir John A. Macdonald Saved More Native Lives Than Any Other Prime Minister," *C2C Journal* (November 27) <https://bit.ly/3wBLSTV>.

21 George Orwell (1949/2001), *Nineteen Eighty-Four* (Project Gutenberg): 33 <https://bit.ly/3wD2TwL>.

22 James Lindsay (2020), "Stealing the Motte: Critical Social Justice and the Principle of Charity," *New Discourses* (May 7) <https://bit.ly/3UAuB7J>.

Chapter 2: Cancel culture harms journalists, journalism, and citizenship

1 Mark Hecht (2019), "Can Social Trust and Diversity Co-exist?" *Vancouver Sun* (September 7) <https://bit.ly/3DwhuxZ>.

2 Merriam Webster Dictionary (2023), "Racist" [entry 2 of 2], Merriam Webster Dictionary <https://bit.ly/3Fe4WMY>.

3 Merriam Webster Dictionary (2023), "Racism," Merriam Webster Dictionary <https://bit.ly/3n57A0w>.

4 Jonathan Goldsbie (2019), "Author of Anti-Immigrant Vancouver Sun Op-Ed Explains How It Got Published," canadaland.com (September 7) <https://bit.ly/3D9QXFp>.

5 Peter Thisted Dinesen, Merlin Schaeffer, and Kim Mannemar Sønderskov (2020), "Ethnic Diversity and Social Trust: A Narrative and Meta-Analytical Review," *Annual Review of Political Science* 23 <https://bit.ly/3Dw2aBn>.

6 Accountable Journalism (Undated), Section 4: Comment and Fact, "Canada: British Columbia Press Council Code of Practice," Accountable Journalism <https://bit.ly/3Dtj8Au>.

7 Canadian Association of Journalists (2011), "Independence," *Ethics Guidelines*, Canadian Association of Journalists <https://bit.ly/3Z0w8Fm>.

8 Ibid., "Diversity."

9 Sean Craig (2019), "You Must Be This Conservative to Ride: The Inside Story of Postmedia's Right Turn," canadaland.com (August 12) <https://bit.ly/3Du4pFu>.

10 Trevor Lautens (Undated), "A Thoughtful, Gentle Reflection on a Sun Apology That Shafted Free Expression," unpublished column.

11 David Beers (2019), "Revolt Grows in Vancouver Sun and Province Newsroom over Op-Ed Policies," *The Tyee* (September 13) <https://bit.ly/3TTQwpf>.

12 Ibid.

13 Robert Hauknes (2019), "It's a Disgrace That Foreigners Are Being Given a Priority to Salmon over Canadians," *Vancouver Sun* (July 22) <https://bit.ly/3svi74w>.

14 Calvin White (2019), "Ban on Face-Covering Niqab Isn't an Attack on Religious Expression," *Vancouver Sun* (June 28) <https://bit.ly/3SxqCXn>.

15 Gordon Clark (2017), "Are We Allowing Too Many People into Canada?" *The Province* (February 9) <https://bit.ly/3THiFjN>.

16 Don Wright (2021), "Rhetoric vs. Results: Shaping Policy to Benefit Canada's Middle Class," Public Policy Forum (June 28) <https://bit.ly/3TR1Xhw>.

17 Gordon Clark (2017), "Richmond Council Right to Ease Off on English Sign Law," *The Province* (June 15) <https://bit.ly/3f4lHPZ>.

18 Gordon Clark (2017), "We Should All Step in to Protect Those Being Bullied in Public," *The Province* (December 7) <https://bit.ly/3DyPny0>.

19 Gordon Clark (2017), "Ignore Them. Just Turn Our Backs on Racist Rally," *The Province* (August 17) <https://bit.ly/3FmmQgN>.

20 Alex Sangha (2018), "Canada Must Reform Sex Trade Laws," *The Province* (August 7) <https://bit.ly/3gIBfJz>.

21 Alex Sangha (2018), "Some Talking Points to Address Domestic Violence in the South Asian Community," *The Province* (August 20) <https://bit.ly/3D9FfdH>.

22 New York Times (Undated), *Ethical Journalism: A Handbook of Values and Practices for the News and Opinion Departments*, *New York Times* <https://nyti.ms/3Wa6pd9>.

23 Peter Zimonjic and Catherine Cullen (2018), "Tories Accuse Trudeau of Bribing Media with Tax Breaks," CBC News (November 23) <https://bit.ly/3THAEXd>.

24 Tara Henley (2022), "Why I Quit the CBC," *National Post* (January 3) <https://bit.ly/3Ttftcm>.

25 Donald G. McNeil Jr. (2021), "NYTimes Peru N-word," (Four-part essay) *Medium* (March 1) <https://bit.ly/3SET9dI>.

26 Jamil Jivani (2022), "Even Black Men Can Be Fired For Not Being 'Woke' Enough," *Substack* (February 1) <https://bit.ly/3fcB0GA>.

27 Bari Weiss [2020], Resignation Letter, *bariweiss.com* <https://bit.ly/3fc5QPw>.

28 Ariel Zilber (2022), "Ex-NY Times Opinion Editor Slams Publisher: 'He Set Me on Fire and Threw Me in the Garbage,'" *The New York Post* (October 18) <https://bit.ly/3gMhmRW>.

29 Committee to Protect Journalists (Undated), "2119 Journalists and Media Workers Killed," Committee to Protect Journalists <https://bit.ly/3SCSXeX>.

30 Bill Maher (2021), "New Rule: The Woke Olympics." <https://bit.ly/3Z44OWK>.

31 Anne Applebaum (2021), "The New Puritans," *The Atlantic* (August 31) <https://bit.ly/3ySAqnv>.

Chapter 3: How a professor was cancelled by academic Stalinists on campus

1 @Ian_Mosby (2020), Twitter post (September 10).

2 @Ian_Mosby (2022), Twitter post (October 20).

3 Leanne Simpson (2010), "Review: Disrobing the Aboriginal Industry: The Deception behind Indigenous Cultural Preservation by Frances Widdowson," Albert Howard: *Wicazo Sa Review*, 25, 1 (Spring): 104-107, 107.

4 Mount Royal University (2023), "History" <https://bit.ly/3Dn4Q4k>.

5 Peter Glenn (2021), "Decolonization Campaign Hits Hard but Finds an Audience at MRU," Mount Royal University (December 8) <https://bit.ly/3goLtPD>.

6 Ray Barnhardt and Angayuqaq Oscar Kawagley (1998), *Culture, Chaos and Complexity: Catalysts for Change in Indigenous Education*, Alaska Native Knowledge Network
<https://bit.ly/3VexPxh>.

7 @Terrilltf [Terrill Tailfeathers] (2021), Twitter post (December 23).

8 Mount Royal University (Undated), "About" <https://bit.ly/3Sw1U9Q>.

Chapter 4: The fight against Critical Race Theory at an Ontario school board

1 Elementary Teachers' Federation of Ontario (2022), "White Privilege Lesson Plans," Elementary Teachers' Federation of Ontario <https://bit.ly/3UvAfHV>.

2 Jonathan Bradley (2022), "Ontario Teacher Union Creates White Privilege Lesson Plans," *Western Standard* (July 7) <https://bit.ly/3tl6RYQ>.

3 John McWhorter (2021), *Woke Racism: How a New Religion Has Betrayed Black America* (Penguin): 16, 27, 30-35.

4 Peter Shawn Taylor (2022), "It's Time to Abolish the Absurd (and Slightly Racist) Concept of 'Visible Minorities,'" *C2C Journal* (February 19) <https://bit.ly/3WSkr3o>.

5 Rebecca Hains (2019), "Dear Fellow White People: Here's What to Do When You're Called Racist," *Washington Post* (August 23) <https://wapo.st/2mHuLPQ>.

6 Heather MacDonald (2017), "The False 'Science' of Implicit Bias," *Wall Street Journal* (October 9) <https://on.wsj.com/3ToSBsI>.

7 Ramesh Ponnuru (2014), "'Check Your Privilege' Means 'Shut Your Mouth,'" *Bloomberg News* (May 8) <https://bloom.bg/3NRgbNP>.

8 Tomiwa Owolade (2020), "The Dangerous Logic of Anti-Racism," *UnHerd* (November 30) <https://bit.ly/3UIoGwD>.

9 Coleman Hughes (2019), "How to Be an Anti-Intellectual," *City Journal* (October 27) <https://bit.ly/3TFc34R>.

10 Ibram X. Kendi (2019), *How to Be an Anti-Racist* (Random House): 19.

11 Brian Balfour and Terry Stoops (2021), *Critical Race Theory: A Primer* (John Locke Foundation) <https://bit.ly/3WTiGD6>.

12 Yaron Steinbuch (2020), "Black Lives Matter Co-founder Describes Herself as 'Trained Marxist,'" *New York Post* (June 25) <https://bit.ly/3NS24aV>.

13 Ian Prior (2022), "The Definitive Proof Critical Race Theory Is Being Taught in Our Schools," Fox News (June 20) <https://fxn.ws/3ULQoZo>.

14 Jon Levine and Dana Kennedy (2021). "NYC Moms Coordinating to Fight Critical Race Theory in Schools," *New York Post* (August 21) <https://bit.ly/3tBvNM9>.

15 Callie Patteson (2021), "Parents Take a Stand Against FBI Crackdown on CRT Opponents," *New York Post* (October 5) <https://bit.ly/3DZeTvq>.

16 Robby Soave (2021), "A.G. Merrick Garland Tells FBI To Investigate Parents Who Yell at School Officials About Critical Race Theory," *Reason* (October 6) <https://bit.ly/3tl8Oo8>.

17 David Smith (2021), "How Did Republicans Turn Critical Race Theory into a Winning Electoral Issue?" *Guardian* (November 3) <https://bit.ly/3hpH4vX>.

18 Alex Seitz-Wald (2021), "In Virginia, Republicans See Education, Curriculum Fears as a Path to Victory," NBC News (October 17) <https://nbcnews.to/3FZRJb3>.

19 Matthew Impelli (2021), "McAuliffe Saying Parents Shouldn't Tell Schools What to Teach Big Factor in Election: Poll," *Newsweek* (November 15) <https://bit.ly/3NTsOro>.

20 Florida (2021), "Governor DeSantis Announces Legislative Proposal to Stop W.O.K.E. Activism and Critical Race Theory in Schools and Corporations," Media release, Government of Florida (December 15) <https://bit.ly/3EkOHNn>.

21 Kiara Alfonseca (2022), "Critical Race Theory Thrust into Spotlight by Misinformation," ABC News (February 6) <https://abcn.ws/3tkhwmK>.

22 Elise Stefanik and Christopher Rufio (2022), "New York's Curriculum Is Critical Race Theory by Another Name," Fox News (June 17) <https://fxn.ws/3NRl5u9>.

23 Élodie Safaris (2021), "FAIR: Intellectuals Critical of Wokism Launch a Foundation to Fight 'Neo-Racism,'" *CTRL-Z Magazine* (March 11) <https://bit.ly/3To2dUD>.

24 Nicole Lampa (2022), "WRDSB Teacher Removed From Virtual Board Meeting After Comments Deemed Transphobic by Chair," CTV News Kitchener (January 18) <https://bit.ly/3G5gnHh>.

25 Sue-Ann Levy (2022), "Cancelled Teacher Launches Second Lawsuit Against Waterloo School Board," *True North News* (June 21) <https://bit.ly/3G9GI7f>.

26 Kate Bueckert (2022), "WRDSB School Board Trustee Barred from Meetings Says Decision 'A Way of Silencing' Him," CBC News Kitchener (June 7) <https://bit.ly/3hqhWFr>.

27 Waterloo Region Record (2022), "Province Needs to Investigate Why Waterloo Region Public School Board Trustee Is Being Censured," Unsigned editorial, Waterloo Region Record (June 6) <https://bit.ly/3ElYNNU>.

28 @_MikeRamsay (2022), "Letter to Parents, Students, and Staff," Twitter post (June 27) <https://bit.ly/3A55EJb>.

29 Sue-Ann Levy (2022), "Waterloo School Board Muzzles Lone Black Trustee," *True North News* (June 28) <https://bit.ly/3UH8RGC>.

30 Johanna Weidner (2022), "Public School Board Trustee Mike Ramsay Called Censure 'Attempt to Silence Him,'" *Waterloo Region Record* (June 7) <https://bit.ly/3A3Mp2J>.

31 Luisa D'Amato (2022), "Mike Ramsay's Offence? Vehemently Disagreeing with Other Trustees," *Waterloo Region Record* (October 5) <https://bit.ly/3WUCRAW>.

32 Ibid.

33 Ibid.

34 Johanna Weidner (2022), "Waterloo Region District School Board Trustee Seeks Details About Lessons on Critical Race Theory," *Waterloo Region Record* (June 2) <https://bit.ly/3DXY2t6>.

35 Johanna Weidner (2022), "Updated: Public School Board Trustees Vote Down Call for Report on Critical Race Theory Lessons," *Waterloo Region Record* (June 20) <https://bit.ly/3EgbbOr>.

36 Waterloo Region District School Board (2020), *Bylaws: Board of Trustees, Waterloo Region District School Board*, Waterloo Region District School Board (September) <https://bit.ly/3hoGjDj>.

37 E. Cooley, et al. (2019), "Complex Intersections of Race and Class: Among Social Liberals, Learning About White Privilege Reduces Sympathy, Increases Blame, and Decreases External Attributions for White People Struggling With Poverty," *Journal of Experimental Psychology: General* 148, 12: 2218–2228 <https://bit.ly/3ElDITO>.

38 Christopher L. Quarles and Lia Bozarth (2022), "How the Term "White Privilege" Affects Participation, Polarization, and Content in Online Communication," *PLoS ONE* 17, 5
<https://bit.ly/3A5ugkR>.

39 Elizabeth Levy Paluck, et al. (2021), "Prejudice Reduction: Progress and Challenges," *Annual Review of Psychology* 72, 1 (January): 533-560 <https://bit.ly/3WItEeG>.

40 Frank Dobbin and Alexandra Kalev (2018), "Why Doesn't Diversity Training Work? The Challenge for Industry and Academia," *Anthropology Now* 10, 48 <https://bit.ly/3zZL5xC>.

41 Ibid, 50.

42 Frank Dobbin, "Why Diversity Programs Fail," *Harvard Business Review*, 2016, July-August <https://bit.ly/3fX3nsI>.

43 David Millard Haskell (2022), "Waterloo Region FAIR Chapter Delegation to the WRDSB" YouTube (June 27) <https://bit.ly/3WP8EmA>.

44 Ritika Goel (2021), "The Perils of Associating 'White' with 'Privilege' in the Classroom," *The Conversation* (January 14) <https://bit.ly/3hrJryq>.

45 Cosmin Dzsurdzsa (2022), "Waterloo School Board Equity Officer Says 'History Is Paved With White-Led Violence,'" *True North News* (February 7) <https://bit.ly/3NSOVyc>.

46 Foundation Against Intolerance and Racism (2022), Home page <https://bit.ly/3NS5Wc2>.

47 Parents as First Educators [PAFE] (2022), "About," PAFE <https://bit.ly/3theqzR>; Action4Canada (Undated), "Frequently Asked Questions," Action4Canada <https://bit.ly/3Ek6uUF>; and Blueprint for Canada (2022), "A Blueprint for Canada – Running for a School Board," Blueprint for Canada <https://bit.ly/3DSRbkF>.

48 Jillian Follert (2022), "Anti-Racism Policy Approved by Durham Catholic, Definitions of Terms Like 'White Supremacy' and 'Colonialism' Removed," *St. Catharines Standard* (May 31) <https://bit.ly/3G4JOt9>.

49 Ontario (2022), "Facts about Elementary and Secondary Education: 2020-2021 School Year," Government of Ontario <https://bit.ly/3tjJdfj>.

50 Ontario Secondary School Teachers' Federation (2022), "2022 Municipal Elections: OSSTF District 24 Waterloo," YouTube (October 21) <https://bit.ly/3UrUHcO>.

51 Kate Bueckert (2022), "Number of Voters Who Cast Ontario Municipal Election Ballots Is Down. Here's Why That Matters," CBC News (October 26) <https://bit.ly/3G5A2aa>.

52 Jonathan Montpetit and Lori Ward (2022), "Scores of Anti-Trans Candidates Running in Ontario School Board Elections," CBC News (October 20) <https://bit.ly/3A7irdZ>; Caroline Alphonso (2022), "Why a Waterloo, Ont., School Board Has Emerged as a Battleground for Ideological Politics," *Globe and Mail* (October 17) <https://tgam.ca/3hwpary>; Kristin Rushowy (2020), "'Anti-Woke' Trustee Candidates Stir Up Concerns Among Educators, Parents" *Toronto Star* (October 23) <https://bit.ly/3WLbo4B>; Alexandra Mae Jones (2022), "Anti-LGBTQ2S+ Groups Trying to Elect 'God-Fearing' and 'Anti-Woke' School Board Trustees, Group Says," CTV News (October 23) <https://bit.ly/3fUAn4O>; and Ian Bickis (2022), "Advocacy Groups Raising Concerns About 'Anti-Trans' School Board Trustee Candidates," *Canadian Press* (October 23) <https://bit.ly/3O1AJmQ>.

53 Tristin Hopper (2022), "Inside the Anti-Hate Materials Saskatchewan Is Trying to Banish from Schools," *National Post* (October 26) <https://bit.ly/3zZNzfq>; Cosmin Dzsurdzsa (2022), "Liberal-Funded "Anti-Hate" Activist Grilled over Misinformation About Freedom Convoy," *True North News* (April 27) <https://bit.ly/3A3B2HU>; and Cosmin Dzsurdzsa (2022), "Court Ruling States Anti-Hate Network 'Did in Fact Assist Antifa,'" *True North News* (November 11) <https://bit.ly/3A6D9e0>.

54 Jones, "Anti-LGBTQ2S+ Groups."

Chapter 5: I know what identity politics does to a nation: I'm from Lebanon

1 Carlo Facci (2014), *At the Origins of the Lebanese State: The Book of Daoud Ammoun through the Works of the Administrative Committee of the Greater Lebanon* (1920 – 1922), Research Book no. 6, Holy Spirit University of Kaslik.

2 Constitution du Liban (1926), Adoption: 23 mai 1926. Entrée en vigueur : 1er Septembre, 1926. Beyrouth: Conseil représentatif libanais [الدستور اللبناني الصادر ي 23 ايارسنة 1926].

3 Rania Maktabi (1999), "The Lebanese Census of 1932 Revisited. Who Are the Lebanese?" *British Journal of Middle Eastern Studies* 26, 2: 219-241 <https://bit.ly/3AizetW>.

4 Tamirace Fakhoury (2014), "Debating Lebanon's Power-Sharing Model: An Opportunity or an Impasse for Democratization Studies in the Middle East?" Special Issue: Cultures of Resistance, *The Arab Studies Journal* 22, 1 (Spring): 230-255 <https://bit.ly/3Ev9SvI>.

5 Totten J. Michael (2013), "Can Beirut Be Paris Again?" *City Journal* (Summer) <https://bit.ly/3AQ3X2X>.

6 Paul Kingston and William L. Ochsenwald (2023), "Lebanese Civil War," *Encyclopedia Britannica* <https://bit.ly/3TtN3gW>.

7 Lauren Lewis (2020),"Remembering the Taif Accord," *Middle East Monitor* (October 22) <https://bit.ly/3CwEdde>.

8 Saleh Machnouk, Hanin Ghhadar, and Matthew Levitt (2020), "The Beirut Disaster: Implications for Lebanon and U.S. Policy," *Policy Analysis*/Policy Watch 3365 (August 18), Washington Institute for Near East Policy <https://bit.ly/3D5DQGy>.

9 BBC News (2009), "Lebanon 'Moves Right Way' on ID," *BBC* (February 24) <https://bbc.in/3Ao6fVK>.

10 CUPE 3912, "Newsletter: The Instructor," CUPE 3912 <https://bit.ly/3Km4X22>.

11 CUPE 3912 (Undated), "About," Web page, CUPE 3912 <https://bit.ly/3PPaEqd>.

12 Rima Azar (2022), "Defending Academic Freedom," *The Instructor* (April). CUPE 3912 newsletter <https://bit.ly/3PSAg5y>.

13 Guy Lawson (2015), "Trudeau's Canada, Again," *New York Times Magazine* (December 8) <https://nyti.ms/3QP77cO>.

14 Jamil Jivani (2020), "A Trailblazing Toronto Judge and the Twitter Mob That Has Come For Him," *National Post* (December 4) <https://bit.ly/3QSb6VX>.

15 Tristin Hopper (2018), "Canadian Schools Facing Blowback for White Privilege Awareness Campaigns," *National Post* (March 8) <https://bit.ly/3PRezCX>.

Chapter 6: Is Canada systemically racist?

1 Canada, Department of Canadian Heritage (2019), *Building a Foundation for Change: Canada's Anti-Racism Strategy 2019-2022,* Government of Canada <https://bit.ly/3Eststv>.

2 Canada, Immigration, Refugees and Citizenship Canada (2022), *Anti-Racism Strategy 2.0 (2021-2024)* Government of Canada <https://bit.ly/3RR1RoX>.

3 Canada, Ministry of Defence (2022), *Minister of National Defence Advisory Panel on Systemic Racism and Discrimination with a Focus on Anti-Indigenous and Anti-Black Racism, LGBTQ2+ Prejudice, Gender Bias, and White Supremacy: Final Report,* Government of Canada <https://bit.ly/3EypMqc>.

4 Canada, Immigration, Refugees and Citizenship Canada (2022), *Anti-Racism Strategy 2.0.*

5 Sowell, Thomas (2013), "Why Racists Love the Minimum Wage Laws," *New York Post* (September 17) <https://bit.ly/3VeFrRf>.

6 University of Manitoba (2016), "Faculty of Education's Diversity Policy Approved by Senate," University of Manitoba (February 11) <https://bit.ly/3VtFJEb>.

7 Canada, Department of Finance (2021), *Budget 2021: A Recovery Plan for Jobs, Growth, and Resilience*, Government of Canada <https://bit.ly/3VdZ7Vo>.

8 Tyler Dawson (2021), "Ontario Teachers' Union Implements Controversial Weighted Voting System to Increase Minority Representation," *National Post* (November 25) <https://bit.ly/3EBjyG5>.

9 Jamie Sarkonak (2022), "CRTC Diversity Quotas Trample Journalistic Independent at CBC," *National Post* (August 11) <https://bit.ly/3rHYJAX>.

10 Milton Friedman (1962/2020), *Capitalism and Freedom* (University of Chicago Press): 131.

11 David R. Henderson (Undated), "Gary Stanley Becker," *Concise Encyclopedia of Economics* <https://bit.ly/3T7rzX6>.

12 Thomas Sowell (2019), *Discrimination and Disparities,* 1.

13 Statistics Canada (2018), *Life Expectancy, 1920-1922 to 2009-2011,* Statistics Canada <https://bit.ly/3T6BQmT>; Wayne J. Millar (1995), "Life Expectancy of Canadians," *Statistics Canada Health Reports* 7, 3 <https://bit.ly/3T7rDGk>; Statistics Canada (2022), "Table 13-10-0014-01: Life Expectancy and Other Elements of the Complete Life Table, Three-Year Estimates, Canada, All Provinces Except Prince Edward Island," Statistics Canada (January 24) <https://bit.ly/3Ew7c1D>.

14 Theresa Qiu and Grant Schellenberg (2022), *The Weekly Earnings of Canadian-Born Individuals in Designated Visible Minority and White Categories in the Mid-2010s*, Statistics Canada (January 26) <https://bit.ly/3V9DFki>.

15 Ibid.

16 Theresa Qiu and Grant Schellenberg (2022), *The Relative Earnings of Individuals in Designated Visible Minority Categories in Canada Across Four Workplace Sectors*, Statistics Canada (February 23) <https://bit.ly/3Cnp3oV>.

17 Valentin Bolotnyy and Natalia Emanuel (2022), "Why Do Women Earn Less than Men? Evidence from Bus and Train Operators," *Journal of Labor Economics* 40, 2 (April) <https://bit.ly/3CnpgZf>.

18 Cody Cook, Rebecca Diamond, Jonathan Hall, et al. (2018), *The Gender Earnings Gap in the Gig Economy: Evidence From over a Million Rideshare Drivers*, Working Paper 24732 (June), National Bureau of Economic Research <https://bit.ly/3erqDhv>.

Chapter 7: Carving out a country: From Magna Carta to Confederation

1 Stephen Harper (2015), "Stephen Harper on Sir John A. Macdonald: Canada's Principled Founder," *National Post* (January 9) <https://bit.ly/3EWc7aU>.

2 See Janet Ajzenstat, Paul Romney, Ian Gentles, and William D. Gairner (eds.) (1999), *Canada's Founding Debates* (Stoddard).

3 Janet Ajzenstat (2007), *The Canadian Founding.* (McGill-Queen's University Press): 50.

4 Harper (2015).

5 UM Today Network (2015), "Ottawa Citizen: Stop Apologizing for John A. Macdonald," *University of Manitoba News* (January 9) <https://bit.ly/3up53yP>.

6 John Ivison (2017), "The Case for John A.," *National Post* (August 25).

7 Greg Piasetzki (2020), "Sir John A. Macdonald Saved More Native Lives Than Any Other Prime Minister," *C2C Journal* (November 27) <https://bit.ly/3VRFge7>.

8 Josephine Tey (1954), *The Daughter of Time* (Penguin Books Canada).

9 Ibid., 33.

10 William McElwee (1968), *The Story of England,* Third Edition (Faber and Faber): 83.

11 "Magna Carta" in *The Selected Writings of Sir Edward Coke Volume II* (Liberty Fund, 2003): 755.

12 On investigating the matter Snopes concludes that he actually did say something of the sort, though he was not the first to do so <https://bit.ly/2lYKedm>.

13 Christopher W. Brooks (1993), "The Ancient Constitution in Sixteenth-Century Legal Thought," in Ellis Sandoz (ed.) (1993), *The Roots of Liberty* (Liberty Fund): 94n.

14 Maurice Hastings (1950) *Parliament House* (Architectural Press): 87. Back then the year started on March 1 so this episode in February counts as 1536 in modern dating.

15 Charles Howard McIlwain (2007), *Constitutionalism: Ancient and Modern* (Liberty Fund): 96.

16 See for instance <https://bit.ly/3gZ2HDI>.

17 See the Canadian Encyclopedia (2022), "1793 Act to Limit Slavery in Upper Canada," <https://bit.ly/3F1Aeox>.

18 Canadian Museum of History (Undated), "Population: Slavery," *Virtual Museum of New France* <https://bit.ly/2LaITXZ>.

19 See for instance Alison F. Gardner (2008), *James Douglas* (Fitzhenry & Whiteside): 31.

20 Canadian Museum for Human Rights (Undated), "The Story of Slavery in Canadian History" <https://bit.ly/3XVHI5c>.

21 "Canadian Museum of History, "Population: Slavery."

22 Sue Ferguson (1999), "Letter from North Buxton: Underground to Freedom: A Historic Black Community Celebrates its 150th Anniversary," *Maclean's* (November 29): 32.

23 Bruce Lenman (1981), *Integration, Enlightenment, and Industrialization; Scotland 1746-1832* (University of Toronto Press): 72.

24 William Blackstone (1979), *Commentaries of the Laws of England,* Volume 1 (University of Chicago Press): 6.

25 Eric Foner (2009), *Give Me Liberty! An American History,* Volume I (2nd Seagull Edition) (W.W. Norton & Co.): 79.

26 See the Sir John A. Macdonald Society entry "Pre Confederation" <https://bit.ly/3XVIcbw>.

27 Ajzenstat (2007), *The Canadian Founding*, 126.

28 See Nova Scotia Legislature (2017), "Responsible Government" <https://bit.ly/3h4Si9t>.

29 See Nova Scotia Legislature (2017), "Twelve Resolutions" <https://bit.ly/3P4u3EJ>.

30 Quoted by the CBC (1999), "Chretien Compares Quebec to Northern Ireland During Visit," CBC News (June 14) <https://bit.ly/3h6gxnx>.

31 Jean-paul Bernard (2015), "Montréal Riots," *Canadian Encyclopedia* <https://bit.ly/3VFTi32>.

32 Dennis Gruending (ed.) (2004), *Great Canadian Speeches* (Fitzhenry & Whiteside): 7.

33 See for instance Maxwell Sucharov (2022), "The Ugly Truth to Canada's Big Lie: A Tale of Ongoing Settler Colonial Genocide of Canada's Indigenous Peoples and the Creation of an Apartheid State," *Psychoanalysis, Self and Context* (March 17) <https://bit.ly/3PapKb9> and Babacar Faye (2021), "The Unsettling Truth Of The Settler State," Canadian Bar Association National <https://bit.ly/3H7dVk6>, the latter being especially noteworthy as it's the national magazine of the Canadian Bar Association not some random Twitter account (like say <https://bit.ly/3F2B30A>).

34 Daniel Hannan (2015), interview with the author (April 25).

35 Winston Churchill (1956), *A History of the English Speaking Peoples,* Volume 1 (Cassell).

Chapter 8: Sir John A. Macdonald saved more indigenous lives than any other prime minister

1 Peter Shawn Taylor (2015), "No Grumpy Old Man," *C2C Journal* (June 1) <https://bit.ly/3dPFba2>.

2 Justin McElroy (2018), "City of Victoria to Remove John A. Macdonald Statue from Front Steps of City Hall," CBC News (August 8) <https://bit.ly/3wzMSaU>.

3 CBC News (2020), "Activists Topple Statute of Sir John A. Macdonald in Downtown Montreal," CBC News (August 29) <https://bit.ly/3PZBzj3>.

4 Queen's Gazette Staff (2020), "Queen's to Remove Sir John A. Macdonald Name from Law School Building," *Queen's Gazette* (October 19) <https://bit.ly/3pNHrkO>.

5 CBC News (2020), "Sir John A. Macdonald High School to Be Renamed to Reflect Inclusivity," CBC News (November 12) <https://bit.ly/3KrvoDt>.

6 Pam Palmater (2017), "Resurgence or Revelation? White Nationalist Legacies in Canada," Canadian Dimension (December 8) <https://bit.ly/3POOKUd>.

7 United States (1890), *Indian Wars and Their Cost and Civil Expenditures for Indians,* Decennial Census <https://bit.ly/3crksZQ>.

8 Colin S. Gillepsie (2017), "Estimating the Number of Casualties in the American Indian War: A Bayesian Analysis Using the Power Law Distribution," *Annals of Applied Statistics 11, 4 (December): 2357-2374* <https://bit.ly/3wCEyr9>.

9 Gregory F. Michno (2003), *Encyclopedia of Indian Wars: Western Battles and Skirmishes 1850-1890* (Mountain Press).

10 Blair Stonechild and Bill Waiser (2010), *Loyal Till Death: Indians and the North-West Rebellion* (Fifth House Books); and Bob Beal and Rod Macleod (2006), "North-West Resistance," *The Canadian Encyclopedia* (February 7) <https://bit.ly/3ReM5nR>.

11 Joseph Howe (1869), Letter from the Office of the Secretary of State for the Provinces to The Very Reverend Grand Vicar, Mr. Thibault (December 4), *Session 1870: Third Session of the First Parliament of the Dominion of Canada,* Volume V: 45 <https://bit.ly/3ARXggT>.

12 United States, House of Representatives, 41st Congress, 2nd Session (1870), *Management of the Indians in British North America by the British Government* (January 21) <https://bit.ly/3R0AWHp>.

13 Canadian Parliamentary Historical Resources (1885), *Commons Debates* (June): 2426 <https://bit.ly/3AUxisY>.

14 Canadian Parliamentary Historical Resources (1870), *Commons Debates* (May 2): 1310 <https://bit.ly/3AUVuLP>.

15 John McDougall (1911), *On Western Trails in the Early Seventies* (Hill Country Books): 186 <https://bit.ly/3YuH9PA >

16 Canadian Parliamentary Historical Resources (1885), *Commons Debates* (June 10): 2442 <https://bit.ly/3coceC0>.

17 Arthur J. Ray (1974), *Indians in the Fur Trade: Their Role as Trappers, Hunters, and Middlemen in the Lands Southwest of Hudson Bay* (University of Toronto Press).

18 Canada, Indian Affairs (1868), *Annual Report of the Secretary of State for the Year 1868,* 12 <https://bit.ly/3PXvNyw>.

19 Canada, Indian Affairs (1883), *Annual Report of the Department of Indian Affairs for the Year Ended 31st December, 1883,* p. 263 <https://bit.ly/3KIpv57>.

20 Canada, Indian Affairs (1886), *Annual Report of the Department of Indian Affairs for the Year Ended 31st December, 1886,* 28 <https://bit.ly/3R2bhy8>.

21 James Daschuk (2013), *Clearing the Plains* (University of Regina Press): 105.

22 Ibid, 123 and 134.

23 Ibid, 99.

24 Canada (1964), *Copy of Treaty No. 6 between Her Majesty the Queen and the Plain and Wood Cree Indians and other Tribes of Indians at Fort Carlton, Fort Pitt and Battle River with Adhesions,* Treaty Texts, Government of Canada <https://bit.ly/3qbDbfv>.

25 Canada (1886), *Official Report of the Debates of the House of Commons of the Dominion of Canada: Fourth Session, Fifth Parliament* (February): 22 <https://bit.ly/3AUHGkq>.

26 Daschuk, *Clearing the Plains,* 117.

27 Canada, Indian Affairs (1880), *Annual Report of the Department of Indian Affairs for the Year Ended 31st December, 1880,* p. 119 <https://bit.ly/3ToYmIc>.

28 Grant A. Brown (2020), "The WE Charity Scandal: One of Many," *C2C Journal* (September 2) <https://bit.ly/3wByQpp>.

29 Canadian Parliamentary Historical Resources, Commons Debate, April 1882, page 1186 <https://bit.ly/3TRkOcK>.

30 Canada (1880), *Debates of the House of Commons of the Dominion of Canada: Second Session, Fourth Parliament* (May): 1942 <https://bit.ly/3pYSoQB>.

31 Daschuk, *Clearing the Plains,* 132.

32 Risa Barkin and Ian Gentles (1990/2013), "Death in Victorian Toronto, 1850-1899," *Urban History Review* 19, 1 (June) <https://bit.ly/3RnrVrT>.

33 Canada (Indian Affairs (1920), *Annual Report of the Department of Indian Affairs for the Year Ended 31st December, 1920,* 106. <https://bit.ly/3QZbEJQ>.

Chapter 9: How a "Maker of Canada" was framed: The unjust treatment of Egerton Ryerson?

1 Nathanael Burwash (1906), *Egerton Ryerson* (Morang).

2 C.B. Sissons (1947), *Egerton Ryerson: His Life and Letters,* volume II (Clarke Irwin): 233-34.

3 Egerton Ryerson (1882), *Canadian Methodism: Its Epochs and Characteristics* (William Briggs): 129-30.

4 Egerton Ryerson (1831), "Upper Canada Academy," *Christian Guardian* II, 23 (April 23): 94.

5 Egerton Ryerson (1848), *Lectures Delivered by the Chief Superintendent of Schools... September to December, 1847. Journal of Education for Upper Canada,* I, 10 (October): 289-94.

6 Egerton Ryerson (1849), "Canadian Mechanics and Manufactures," An Address Delivered before the Mechanics Institute, Toronto, Jan. 12, 1849, by the Chief Superintendent of Schools of Upper Canada," *Journal of Education for Upper Canada* I, 10 (February 18): 289.

7 Sissons, 1947, 246.

8 Egerton Ryerson (1833), "House of Commons, 14 May, Colonial Slavery," *Christian* IV, 33, (June 26): 131.

9 Egerton Ryerson (1838), *A Discourse on Civil Government—The Late Conspiracy: Delivered in Kingston, UC, December 31, 1837* (Joseph H. Lawrence): 12.

10 Ibid, 19.

11 Ibid, 3.

12 Ibid, 12.

13 Ibid, 20.

14 Ibid, 19.

15 Ryerson (1882), *The Story of My Life*, 64.

16 Neil Semple (1996), *The Lord's Dominion: The History of Canadian Methodism* (McGill-Queen's University Press): 154.

17 Ryerson (1882), *The Story of My Life*, 56.

18 Ryerson letter (1839, 2 October), *Credit Mission Letterbook, 1825-1842:* 121-2. RG 10, vol. 1011, on microfilm reel T-1456, Library and Archives Canada.

19 Donald B. Smith (2013), *Sacred Feathers: The Reverend Peter Jones (Kahkewaquonaby) and the Mississauga Indians,* 2nd edition (University of Toronto Press): 65.

20 *Christian Guardian I* (1830), "Religious Intelligence," 30 (January 30): 83.

21 *Christian Guardian II* (1830), "John Sunday's Journal of a Missionary Tour among the North-Western Tribes of Indians," 50 (October 29): 201.

22 C.B. Sissons (1937-1947), *Egerton Ryerson: His Life and Letters,* 2 volumes (Clarke Irwin).

23 Burwash, *Egerton Ryerson,* 11905; Clara Thomas (1969), *Ryerson of Upper Canada* (Ryerson Press); Laura Damamaia (1975), *Egerton Ryerson* (Fitzhenry & Whiteside).

24 Smith (2013), *Sacred Feathers.*

25 Hope MacLean (2002), "A Positive Experiment in Aboriginal Education: The Methodist Ojibwa Day Schools in Upper Canada 1824-1855," *Canadian Journal of Native Studies* XXII, 1: 57.

Chapter 10: A crime against Sir Matthew Begbie's humanity

1 House of Commons (2018), Debates (Hansard number 275) (March 26) <https://bit.ly/3UxpiW7>.

2 British Columbia Legislative Assembly (2014), Debates of the Legislative Assembly, Volume 16, number 2 (October 23) <https://bit.ly/3sLoctU>.

3 David R. Williams (1977), *The Man for a New Country: Sir Matthew Baillie Begbie* (Gray's Press).

4 David R. Williams (1980), "Sir Matthew Baillie Begbie," *Pacific Northwest Quarterly* (July).

5 Williams, 1977.

6 Williams, 1980.

7 Stacy Chappel (2009), "Begbie Statue Stolen," *UVIC Graduate Students' Blog* (May 25) <https://bit.ly/3WpVc8p>.

8 Kamloops This Week (2008), "Controversial Murals being hidden in Victoria," *Kamloops This Week* (June 10) <https://bit.ly/3U0ZWzJ>.

9 Law Society of British Columbia (2017), "Law Society Addresses Colonial Symbolism as Part of Commitment to Truth and Reconciliation" (April 12) <https://bit.ly/3FyFl1q>.

10 Tsilqot'in National Government (2016), "Tsilqot'in Nation Commends Law Society of B.C. for Removing Begbie Statue," *NationTalk* (June 3) <https://bit.ly/3DTYlWR>.

11 Chartres Brew (1864), "Letter to the Colonial Secretary of British Columbia, May 23," *Nobody Knows Him: Lhatŝ'aŝʔin and the Chilcotin War*, CanadianMysteries.ca. <https://bit.ly/3Ys3NIv>.

12 Mel Rothenburger (1978), *The Chilcotin War* (Mr. Paperback).

13 Matthew Begbie (1864), "Begbie to the Governor of British Columbia Including Notes Taken by the Court at the Trial of 6 Indians," *Nobody Knows Him: Lhatŝ'aŝʔin and the Chilcotin War*, CanadianMysteries.ca <https://bit.ly/3DPTbuV>.

14 Begbie (1864), "Begbie to the Governor."

15 Williams, 1977.

16 Begbie (1864), "Begbie to the Governor."

17 Begbie (1864), "Begbie to the Governor."

18 "Executive Council Minutes, Monday the 10th day of October, 1864," *Nobody Knows Him: Lhatŝ'aŝʔin and the Chilcotin War*, CanadianMysteries.ca <https://bit.ly/3sMb1sH>.

19 Anthony Sarich (1993), *Report on the Cariboo-Chilcotin Justice Inquiry* (Province of British Columbia).

20 Matthew Hayday (2017), "Sir Hector-Louis Langevin, 'Architect' of Residential Schools?" *Active History* (June 23) <https://bit.ly/3xhlUF9>.

21 Peter Shawn Taylor (2017), "One Canadian Bears the Weight of Nation's Sin of Scalping," *National Post* (August 24) <https://bit.ly/2JkqR7X>.

22 House of Commons (2018), Debates (March 26).

Chapter 11: Halifax cancels its founding father: The case of Edward Cornwallis

1 Leo J. Deveau (2020), "Counterpoints: History Thrown Overboard with Cornwallis Course Corrections," *Chronicle-Herald* (July 22) <https://bit.ly/3fntsAK>.

2 Daniel Paul (2006), *We Were Not the Savages* (Fernwood Publishing): 117.

3 Moses Harris and D'Anville, "A View of Halifax Drawn from Ye Topmasthead [1750]," *Historical Maps of Nova Scotia,* published according to an Act of Parliament, 25 January 1750; printed for T[homas] Jefferys, St. Martin's Lane, Charing Cross [London, England], Nova Scotia Archives <https://bit.ly/3fxTAZV>.

4 Paul, *We Were Not,* 113.

5 CBC News (2014), "Cornwallis Park Should Be Renamed, Say Halifax Protestors," *CBC News* (May 29) <https://bit.ly/3NCAaiR>.

6 Ibid.

7 CBC News (2020), "Activists Topple Statue of Sir John A. Macdonald in Downtown Montreal," *CBC News* (August 29) <https://bit.ly/3zFLiG4>.

8 Ibid.

9 Jean Laroche (2015), "Cornwallis Statue Removal from Park Should Be Considered, Says Premier," *CBC News* (December 11) <https://bit.ly/3hcN8rJ>.

10 Ibid.

11 Adina Bresge (2016), "Halifax to Consider Scrubbing City of Edward Cornwallis," *CBC News* (May 5) <https://bit.ly/3U6rAvr>.

12 Anjuli Patil (2016), "Edward Cornwallis Naming Motion Narrowly Defeated at Halifax Council," *CBC* News (May 10) <https://bit.ly/3T4lpXu>.

13 Samantha Schwientek (2017), "Moved by Poem, Councillor Wants Halifax to Revisit Cornwallis Controversy," *CBC News* (April 13) <https://bit.ly/3U4Dupn>.

14 Ibid.

15 Halifax (2017), *Halifax Regional Council Minutes* (April 25): 15 <https:// bit.ly/3FL7CSo>.

16 Ibid.

17 Frances Willick (2017), "Most Haligonians Say Edward Cornwallis Should Stay, Survey Suggests," *CBC News* (May 23) <https://bit.ly/3hb6kpQ>.

18 Ibid.

19 Halifax (2018), "Update and Next Steps – HRM Activity Related to Indigenous Affairs, June 28, 2017." Item Number 14.1.5. Halifax Regional Council (January 16) <https://bit.ly/3UHVJRN>.

20 Halifax (2017), "Statement from Mayor Mike Savage on the Planned Protest for July 15," Halifax Regional Municipality (July 11) <https://bit.ly/3FFE6O6>.

21 Ibid.

22 Frances Willick (2017), "'Offensive and Disgraceful.' Protestors Cheer as City of Halifax Shrouds Cornwallis Statue," CBC News (July 15) <https://bit.ly/3U8iL4j>.

23 Halifax (2017), *Halifax Regional Council Minutes* (October 3): 4-5 <https://bit.ly/3sZL20N>.

24 Ibid.

25 Assembly of Nova Scotia Mi'kmaq Chiefs (2018), "The Assembly Calls for Cornwallis Statue to be Removed Immediately," Assembly of Nova Scotia Mi'kmaq Chiefs (January 26).

26 Ibid.

27 Halifax (2018), "Statement from Mayor Savage Regarding Decision by Assembly of Nova Scotia Mi'kmaq Chiefs." Halifax Regional Municipality (January 27) <https:// bit.ly/3NCdIqj>.

28 Halifax (2018), *Halifax Regional Council Minutes* (January 30): 12 <https://bit.ly/3Wyzkrs>.

29 Ibid.

30 Canadian Press Staff (2018), "Halifax Council Votes to Temporarily Remove Edward Cornwallis Statue." *Global News* (January 30) <https://bit.ly/3TbmZ9L>.

31 Ibid.

32 Halifax (2022), "Task Force on the Commemoration of Edward Cornwallis and the Recognition and Commemoration of Indigenous History," Halifax Regional Municipality (September 7 update) <https://bit.ly/3NEmKmO>.

33 Ibid (2020), *Report* [link] (April): 59-68.

34 Gareth Hampshire (2021), "Peace and Friendship Park Officially Replaces Cornwallis Park Name," CBC News (June 9) <https://3TeAwha>.

35 Andrea Jerrett (2022), "Halifax's Cornwallis Street to Be Renamed Nora Bernard Street," CTV News (December 14) <https://bit.ly/3Wq7g8D>.

Chapter 12: Struggle and success: A balanced account of women in early Canada

1 W.L. Morton (1943), "The Extension of the Franchise in Canada: A Study in Democratic Nationalism," *Report of the Annual Meeting/Rapports de la Société historique du Canada* 22, 1: 72-81 <http://bit.ly/3JKrmaK>.

2 Catherine L. Cleverdon (1950), *The Woman Suffrage Movement in Canada* (University of Toronto Press): 7.

3 Ibid., 7.

4 Garth Grafton (1885), "Other People and I," *The Globe* (July 15): 3.

5 Ibid., 3.

6 Susanna Moodie (1871/2007), *Roughing It in the Bush* (W.W. Norton): 275.

7 Moodie, *Roughing It*, 275.

8 Audrey Saunders Miller (ed.) (1968), *The Journals of Mary O'Brien, 1828-1838* (Macmillan): 198.

9 Miller, *Journals*, 197.

10 Lucy Peel (2001), *Love Strong as Death: Lucy Peel's Canadian Journal, 1833-1836* (Wilfrid Laurier University Press): 82.

11 Catharine Parr Traill (1836/1989), *The Backwoods of Canada* (McClelland and Stewart): 11.

12 Traill, *Backwoods*, 90.

13 Thomas Tausky (1978), *Sara Jeannette Duncan: Selected Journalism* (Tecumseh Press): 6.

14 Sara Jeannette Duncan (1886), "W.D. Howells at Washington," *The Week* (April 22): 327.

15 Kathleen Blake [Kit] Coleman (1890), "Woman's Kingdom," *Toronto Daily Mail* (July 5).

16 Ibid (1890, October 25): 5.

17 Ibid (1896, May 23): 5.

18 Flora MacDonald Denison (1909), "Under the Pines," *Toronto Sunday World* (November 7).

19 Ibid (1910, April 24).

20 Ibid (1909, October 17).

21 Ibid (1910, May 15).

22 Ibid (1910, January 16).

23 E. Pauline Johnson (2000), "A Cry from an Indian Wife" [1885] in *E. Pauline Johnson, Tekahionwake: Collected Poems and Selected Prose* (University of Toronto Press): 14-15.

24 Johnson, "The Cattle Thief," *Collected Poems*, 97-99.

25 Nellie L. McClung (1915/1972), *In Times Like These* (University of Toronto Press): 22.

26 Ibid., 23.

27 Ibid., 48.

Chapter 13: The British colonial achievement and its deniers

1 BBC (Undated), "Abolition of the Slave Trade in Britain," *Bitesize*, BBC Online <http://bit.ly/3GFnneg> inter alia.

2 Richard Grenier (1991), "Indian Love Call," *Commentary* (March) <https://bit.ly/3MZCIaw>.

3 Robert Kee, quoted in Richard Grenier (1994), "In the Name of the IRA," *Commentary* (April): 51 <https://bit.ly/3DmXZXB>.

4 Robin Winks, ed. (2001), *Oxford History of the British Empire: volume 5: Historiography*. Oxford.

5 Bernard Lewis (1982/2001), *The Muslim Discovery of Europe* (W.W. Norton): 192.

6 Bernard A. Cook (2006), *Women and War: A Historical Encyclopaedia from Antiquity to the Present* (ABC-CLIO): 28; and Alexis Demirdjian (ed.) (2016), *The Armenian Genocide Legacy* (Springer).

7 Eric Williams (2021), *Capitalism and Slavery*, 3rd ed. (University of North Carolina Press); Barbara Lewis Solow and Stanley L. Engerman (2004), *British Capitalism and Caribbean Slavery: The Legacy of Eric Williams* (Cambridge University Press).

8 William R. Cotter (1994), "The Somerset Case and the Abolition of Slavery in England," *History* 79, 255: 31–56.

9 G.K. Chesterton, "Shaw, The Philosopher," in Alberto Manguel (ed.) (2000), *On Lying in Bed and Other Essays by G.K. Chesterton* (Bayeux Arts): 256.

10 Lewis S. Feuer (1987), *Imperialism and the Anti-Imperialist Mind* (Transaction).

11 J.R. Seeley (1891), *The Expansion of England: Two Courses of Lectures* (Macmillan): 8.

12 Roy MacLaren (2019), *Mackenzie King in the Age of the Dictators: Canada's Imperial and Foreign Policies* (McGill-Queen's University Press): 55.

13 John M. Carroll (2007), *A Concise History of Hong Kong* (Rowman & Littlefield): 79.

14 Adam Hochschild (1998/1999), *King Leopold's Dream: A Story of Greed, Terror, and Heroism in Colonial Africa* (Houghton Mifflin/Mariner Books): 175.

15 Ibid., 318.

16 Ibid.

17 Suzanne Miers and Igor Kopytoff (1977), *Slavery in Africa: Historical and Anthropological Perspectives* (University of Wisconsin Press): 12.

18 Richard J. Chacon and Rubén G. Mendoza (eds.) (2007), *North American Indigenous Warfare and Ritual Violence* (University of Arizona Press); Leland Donald (1997), *Aboriginal Slavery on the Northwest Coast of North America* (University of California Press).

19 Miers and Kopytoff, 5-6.

20 E.V. Walter (1969), *Terror and Resistance: A Study of Political Violence, With Case Studies of Some Primitive African Communities* (Oxford); John Wright (1989), "Political Mythology and the Making of Natal's Mfecane," *Canadian Journal of African Studies* 23, 2: 272-291; and cf. J.B. Peires (1993), "Paradigm Deleted: The Materialist Interpretation of the Mfecane," *Journal of Southern African Studies* 19, 2 (June): 295-313; cf. Leland Donald, op. cit.

21 Rodney Stark (2005), *The Victory of Reason: How Christianity Led to Freedom, Capitalism, and Western Success* (Random House); Rodney Stark (2014), *How the West Won: The Neglected Story of the Triumph of Modernity* (Intercollegiate Studies Institute).

22 Michael Oakeshott (1962/1991), *Rationalism in Politics and Other Essays* (Liberty Fund): 9.

23 Nicholas St. Fleur (2019), "Massacre of Children in Peru Might Have Been a Sacrifice to Stop Bad Weather," *New York Times* (March 6) <http://bit.ly/3F1uSes>.

24 National Park Service (Undated), "Civil War Facts, 1861-1865" <https://bit.ly/3ItoMW8>.

25 Winston Churchill (1956), *The Great Democracies,* volume 4 of *A History of the English-Speaking Peoples* (Cassell): 239-40.

26 Alexander Henry (1921), *Alexander Henry's Travels and Adventures in the Years 1760-1776,* Milo M. Quaife (ed.) (The Lakeside Press).

27 Alan Taylor (2007), *The Divided Ground: Indians, Settlers, and the Northern Borderland of the American Revolution* (Knopf Doubleday).

28 Christopher F. Minty (2015), "The Future of Loyalist Studies," Blog post (Nov. 23), *Borealia/Early Canadian History* <http://bit.ly/3ieLq9u>.

29 Arthur Einhorn (1999), "Warriors of the Sky: The Iroquois Iron Workers," *European Review of Native American Studies* 13, 1: 25-34 (p. 27).

30 Edward Butts (2006/2023), "North-West Mounted Police," *Canadian Encyclopedia* <https://bit.ly/3Tuz8ba>.

31 Cf. archeological evidence in William Whipple Warren (1897), *History of the Ojibway Nation* (Minnesota Historical Society/University of Michigan): 99.

32 Robert McGhee (2008), "Aboriginalism and the Problems of Indigenous Archaeology," *American Antiquity,* 73: 4 (October): 579-597.

33 Joachim Fromhold (2010), *The Western Cree (Pakisimotan Wi Iniwak)* (Lulu Enterprises): xii; Wilson D. Wallis and Ruth S. Wallis (1955), *The Micmac Indians of Eastern Canada* (University of Minnesota Press): 14; and Basil Johnston (1990), *Ojibway Heritage* (University of Nebraska Press).

34 Edward L. Dreyer (2007), *Zheng He: China and the Oceans in the Early Ming Dynasty, 1405-1433* (Pearson Longman); Philip T. Hoffman (2017), *Why Did Europe Conquer the World?* (Princeton University Press): 175, cf. Hoffman's footnote 32 which cites others who discuss why China did not undertake additional voyages and world conquest due, perhaps, to the effects of the Mongol invasions.

35 Ernesto Novato and Charles River (eds.) (2019), *Huitzilopochtli: The History of the Aztec God of War and Human Sacrifice* (independently published); David Roos (2018), "Human Sacrifice: Why the Aztecs Practised This Gory Ritual," *History.com,* (October 11) <https://bit.ly/3VYSBSU>.

36 David Malouf (2003), "Made in England: Australia's British Inheritance," *Quarterly Essay* (Black Inc.): 52.

37 Freeman M. Tovell (2009), *At the Far Reaches of Empire: The Life of Juan Francisco de la Bodega y Quadra* (UBC Press).

38 Leland Donald (1997), *Aboriginal Slavery on the Northwest Coast of North America* (University of California Press): 113 and passim.

39 Barry M. Gough (1978), "Send a Gunboat! Checking Slavery and Controlling Liquor Traffic among Coast Indians of British Columbia in the 1860s," *Pacific Northwest Quarterly* 69, 4 (October): 159.

40 Matthias Häussler (2021), *The Herero Genocide: War, Emotion, and Extreme Violence in Colonial Namibia* (Berghahn Books); Jeremy Sarkin-Hughes (2011), *Germany's Genocide of the Herero: Kaiser Wilhelm II, His General, His Settlers, His Soldiers* (UCT Press).

41 Nina Green (2022), "'Our Dear Children': Sisters' Chronicles of Indian Residential School," *The Dorchester Review* (April 1) <https://bit.ly/3P7QSHE>; Rodney Clifton (2022), "My Life in Two Indian Residential Schools," *C2C Journal* (Sept. 5) <https://bit.ly/3BhvQAC>.

42 First Nations Centre (2005), *First Nations Regional Longitudinal Health Survey, 2002-03* (First Nations Centre): 32.

43 Barry M. Gough (ed.) (2011), *Historical Dictionary of Canada* (Scarecrow Press): 342.

44 Jean Chretien (1985), *Straight from the Heart* (Key Porter): 145.

45 Michel Ducharme (2014), *The Idea of Liberty in Canada during the Age of Atlantic Revolutions, 1776-1838* (McGill-Queen's University Press).

46 Peter M. Doll (2000), *Revolution, Religion, and National Identity: Imperial Anglicanism in British North America, 1745-1795* (Fairleigh Dickinson University Press).

47 A.P. Thornton (1985), *The Imperial Idea and Its Enemies: A Study in British Power* (Palgrave Macmillan): 212-13.

48 Hannah Weiss Muller (2017), *Subjects and Sovereign: Bonds of Belonging in the Eighteenth-Century British Empire* (Oxford University Press): 122, cited by Mark R. Anderson (2022), "The Quebec Act, Two Fights, and Relative Subjecthood," Blog post (June 30) *Borealia/Early Canadian History* <http://bit.ly/3V3gzvq>.

49 Ducharme, 52.

50 W. J. Eccles (1969), *The Canadian Frontier, 1534-1760* (Holt, Rinehart and Winston).

51 Andrée Désilets (1976), "Taché, Sir Étienne-Paschal," *Dictionary of Canadian Biography*, Volume IX (1861-1870).

52 Lucie K. Morisset and Luc Noppen (1998), "Taché, Eugène-Étienne," *Dictionary of Canadian Biography*, Volume XIV (1911-1920).

53 Assemblée nationale du Québec (2015), *Mémoire de bronze : Les statues de la façade de l'hôtel du Parlement*, Direction des communications, des programmes éducatifs et de l'accueil (de l'Assemblée nationale) (Novembre) <https://bit.ly/3Whzp2w>.

54 Damien-Claude Bélanger (2022), "The Rise and Fall of French Canadian Loyalism," in D. Michael Jackson and Christopher McCreery (eds.), *A Resilient Crown: Canada's Monarchy at the Platinum Jubilee* (Dundurn).

55 Frédéric Bastien (2014), *The Battle of London: Trudeau, Thatcher, and the Fight for Canada's Constitution* (Dundurn).

56 Ibid.; and Brian Smith (2022), "Behind the Constitutional Curtain," *The Dorchester Review* (Spring/Summer): 88-92.

57 Feuer, 33, and 222, note 93.

58 "Some Considerations on the Colonial Question," *l'Humanité* (May 25, 1922), reprinted in Bernard B. Fall (ed.) (1967), *Ho Chi Minh on Revolution: Selected Writings 1920-66* (Signet/New American Library): 27 <https://bit.ly/3WHw3pj>.

59 Nirad C. Chaudhuri (1975), *Clive of India: A Political and Psychological Essay* (Barrie & Jenkins): 11.

60 Nirad C. Chaudhuri (1951), *The Autobiography of an Unknown Indian* (Macmillan): v.

61 Erik von Kuehnelt-Leddhin (1985), "The Problems of a Successful American Foreign Policy," *Imprimis*, 14, 11 (November) <https://bit.ly/3PKv1GJ>. Cf. his wide-ranging 1974 book *Leftism: From de Sade and Marx to Hitler and Marcuse* (Arlington House).

62 Edwin Rios (2022), "Queen's Death Intensifies Criticism of British Empire's Violent Atrocities," *The Guardian* (September 10) <https://bit.ly/3YIfM5f>.

63 Penderel Moon (1961), *Divide and Quit: An Eye-witness Account of the Partition of India* (Chatto & Windus).

64 C. Northcote Parkinson (1967), *Left Luggage: A Caustic History of British Socialism from Marx to Wilson* (Houghton Mifflin): 133.

65 Caroline Elkins (2005), *Britain's Gulag: The Brutal End of Empire in Kenya* (Pimlico).

66 James Franks (2004), *Scram from Kenya! From Colony to Republic* (Pomegranate): 107.

67 Audrey Dermawan (2022). "No Justification to Change George Town's Name to Tanjong Penaga," *New Straits Times* (March 15).

68 Swati Bhat (2022), "India on Course to Become World's Fastest-Growing Economy, Says RBI," *Reuters* (July 16).

69 First broadcast on August 15, 2022 on Tom Holland's "The Rest Is History" podcast <https://bit.ly/3PJEcY5>.

70 Parkinson, *Left Luggage,* 10.

71 H.W. Crocker (2011), *The Politically Incorrect Guide to the British Empire* (Regnery): 4.

72 Feuer, 15.

73 Armando Valladares (1986), *Against All Hope: The Prison Memoirs of Armando Valladares* (Alfred A. Knopf).

74 Stéphane Courtois, Nicolas Werth, Jean-Louis Panné, et al. (eds.) (1999), *The Black Book of Communism* (Harvard): 697; Peter Gill (2010), *Famine and Foreigners: Ethiopia Since Live Aid* (Oxford University Press): 36, 43.

75 Alan Clark (2002), *The Last Diaries: In and Out of the Wilderness* (Weidenfeld & Nicolson): 330.

76 Cf. Core Knowledge Foundation <https://bit.ly/2Ro3FpU>.

77 Amrit Dhillon (2020), "Selective Abortion in India Could Lead to 6.8m Fewer Girls Being Born by 2030," *The Guardian* August 21) <https://bit.ly/3ioEojg>.

78 Monty Python (1979), "What Have the Romans Ever Done for Us?" *The Life of Brian,* YouTube <http://bit.ly/3VGHI7p>.

Chapter 14: A new challenge for Canadians of any colour: Remixed racism

1 Brian Lilley (2021), "Feds' Anti-Racism Training Deals with Political Agendas, Nothing Else," *Toronto Sun (*April 8). <https://bit.ly/3GW0cMq>.

2 Rohan Deb Roy (2018), "Science Still Bears the Fingerprints of Colonialism," *Smithsonian Magazine* (April 9) <https://bit.ly/3VZ8fwo>.

3 Maan Alhmidi (2021), "Rejection Letter ESC Sent to Black Organizations 'Completely Unacceptable," *National Post* (January 15). <https://bit.ly/3Iw0drI>.

4 Ibid.

5 @cityofhamilton [City of Hamilton] (2021), Twitter post (April 23) <https://bit.ly/3W2oXuO>.

6 Eliza Griswold (2021), "A Pennsylvania Lawmaker and the Resurgence of Christian Nationalism," *New Yorker* (May 9) <https://bit.ly/3CDeSNS>.

7 CBC News (2021), "Ontario Judge Cleared of Perjury Allegations over Ties to Black Federation" (June 2) <https://bit.ly/3k16G3D>.

8 Ontario Judicial Council (2021), *Reasons for Decision,* Concerning a Complaint about the Conduct of the Honourable Justice Donald McLeod: 228. <https://www.ontariocourts.ca/ocj/files/ojc/decisions/2021-mcleod-decision.docx>

9 Jennifer Pagliaro and Wendy Gillis (2022), "'You Have To Show Me': Black Toronto Voices Reject Police Chief's Apology for 'Systemic' Discrimination," *Toronto Star* (June 15) <https://bit.ly/3IF5mh9>.

10 Wendy Gillis (2022), "They've Known for 'Quite Literally Decades.' Why a Landmark Police Apology Fell Flat for So Many Black Torontonians" *Toronto Star* (June 21) <https://bit.ly/3Gudxdn>.

11 Statistics Canada (2023), "Black History Month 2022... By the Numbers," Government of Canada <https://bit.ly/3GSK526>.

12 CTV News (2021), "Sandy Hudson 'Enraged' by Justin Trudeau's Comments on BLM," YouTube (May 5). <https://bit.ly/3Qypqnu>.

13 Coleman Hughes (2018), "The Racism Treadmill," *Quillette* (May 14) <https://bit.ly/3vTWrRp>.

14 Silla Brush and Russel Ward (2022), "BlackRock CEO Says Stakeholder Capitalism Isn't "Woke," *Bloomberg,* (January 17) <https://bit.ly/3CztZb1>.

15 Paul Polman (2022), "Critics of 'Woke' Capitalism are Wrong," *Becoming Net Positive* (January 26), LinkedIn <https://bit.ly/3k7IkFu>.

16 Vivek Ramaswamy (2020), "The 'Stakeholders' vs. the People," *Wall Street Journal* (February 12) <https://bit.ly/3IJpcrL>.

17 Andrew Stuttaford (2022), "The CEO as 'Lawmaker': A Corporatist Manifesto," *National Review* (January 28) <https://bit.ly/3X6VGQT>.

18 iShares by BlackRock (2022), *2022 Interim Management Report of Fund Performance*, BlackRock (June 30) <https://bit.ly/3vUJU02>.

19 Bell Canada Enterprises (BCE Inc.) (2021), *Notice of 2021 Annual General Shareholder Meeting and Management Proxy Circular* (April), <https://bit.ly/3Gy2WOx>.

20 Bell Canada Enterprises (BCE Inc.) (2022), *Advancing How Canadians Connect with Each Other and the World. Annual General Shareholder Meeting and Management Proxy Circular*, BCE (May 5) <https://bit.ly/3GWkKo2>.

21 Yaron Steinbuch (2020), "Black Lives Matter Co-Founder Describes Herself as 'Trained Marxist,'" *New York Post* (June 25) <http://bit.ly/3XoYYhI>.

22 Kiley Hurst and Kim Parker (2021), "Growing Share of Americans Say They Want More Spending on Police in Their Area," Pew Research (October 26) <http://bit.ly/3YhxWKD>.

23 Benjamin Fearnow (2023), "Twitter Elitists: Three-Quarters of All US Political Tweets Come from Very Few," *Newsweek* (February 9) <http://bit.ly/3jQmEOb>.

24 Jacey Fortin (2021), "Critical Race Theory: A Brief History," *New York Times* (November 8) <https://bit.ly/3GAadgS>.

25 Derrick Bell (1993), "The Racism is Permanent Thesis: Courageous Revelation or Unconscious Denial of Racial Genocide." *Capital University Law Review* (Summer) <https://bit.ly/3ZtnnVs>.

26 Colton Wiens (2022), "Kitchener MPP's Anti-Racism Bill Receives Nearly Unanimous Support," CTV News (March 3) <https://bit.ly/3Gy65xQ>.

27 Breck Dumas (2022), "'Woke' Home Depot Flyer Causes Online Stir," Fox Business (March 23) <https://bit.ly/3XhsMxL>.

28 Jamil Jivani (2021), "What Black Conservatives Are Saying Following the Derek Chauvin Verdict," *National Post* (April 21) <https://bit.ly/3W0Fy22>.

29 @SlowToWrite [Samuel Sey] (2021), Twitter Post (April 20) <https://bit.ly/3HLI4Eh>.

30 Ambrose Student Council (2021), "ASC and Student Life Statement/Apology)," Ambrose University (April 19). Republished by Samuel Sey on the *Slow to Write* blog <https://bit.ly/3XjcHqS>.

31 Tyler Dawson (2021), "Black Conservative Addresses an Alberta Christian University and a Free Speech Fight Breaks Out." *National Post (*April 27) <https://bit.ly/3io0kuR>.

32 Ibid.

33 Timothy P. Carney (2022), "Of Course Fatherlessness Contributes to Violent Crime, Including Mass Shootings," *Washington Examiner* (May 26) <https://bit.ly/3CDk0Bw>.

34 Adam B. Coleman (2022), "We Overlook a Significant Factor in Mass Shootings: Fatherlessness," *New York Post* (May 27) <https://bit.ly/3W3i0JZ>.

35 Ron DeSantis (2022), "Governor Ron DeSantis Signs Groundbreaking Legislation to Support Involved Fatherhood in Florida," News Release (April 11) <https://bit.ly/3W6bkL0>.

36 Tony Dungy, (2022). Twitter. (April 22). <https://bit.ly/3SfOP5Z>.

37 Tamara Khandaker (2015). "Canada's Liberal Leader Blasted for Blaming Misogyny on 'Certain Types of Music' and Porn," *Vice News* (September 22) <https://bit.ly/3ZF8nE8>.

38 Anna Livsey (2018), "Justin Trudeau Tells People to Say 'Peoplekind' Not 'Mankind.'" *The Guardian* (February 7) <https://bit.ly/2FUAFke>.

39 Statistics Canada (2017), *Portrait of Children's Family Life in Canada in 2016: Census of Population, 2016*, Statistics Canada (August 2) <https://bit.ly/3XodNlg>.

40 Gary Pieters (2007), "Character, Not Colour, Matters," *Toronto Star* (January 11) <https://bit.ly/3GWxDhK>.

Chapter 15: How the Yukon Court of Appeal denied Charter rights to an Aboriginal Canadian

1 Cindy Dickson (2022), Interview with Peter Shawn Taylor, *C2C Journal* (November 15).

2 *Dickson v. Vuntut Gwitchin First Nation, 2021 YKCA 5*, Court of Appeal of Yukon (2021) <https://bit.ly/3ieZ64S>.

3 Alan C. Cairns (2001), *Citizens Plus: Aboriginal Peoples and the Canadian State* (UBC Press).

4 Gordon Gibson (2009), *A New Look at Canadian Indian Policy: Respect the Collective—Promote the Individual* (Fraser Institute): 79.

5 Ibid., 80.

6 *Dickson v. Vuntut Gwitchin First Nation*, 20.

7 *Dickson v. Vuntut Gwitchin First Nation*, 49.

8 Lynne Cohen (2021), "Canada's Newest and Deadliest Human Right: Assisted Suicide for All," *C2C Journal* (January 10) <https://bit.ly/3jRnji7>; and Grant A. Brown (2022), "Doug Ford's Use of the 'Notwithstanding' Clause: Keeping Ontario's Schools Open," *C2C Journal* (November 10) <https://bit.ly/3VIvLh3>.

9 Canadian Constitution Foundation (2022), "Supreme Court to Hear Case on Whether Indigenous Governments are Subject to Charter Scrutiny: CCF to Intervene," Press Release (October 2) <https://bit.ly/3CmZxks>.

10 Government of Canada and Nisga'a Nation (1999), *Nisga'a Final Agreement* <https://bit.ly/3Qht7NX>.

11 Graeme Hamilton (2018), "Mohawk Community By-Law Against Mixed Race Couples on Reserve Ruled Unconstitutional," *National Post* (April 30) <https://bit.ly/3CsPoCK>.

12 Peter Best (2021), The Myth of Aboriginal Law in Canada," Frontier Centre for Public Policy (August 11) <https://bit.ly/3W3IcEp>.

13 Rob Louis (2022), "First Nations Don't Live in a Harmony Hut," *The Lawyer's Daily* (July 22) <https://bit.ly/3GmDkEx>.

14 Tom Flanagan (2016), "Corruption and First Nations in Canada," *Canadian Foreign Policy Journal* (October 24) <https://bit.ly/3igW3sZ>.

15 Gordon Gibson (2014), "Canada Enables the Sickness of the Reserves," *Globe and Mail* (September 8) <https://tgam.ca/3Gj0ITg>.

16 Calvin Helin (2008), *Dances with Dependency: Out of Poverty Through Self-Reliance* (Ravenscrest Publishing): 146.

17 Philippe Sands (2017), *East West Street: On the Origins of "Genocide" and "Crimes Against Humanity"* (Vintage Books): 63.

Chapter 16: Indigenous peoples have a chance, if they grasp it

1 Diane Francis (2022), "A First Nations' 'Quiet Revolution' Has Begun," *National Post* (July 11) <http://bit.ly/3jEepoC>.

2 Gordon Gibson (2004), "Conversation," Frontier Centre for Public Policy (April 5). <http://bit.ly/3x7PVqJ>.

3 Standing Committee on Indigenous and Northern Affairs (2017), "Evidence (42-1) – No. 53," House of Commons of Canada. https://bit.ly/3EryZQ9.

4 Public Policy Forum (2016), *Improving Access to Capital for Canada's First Nation Communities*, Public Policy Forum (February) <https://bit.ly/40Fqo5O>.

5 Joseph Quesnel (2009), "Property Rights: The Nisga'a Pave the Way," *Globe and Mail* (July 7) <http://bit.ly/3DOSNMY>.

6 Joseph Quesnel (2016), "The B.C. First Nation That's Experimenting with Private Property," *National Post* (August 2) <http://bit.ly/3Eg1CQn>.

7 Standing Senate Committee on Aboriginal Peoples (2015), *Housing on First Nation Reserves: Challenges and Successes. Interim Report.* Senate of Canada (February) <https://bit.ly/40KrXiP>.

8 John Ibbitson (2012), "Harper Government to Introduce Law to Allow Private Property on Reserves," *Globe and Mail* (August 6) <https://tgam.ca/3YJqFD3>.

9 Joseph Quesnel (2010), *Respecting the Seventh Generation: A Voluntary Plan for Relocating Non-Viable Native Reserves*, Frontier Centre for Public Policy <http://bit.ly/3lk3pNu>.

10 Ravina Bains and Kayla Ishkanian (2016), *Government Spending and Own Source Revenue for Canada's Aboriginals: A Comparative Analysis*, Fraser Institute <https://bit.ly/3YxXkeE>.

11 Ravina Bains (2013), *Opportunities for First Nation Prosperity Through Oil and Gas Development*, Fraser Institute <https://bit.ly/40HiDMB>. See also Gregory John and Martk Milke (2020), *Pro or Con? Measuring First Nations Support of Opposition to Resource Development*, Canadian Energy Centre (July) <https://bit.ly/3RS9KMk>.

12 Dominique Collin and Michael L. Rice (2019), *Evening the Odds: Giving Indigenous Ventures Access to the Full Financial Toolkit.* Macdonald-Laurier Institute <https://bit.ly/40EkVfB>.

13 Mark Milke (2013), *Ever Higher: Government Spending on Canada's Aboriginals Since 1947,* Fraser Institute <https://bit.ly/2XQk92h>.

Chapter 17: How teaching the full history of world slavery frees us from selective guilt

1 John R. Jewitt (1815/2000), *White Slaves of Maquinna: John R. Jewitt's Narrative of Capture and Confinement at Nootka* (Heritage House): 31.

2 Marjorie Gann and Janet Willen (2011), *Five Thousand Years of Slavery* (Tundra).

3 Elementary Teachers' Federation of Toronto (Undated), *My Community* (Slow to Write): 1, 5 <bit.ly/3GXDTGN>.

4 Elementary Teachers' Federation of Toronto (Undated), *My Classroom* (Slow to Write): 5 <http://bit.ly/3XFkOPd>.

5 John Gyles [1736], *Memoirs of odd adventures, strange deliverances, &c. in the captivity of John Gyles, Esq; commander of the garrison on St. George's River. Written by himself. ; Eight lines in English from Homer's Odyssey* (S. Kneeland and T. Green) <http://bit.ly/3gHDpK1>.

6 See *Five Thousand Years of Slavery,* p. 61 for Baquaqua's story and pp. 86-87 for Equiano's. Northup's story was later made into a major Hollywood film, *Twelve Years a Slave.*

7 See http://bit.ly/3iiNrlo for full text of Drew's collection.

8 Archives of Ontario (Undated), "Sophia Burthen Pooley: Part of the Family?" Government of Ontario, Ministry of Public and Business Service Delivery <bit.ly/3VucTDf>.

9 Henry Louis Gates Jr. (2010). "Ending the Slavery Blame-Game," *New York Times* (April 23) <bit.ly/3XRlQYT>.

10 The full story of the Robin Johns is told in Randy L. Sparks (2004), *The Two Princes of Calabar: An Eighteenth-Century Atlantic Odyssey* (Harvard University Press).

11 Sparks, 130.

12 Murray Gordon (1989), *Slavery in the Arab World* (New Amsterdam Books): 50.

13 Ronald Segal (2001), *Islam's Black Slaves: The Other Black Diaspora* (Farrar, Straus and Giroux): 162-168; and Seymour Drescher and Stanley L. Engerman (eds.) (1998), *A Historical Guide to World Slavery* (Oxford University Press): 35.

14 The *Slave Voyages* website (bit.ly/3ARqSKJ) dates the very first transatlantic slave voyage to 1526.

15 Marcia Wright (1993), *Strategies of Slaves & Women: Life Stories from East/Central Africa* (Lilian Barber Press). *Includes the quotations from the narrative of Meli (pp. 50–51). Used in Five Thousand Years of Slavery with permission.*

16 Janet Willen and Marjorie Gann (2015), *Speak a Word for Freedom: Women Against Slavery* (Tundra): 91-100.

17 Adam Hochschild (1998), *King Leopold's Ghost* (Houghton Mifflin): 278.

18 Janet Lim (2004), *Sold for Silver: An Autobiography of a Girl Sold into Slavery in Southeast Asia* (Singapore): 33.

19 Ibid.

20 *Macmillan Encyclopedia of World Slavery,* s.v. "Maori"

21 *Macmillan Encyclopedia of World Slavery,* s.v. "Hawaii"

22 Gann and Willen, *Five Thousand Years,* 134-135.

23 Samuel Sewall (2000), "The Selling of Joseph: A Memorial," in Mason Lowance (ed.), *Against Slavery: An Abolitionist Reader* (Penguin): 12.

24 Sarah M. Grimké (2000), "An Epistle to the Clergy of the Southern States," in *Against Slavery*, 206.

25 Theodore Dwight Weld (2000), "The Bible Against Slavery," in *Against Slavery*, 53-58.

26 Author's transcription of letter from John Harris to Dr. Harry Guinness, May 19, 1904. Bodleian/Rhodes House Mss. Brit.emp.Anti-Slavery Society S19, D5/9.

27 @VidyaShah6 (2020), Twitter post (March 15).

28 Vidya Shah (2020), "Opportunism or Opportunity? Navigating Educational Equity in the Time of COVID-19," EdCan Network (October 21) <bit.ly/3u8lOOm>.

29 Deuteronomy: 23:7.

30 Rabbi Jonathan Sacks (2015), *Not in God's Name: Confronting Religious Violence* (Schocken Books): 251.

Chapter 18: The problem with Canada's "woke" self-loathing: A view from abroad

1 Ian Holliday (2021), "Vancouver Police, Mayor Apologize for Handcuffing of B.C.'s First Black Supreme Court Justice," CTV News (May 15) <https://bit.ly/3AZsRNq>.

2 Peel District School Board Calendar <https://bit.ly/3Vr29p4>.

3 Roshan Rivetna (2013), "The Zarathushti World: A 2012 Demographic Picture," *FEZANA Journal* (Fall) <https://bit.ly/3AZslis>.

4 Statistics Canada (2021), "Religion in Canada," Statistics Canada <bit.ly/3BsPQRh>.

Chapter 19: Ideas, immigrants, and the future of Canada

1 Iris Chang (2003), *The Chinese in America: A Narrative History* (Viking): 17-26.

2 Jens Manuel Krogstag (2020), "Most Cuban-Americans Identify as Republican in 2020," Pew Research Center (October 2), <https://pewrsr.ch/3SD1lwO>.

3 There has been always a debate about the difference between "migrant" and "immigrant." In fact, there is no distinction between the two in law. See The Migration Observatory (2019), "Who Counts as a Migrant? Definitions and their Consequences," University of Oxford (July 10) <https://bit.ly/3wXvxsX>.

4 Statistics Canada, Table 17-10-0014-01 <https://bit.ly/3PWeo9n>.

5 Government of Canada (2022), "An Immigration Plan to Grow the Economy," News Release (November 1), Immigration, Refugees and Citizenship Canada <https://bit.ly/3WL3IiH>.

6 Statistics Canada (2017), "Number and Proportion of Foreign-Born Population in Canada, 1871 to 2036," Graph, *The Daily* <https://bit.ly/3pS7He6>.

7 Broadly speaking, immigrants to Canada are granted entry as either temporary residents or permanent residents. Temporary residents are migrants who enter Canada for a defined period of time and include visitors, temporary workers, and students. Permanent residents are economic immigrants, family-class immigrants, or refugees.

8 Statistics Canada (2022), "Canada in 2041: A Larger, More Diverse Population with Greater Differences between Regions," *The Daily* (September 8) <https://bit.ly/3UqkC4m>.

9 Statistics Canada (2022), "Focus on Geography Series, 2021 Census of Population" <https://bit.ly/3DYbugo>.

10 Statistics Canada (2017), "Distribution of Foreign-Born Population, by Region of Birth, Canada, 1871 to 2036," Graph, *The Daily* (October 25) <https://bit.ly/3DpCtCj>.

11 Statistics Canada (2013), *Immigration and Ethnocultural Diversity in Canada: National Household Survey, 2011*. <https://bit.ly/3kXExes>.

12 Recent immigrant (or new immigrant, or newcomer) refers to a person who has been admitted to the country permanently in the five years preceding a census. In the 2021 Census, this period was from January 1, 2016, to May 11, 2021 (see Statistics Canada (2022), "Immigrants Make Up the Largest Share of the Population in over 150 Years and Continue to Shape Who We Are as Canadians," *The Daily* (October 26) <https://bit.ly/3x5DL1t>.

13 Statistics Canada (2022), "Focus on Geography Series, 2021 Census."

14 Statistics Canada (2013), *Immigration and Ethnocultural Diversity in Canada.*

15 Neli Esipova, Julie Ray, and Dato Tsabutashvili (2020), "Canada No. 1 for Migrants, U.S. in Sixth Place," Gallup (September 23) <https://bit.ly/3KAu1m8>.

16 Transparency International (2023). Corruptions Perceptions Index 2022. <https://bit.ly/3IPGyBl>.

17 Thomas Sowell (1994), *Race and Culture*: 8.

Chapter 20: Renewing the peaceable kingdom: Why ideas and not identities should matter

1 Immigration, Refugees and Citizenship Canada (2021), *Discover Canada: The Rights and Responsibilities of Citizenship*, Study Guide (Government of Canada): 9 <https://bit.ly/2t3SWah>.

2 Daniel Proussalidis (2011), "Liberals: Don't Call Honour Killings 'Barbaric,'" Newstalk 1010 (March 14) <https://bit.ly/3Jbzh0b>.

3 Bryn Weese (2011), "Trudeau Blasts Feds for Calling Honour Killings 'Barbaric,'" Parliamentary Bureau (March 14).

4 Jane Taber (2011), "Justin Trudeau's Honour-Killing Unease Fans Cultural-Relativist Flames," *Globe and Mail* (March 15) <https://tgam.ca/3HfFCH1>.

5 Guy Lawson (2012), "Trudeau's Canada, Again," *New York Times Magazine* (December 8) <https://nyti.ms/2wMoQcW>.

6 Tabitha De Bruin (2021), "Battle of the Plains of Abraham," *Canadian Encyclopedia* (August 20) <https://bit.ly/2B5PTD6>.

7 Jacques Monet (2019), "Act of Union," *Canadian Encyclopedia* (September 27) <https://bit.ly/2I2ZZuo>.

8 Janet Ajzenstat, Paul Romney, Ian Gentles and William D. Gairdner, editors (1999), *Canada's Founding Debates*, (Stoddart Publishing), 384.

9 John Duffy (2002). *Fights of Our Lives*. HarperCollins, 48-49.

10 Trudeau (1992): 57.

11 Trudeau (1992): 58.

12 Trudeau (1992): 58.

Index

D

E

I

J

K

L

V

W

Z

ALSO BY MARK MILKE

The Victim Cult

Ralph vs. Rachel

Tax Me I'm Canadian

Stealth Confiscation

A Nation of Serfs?

Barbarians in the Garden City

About the
Aristotle Foundation for Public Policy

The Aristotle Foundation for Public Policy is a new educational and public policy think tank that aims to renew a common-sense approach to public discourse and public policy in Canada. The Aristotle Foundation is a federally registered Not for Profit Corporation and a registered charity under the federal Income Tax Act. Donations are eligible for a charitable tax receipt.

Our mission

Championing reason, democracy, and civilization so all can participate in a free, flourishing Canada.

Our vision

A Canada where the sacrifices and successes of past generations are cherished and built upon; where citizens value each other for their character and merit; and where open inquiry and free expression are prized as the best path to a flourishing future for all.

Why name it after Aristotle?

Aristotle asserted that reality and reason matter to solving problems; ancient Greece was an incubator for experiments in democracy; Athenian citizens debated justice and the good life. All such elements—reason, democracy, and civilization—yet matter today to human flourishing.

ARISTOTLE
FOUNDATION FOR PUBLIC POLICY
Championing Reason, Democracy and Civilization

www.aristotlefoundation.org

Manufactured by Amazon.ca
Bolton, ON

34606455R00190